CAREER OPPORTUNITIES IN ENGINEERING

CAREER
OPPORTUNITIES
IN ENGINEERING

R<small>ICHARD</small> A. M<small>c</small>D<small>AVID</small>

S<small>USAN</small> E<small>CHAORE</small>-M<small>c</small>D<small>AVID</small>

Ferguson

An imprint of Infobase Publishing

Career Opportunities in Engineering

Ferguson
An imprint of Infobase Publishing
132 West 31st Street
New York NY 10001

Library of Congress Cataloging-in-Publication Data
McDavid, Richard A.
   Career opportunities in engineering / by Richard A. McDavid and Susan Echaroe-McDavid.
      p. cm.
   Includes bibliographical references and index.
   ISBN 0-8160-6152-1 (hc: alk.paper)
   1. Engineering—Vocational guidance. I. Echaroe-McDavid, Susan. II. Title.
   TA157.M2135 2006
   620.0023—dc22   2006000092

Ferguson books are available at special discounts when purchased in bulk quantities for businesses, associations, institutions, or sales promotions. Please call our Special Sales Department in New York at (212) 967-8800 or (800) 322-8755.

You can find Ferguson on the World Wide Web at http://www.fergpubco.com

Cover design by Cathy Rincon

Printed in the United States of America

VB Hermitage 10 9 8 7 6 5 4 3 2 1

This book is printed on acid-free paper.

To our parents:
Betty and James McDavid & Frances and Santiago Echaore

CONTENTS

INTRODUCTION

Do you like to solve problems? Are you fascinated by technology? Do you like to design and build things? Are science and math your favorite subjects? If you answered "yes" to any or all of these questions, then engineering may very well be the profession for you. Engineers make modern life possible—and they have fun doing so.

You are probably familiar with what engineers do, such as build bridges, roads, or skyscrapers. Perhaps you are also aware that engineers design automobiles, large ships, and space vehicles. Did you know that engineers also work in the food, city planning, pharmaceutical, and forestry industries? Did you know that engineers help to raise seafood, keep traffic running smoothly, and design roller coasters? Engineers are involved in all these different activities and much more. Just look around you. Engineers were part of the development and production of everything that was built and made.

Engineering is comprised of many different disciplines—civil engineering, mechanical engineering, electrical engineering, chemical engineering, and biomedical engineering, to name just a few—and within each field are several subdisciplines. Regardless of their engineering background, engineers are engaged in solving problems in most, if not all, industries, including manufacturing, energy, utilities, petroleum, construction, telecommunications, the environment, automotive, entertainment, aerospace, mining, welding, health, education, and government.

In *Career Opportunities in Engineering,* you will learn about 84 career options that are available in the wide world of engineering. Most of the career profiles are about different types of engineers. A few other profiles are about professionals who work with engineers as well as alternative careers for engineers. The profiles give you basic information about 84 occupations. You will learn what people in these 84 professions do, where they work, and how much they earn. You will also learn about job prospects, advancement opportunities, and the requirements for obtaining entry-level jobs. Perhaps as you read the profiles, you will come across engineering professions that interest you. We provide you with suggestions to help you learn more about them.

As our population grows, and as we develop new technologies, engineers will be at the forefront of the creation of new products and modern conveniences. Maybe you will be one of these engineers. This book can help you make that important decision.

Job Outlook

According to the U.S. Bureau of Labor Statistics, 1.4 million engineers were employed in the United States in 2004. This federal agency predicted that over the period between 2004 and 2014, overall job growth for engineers will increase by only 9 to 17 percent. Job opportunities are expected to remain favorable for this profession because the number of graduating students from engineering programs should be about equal to the number of job openings expected to become available.

Most job opportunities become available as engineers retire, advance to higher positions, or transfer to other positions. A large number of engineers throughout the different engineering disciplines will soon become eligible for retirement, which should create more openings for both experienced and entry-level positions.

Keep in mind that the job market fluctuates with the health of the nation's economy. When the economy is in a downturn, many employers lay workers off and hire fewer employees. However, even during periods when the job outlook seems poor, opportunities will continue to be available as employers need the experience, skills, and talents of engineers to help run their organizations more productively, efficiently, and safely. Because technologies are constantly changing and becoming more complex and sophisticated, individuals need to continually update their skills and knowledge to remain employable.

A Note to High School Students

It is never too early to start preparing for your future career. The first step begins in high school by taking courses that can help you succeed in college, and doing well in those courses. For any college program, you need to have at least a foundation in English, mathematics, science, history, and social science. Many engineering professionals recommend that high school students take as many science and math classes as possible to prepare for college engineering courses.

Other courses that can help you meet the challenges of college include computer, public speaking, and foreign language classes. In fact, some colleges may require that you have taken two years of a foreign language while in high school. Also be sure to develop your writing, critical thinking, and problem-solving skills, which will be essential to performing well in college as well as in your future jobs.

You can start getting an idea of what lies ahead for you in college by checking out various college catalogs. (School and public libraries usually carry catalogs of colleges and universities that are nearby.) In addition to describing campus life and explaining how to enroll in a college, college catalogs detail the different majors that a school offers, along with the courses that are required for each major.

Talk with your high school counselor or teachers. Let them know about your interest in going to college and perhaps pursuing an engineering career. They can help you choose the best courses to take while you are in high school, as well as advise you on the different college and career options that are available.

Start Exploring Your Options

Career Opportunities in Engineering provides you with basic information about 84 engineering and engineering-related professions. When you come across occupations that look intriguing, take the time to learn more about them. The references mentioned throughout the book and in the appendixes can help you further research careers that interest you. In addition, here are a few other things you might do to explore a profession or field in more depth:

- read books about the profession or field
- read professional and trade magazines, journals, newspapers, and other print and online periodicals
- visit Web sites for professional societies, trade associations, and other organizations related to your desired occupation
- talk with professionals who work in those jobs that interest you
- visit workplaces where engineers, surveyors, or other professionals work
- enroll in courses related to the profession
- browse through career resources that are available at libraries and career centers
- obtain part-time, seasonal, volunteer, or internship positions at private companies or other organizations that interest you

As you explore various occupations, you will discover the kinds of careers you might like—and will not like. You will also be gaining valuable knowledge and experience. Furthermore, you will be building a network of contacts who may be able to help with your next steps—obtaining further education and training, as well as future jobs.

Remember, only you can make your career goals and dreams come true. You can do it!

ACKNOWLEDGMENTS

We could not have done this book without the help of many people who took the time out of their busy schedules to talk to a stranger over the phone and through e-mail. In particular, we would like to thank the following individuals and organizations:

Lee Adler, Executive Director, Structural Engineers Association of California; American Institute of Aeronautics and Astronautics; William H. Allen, Ph.D., P.E., Professor, Chair, Agricultural and Biological Engineering Department, Clemson University; Gordon T. Arnold, Esq., Arnold & Ferrera, L.L.P.; Ed Aulerich, Council on Forest Engineering; Richard A. Behr, P.E., Ph.D., Professor and Department Head, Architectural Engineering Department, Pennsylvania State University; Professor Michael M. Bernitsas, Ph.D., Undergraduate Program Advisor, Naval Architecture and Marine Engineering, University of Michigan, Ann Arbor.

Michael E. Bonner, Master Instructor, Engineer Development Office, Edwards Air Force Base; Timothy J. Bowser, Ph.D., P.E., Associate Professor, Biosystems and Agricultural Engineering Department, Oklahoma State University; Dr. Brian L. Brazil, Supervisory Environmental Engineer, United States Department of Agriculture; Michael S. Bruno, Professor of Ocean Engineering, Stevens Institute of Technology; Joy L. Bryant, Esq., Executive Director of the National Association of Patent Practitioners; John Colt, NOAA National Marine Fisheries Service, Seattle; Scott Danielson, Ph.D., P.E., Chair, Mechanical and Manufacturing Engineering Technology, Arizona State University.

Arden Davis, Ph.D., P.E., Chair, Department of Geology and Geological Engineering, South Dakota School of Mines and Technology; Richard Felder, Hoechst Celanese Professor Emeritus of Chemical Engineering, North Carolina State University; Franklin Fong, G.E., Consulting Geotechnical Engineer; Louis E. Freund, Ph.D., Professor and Chair, Department of Industrial and Systems Engineering, San Jose State University; Izabella A. Gieras, M.S., M.B.A., Clinical Engineering Manager, Beaumont Services Company.

Marina Gonzalez, Recruiting and Employment Manager, Staffing and Employee Development, Lawrence Livermore National Laboratory; Cecilia Haskins, CSEP, Associate Director of Communications, International Council on Systems Engineering; David Ho; International Council on Systems Engineering; Dan Jilka, Vice President and Senior Account Manager, Avionics and Aerospace Engineering and Management, Management Recruiters of Seattle; John M. Joyce, P.E., President, Engineering Solutions.

Dr. Robert Kaplan, Principal, Usernomics; Kevin M. Keener, Ph.D., P.E., Associate Professor, North Carolina State University; Al Lawless, Technical Council Chairman, Society of Flight Test Engineers; John D. Lee, Associate Professor of Industrial Engineering, University of Iowa; William Malinowski, P.E., S.E.; Phillip B. Messersmith, Ph.D., Associate Professor, Biomedical Engineering Department, Northwestern University; Richard C. Moeur, P.E., Traffic Engineer; Dr. Pierre Mousset-Jones, Department of Mining Engineering, University of Nevada, Reno.

Steve Mueller, Senior Environmental Engineer, Black Hills Corporation; Tara Mulligan, Member Services Manager, USENIX Association; National Association of Patent Practitioners; Michael Papp, Rehabilitation Technology Specialist II, Alabama Department of Rehabilitation Services; Richard L. Parish, Ph.D., P.E., Professor of Agricultural Engineering, Louisiana State University; Dr. James Rankin, P.E., Director, Avionics Engineering Center, Ohio University; Carol Richardson, Miller Professor and Vice Dean, College of Applied Science and Technology, Rochester Institute of Technology; Jon A. Schmidt, P.E., Senior Structural Engineer, Burns and McDonnell; Randy Shingai, Software Development Engineer; R. Paul Singh, Professor of Food Engineering, Department of Biological and Agricultural Engineering, University of California at Davis.

Joe Siudzinski; Kathy Ferguson Siudzinski; Norman Smith, Chief Chemical Engineer/CEO, Biotek Associates International; Linda Vaccarezza; Jeanne Vogelzang, Executive Director, National Council of Structural Engineers Associations; Robert W. Warke, Assistant Professor, Welding and Materials Joining, School of Engineering and Engineering Technology, LeTourneu University, Texas; Mike Warren, District Engineer, Air Quality Division, Wyoming Department of Environmental Quality; and G.K. Yuill, Ph.D., Professor, Architectural Engineering, University of Nebraska.

Our thanks and appreciation also go to Sarah Fogarty and Vanessa Nittoli, among others who play essential roles at Ferguson Publishing to getting this book to you, our readers.

And, most of all, thank you, James Chambers! You are a one-of-a kind editor!

HOW TO USE THIS BOOK

How to Use This Book

In *Career Opportunities in Engineering,* you will learn about 84 engineering and engineering-related professions. The majority of the job profiles in this book are about the various types of engineers that work in such fields as civil engineering, electrical engineering, mechanical engineering, chemical engineering, and biomedical engineering, among others. A few profiles describe occupations that support these engineers, and several other profiles discuss alternative occupations that individuals with engineering training or backgrounds may enter.

Career Opportunities in Engineering provides basic information about the different occupations described in this book. You will read about what the occupations are like and which job requirements are needed. You will also get a general idea of the salaries, job markets, and advancement prospects for each occupation.

Sources of Information

The information presented in *Career Opportunities in Engineering* comes from a variety of sources—engineers, educators, professional societies, trade associations, government agencies, and others. In addition, books and periodicals related to the different occupations were read along with materials created by professional associations, federal agencies, businesses, and other organizations. Job descriptions, work guidelines, and other work-related materials for the different occupations were also studied.

The World Wide Web was also a valuable information source. A wide range of Web sites was visited to learn about each of the occupations that are described in this book. These Web sites included engineering departments at colleges and universities, societies, trade associations, regulatory agencies, engineering firms, private companies, online periodicals, and so forth.

How This Book Is Organized

Career Opportunities in Engineering is designed to be easy to use and read. Altogether there are 84 job profiles in fourteen sections. A section may have as few as three profiles or as many as 14 profiles, and the profiles are usually two or three pages long. All profiles follow the same format so that you may read the job profiles or sections in whatever order you prefer.

Sections one through 10 cover several career options that are available in each of the major engineering disciplines,

such as civil engineering, mechanical engineering, and agricultural engineering. Section 11 describes eight additional engineering disciplines, while section 12 discusses some of the engineering specialties, such as design and research, in which engineers work. Section 13 describes a few of the professions that provide technical support to engineers, and section 14 covers several alternative career options that are available to engineers.

The Job Profiles

The job profiles give you basic information about 84 career opportunities. Each profile starts with the *Career Profile*—a summary of the job's major duties, salary, employment outlook, and opportunities for promotion. It also sums up general requirements and special skills needed for a job, as well as personality traits that successful professionals may share. The *Career Ladder* section is a visual presentation of a typical career path.

The rest of each occupational profile is divided into the following parts:

- The "Position Description" details major responsibilities and duties of an occupation.
- "Salaries" presents a general idea of the wages that professionals may earn.
- "Employment Prospects" provides a general idea of the job market for an occupation.
- "Advancement Prospects" discusses some options in which individuals may advance in their careers.
- "Education and Training" describes the type of education and training that may be required to enter a profession.
- "Special Requirements" covers any professional license, certification, or registration that may be required for an occupation.
- "Experience, Skills, and Personality Traits" generally covers the job requirements needed for entry-level positions. It also describes some basic employability skills that employers expect job candidates to have. In addition, this part describes some personality traits that successful professionals have in common.
- "Unions and Associations" provides the names of some professional associations and labor unions that professionals are eligible to join.
- "Tips for Entry" offers general advice for gaining work experience, improving employability, and finding jobs. It also provides suggestions for finding more information on the World Wide Web.

Additional Resources

At the end of the book are four appendixes that provide additional resources for the occupations described in *Career Opportunities in Engineering*. Appendix I provides Web resources to learn about educational programs for some of the professions described in this book. Appendix II gives a list of state licensing agencies that grant licensure to professional engineers and professional surveyors, while Appendix III provides contact information for professional unions and associations. In Appendix IV, you will find a listing of resources on the World Wide Web, which can help you learn more about the many engineering and engineering-related professions.

In addition, you will find a glossary, which defines some of the abbreviations and terms that are used in this book. You will also find a bibliography in which you can find titles of periodicals and books to help you learn more about the professions that interest you.

The World Wide Web

Throughout *Career Opportunities in Engineering,* Web site addresses for various online resources are provided so that you can learn more on your own. All the Web sites were accessible as this book was being written. Keep in mind that Web site owners may change Web site addresses, remove the web pages to which you have been referred, or shut down their Web sites completely. Should you come across a URL that is unavailable, you may still be able to find the Web site by entering its title or the name of the organization or individual into a search engine.

This Book Is Yours

Career Opportunities in Engineering is your reference book. Use it to read about jobs you have often wondered about. Use it to learn about engineering professions that you never knew existed. Use it to start your search for the career of your dreams.

Good luck!

CIVIL ENGINEERING

CIVIL ENGINEER

CAREER PROFILE

Duties: Plan, design, and oversee the construction of buildings, public works, water systems, transportation systems, and other structures or elements of the infrastructure; perform duties as required

Alternate Title(s): A title that reflects a specialty (such as Structural Engineer) or an engineering function (such as Project Engineer)

Salary Range: $44,000 to $98,000

Employment Prospects: Fair

Advancement Prospects: Good

Prerequisites:

    Education or Training—Bachelor's degree in civil engineering; on-the-job training

    Experience—Previous work experience generally required

    Special Skills and Personality Traits—Communication, writing, computer, teamwork, interpersonal, customer service, leadership, analytical, and problem-solving skills; curious, creative, reliable, composed, honest, self-motivated, detail-oriented, and persistent

    Special Requirements—Professional engineer (P.E.) license usually required

CAREER LADDER

```
┌─────────────────────────────┐
│    Senior Civil Engineer    │
└─────────────────────────────┘

┌─────────────────────────────┐
│        Civil Engineer       │
└─────────────────────────────┘

┌─────────────────────────────┐
│    Junior Civil Engineer    │
└─────────────────────────────┘
```

Position Description

Civil engineering is often described as the oldest engineering profession. Evidence of this can be found all around the world. The Great Wall of China, the pyramids of Egypt and Central America, and the Coliseum of Rome are just a few examples of magnificent ancient civil engineering projects.

Today, Civil Engineers are the professionals who plan, design, and oversee the construction of the public works projects that comprise a society's infrastructure. For example, Civil Engineers are involved with the creation and maintenance of roads, tunnels, bridges, railroads, airports, harbors, dams, irrigation projects, pipelines, and waste disposal systems. They are also involved in private projects, such as the construction of shopping malls, apartment buildings, and industrial facilities. Their designs range from the simple to the complex: from bike paths to highways; from buildings to cities; from embankments to space stations.

Civil engineering is divided into several subdisciplines, in which many Civil Engineers choose to specialize. The following are a few of these professionals:

• Structural engineers are experts in the properties of building materials and how they behave in all sorts of conditions. They are typically involved with the design and construction of large projects such as skyscrapers, freeway overpasses, and airplanes that are mainly built with steel or such other materials as plastics, other metals, and concrete.

• Environmental engineers use their understanding of biology and chemistry to develop pollution-reduction systems. For example, an environmental engineer seeks ways to clean air and water, remove contamination from the soil, and dispose of various waste products. They also design industrial facilities that reduce the production of by-products that pollute the environment.

- Geotechnical engineers design structures built from, on, or under the ground. They apply their knowledge about the nature and use of soils, minerals, and water to construct or support structures. Tunnels, river levees, and building foundations are among the structures with which these engineers work.
- Construction engineers plan and oversee designs created by other Civil Engineers. They understand all practical aspects of construction from planning and financing to building methods and project management. Their expertise makes it possible to convert designs into finished facilities.
- Water resources engineers help to protect precious water resources and ensure that water is adequately supplied to cities and agricultural areas. They design and oversee the construction of such projects as reservoirs, canals, pipelines, and hydroelectric facilities. They maintain seaports and freshwater pumping stations. They are also concerned with water conservation and flood control projects.
- Ocean engineers combine engineering with oceanography to design systems for such aspects of oceanographic operations as research, oil production, mineral exploration, marine transportation, commercial fishing, ocean resources management, and coastline protection. These engineers also design and build equipment, vessels, structures, and instruments that can function in ocean environments.
- Transportation engineers are involved with the transport of people and things over roadways, railroads, and waterways. They design, plan, estimate costs, and make specifications for a variety of transportation projects, as well as work to improve older systems and structures.
- Government and urban planning engineers oversee public works projects in municipalities and regional areas. They work to solve problems with traffic patterns, neighborhood layouts, zoning issues, and other matters.

Throughout their careers, Civil Engineers also perform various engineering functions, or roles, in the different phases of their projects. For example, they may be employed as field engineers, designers, research engineers, development engineers, test engineers, project managers, regulatory specialists, forensic engineers, and consultants. Some Civil Engineers teach engineering students at colleges and universities on a full- or part-time basis. Most full-time instructors also conduct research to add new knowledge and understanding about civil engineering topics, or to seek new and better ways to apply basic knowledge of civil engineering.

Regardless of their specialty or function, Civil Engineers perform a variety of duties that are similar. For example, they might:

- plan and design new structures and systems
- plan and direct the maintenance and improvement of older projects
- test construction materials and soils for strength, durability, or safety
- survey or oversee the surveying of construction sites
- conduct studies of the feasibility of a new project such as a road, water treatment plant, or tunnel as well as the environmental conditions surrounding a project site
- analyze information such as planning reports, design specifications, maps, and photographs to facilitate their planning of projects as well as to understand the impact of a project on the surrounding area
- estimate the quantities and costs of the materials, equipment, or labor needed to complete projects
- prepare environmental impact reports, financial statements, and other reports
- prepare designs, blueprints, and project specifications
- direct the building of a project site
- schedule work and activities
- supervise or manage other engineers or departments
- inspect project sites to monitor work progress and to ensure that the construction conforms to the design and that safety standards are met
- provide technical advice to clients about the design, materials, and maintenance of a project
- consult with other engineers during the life of a project
- update and use job-related knowledge by reading, studying, and taking refresher courses

Civil Engineers work closely on teams made up of other Civil Engineers, technicians, and engineers from other fields. Their work involves the use of computers to complete a variety of tasks. For example, they utilize design, word processing, drawing, and image editing software, as well as other computer technologies such as Global Positioning Satellite (GPS) and geographical information systems (GIS).

Civil Engineers are employed in both the public and private sectors. Junior engineers typically work under the guidance and supervision of senior engineers. Their focus is to develop their skills and their understanding of the rules, regulations, standards, and practices of their area of concern. Junior Civil Engineers are given specific directions on their assignments along with clearly defined priorities and goals.

As engineers gain experience and knowledge, they receive more complex assignments and are able to exercise greater levels of authority. They may work as lead persons in certain assignments while directing the activities of other engineers and technicians. Some decisions are made at this level.

Senior engineers are more actively involved with the decision-making process and are more likely to be team leaders. Their decisions are made without direct supervision. Senior engineers are more aware of program needs and work independently in response to those needs. They are expected to implement departmental customer service and partnership concepts, for example.

Advanced and executive-level Civil Engineers are the primary engineers for project divisions, or for an entire geographical area. As their level of expertise is wider in scope, these professionals perform the most difficult engineering tasks. They make policy decisions and consult with clients or government agencies at the highest levels. They are responsible for top-level project management. For example, a principal engineer in a consulting firm might oversee all of the aspects of planning, design, and consultation. In addition, they have the responsibility to perform client management, business development, and administration duties.

Civil Engineers usually work in or near industrial centers. They might be required to be outdoors at construction sites. Some engineers work in a variety of locations. For some, their work takes them to remote areas and even to other countries. Civil Engineers are sometimes required to physically exert themselves by lifting moderate weights, kneeling, stooping, climbing, or walking. Civil Engineers might be exposed to dust, temperature extremes, noise, and other environments when they work away from their desks. A 40-hour workweek is standard for Civil Engineers, but they may be required to work additional hours to meet deadlines and complete their various tasks.

Salaries

Salaries for Civil Engineers vary, depending on such factors as their education, experience, job duties, employer, industry, and geographical location. According to the November 2004 *Occupational Employment Statistics* survey by the U.S. Bureau of Labor Statistics (BLS), the estimated annual salary for most Civil Engineers ranged between $43,530 and $97,450.

Employment Prospects

The BLS reported that about 226,100 Civil Engineers were employed in the United States as of November 2004. The highest level of employment was in the architectural and engineering services industry. Other major employers include the local, state, and federal governments as well as the nonresidential building construction industry. Some Civil Engineers are employed as professors and instructors in academic institutions, and some are self-employed consultants.

In general, opportunities will continually be available for Civil Engineers, as they will be needed to design, construct, maintain, and repair roads, bridges, water supply systems, and other public works. The BLS predicts that the employment of Civil Engineers is expected to grow by 9 to 17 percent through 2014. Additionally, job openings will become available as engineers advance to higher positions, transfer to other occupations, retire, or leave the workforce for other reasons. Although the job market for this occupation is expected to be average, opportunities should be favorable for experienced engineers.

Advancement Prospects

Civil Engineers may advance in any number of ways, depending on their ambitions and interests. For example,

they can specialize in a particular field, such as traffic engineering or geotechnical engineering, or pursue a career in finance, marketing, or other business areas within their organizations.

Engineers with management and administrative interests and talents can seek positions as supervisory, project, and chief engineers. In addition, Civil Engineers can advance to executive officer positions within their organization. Civil Engineers with entrepreneurial ambitions can become independent consultants or owners of firms that offer civil engineering services. These engineers can also pursue teaching and research careers in academic institutions.

Education and Training

Minimally, a bachelor's degree in civil engineering, math, physical science, or another related field is needed for entry-level civil engineering positions. A master's or doctoral degree is usually required for engineers to advance to careers in management, consulting, research, or teaching. Engineers must possess a doctorate to teach civil engineering at the college level. Many Civil Engineers obtain advanced degrees in a civil engineering specialty that interests them.

Employers typically provide entry-level engineers with training programs, which may include both on-the-job training and formal classroom training.

Throughout their careers, Civil Engineers enroll in continuing education and training programs to update their skills and keep up with advancements in their field.

Special Requirements

Because their work affects the public safety and welfare, Civil Engineers must be licensed as professional engineers (P.E.) where they practice. The P.E. licensing process consists of two stages. At the first level, qualifying individuals become licensed as engineers-in-training (E.I.T.). After working several years under the supervision of licensed Civil Engineers, E.I.T.s become eligible to apply for the P.E. license.

The requirements for P.E. licensure differ in each state and territory, as well as in Washington, D.C. For specific information, contact the board of engineering examiners for the area where you wish to practice. See Appendix II for a list of boards.

Experience, Special Skills, and Personality Traits

Entry-level candidates should have work experience related to the positions for which they apply. They may have gained their experience through internships, work-study programs, student research projects, or summer employment.

Civil Engineers need strong communication, writing, and computer skills for their jobs. They must also have effective interpersonal and customer service skills to work well with many people with different backgrounds. In addition, they should have excellent leadership, analytical, and problem-solving skills. Being curious, creative, reliable, composed, honest, self-motivated, detail-oriented, and persistent are some personality traits that successful Civil Engineers share.

Unions and Associations

Many Civil Engineers belong to local, state, and national societies to take advantage of networking opportunities, continuing education programs, and other professional services and resources. Some national societies that serve the general interests of these engineers include the American Society of Civil Engineers, the National Society of Professional Engineers, the Society of Women Engineers, and the American Public Works Association. Many Civil Engineers also belong to professional societies that serve their particular specialties. For example, transportation engineers might join the Institute of Transportation Engineers, while water resources engineers might join the American Water Resources Association.

For contact information for all the above organizations, see Appendix III.

Tips for Entry

1. While in college, explore the different types of work environments in which you are interested. Contact companies about available internship, work experience, or summer job programs.

2. Join a student chapter of a professional engineering society and participate in its various activities.

3 Some companies visit college campuses to conduct job interviews. To learn about such visits, contact your college career center and engineering department.

4 Many government agencies have a job hotline that you can call at any time. Many agencies also post job vacancies at their Web sites. To learn about federal government openings, visit the government's official jobs site at http://www.usajobs.opm.gov.

5 Use the Internet to learn more about Civil Engineers. You might start by visiting these Web sites: American Society of Civil Engineers, http://www.asce.org; and iCivilEngineer: The Civil Engineering Portal, http://www.icivilengineer.com. For more links, see Appendix IV.

STRUCTURAL ENGINEER

CAREER PROFILE

Duties: Plan, design, and oversee the construction of safe and sound structural systems; perform duties as required

Alternate Title(s): Civil Engineer; Bridge Engineer; a title that reflects an engineering function such as Project Engineer

Salary Range: $44,000 to $98,000

Employment Prospects: Good

Advancement Prospects: Good

Prerequisites:

Education or Training—Bachelor's degree in civil engineering; on-the-job training

Experience—Previous work experience generally required

Special Skills and Personality Traits—Leadership, decision-making, organizational, negotiation, writing, communication, interpersonal, teamwork, and computer skills; creative, flexible, reliable, tactful, honest, self-motivated, and persistent

Special Requirements—Professional engineer (P.E.) license usually required; structural engineer (S.E.) license required in some states

CAREER LADDER

```
┌─────────────────────────────┐
│  Senior Structural Engineer │
└─────────────────────────────┘

┌─────────────────────────────┐
│    Structural Engineer      │
└─────────────────────────────┘

┌─────────────────────────────┐
│    Junior Civil Engineer    │
└─────────────────────────────┘
```

Position Description

In our modern society, we often live or work in large, steel-enforced, multistoried buildings. We cross enormous bridges made of steel and concrete. We use water that is stored behind huge dams. We run our vehicles on petroleum products that are sometimes extracted with gigantic offshore oil rigs. Professionals who work in the field of structural engineering are involved in the design of all of these larger-than-life structures. These men and women are called Structural Engineers.

Structural engineering is a specialty of civil engineering. It is the discipline that focuses on the design of large construction projects and the analysis of the forces and stresses that such structures endure. Structural engineering is also concerned with other fields besides civil engineering when it is involved in the design of large movable objects such as space stations, ships, or airplanes. However, Structural Engineers are mostly engaged in planning unchangeable objects that range in size from houses to skyscrapers.

Many of Structural Engineers' clients are architects. Architects design how a building will look. Structural Engineers design the framework—the support system of beams and columns. Their designs specify how and where the various components of the framework are made and installed. It is their responsibility to design a structure in a manner that ensures that it will be strong and safe.

Massive buildings need to be able to support their own weight, which Structural Engineers refer to as "dead loads." Further, they need to be able to withstand the forces of nature, particularly strong winds and earthquakes, as well as the weight of the people and furnishings within. These stress factors are known as "live loads." The vibrations from the movement of people, machines, and vehicles must also be withstood by large structures. Structural Engineers utilize their understanding of mathematics and physics to design structures that can withstand the various stresses. They use computers to make the necessary calculations in a quick and efficient manner.

888

рррё

Structural Engineers are knowledgeable about the properties of strong building materials such as wood, aluminum, concrete, and steel. Structural Engineers use their thorough understanding of materials and their behaviors to oversee the construction of their projects, but they also apply such knowledge to the repair and rehabilitation of large structures as well as to their demolition. They take this knowledge into consideration when making their calculations to solve the problems of how structures are to withstand the stresses placed upon them. The sizes and strengths of the various components of the framework are established in preparation for construction.

Structural Engineers are on hand during construction to inspect the structures and to ensure that the materials used in the construction are being used properly. The inspections focus on certain specifications for the various purposes of the building. For example, some floors in a large office building house sensitive equipment that requires a minimum amount of vibration. Those areas of the building would be constructed differently than the other areas. Structural Engineers continue their inspections after construction is completed to ensure that the structure functions properly.

Some Structural Engineers specialize according to a type of structure or a type of structural engineering. For example, they may be involved in any of the following:

- new bridge construction or bridge repair
- building design, construction, or renovation
- structural analysis
- construction of specific types of buildings such as educational buildings
- historic preservation of buildings, roadways, and other sites
- building relocation

Many Structural Engineers are employed by governmental regulatory agencies. In that working environment, their duties include reviewing construction plans and other pertinent documents for compliance with various regulations including zoning codes. They provide reports about such regulations to their local governments and planning boards. Structural Engineers also inspect buildings and their renovations. In addition, they appear before various groups, schools, and government entities to share their expertise about structural engineering.

Many other Structural Engineers work for private companies. They are responsible for completing such duties as investigating, analyzing, designing, and engineering all of the structural systems for projects and being involved in all phases of the projects. In private companies, some Structural Engineers are involved in the processes of client development and marketing of their services.

In both public and private settings, Structural Engineers complete general tasks that include:

- conducting research that involves asking for field tests and evaluating their results
- preparing documentation of design specifications, engineering standards, and construction costs and methods
- compiling all the data that is needed for preparing drawings and specifications
- ensuring compliance with applicable laws, regulations, and codes and including them in their designs, drawings, and specifications
- documenting and providing cost estimates and contract documents
- coordinating structural system designs and drawings with those of other professionals involved on a project
- calculating structural loads and incorporating them into their designs
- reviewing and approving drawings, plans, and specifications submitted by staff members and consulting engineers or architects
- visiting construction sites and performing site inspections
- providing technical expertise to clients, governments, as well as to other engineers and professionals
- preparing engineering reports

Experienced Structural Engineers lead project teams, occasionally direct other Structural Engineers, and mentor junior engineers. Those working in the capacity of the structural engineer of record are responsible for providing approval of all plans, calculations, specifications, and drawings for projects. Senior engineers are expected to keep up-to-date with the latest developments in their field and share this information with their staff members.

Structural Engineers must work well with a wide range of people in a variety of situations. They sometimes have to settle disputes or resolve problems that arise regarding both technical and nontechnical issues. The reports and reviews that Structural Engineers prepare must be written in a way that everyone involved with a project can read and comprehend.

Much of the work done by Structural Engineers requires the use of computers. Creating and analyzing designs, testing structural systems, and writing documents are all tasks that are done with the aid of computers.

Structural Engineers work in offices as well as at project sites. Their site inspections may require them to climb ladders or scaffolds, move through crawl spaces, or walk on beams and roofs. They generally work a 40-hour week but may be required to put in additional hours to meet deadlines and complete their various tasks.

Salaries

Salaries for Structural Engineers vary, depending on such factors as their education, experience, employer, and geographical location. The estimated annual salary for most civil engineers, including Structural Engineers, ranged between $43,530 and $97,650, according to the November

2004 *Occupational Employment Statistics* survey by the U.S. Bureau of Labor Statistics.

Employment Prospects

Besides consulting firms and regulatory agencies, Structural Engineers are employed by construction companies and suppliers of specific components and systems (such as pre-cast concrete, steel joists, and cold-formed steel). Many engineers also find employment in steel mills, oil refineries, and other large industrial facilities. Some Structural Engineers work as teachers and researchers in academic institutions. Others are independent contractors.

The job market in structural engineering is generally stable, as buildings, bridges, and roads continually need to be built and repaired. However, during economic slowdowns, construction usually slows down and that may lead to fewer employment opportunities. Job openings also become available as Structural Engineers advance to higher positions, transfer to other jobs, retire, or leave the workforce for other reasons.

Advancement Prospects

Structural Engineers with management and administrative interests and talents can seek positions as supervisory, project, and chief engineers. They can also advance to executive officer positions within their organization. Some engineers choose to advance by seeking teaching and research opportunities. A master's or doctoral degree is usually required for engineers to obtain management, teaching, and research positions. Engineers with entrepreneurial ambitions can become independent practitioners or owners of firms that offer consulting or contracting services.

Education and Training

Minimally, Structural Engineers must possess a bachelor's degree in civil engineering, preferably with an emphasis in structural engineering, physical science, or another related field. Some employers require that applicants possess a master's degree in structural or civil engineering. To teach engineering at the college and university level, Structural Engineers must possess a doctoral degree.

Employers typically provide entry-level engineers with training programs, which may include both on-the-job and classroom training. New engineers work under the supervision and direction of experienced engineers.

Throughout their careers, Structural Engineers enroll in continuing education and training programs to update their skills and keep up with advancements in their fields.

Special Requirements

Structural Engineers must be licensed professional engineers (P.E.) where they practice.

As of June 2005, Illinois, Nebraska, New Mexico, Utah, Nevada, Idaho, Washington, Oregon, California, and Hawaii had separate licensure requirements for structural engineers (S.E.). Some states require that structural engineers possess both P.E. and S.E. licenses.

The requirements for engineering licensure differ in each state and territory, as well as in Washington, D.C. For specific information, contact the board of engineering examiners for the area where you wish to practice. See Appendix II for a list of boards.

Experience, Special Skills, and Personality Traits

Many employers prefer that entry-level candidates have some work experience related to the position for which they apply. They may have gained their experience through internships, work-study programs, student research projects, or summer employment.

To perform well at their job, Structural Engineers need strong leadership, decision-making, organizational, and negotiation skills. In addition, they must have effective writing, communication, interpersonal, and teamwork skills. Having strong computer skills is also essential. Being creative, flexible, reliable, tactful, honest, self-motivated, and persistent are some personality traits that successful Structural Engineers have in common.

Unions and Associations

Many Structural Engineers join local, state, and national societies to take advantage of continuing education programs, networking opportunities, and other professional services and resources. Some national societies to which they might belong include the Structural Engineering Institute, the American Concrete Institute, the American Wood Council, the American Society of Civil Engineers, and the National Society of Professional Engineers. For contact information, see Appendix III.

Tips for Entry

1. If you are in high school, learn carpentry skills. Gain experience by taking construction jobs.
2. In college, take advantage of your part-time jobs and internships by learning as much as you can about a project.
3. If you want to work abroad, make yourself employable. Learn the main language as well as about the culture of the area where you wish to work.
4. Check out professional associations and professional journals for job listings.
5. Use the Internet to learn more about Structural Engineers. You might start by visiting these Web sites: National Council of Structural Engineers Associations, http://www.ncsea.com, and iCivilEngineer—Structural Engineering Portal, http://www.icivilengineer.com/Structural_Engineering. For more links, see Appendix IV.

GEOTECHNICAL ENGINEER

Duties: Plan, design, and oversee the construction of underground structures and parts of infrastructure; perform duties as required

Alternate Title(s): Civil Engineer, Soil Engineer, Foundation Engineer; a title that reflects an engineering function such as Field Engineer or Forensic Engineer

Salary Range: $44,000 to $98,000

Employment Prospects: Fair

Advancement Prospects: Good

Prerequisites:

Education or Training—Bachelor's degree in civil engineering; on-the-job training

Experience—Previous work experience generally required

Special Skills and Personality Traits—Leadership, interpersonal, teamwork, problem-solving, judgment, writing, communication, and self-management skills; trustworthy, reliable, creative, innovative, and self-motivated

Special Requirements—Professional engineer (P.E.) license usually required

Senior Geotechnical Engineer

Geotechnical Engineer

Junior Geotechnical Engineer

Position Description

Geotechnical engineering is a specialty of civil engineering that utilizes knowledge and expertise about the properties of underground water, soil, and rock to design structures on, in, and under the ground. This area of civil engineering is also known as ground engineering or soil engineering.

Geotechnical Engineers are knowledgeable about geology, but they are not to be confused with engineering geologists, who concentrate on applying principles of geology to understand the conditions and properties of earth materials. Geotechnical Engineers apply their specialized understanding of geology toward the use of earth materials to design and build public works projects.

Nearly our entire infrastructure is composed of structures that are situated in or under the earth, or are made of earth materials. For example, buildings sit on the earth, but are supported by unseen foundations that are constructed beneath the surface. Tunnels and pipelines are located underneath the ground surface. Some structures, such as river embankments and earth-filled dams, are constructed with soil and other earth materials. Geotechnical Engineers may be involved in the planning, design, and construction phases of such projects.

Geotechnical Engineers study the properties of the soil, rock, and underground water in a specific location to evaluate their use for construction as well as how they would impact or be impacted by future structures. Their mission is to determine whether the rocks and soils below a site can support a proposed structure; to decide whether groundwater conditions will change and how such changes will affect the project; and to understand how an earthquake would impact the structure.

They visit the proposed construction site and drill into the ground to take samples of the soil. These are analyzed in a laboratory to determine soil consistencies and other characteristics that suggest their appropriateness as building materials. The samples are also tested for strength to determine how a structure's weight will impact it. Geotechnical

Engineers create reports of their findings, and submit project designs to their clients before proceeding further with the projects.

Geotechnical Engineers monitor the construction process to make sure that their findings and recommendations are correct. If they are incorrect, they make adjustments to the construction plans. They determine what sort of foundations and retaining walls are needed, and how they should be designed. Geotechnical Engineers make sure that groundwater will not be contaminated by the construction process, or by the future function of the structure. They use heavy equipment on the project site to move the earth and ensure its reliability as a building material.

During the construction process, Geotechnical Engineers work closely with their clients to solve various geotechnical, financial, or planning problems to ensure that the projects are completed within costs and schedules.

Geotechnical Engineers provide further geotechnical engineering studies for completed projects or older structures such as underground storage facilities, water treatment systems, pipelines, roads, and harbor facilities. These studies lead to retrofitting, improvements, or repairs to these structures.

Geotechnical Engineers work in teams to complete their projects. Each team may consist of a project director or a senior engineer who is assisted by one or more staff engineers and geologists, as well as by technicians and other support staff including personnel who check the team's work for correctness and accuracy.

Geotechnical Engineers work in office settings and in the field. Field operations involve soil sampling, monitoring of geotechnical instrumentation, and construction work. Office operations involve design work and lab duties. Geotechnical Engineers use computers for many aspects of their office work, including for writing their reports. They also use computer-aided design (CAD) programs to design and draft project plans.

Throughout their careers, Geotechnical Engineers work in different engineering functions. For example, they may be engaged as design engineers, project managers, research engineers, or consultants. Some engineers teach and conduct research in colleges and universities.

Geotechnical Engineers perform work in highly populated areas, as well as in remote locations. They may be required to work in outdoor settings and in all sorts of weather conditions. They may also be required to lift moderate weights, and to operate vehicles or construction equipment.

Geotechnical Engineers generally work a 40-hour workweek, but they may be required to put in additional hours to complete various tasks or to meet deadlines.

Salaries

Salaries for Geotechnical Engineers vary, depending on such factors as their education, experience, employer, and geographical location. According to the November 2004 *Occupational Employment Statistics* survey by the U.S. Bureau of Labor Statistics, the estimated annual salary for most civil engineers, such as Geotechnical Engineers, ranged between $43,530 and $97,650.

Employment Prospects

Opportunities are available for qualified Geotechnical Engineers in both the public and private sectors. Some governmental employers include local public works departments, flood control districts, utilities, state highway and water resources departments, the U.S. Forest Service, and the U.S. Army Corps of Engineers. Besides consulting firms, Geotechnical Engineers are hired by such private companies as land and real estate developers, engineering contractors, and research organizations. Some Geotechnical Engineers are self-employed practitioners, and some work in academic institutions as professors and researchers.

Job openings usually become available to replace engineers who advance to higher positions, transfer to other occupations, retire, or leave the workforce for other reasons. In general the job demand for Geotechnical Engineers should remain stable, as houses, commercial property, and public works are continually being built, renovated, and repaired.

Advancement Prospects

As Geotechnical Engineers gain experience, they are assigned to more complex projects and receive increasingly greater responsibilities. They can advance in any number of ways. They can become specialists in a particular area, such as soil dynamics, earthquake engineering, or computer modeling. Engineers with management and administrative interests and talents can seek positions as supervisory, project, and chief engineers. To advance to higher positions, engineers usually are required to possess a master's or doctoral degree. Geotechnical Engineers with entrepreneurial ambitions can become independent practitioners or business owners who provide geotechnical engineering services.

Education and Training

Geotechnical Engineers hold at least a bachelor's degree in civil engineering, geology, or another related field. Many of them also possess a master's degree in geotechnical engineering or in civil engineering with an emphasis in geotechnical engineering.

Engineers who wish to teach in academic institutions must have a doctorate.

Employers typically provide entry-level engineers with training programs, which may include both on-the-job and classroom training. New engineers work under the supervision and direction of experienced engineers.

Throughout their careers, Geotechnical Engineers enroll in continuing education and training programs to update their skills and keep up with advancements in their fields.

Special Requirements

Because their work affects the public safety and welfare, Geotechnical Engineers must be state-licensed professional engineers (P.E.) where they practice. In California, they must also be licensed geotechnical engineers. The requirements for P.E. licensure differ in each state and territory, as well as in Washington, D.C. For specific information, contact the board of engineering examiners for the area where you wish to practice. See Appendix II for a list of boards.

Experience, Special Skills, and Personality Traits

Entry-level candidates should have work experience related to the positions for which they apply. They may have gained their experience through internships, work-study programs, student research projects, or summer employment.

Geotechnical Engineers must have effective leadership, interpersonal, teamwork, problem-solving, and judgment skills to perform well at their job. In addition, they need strong writing and communication skills, as well as excellent self-management skills, such as the abilities to handle stressful situations, work independently, prioritize multiple tasks, and meet deadlines.

Some personality traits that successful Geotechnical Engineers share include being trustworthy, reliable, creative, innovative, and self-motivated.

Unions and Associations

Many Geotechnical Engineers join professional associations to take advantage of networking opportunities, continuing education programs, and other professional services and resources. Societies are available at the local, state, and national levels. For example, the Geo-Institute, the American Society of Civil Engineers, and the National Society of Professional Engineers are some national organizations. For contact information, see Appendix III.

Tips for Entry

1. Obtain an internship or part-time job with a geotechnical engineering firm to determine if that is the field you want to enter.
2. Employers like to hire candidates who demonstrate that they have a willingness to learn what the employers have to teach them.
3. Many employers prefer to hire candidates who possess a master's degree in geotechnical engineering.
4. Contact local, state, and national professional associations for information about scholarships, internships, fellowships, and employment.
5. Use the Internet to learn more about Geotechnical Engineers. You might start by visiting these Web sites: The Geo-Institute, http://www.geoinstitute.org, and The World Wide Web Virtual Library of Geotechnical Engineering, http://www.ejge.com/GVL. For more links, see Appendix IV.

CONSTRUCTION ENGINEER

CAREER PROFILE

Duties: Plan and oversee the various phases of construction projects; perform duties as required

Alternate Title(s): Project Engineer, Construction Manager; a title that reflects an engineering function such as Estimator, Scheduler, Field Engineer, or Assistant Project Manager

Salary Range: $44,000 to $98,000

Employment Prospects: Fair

Advancement Prospects: Good

Prerequisites:

Education or Training—Bachelor's degree in civil engineering; on-the-job training

Experience—Previous work experience not necessary, but preferred

Special Skills and Personality Traits—Leadership, teamwork, analytical, problem-solving, writing, presentation, interpersonal, and communication skills; confident, self-motivated, detail-oriented, organized, ethical, creative, and persistent

Special Requirements—Professional engineer (P.E.) license usually required

CAREER LADDER

```
Senior Construction Engineer
```

```
Construction Engineer
```

```
Junior Construction Engineer
```

Position Description

Whenever any part of our infrastructure is built, someone needs to coordinate all of the planning and application of design specifications that are contributed by a variety of engineers. Construction engineering is the field to which that individual, a Construction Engineer, belongs. Hospitals, office buildings, and factories are just a few of the private projects with which Construction Engineers are involved. They also administer such public works projects as recreation facilities, airports, parks, water and sewage treatment plants, highways, bridges, and other structures and installations. In addition to new construction projects, they are also engaged in the rehabilitation of existing structures.

Construction engineering is a specialty of civil engineering. It applies business science and management to the development of construction projects from design to completion. Construction Engineers are guided by the standards of planning, organizing, financing, managing, and operating construction ventures in close association with construction methods, equipment, and the likely results of their use. They use this knowledge to convert designs created by other engineers into finished facilities. It is the job of Construction Engineers to coordinate and efficiently integrate such factors as labor, materials, equipment, and supplies to finish construction projects within scheduling and budgetary limitations. They ensure that the designer's specifications for quality are met.

The Construction Engineers' grasp of mathematics and science is used to determine the need for building site modifications. They suggest which materials to use during all stages of construction. They may design some of the components, such as utility systems, that will be included in the structure.

Construction Engineers are also responsible for designing temporary structures such as scaffolding, systems for lifting, and material handling, and work platforms, as well as ramps and earthwork structures. They design the layout of each project, procure materials and supplies, select equipment, and continually monitor the costs and quality of the work. Sometimes the Construction Engineer assigns the design work to a design specialist.

Some Construction Engineers specialize in specific areas of the construction field, such as construction costs and financing; computerized scheduling and control; construction equipment design; and international construction.

Construction Engineers fill a variety of roles in the course of their careers, many of which require specialized training in the areas of construction programming, cost control, construction quality control, and management. Some of these engineering functions include superintendent, project manager, sales engineer, field engineer, cost engineer, design engineer, safety engineer, and company executive.

Construction Engineers are responsible for performing many tasks on the job. For example, they:

- analyze and interpret data such as construction modifications and specifications to better make decisions as well as to resolve disputes or settle costs
- test and evaluate construction facilities to ensure compliance with municipal, state, and federal standards
- review work schedules, technical reports, and correspondence
- plan such construction operations as site layout, scheduling of tasks, selecting equipment, organizing crews, managing materials, and safeguarding the environment
- check plans for the feasibility of construction with an eye toward utilizing efficient methods and safety considerations
- prepare bids and cost estimates
- manage subcontractor firms
- resolve job site and engineering problems
- prepare construction proposals, specifications, and provisions as well as other necessary documents throughout the construction process
- negotiate agreements with contractors, property owners, and officials
- write and process various pertinent documents such as work orders and agreements
- use computers to work with database or project management software
- supervise and provide technical direction to personnel in the office or in the field
- represent their employer at meetings with clients and government officials
- maintain positive relationships with coworkers, subordinates, clients, and subcontractors, as well as with the general public

Construction Engineers may be responsible for several jobs, which will therefore take them to different work sites. They work indoors in office buildings or in on-site temporary buildings. Their work requires long hours at a computer or desk. Construction Engineers also spend a lot of their time outdoors where they work with heavy equipment in an environment of noise, dust, and a variety of weather conditions. They work in all types of terrain, sometimes among mosquitoes and other insects.

Construction Engineers typically work 40 hours per week but on occasion put in additional hours to complete tasks, meet deadlines, or attend meetings.

Salaries

Salaries for Construction Engineers vary, depending on such factors as their education, experience, position, employer, and geographical location. The U.S. Bureau of Labor Statistics (BLS) reported in its November 2004 *Occupational Employment Statistics* survey that the estimated annual salary for most civil engineers, including Construction Engineers, ranged between $43,530 and $97,650.

Employment Prospects

According to the BLS, the employment of construction managers is predicted to increase by 9 to 17 percent through 2014. In addition to job growth, openings for Construction Engineers will become available as individuals retire, advance to higher positions, or transfer to other occupations.

In general, the demand for qualified Construction Engineers should remain steady, as buildings, bridges, public works, and other structures continually need to be built, improved, or repaired. However, during economic downturns, construction usually slows down and that may lead to fewer employment opportunities.

Opportunities for Construction Engineers are favorable throughout the world as many American firms are becoming involved in construction in other nations.

Advancement Prospects

Novice Construction Engineers generally start their careers as assistants to field engineers, estimators, project managers, and other senior Construction Engineers. As they gain experience, they receive increasingly greater responsibilities.

Construction Engineers may advance in any number of ways, depending on their ambitions and interests. They may specialize in a particular area, such as project scheduling, construction equipment design, or construction costs and financing. They may pursue management and leadership positions. Engineers with entrepreneurial ambitions may become independent consultants or owners of firms that provide construction engineering services.

Education and Training

To become a Construction Engineer, one must possess at least a bachelor's degree in construction engineering, or in civil engineering with an emphasis in construction engineering, or in another related field. Some engineers continue on to earn a master's degree in construction management. Those engineers wishing to teach and conduct research in academic institutions obtain their doctorate.

The curriculum of construction engineering programs includes engineering, management, and business science courses. Students learn how to plan, design, and build structures as well as learn about construction methods, materials, and project management.

Throughout their careers, Construction Engineers enroll in continuing education and training programs to update their skills and keep up with advancements in their fields.

Special Requirements

All engineers who offer engineering services directly to the public or perform work that affects the life, health, or property of the public must be licensed as professional engineers (P.E.) in the states where they practice.

The P.E. licensing process consists of two stages. At the first level, qualifying engineers become licensed as engineers-in-training (E.I.T.). After working several years under the supervision of licensed engineers, E.I.T.s become eligible to apply for the P.E. license.

All U.S. states, territories, and Washington, D.C., have their specific requirements for P.E. licensure. For specific information, contact the board of engineering examiners for the area where you wish to practice. See Appendix II for a list of boards.

Experience, Special Skills, and Personality Traits

Entry-level candidates do not necessarily need any prior work experience, but they should possess a professional level of technical competence to handle the various phases of construction projects. They may have gained their experience through internships, work-study programs, student research projects, or part-time employment.

To perform their various tasks well, Construction Engineers must have excellent leadership, teamwork, analytical, and problem-solving skills. Having strong writing and presentation skills is also essential. In addition, they need superior interpersonal and communication skills, as they must be able to work effectively with clients, colleagues, staff, government agencies, and others. Being confident, self-motivated, detail-oriented, organized, ethical, creative, and persistent are some personality traits that successful Construction Engineers share.

Unions and Associations

Many Construction Engineers belong to local, state, and national societies to take advantage of networking opportunities and other professional services and resources. Some national societies that serve the interests of Construction Engineers include the Construction Management Association of America, the American Society of Civil Engineers, the National Society of Professional Engineers, and the American Water Resources Association. For contact information, see Appendix III.

Tips for Entry

1. Taking some courses in business subjects may enhance your employability. Talk with professionals for suggestions about courses that may be helpful.
2. Stay up-to-date with developments, trends, and issues in the construction industry.
3. On your job search, take advantage of the different job banks that are available on the Internet. Along with job banks such as America's Job Bank (http://www.ajb.dni.us), check out those offered by professional associations on their Web sites.
4. Learn more about Construction Engineers on the Internet. You might start by visiting these Web sites: Construction Management Association of America, http://www.cmaanet.org; and The Civil Engineering Portal—Construction, http://www.icivilengineer.com/Construction. For more links, see Appendix IV.

WATER RESOURCES ENGINEER

CAREER PROFILE

Duties: Plan, design, and manage water systems for providing drinking water, controlling flooding, protecting water quality, and storing water; perform duties as required

Alternate Title(s): Civil Engineer, a title that reflects an engineering function such as Project Engineer or Water Resources Planner

Salary Range: $44,000 to $98,000

Employment Prospects: Good

Advancement Prospects: Good

Prerequisites:

    Education or Training—Bachelor's degree in civil engineering; on-the-job training

    Experience—Previous work experience generally required

    Special Skills and Personality Traits—Communication, writing, project management, problem-solving, computer, interpersonal, and teamwork skills; flexible, analytical, inquisitive, detail-oriented, dedicated, and creative

    Special Requirements—Professional engineer (P.E.) license usually required

CAREER LADDER

```
┌─────────────────────────────────────┐
│  Senior Water Resources Engineer     │
└─────────────────────────────────────┘

┌─────────────────────────────────────┐
│  Water Resources Engineer            │
└─────────────────────────────────────┘

┌─────────────────────────────────────┐
│  Junior Water Resources Engineer     │
└─────────────────────────────────────┘
```

Position Description

Water is our most precious resource. We cannot live without it. We need it to drink, bathe, grow our food, run our industries, and much more. However, we do not always live in areas where water is plentiful. Sometimes the available water is contaminated and therefore useless. Treating our water, finding new sources of water, and distributing it to wherever it is needed is the vital role of water resources engineering.

Water resources engineering, a specialty of civil engineering, is the profession that develops, designs, and manages systems for providing drinking water, controlling flooding, protecting water quality, and storing water. The professionals who work in this field are known as Water Resources Engineers.

Water Resources Engineers ensure that communities have sufficient supplies of water to fulfill their every need, and that it is readily available at low cost. They study a community's need for water, and analyze how it will be delivered and used. They plan, design, and construct systems that the community will use to control and manage their water supply.

Water Resources Engineers are involved with many types of water systems, including reservoirs, irrigation and sewer systems, and drinking water processing plants. They involve themselves in a wide range of projects, from helping people to more efficiently use water in their homes to building enormous water projects that span several states. They ensure that new water system projects do not upset the natural behavior of their local water supply.

All of the water in the world moves from an original source to where it is used and then returns to its source. This is called the hydrological cycle. Water Resources Engineers deal with every phase of this cycle. They study local water supplies and help plan for their use and development. They find out why flooding erodes soil, how waterways become polluted, and why water sources are being overused, and then they seek preventative measures or solutions to these problems. They consider how a proposed or existing water project will impact the environment and be cost effective.

Water Resources Engineers design projects and equipment with an eye toward improved water quality at its source as well as at the various delivery points, whether they would be a farm's irrigation system, a city's drinking water reservoir, or a factory's water supply. They consider such aspects of water usage as the runoff of excess water, the collection of sediments in river bottoms, and the concentration of salts and other substances carried into the soil by water. They also collect data about water quality, rainfall, and general weather patterns, which they analyze to determine what needs to be done to improve the water supply. Furthermore, they help to resolve conflicts that may arise among various groups that want access to a certain water source.

Throughout their careers, Water Resources Engineers fulfill specific engineering functions on projects. They may be involved as researchers, designers, planners, managers, and consultants, for example. Some engineers focus on a particular function. Some may work in two or more functions.

Their tasks within each function are as equally varied. Each of the tasks they perform serves to help them develop their knowledge and skill in engineering, and prompts them to apply engineering standards and procedures to every aspect of their work.

In the area of research, Water Resources Engineers compile, analyze, and interpret technical studies and data. Some of their duties include mapping floodplains, conducting flood insurance studies, calculating water flow rates, determining the appropriate equipment to use to pump excess water, evaluating the management of watersheds, and developing computer models and programs for use in scheduling or interpreting water quality data. Research engineers also assist with civil engineering studies of water management facilities.

As design engineers, Water Resources Engineers perform such tasks as designing irrigation, drainage, and waste water systems for agriculture, cities, and industries. They are also involved with preparing working plans and various detailed drawings and graphics through the use of computer-aided design (CAD) programs. When there are several proposed designs for a project, Water Resources Engineers compare the costs of these alternatives while giving consideration to environmental or regulatory requirements.

For Water Resources Engineers who work as planners, their job involves working with their staff to plot project schedules and construction specifications, preparing cost estimates, assisting in the bidding process, and drawing up contract documents. They study and report on the environmental impact of a project. Writing is a major part of the planning process. Water Resources Engineers prepare a variety of documents, such as reports from their analyses

about issues pertaining to surface and ground water resources as well as about water rights. They write proposals for projects, which include budget analyses. Water Resources Engineers must be able to write clearly, concisely, and in layman's terms. Those who read these documents, such as their clients, are not engineers or technical experts, but they need to understand the reports.

In the area of management, Water Resource Engineers may oversee the work of their staff in the office as well as at project sites. They give direction with technical matters as well as set the course for the completion of any or all phases of a project. When necessary, they prepare presentations to impart needed information or guidance.

Most Water Resources Engineers meet with clients, local officials, community groups, and other interested parties to consult and advise about their projects. Such issues as water quality, waste management, water treatment, and the control of rivers and other water resources are discussed in these consultation settings. Water Resources Engineers also consult with other engineers and professionals in related water management programs.

Much of the work performed by Water Resources Engineers is done in an office setting. In the office, computers are the main tools they use to complete such tasks as writing documents, analyzing field data, and preparing modeling studies to predict flooding or the consequences of water leakage from storage facilities. They use computers to draw and analyze designs for future projects as well as to test the performance of their projects. Water Resources Engineers develop some of the software they need to complete their tasks.

Water Resources Engineers also spend lots of time in the field. They leave the office to survey future water project sites, take samples, test water quality, and confer with clients about planning, designing, and constructing the projects. Once construction begins, Water Resources Engineers return to the field to oversee the construction process and inspect the structures that are being built.

Water Resources Engineers generally work a 40-hour week. They occasionally work additional hours to meet deadlines, complete tasks, or attend conferences. They may be given assignments that require them to travel to other cities, states, or countries, where they may be required to live for several days, weeks, or months.

Salaries

Salaries for Water Resources Engineers vary, depending on such factors as their education, experience, employer, industry and geographical location. According to the November 2004 *Occupational Employment Statistics* survey by the U.S. Bureau of Labor Statistics (BLS), the estimated annual salary for most Water Resources Engineers and other civil engineers ranged between $43,530 and $97,650.

Employment Prospects

Water Resources Engineers are employed by governmental regulatory agencies and research organizations at the local, state, and federal level. They also find employment with utilities, nonprofit organizations, consulting engineering firms, and industrial facilities. Some Water Resources Engineers are employed as teachers and researchers at academic institutions. Furthermore, some Water Resources Engineers are independent practitioners.

Many job opportunities become available as engineers advance to higher positions, retire, or transfer to other occupations. Additional positions are also expected to be created due to predicted job growth of 27 percent or more through 2014 in the area of environmental engineering, according to the BLS. However, the job market can be affected by downturns in the economy as well as by changes in governmental policies and priorities. For example, when policy makers enact looser environmental regulations, fewer jobs may become available.

Advancement Prospects

Water Resources Engineers with management and administrative interests and talents can seek positions as supervisory, project, and chief engineers. In addition, Water Resources Engineers can advance to executive officer positions within their organization. To advance to higher positions, engineers are usually required to hold a master's or doctoral degree. Engineers with entrepreneurial ambitions can become independent consultants or owners of companies that offer water resources engineering services.

Education and Training

Water Resources Engineers usually possess a bachelor's degree in civil engineering, environmental engineering, geology, or another related field with course work in water resources. Many also possess a master's degree in water resources engineering.

Employers require that Water Resources Engineers have at least a bachelor's degree, but many prefer to hire those with advanced degrees.

To teach and conduct research in academic institutions, engineers must possess a doctorate.

Employers typically provide entry-level engineers with on-the-job training. Many also have formal classroom training programs for novice engineers.

Throughout their careers, Civil Engineers enroll in continuing education and training programs to update their skills and keep up with advancements in their fields.

Special Requirements

All engineers who offer engineering services directly to the public or perform work that affects the life, health, or property of the public must be licensed as professional engineers (P.E.) where they practice. Every U.S. state and territory, as well as Washington, D.C., has its own requirements for P.E. licensure. For specific information, contact the board of engineering examiners for the area where you wish to practice. See Appendix II for a list of boards.

Experience, Special Skills, and Personality Traits

Entry-level candidates should have work experience related to the positions for which they apply. They may have gained their experience through internships, work-study programs, student research projects, or summer employment.

Water Resources Engineers need effective communication, writing, project management, and problem-solving skills for their work. Having strong computer skills is important as well. In addition, they need excellent interpersonal and teamwork skills. Some personality traits that successful Water Resources Engineers share include being flexible, analytical, inquisitive, detail-oriented, dedicated, and creative.

Unions and Associations

Many Water Resources Engineers join local, state, and national societies to take advantage of networking opportunities, continuing education programs, and other professional services and resources. The American Water Resources Association, the American Society of Civil Engineers, the American Academy of Environmental Engineers, and the National Society of Professional Engineers are some national societies that serve the interests of these engineers. For contact information, see Appendix III.

Tips for Entry

1. In high school, start learning about various water systems. Find out about your local water systems and how they work in your community.
2. You can take the engineer-in-training exam, the first level of P.E. licensure, when you graduate. Having this license may enhance your employability.
3. When you are a college senior, contact government agencies and companies directly to find out about job vacancies and application processes.
4. Attend professional conferences to learn about issues and trends, as well as to develop a network of professional contacts.
5. Learn more about Water Resources Engineers on the Internet. You might start by visiting these Web sites: American Water Resources Association, http://www.awra.org; and U.S. Geological Survey—Water Resources of the United States, http://water.usgs.gov. For more links, see Appendix IV.

TRANSPORTATION ENGINEER

CAREER PROFILE

Duties: Plan, design, and oversee the construction of road, air, water, and other types of transportation systems; perform duties as required

Alternate Title(s): A title that reflects a specialty (such as Traffic Engineer or Airport Engineer) or an engineering function (such as Planner or Project Engineer)

Salary Range: $44,000 to $98,000

Employment Prospects: Fair

Advancement Prospects: Good

Prerequisites:

Education or Training—Bachelor's degree in transportation engineering or a related field

Experience—Previous work experience generally required

Special Skills and Personality Traits—Interpersonal, communication, computer, writing, mathematical, leadership, teamwork, problem-solving, and analytical skills; curious, creative, detail-oriented, analytical, reliable, ethical, and persistent

Special Requirements—Professional engineer (P.E.) license usually required

CAREER LADDER

```
┌─────────────────────────────────────┐
│   Senior Transportation Engineer     │
└─────────────────────────────────────┘

┌─────────────────────────────────────┐
│     Transportation Engineer          │
└─────────────────────────────────────┘

┌─────────────────────────────────────┐
│   Junior Transportation Engineer     │
└─────────────────────────────────────┘
```

Position Description

The movement of goods and people is an aspect of life that we sometimes take for granted. Each day, we travel to and from our schools or jobs, or purchase needed items that came from somewhere else by way of cars, trucks, trains, airplanes, and other modes of transportation. The needs of individuals, communities, and regions, along with their movement and commercial activities, are served by a highly intricate infrastructure of roadways, subways, rail lines, airways, canals, sea-lanes, and other systems. Transportation engineering is the civil engineering specialty that pertains to the planning, design, and construction of the various road, mass transit, rail, air, river, marine, and other transportation systems. The civil engineers who specialize in this field are called Transportation Engineers.

The application of engineering standards, theories, and principles to every phase of their projects is essential for Transportation Engineers to be effective and successful. The complexity of combined components of the transportation infrastructure is closely studied, monitored, designed, built, and understood by Transportation Engineers. They are instrumental in ensuring that our transportation systems are efficient and safe. They plan for future transportation systems but just as importantly, they maintain and improve the systems that are already in place. These engineers continually seek ways to improve or oversee the function, implementation, assessment, upkeep, and rehabilitation of these facets of the transportation infrastructure.

Transportation Engineers have many responsibilities. In general, they assess the travel needs for transportation systems in their vicinity. They plan and design streets, highways, public transit lines, railroads, airports, harbors, and so forth, along with such facilities and structures as depots, distribution centers, and passenger terminals that all work together to fulfill those needs. Transportation Engineers are responsible for the safe, efficient construction and operation of these facilities and systems, as well as their maintenance and administration. The potential, current, and future impact of these systems on the local environment is also an aspect of the involvement of Transportation Engineers.

Transportation Engineers have more specific duties to perform in fulfilling their basic responsibilities. They perform other engineering design and maintenance work. They attend to the details of integrating land, roadways, railroads, water and sanitary systems, as well as the structures associated with transportation systems. For example, they may be engaged in:

- creating and putting into operation such projects as special lanes for buses or carpools to alleviate bottlenecks on highways
- compiling studies of the impact of new transportation projects with the intent to relieve traffic congestion
- investigating ways to reduce the environmental impact of transportation projects
- working to find ways to reduce traffic accidents and fatalities
- planning parking facilities
- designing pedestrian walkways
- developing better navigation systems (such as air navigation systems for commercial pilots)
- formulating methods of improving traffic safety while allowing for an increase in traffic volume
- creating and managing computerized traffic signal systems for city streets

Transportation Engineers can specialize in a number of ways within their profession. They may specialize in a particular type of transportation system, such as highways, railways, or mass transit. As engineers gain experience, they may further concentrate on a particular specialty within their field. Traffic engineering, planning for highway upkeep, analyzing environmental issues, and designing automated electronic toll payment systems or intelligent transportation systems are just a few examples of the diverse specialty areas that Transportation Engineers may choose. Some Transportation Engineers work in the field of operations, in which they monitor the flow of traffic, work with public transportation, and coordinate traffic signs, signals, and markers to ensure the orderly and efficient use of the transportation infrastructure.

Most Transportation Engineers perform different engineering functions throughout their careers. Depending on their experience, skills, and interests, they may be employed as designers, analysts, project managers, researchers, planners, consultants, or forensic engineers, for example. Some engineers become part-time or full-time teachers in colleges and universities. Full-time instructors typically conduct basic or applied research to further understand, create, or improve transportation systems.

Regardless of the function they perform, Transportation Engineers work and collaborate with many people. For example, planners work with other transportation professionals and technicians to collaborate on the aspects of

designs in which each discipline specializes. For another example, some project managers supervise staffs of other engineers, technicians, project leaders, and support personnel. These managers provide technical guidance as well.

All Transportation Engineers prepare a variety of documents such as reports, surveys, and analyses, which may be presented to clients, government officials, or the general public. Transportation Engineers also examine and review such documents written by other transportation professionals for accuracy and thoroughness. Contracts, proposals, designs, and files are all subject to this process.

Transportation Engineers use computers to help them perform their various duties. Transportation designers, for example, utilize computer-aided design (CAD) software to draw, revise, and fine-tune their concepts for structures and facilities. Computers allow Transportation Engineers to create many variations of each design, as well as to effect exacting details.

Transportation Engineers work in offices or at project job sites. Their work can be stressful. Unexpected developments such as cost overruns, scheduling difficulties, or inaccurate designs can contribute to an engineer's stress level. A 40-hour work week is standard for Transportation Engineers, but additional hours may be required of them to meet deadlines and complete their various tasks.

Salaries

Salaries for Transportation Engineers vary, depending on such factors as their education, experience, job duties, employer, and geographical location. According to the November 2004 *Occupational Employment Statistics* survey by the U.S. Bureau of Labor Statistics, the estimated annual salary for most civil engineers, which includes Transportation Engineers, ranged between $43,530 and $97,650.

Employment Prospects

The majority of Transportation Engineers work in government agencies at the local, state and federal levels. Others are employed in the private sector for consulting firms, contractors, or other transportation-related companies. Some engineers are employed as teachers and researchers at academic institutions. Some are independent practitioners.

The job market for Transportation Engineers is generally steady, as transportation systems continually need to be built, improved, repaired, and rehabilitated throughout the United States. Job openings usually become available as Transportation Engineers advance to higher positions, transfer to other jobs, retire, or leave the workforce for other reasons.

Advancement Prospects

Transportation Engineers may advance in any number of ways, depending on their ambitions and interests. They can become specialists in a particular field, such as traffic engineering. Engineers with management and administrative interests and talents can seek positions as supervisory, project, and chief engineers. Transportation Engineers with entrepreneurial ambitions can become independent consultants or owners of engineering consulting firms.

Education and Training

Minimally, Transportation Engineers must possess a bachelor's degree in transportation engineering, civil engineering, or another related field. Some employers may prefer to hire applicants with an advanced degree. A master's or doctoral degree is usually required for engineers to advance to careers in management, consulting, research, or teaching. Engineers must possess a doctorate to teach engineering at the college and university level.

Throughout their careers, Transportation Engineers enroll in continuing education and training programs to update their skills and keep up with new developments in their fields.

Special Requirements

Transportation Engineers who offer their services directly to the public must possess a valid professional engineer (P.E.) license in the state or territory where they practice. The P.E. licensing process consists of two stages. At the first level, qualifying individuals become licensed as engineers-in-training (E.I.T.). After working several years under the supervision of licensed engineers, E.I.T.s become eligible to apply for the P.E. license.

The requirements for P.E. licensure differ in each state and territory, as well as in Washington, D.C. For specific information, contact the board of engineering examiners for the area where you wish to practice. See Appendix II for a list of boards.

Experience, Special Skills, and Personality Traits

Entry-level candidates should have work experience related to the positions for which they apply. They may have gained their experience through internships, work-study programs, student research projects, or summer employment. Applicants for journey-level positions are expected to have several years of work experience in transportation projects.

Transportation Engineers should have effective interpersonal and communication skills, as they must be able to work well with different people from diverse backgrounds. In addition, they must have strong computer, writing, and mathematical skills. Other essential skills are leadership, teamwork, problem-solving, and analytical skills. Being curious, creative, detail-oriented, analytical, reliable, ethical, and persistent are some personality traits that successful Transportation Engineers share.

Unions and Associations

Many Transportation Engineers join local, state, and national societies to take advantage of networking opportunities, continuing education programs, and other professional services and resources. Some national societies to which Transportation Engineers might belong include the Institute of Transportation Engineers, the American Society of Civil Engineers, and the American Public Works Association. For contact information, see Appendix III.

Tips for Entry

1. Ask your engineering professors for help in finding internship or summer employment positions.
2. Many government agencies post job vacancies as well as information about their job selection process at their Web site. You may also be able to download or complete job applications at a site.
3. Use the Internet to learn more about Transportation Engineers. You might start by visiting these Web sites: Institute of Transportation Engineers, http://www.ite. org; and iCivilEngineer—Transportation Engineering, http://www.icivilengineer.com/Transportation_ Engineering. For more links, see Appendix IV.

TRAFFIC ENGINEER

CAREER PROFILE

Duties: Plan, design, execute, and preserve traffic controls within a particular jurisdiction; perform duties as required

Alternate Title(s): Civil Engineer, Transportation Engineer; a title that reflects an engineering function such as Traffic Planner or Design Engineer

Salary Range: $44,000 to $98,000

Employment Prospects: Good

Advancement Prospects: Good

Prerequisites:

Education or Training—Bachelor's degree in civil engineering, with an emphasis in transportation engineering

Experience—Previous work experience generally required

Special Skills and Personality Traits—Computer, writing, interpersonal, communication, leadership, teamwork, and problem-solving skills; creative, curious, analytical, detail-oriented, reliable, and ethical

Special Requirements—Professional engineer (P.E.) license usually required

CAREER LADDER

```
┌─────────────────────────────┐
│   Senior Traffic Engineer   │
└─────────────────────────────┘

┌─────────────────────────────┐
│      Traffic Engineer       │
└─────────────────────────────┘

┌─────────────────────────────┐
│   Junior Traffic Engineer   │
└─────────────────────────────┘
```

Position Description

Whenever we travel in, through, or among our communities, whether as pedestrians, cyclists, drivers, or riders, we find our way with the help of various means such as street signs, sidewalks, special lanes, and ramps. These are the result of traffic engineering, which is a type of engineering that specializes in planning and operating this coordinated system of traffic control. Historical evidence of traffic engineering can be traced as far back as ancient Rome, which had road signs, one-way streets, and vehicle-free zones. With increased population over the centuries along with the development of railroads, roadways, and automobiles, traffic engineering has grown to be a more vital aspect of the world's infrastructure. The men and women who are employed in this profession are called Traffic Engineers.

Traffic Engineers provide support to agencies of their local government that have an interest in maintaining an efficient, smooth-flowing traffic system. Such agencies as police and fire departments and community development programs, as well as public facilities, parking agencies, and historical marker programs all work closely with Traffic Engineers to guarantee public access, safety, and the enforcement of traffic laws. Traffic engineering, or transportation operations, is one of several subspecialties of transportation engineering.

Traffic Engineers are experts in all aspects of traffic systems and control. Their research in such areas as road conditions, traffic patterns, accident statistics, and safety, as well as traffic impact studies and traffic impact analysis, contributes to their understanding of the need for plans that fit every requirement. Traffic Engineers invent or improve traffic signals and coordinate their timing. They design signs and determine where they should be placed. They oversee the development of transit systems, parking structures, and highway on-ramps. They design transit routes, decide where to place the stops, and develop schedules. Traffic Engineers also study how other professionals approach similar problems and evaluate their results. Their mission is to improve and hasten the flow of traffic while maximizing safety and maintaining a low accident rate.

Traffic Engineers are directly involved with the planning, execution, and preservation of all types of traffic controls. Their job is to alleviate traffic congestion and to devise new systems or improvements to prevent increased problems. They study traffic conditions and make note of various measurements. They meet with people to discuss the problems they have with moving about their particular neighborhood or their community in general. For example, citizens might discuss the need for special lanes for buses or trucks, better crosswalks for pedestrians, or left-turn-only traffic signals. Traffic Engineers also confer with government and business leaders, as well as with planners, developers, and environmental agency representatives before putting forth a proposal for necessary action. Their proposal includes a scheme to ensure safety and efficiency in addition to the physical improvements that need to be made. Upon approval, Traffic Engineers oversee the implementation of their plan. They observe the construction process to make sure that the project proceeds within the specified schedule and adheres to regulations. They delegate some of their responsibilities to engineering assistants or technicians and manage their performance.

Traffic Engineers perform a range of duties in the process of improving traffic conditions in their area, including:

- determining the impact of an area's growth on traffic patterns
- preparing formal impact and feasibility studies
- managing planning programs
- reviewing the input of other professionals
- soliciting proposals for transportation consultants
- investigating traffic complaints
- coordinating and working with government departments and other entities on transportation matters
- supervising the design and implementation of traffic control measures and devices
- training a staff in matters of traffic safety, traffic control, and traffic design
- serving on traffic commissions

The complexity of traffic networks and systems, combined with the increasing number of such systems, has led to a need for specialization. Some Traffic Engineers specialize in one or more engineering functions, such as traffic design, research, consulting, or project management. Others combine several functional specialties. For example, a Traffic Engineer might work in the area of traffic studies, along with the design of highway interchanges and lighting. Another engineer may be involved in the areas of administration, traffic laws, and public relations.

Traffic Engineers are well versed in a variety of areas of expertise within their profession. They are knowledgeable about equipment and methods used to monitor traffic, procedures and ethics of traffic engineering, as well as traffic laws and regulations. They keep up-to-date with the latest developments in their profession by reading books, articles, and papers written by experts in their field. They write reports, proposals, and reviews in a clearly written fashion. They make drawings and diagrams that include concise specifications for the projects they design.

Traffic Engineers begin their careers at an entry level that requires them to assist in the design of traffic control projects, analyze field studies such as traffic patterns or accident statistics, conduct basic transportation research, participate in extended studies regarding various traffic issues, and oversee the work of assistant engineers to collect and analyze traffic study data.

More experienced Traffic Engineers engage themselves in such tasks as selecting the position of traffic signals, taking action on complaints, overseeing the acquisition of materials and equipment, preparing budget estimates and distributing project funds, appearing as expert witnesses in court, and supervising a staff of engineers, technicians, and support personnel.

Traffic Engineers work in offices, but visit project sites as well. They work 40-hour weeks but occasionally put in additional hours when necessary.

Salaries

Salaries for Traffic Engineers vary, depending on such factors as their education, experience, and geographical location. According to the November 2004 *Occupational Employment Statistics* survey by the U.S. Bureau of Labor Statistics, the estimated annual salary for most civil engineers ranged between $43,530 and $97,650. Traffic Engineers are classified as part of this occupation.

Employment Prospects

Most Traffic Engineers are employed by government agencies. They may also find employment with private consulting firms, which perform contractual work for the government. Some Traffic Engineers are self-employed practitioners.

Because traffic congestion and safety are serious issues throughout the United States, the job market for Traffic Engineers is relatively stable. Most opportunities become available as engineers advance to higher positions, transfer to other jobs, retire, or leave the workforce for other reasons.

Advancement Prospects

As Traffic Engineers gain experience, they can become technical specialists and project managers. They may also seek administrative and managerial positions within their organizations, as well as pursue opportunities as consultants with engineering consulting firms. Some Traffic Engineers become independent practitioners, while others choose to teach and conduct research in academic institutions.

Education and Training

Traffic Engineers must possess at least a bachelor's degree in civil engineering, preferably with an emphasis in transportation or traffic engineering. Some employers prefer to hire Traffic Engineers who have a master's degree in transportation engineering, civil engineering, or a related field.

An advanced degree is usually required for engineers to pursue careers in management, consulting, or research. To teach at the college and university level, engineers must possess a doctorate.

Employers typically provide entry-level engineers with training programs, which may include both on-the-job and classroom training.

Throughout their careers, Traffic Engineers enroll in continuing education programs and training programs to update their skills and keep up with advancements in their fields.

Special Requirements

All individual states, territories, and Washington, D.C., require engineers to be licensed professional engineers (P.E.) if their work affects the public safety and welfare or if they offer engineering services directly to the public. The requirements for P.E. licensure differ in every location. For specific information, contact the board of engineering examiners where you wish to practice. See Appendix II for a list of boards.

Experience, Special Skills, Personality Traits

Entry-level candidates should have work experience related to the positions for which they apply. They may have gained their experience through internships, work-study programs, student research projects, or summer employment. For jour-

ney-level positions, employers usually prefer to hire applicants who have several years of traffic or transportation engineering experience.

To be effective in their work, Traffic Engineers must have strong computer and writing skills. Because they must work well with colleagues, customers, clients, and the public, they need excellent interpersonal and communication skills. In addition, they should have adequate leadership, teamwork, and problem-solving skills. Being creative, curious, analytical, detail-oriented, reliable, and ethical are some personality traits that successful Traffic Engineers share.

Unions and Associations

The Institute of Transportation Engineers and the American Society of Civil Engineers are two national societies that serve the interests of Traffic Engineers. Professional associations are also available at the local and state levels. Many engineers join one or more societies to take advantage of networking opportunities, continuing education programs, and other professional services and resources. (For contact information for the above groups, see Appendix III.)

Tips for Entry

1. Talk with professionals to learn more about the job.
2. Obtain an internship or part-time job with a traffic engineering agency or firm to help you determine if traffic engineering is the field for you.
3. To enhance your employability, you might consider obtaining the Professional Traffic Operations Engineer (PTOE) certification, granted by the Institute of Traffic Engineers. For information, visit its Web page at http://www.ite.org/certification.
4. You can learn more about traffic engineering on the Internet. Many local agencies have Web sites for their traffic engineering departments. To get a list of Web sites, enter the keyword *traffic engineering* in a search engine. To learn about some links, see Appendix IV.

URBAN PLANNER

CAREER PROFILE

Duties: Develop plans and programs for the use of land and resources in cities, rural areas, regions, and other jurisdictions; perform duties as required

Alternate Title(s): Regional Planner; a title that reflects a specialty such as Environmental Planner or Airport Planner

Salary Range: $35,000 to $85,000

Employment Prospects: Fair

Advancement Prospects: Good

Prerequisites:

Education or Training—Master's degree in planning or a related field

Experience—Previous work experience generally required

Special Skills and Personality Traits—Interpersonal, communication, public speaking, writing, computer, teamwork, mediation, problem-solving, and organizational skills; energetic, self-motivated, analytical, objective, flexible, and creative

CAREER LADDER

```
┌─────────────────────────────┐
│    Senior Urban Planner     │
└─────────────────────────────┘

┌─────────────────────────────┐
│       Urban Planner         │
└─────────────────────────────┘

┌─────────────────────────────┐
│    Junior Urban Planner     │
└─────────────────────────────┘
```

Position Description

Communities of all sizes are not built in random fashion; they are the result of careful preparation. The layouts of streets, transportation systems, power and water delivery systems, parks, residential areas, and business districts are designed and planned before they are actually constructed. This design and planning work is called urban planning, even when it applies to suburban or rural areas. Expanding communities continue to utilize urban planning to facilitate their growth as well as make improvements. The men and women who perform this planning work are called Urban Planners. Their profession is a specialty of civil engineering.

One could call Urban Planners visionaries, because they work with communities to create a pleasant, functional, and efficient place to live and work. They think about and help design many facets of the neighborhoods, towns, and cities that already exist as well as those that are planned for the future. They give thought to economic, environmental, and social considerations and how they relate to one another. They also work toward resolving such social issues as homelessness, protecting the environment, and the impact of a changing community on its residents.

Urban Planners consider current conditions and analyze how they indicate future trends for the area. Topics such as housing and recreational needs, transportation, employment needs, population growth, and the natural resources of an area are some of the things that Urban Planners need to understand in the process of planning a community.

Urban Planners follow a procedure that starts with their analysis and study. They begin by surveying the site or sites that are slated for development. They carefully consider unused land and vacant buildings to see how they might be incorporated into the overall plan. They contemplate about whether an area should be zoned for business, industrial, or residential use. Urban Planners give thought to such factors as traffic patterns, air or water pollution, land use patterns, social trends, government policies, financing, and other issues that may arise in the future. The analysis is very detailed and their considerations range from the sizes of buildings and streets to where to place street signs, fireplugs, and light poles. Urban planners work with an understanding about how all these elements fit together.

Their completed analysis is then formulated into a cohesive plan, which they present in a report to local officials.

Urban Planners present both an immediate and long-term plan. Their goal is to encourage officials to provide input as well as make decisions about problems that may arise in their cities or towns. Upon the officials' approval, Urban Planners begin to put their plans into operation.

Urban Planners keep up-to-date with legal issues, economic conditions, and all local, state, and federal regulations pertaining to building, zoning, environmental protection, and other matters. They offer the assurance that developers will comply with these regulations. Urban Planners are prepared to encounter opposition and thus need to mediate disputes and meet with the public to discuss a variety of opinions about their plans. They are ready to achieve a unity of social, budgetary, and developmental concerns in response to this input.

Urban Planners must understand engineering concepts and the principles of mathematics, science, and logic to work in coordination with other civil engineering specialists in implementing their plans. They also work closely with architects, real estate developers, and various business entities in addition to their local governments.

The work of Urban Planners requires creativity. Their plans are drawn up with a sense of artistry of design as well as their utility and function, while remaining economically practical. They design and manage their entire planning process. They are able to work with a variety of people representing different viewpoints, expertise, and backgrounds. Urban Planners "see the big picture," and are therefore equipped to solve many problems in a wide range of areas, or find someone who can solve a particular problem.

Some Urban Planners specialize in one or more specific areas of urban planning, depending on the size of the organization in which they work. These specialties include transportation, demographics, housing, historic preservation, urban design, economic development, and environmental or regulatory issues. Urban Planners also specialize in their functions. They can play the role of educator, researcher, analyst, designer, or manager, to name a few.

Urban Planners work in offices most of the time. However, they also spend part of their working lives outside the office to attend meetings or visit development sites. They often travel to some of the areas that are being discussed for development.

Urban Planners typically work a 40-hour workweek, although they often attend meetings or public hearings in the evenings or on weekends. They also put in additional hours to meet deadlines and deal with tight work schedules.

Salaries

Salaries for Urban Planners vary, depending on such factors as their education, experience, employer, and geographical location. According to the November 2004 *Occupational Employment Statistics* (OES) survey by the U.S. Bureau of Labor Statistics (BLS), the estimated annual salary for most Urban Planners ranged between $34,890 and $84,820.

Employment Prospects

The BLS reported in its November 2004 OES survey that an estimated 30,950 Urban Planners were employed in the United States. The majority of planners were employed by local government agencies. Some Urban Planners worked at the state government level, where they mainly deal with environmental, housing, and transportation concerns. The federal government also hired a small number of Urban Planners. Private sector employers included architectural and engineering services firms as well as management and technical consulting companies.

According to the BLS, the job market for Urban Planners should increase by 9 to 17 percent through 2014. Most opportunities are expected to be found in affluent areas of the United States that will be experiencing rapid growth. The BLS further reports that opportunities should increase due to the growing interest in historic preservation, urban renewal projects, and increased local government compliance with regulations regarding the environment, transportation, housing, commercial development, and land use. However, keep in mind that job growth in government agencies fluctuates with the economy. During periods of economic downturns, opportunities with government agencies may be limited due to restrictive budgets. In addition to job growth, openings will become available as Urban Planners retire, advance to higher positions, or transfer to other occupations.

Advancement Prospects

Urban Planners may advance in various ways. Those with managerial ambitions can rise through the ranks as supervisors, managers, directors, or partners. Some planners choose to advance by seeking positions in larger cities, where they find employment in either private firms or government agencies, or by teaching in academic institutions. Others set a goal to become successful independent consultants.

Education and Training

Most employers generally require entry-level applicants to possess a master's degree in planning or another related field, or a bachelor's degree in planning along with a master's degree in such fields as civil engineering or architecture. Employers sometimes hire applicants with only a bachelor's degree, but promotional opportunities are limited for those without an advanced degree. A doctorate is needed for Urban Planners to teach in academic institutions.

Planning students complete courses in such areas as land use, environmental planning, housing, and historic preservation. They may also be required to take relevant courses in law, economics, architecture, demography, earth sciences, and other related fields.

Throughout their careers, Urban Planners enroll in continuing education programs and training programs to update their skills and keep up with advancements in their fields.

Experience, Special Skills, Personality Traits

Entry-level candidates should have work experience related to the positions for which they apply. They may have gained their experience through internships, work-study programs, student research projects, or summer employment.

Because they must be able to work well with colleagues, technical experts, politicians, and the general public, Urban Planners need excellent interpersonal, communication, and public speaking skills. Having strong writing and computer skills is also essential. In addition, they must have effective teamwork, mediation, problem-solving, and organizational skills.

Some personality traits that successful Urban Planners share include being energetic, self-motivated, analytical, objective, flexible, and creative.

Unions and Associations

Many Urban Planners join professional associations to take advantage of networking opportunities and other professional services and resources. Societies are available at the local, state, and national level. For example, the American Planning Association is a national organization that serves the general interests of Urban Planners. For contact information, see Appendix III.

Tips for Entry

1. Internships and part-time employment can sometimes lead to full-time jobs after graduation.
2. Take advantage of your college career center. There, you can find job announcements, and career counselors can help you develop effective job search skills, such as writing your resume and preparing for a job interview.
3. A willingness to relocate to other cities or regions may provide you with greater job opportunities.
4. Learn more about urban planning on the Internet. You might start by visiting these Web sites: American Planning Association, http://www.planning.org; and Cyburbia: The Planning Portal, http://www.cyburbia.org. For more links, see Appendix IV.

ENVIRONMENTAL ENGINEERING

ENVIRONMENTAL ENGINEER

CAREER PROFILE

Duties: Design solutions to prevent, control, and remediate problems related to air quality, water quality, waste management, and other environmental issues; perform duties as required

Alternate Title(s): Civil Engineer, Chemical Engineer, Mechanical Engineer; a title that reflects a specialty (such as Hazardous Waste Engineer) or an engineering function (such as Project Engineer or Environmental Analyst)

Salary Range: $42,000 to $99,000

Employment Prospects: Good

Advancement Prospects: Good

Prerequisites:

Education or Training—Bachelor's degree in environmental engineering or another related field; on-the-job training

Experience—Previous work experience generally required

Special Skills and Personality Traits—Communication, interpersonal, teamwork, writing, problem-solving, leadership, and computer skills; dependable, cooperative, curious, analytical, detail-oriented and persistent

Special Requirements—Professional engineer (P.E.) license may be required

CAREER LADDER

```
┌─────────────────────────────────────┐
│   Senior Environmental Engineer      │
└─────────────────────────────────────┘

┌─────────────────────────────────────┐
│      Environmental Engineer          │
└─────────────────────────────────────┘

┌─────────────────────────────────────┐
│   Junior Environmental Engineer      │
└─────────────────────────────────────┘
```

Position Description

Human beings have always produced waste products that have been discarded into the air, water, and soil. Over the centuries, the processes of nature have accommodated these materials by utilizing them and cleansing them. However, with our larger population and increased industrial activity, our wastes are accumulating too quickly. We call these collective wastes *pollution*. Many of us are very concerned about the impact of our activities on the environment, but Environmental Engineers work specifically to alleviate this problem. They are also concerned with problems created by natural environmental hazards, such as the damaging effects of storms, floods, or droughts. They design systems and methods to proactively correct the effects of environmental degradation and seek ways to prevent further damage.

Environmental engineering is a newer name for an established field that was once known as sanitary engineering, a subdiscipline of civil engineering. This field has expanded from one that was traditionally concerned with water, wastewater, and sewage treatment to one that is characterized by a wider scope of involvement with all kinds of environmental problems. For example, Environmental Engineers are involved with such issues as air and water quality, solid waste management, toxic waste disposal, recycling, and public health, as well as land and wildlife management.

Environmental Engineers are well versed in a variety of other disciplines besides engineering. Principles of biology, chemistry, and mathematics are all applied to conserve natural resources and protect the environment. Environmental Engineers also draw from the fields of engineering design, physics, microbiology, ecology, and public health.

They work locally, regionally, and globally in the public and private sectors to find solutions to prevent, control, and fix environmental problems. They are engaged in a wide range of activities. For example, they may be involved in:

- providing safe drinking water, maintaining air quality, treating and disposing wastes, controlling water pollution, and cleaning up hazardous waste sites
- inventing devices and developing systems to reduce the release of pollutants and wastes into the environment, as well as to protect the public health
- planning, designing, and constructing facilities such as landfills, recycling centers, dams, canals, and wastewater treatment plants, as well as overseeing their operations
- helping to clean up and restore contaminated sites and damaged ecosystems
- protecting wildlife
- preventing the production of hazardous wastes and the results of their consequential misuse, such as acid rain, ozone depletion, and global warming
- managing the construction of facilities
- implementing the operations of treatment systems and production processes

Environmental Engineers fulfill many engineering functions in the process of managing the environment as researchers, designers, project managers, regulatory specialists, or consultants. Some Environmental Engineers are involved with basic research at universities or for the government. They develop new theories and practices, or invent new technologies. Elsewhere in academic settings, Environmental Engineers teach engineering courses. Full-time professors add independent research and counseling duties to their teaching responsibilities.

Environmental Engineers sometimes specialize in specific fields of interest within their profession. Some of these specialties are air pollution control engineering, water and wastewater engineering, hazardous and solid waste management engineering, as well as biotechnology and bioremediation. Other specialized areas include industrial hygiene, radiation protection, emissions engineering, and sediment analysis and evaluation.

Environmental Engineers perform a variety of general duties in the process of fulfilling their responsibilities. Examples of their tasks include:

- conducting research on proposed environmental systems and projects
- creating computer models to predict the behavior or flow of waste materials in ground or surface waters
- analyzing the risks of utilizing new methods to contain and treat environmental hazards
- responding to environmental emergencies such as oil spills, industrial accidents, and poisoned water supplies
- identifying particular problems to be solved with a new project
- obtaining samples of soil, water, or substances that cause pollution

- assessing the extent of contamination at a particular site
- developing project objectives
- evaluating data regarding environmental problems and recommending solutions, as well as procedures to follow
- determining the environmental impact of a construction project
- acquiring plans and permits and keeping them up-to-date
- developing operating procedures for projects and systems
- developing risk management or prevention plans for environmental systems, processes, or facilities
- preparing such reports as bid proposals or evaluations to help employers or clients arrive at decisions
- inspecting industrial and municipal facilities to make sure they are meeting goals for effectiveness
- ensuring compliance with government regulations of all systems and projects
- completing paperwork required by government agencies

Some Environmental Engineers perform specialized tasks within the general field of environmental engineering or within their specialties. For example, regulatory specialists, who are employed by government agencies, perform such duties as enforcing environmental regulations, monitoring corporate or organizational activities, and developing environmental policies.

There are several levels of expertise within the environmental engineering profession. Junior engineers typically work under the guidance and supervision of senior engineers, to develop their skills as well as their understanding of the rules, regulations, standards, and practices of their area of concern. As they gain experience and knowledge, they receive more complex assignments and are able to exercise greater levels of authority. For example, they may work as lead persons in certain assignments while directing the activities of other engineers and technicians.

Senior Environmental Engineers are more aware of program needs and work independently in response to those needs. They are more actively involved with the decision-making process and are more likely to be team leaders. Advanced and executive-level engineers perform the most difficult engineering tasks. They are the primary engineers for project divisions, or for an entire geographical area. Their responsibilities involve making policy decisions and consulting with clients or government agencies at the highest levels.

All levels of Environmental Engineers work together with scientists and technicians, as well as with other engineers and specialists. They also work with legal and business leaders to seek solutions to environmental problems.

Their job may require them to work in offices or in the field. Consultants often travel to other cities, states, or countries.

Environmental Engineers generally work 40-hour weeks, unless their work requires them to put in extra hours.

Salaries

Salaries for Environmental Engineers vary, depending on such factors as their education, experience, position, employer, and geographical location. The U.S. Bureau of Labor Statistics (BLS) reports in its November 2004 *Occupational Employment Statistics* (OES) survey that the estimated annual salary for most Environmental Engineers ranged between $41,570 and $99,120.

Employment Prospects

The BLS reported in its November 2004 OES survey that an estimated 50,120 Environmental Engineers were employed in the United States. The highest levels of employment for Environmental Engineers were in the architectural and engineering services industry, followed by the management and technical consulting services industry, state government, federal government, and local government. In addition, these engineers can find employment in manufacturing industries, construction industries, research institutions, academic institutions, and public interest organizations that are involved in environmental issues. Some engineers are independent practitioners.

According to the BLS, the job growth for this occupation is expected to increase by 27 percent or more through 2014. New employees will also be needed to replace Environmental Engineers who retire, advance to higher positions, transfer to other occupations, or leave the workforce for various reasons.

The job market for this occupation can be affected by downturns in the economy as well as changes in governmental policies and priorities. For example, when policy makers enact looser environmental regulations, fewer jobs may become available.

Advancement Prospects

Environmental Engineers may advance in any number of ways, depending on their ambitions and interests. They can become technical specialists as well as pursue such managerial positions as supervisory, project, and chief engineers. Some engineers choose to move into positions in marketing, technical sales, and other business areas. Engineers with entrepreneurial ambitions can become independent practitioners or owners of firms that offer various types of environmental engineering services.

Education and Training

Environmental Engineers possess at least a bachelor's degree in environmental engineering, civil engineering, chemical engineering, mechanical engineering, physical science, or another related field. Many also hold a master's or doctoral degree in environmental education. An advanced degree is usually required for Environmental Engineers to advance to careers in management, consulting, and research.

To teach or conduct research at the college and university level, engineers must possess a doctorate.

Entry-level engineers typically receive on-the-job training; some also participate in formal classroom training programs.

Throughout their careers, Environmental Engineers enroll in continuing education and training programs to update their skills and keep up with advancements in their fields.

Special Requirements

All engineers who offer engineering services directly to the public or perform work that affects the life, health, or property of the public must be licensed as professional engineers (P.E.) where they practice. Every U.S. state and territory, as well as Washington, D.C., has its particular requirements for P.E. licensure. For specific information, contact the board of engineering examiners for the area where you wish to practice. See Appendix II for a list of boards.

The P.E. licensing process consists of two stages. At the first level, qualifying engineers become licensed as engineers-in-training (E.I.T.). After working several years under the supervision of licensed engineers, E.I.T.s become eligible to apply for the P.E. license.

Experience, Special Skills, and Personality Traits

Entry-level candidates should have work experience related to the positions for which they apply. They may have gained their experience through internships, work-study programs, student research projects, or summer employment. Employers also expect applicants to be knowledgeable about environmental laws and safety.

Because they work with people from diverse backgrounds, Environmental Engineers must have effective communication, interpersonal, and teamwork skills. They also need excellent writing, problem-solving, and leadership skills. Additionally, they must have adequate computer skills as their work requires them to use computers to devise and run software programs, design facilities, write reports, and process and analyze data.

Being dependable, cooperative, curious, analytical, detail-oriented and persistent are some personality traits that successful Environmental Engineers have in common.

Unions and Associations

Many Environmental Engineers join local, state, and national societies to take advantage of networking opportunities, continuing education programs, certification programs, and other professional services and resources. Some national societies that serve the diverse interests of these engineers include:

- American Academy of Environmental Engineers
- American Society of Civil Engineers
- American Institute of Chemical Engineers

- American Society of Agricultural Engineers
- Air and Waste Management Association
- National Society of Professional Engineers
- Society of Women Engineers

For contact information for these organizations, see Appendix III.

Tips for Entry

1. As a high school student, volunteer or work part-time with environmental organizations to learn about environmental issues and to gain practical experience.
2. In college, take advantage of internship or work experience programs to obtain work experience. To learn about such programs, talk to your professors or your college career center.
3. The selection process for government positions usually involves several steps, including completing a job application and interview, scoring well on a written examination, and passing a medical exam, a drug screening, and a comprehensive background check.
4. Use the Internet to learn more about Environmental Engineers. You might start by visiting these Web sites: American Academy of Environmental Engineers, http://www.aaee.net; and The Civil Engineering Portal—Environmental Engineering, http://www. icivilengineer.com/Environmental_Engineering. For more links, see Appendix IV.

AIR QUALITY ENGINEER

CAREER PROFILE

Duties: Research, plan, design, and implement systems and technologies to prevent, control, and correct air pollution; perform duties as required

Alternate Title(s): Environmental Engineer, Chemical Engineer, Air Pollution Control Engineer, Air Management Engineer; a title that reflects an engineering function such as Air Quality Planner

Salary Range: $42,000 to $99,000

Employment Prospects: Good

Advancement Prospects: Good

Prerequisites:

Education or Training—Bachelor's degree in environmental engineering; on-the-job training

Experience—Previous work experience generally required

Special Skills and Personality Traits—Writing, computer, communication, analytical, problem-solving, interpersonal, teamwork, and self-management skills; self-motivated, honest, persistent, detail-oriented, cooperative, and dependable

Special Requirements—Professional engineer (P.E.) license may be required

CAREER LADDER

```
┌─────────────────────────────────┐
│  Senior Air Quality Engineer    │
└─────────────────────────────────┘

┌─────────────────────────────────┐
│  Air Quality Engineer           │
└─────────────────────────────────┘

┌─────────────────────────────────┐
│  Junior Air Quality Engineer    │
└─────────────────────────────────┘
```

Position Description

Air pollution is the result of the presence of an unbalanced proportion of natural and manmade substances in the atmosphere. Normally, our atmosphere is composed primarily of oxygen and nitrogen as well as smaller proportions of carbon dioxide, other gases, and microscopic particulates (particles of liquids or solids). Nature has mechanisms whereby these components of the atmosphere are kept in a balance that helps sustain life. However, as the human race has grown in numbers and increased the intensity of our industrial activities, we produce and add too many chemicals and particulates to the air to be kept in balance by the forces of nature. Today, we are continually exposed to both indoor and outdoor air pollution. It is detrimental to our health and to that of the plants and animals with which we share our planet. Although not all pollutants are poisonous, they can cause damage simply by having altered the composition of the atmosphere. Laws have been passed in an effort to alleviate this growing problem.

Air Quality Engineers specialize in preventing, controlling, and correcting atmospheric pollution. (These environmental engineers are also known as air pollution control engineers or air management engineers.) They utilize a variety of engineering disciplines to design, plan, and implement ways to solve our air pollution problems. In addition to engineering, Air Quality Engineers are knowledgeable about mathematics, chemistry, physics, meteorology, thermodynamics, and life sciences. They apply this knowledge to better understand the sources of pollution and how to control them. Their goal is to improve air quality.

Air Quality Engineers measure and monitor air quality and track where pollution is located, from where it originates, and to where it travels. In addition, they understand the local, regional, and federal governmental laws and regulations pertaining to air quality. They keep these factors in mind when tackling air pollution issues. In doing so, they give due consideration to the economic and social impact of the presence of pollution in our atmosphere, as well as the impact of the remediation efforts they propose and implement.

Air Quality Engineers work in both urban and rural settings. Their responsibilities vary, depending on their position, level of expertise, and which engineering function they perform as designer, project manager, researcher, regulatory specialist, consultant, or other function. For example, Air Quality Engineers may be involved in conducting research on the effects of pollution on health; designing new control technologies for such emissions as sulfur dioxide, nitrogen oxides, mercury, and dust; or assisting industries to stay in compliance with air quality and health regulations in all aspects of their business, from inception to implementation and continued operation.

Air Quality Engineers perform various tasks, many of which are specific to their particular function. Other duties are commonly performed by most engineers. Examples of such general tasks include:

- planning and overseeing analytical and evaluation studies to identify pollution problems, determine control methods, and assess the reliability or effectiveness of pollution control systems
- collecting samples to test for polluting substances
- reviewing the information provided by research and study activities
- creating or modifying pollution control methods
- ensuring that monitoring and measuring equipment is properly calibrated
- ensuring that industries comply with air quality regulations, and advising about the appropriate enforcement of regulations where needed
- serving as expert witnesses for courts, advisory boards, or commissions
- utilizing complex computation methods to evaluate industrial processes in order to determine their emission rates
- using computers to perform computations, create graphs and models, analyze data, and maintain data bases
- writing various documents such as data analyses, reports, and regulation proposals

Air Quality Engineers stay up-to-date with current information about air pollution. They read journals, books, and articles about current air quality issues. They stay current with government environmental regulations as well as study new technologies pertinent to their field. Their reading enables them to propose new regulations and develop new pollution control technologies.

Air Quality Engineers work with other engineers as well as technicians, government officials, business leaders, and many others in a variety of occupations. Senior Air Quality Engineers who supervise others are responsible for maintaining discipline, solving staff problems, and appraising their employees' performance, as well as recommending the hiring or terminating of employees.

Air Quality Engineers work in offices for the most part, but are often required to work away from the office. Sometimes they travel to other parts of the world. Some of their work locations are in rough terrain, or in industrial facilities. Air Quality Engineers are regularly exposed to chemicals, dust, grease, and mechanical dangers. They may be expected to use protective gear to minimize the hazards they encounter.

A 40-hour week is normal for Air Quality Engineers, but they may occasionally be required to put in longer hours.

Salaries

Salaries for Air Quality Engineers vary, depending on such factors as their education, experience, employer, and geographical location. According to the November 2004 *Occupational Employment Statistics* survey by the U.S. Bureau of Labor Statistics (BLS), the estimated annual salary for most environmental engineers, such as Air Quality Engineers, ranged between $41,570 and $99,120.

Employment Prospects

Employers of Air Quality Engineers include governmental agencies (at the federal, state, and local levels), architectural and engineering services, management and technical consulting services, manufacturers, research institutions, academic institutions, and environmental public-interest organizations. Some Air Quality Engineers are independent practitioners.

Opportunities should be strong for Air Quality Engineers. According to the BLS, the job growth for environmental engineers, in general, is expected to increase by 27 percent or more through 2014. In addition, openings will be created to replace engineers who retire, advance to higher positions, transfer to other occupations, or leave the workforce for various reasons.

Keep in mind that the job market for Air Quality Engineers can be affected by downturns in the economy as well as by changes in governmental policies and priorities. For example, when policy makers enact looser environmental regulations, fewer jobs may become available.

Advancement Prospects

Air Quality Engineers may advance in any number of ways, depending on their ambitions and interests. As they gain experience, they are assigned to more complex projects and receive increasingly greater responsibilities. Additionally, they can become technical specialists as well as advance to such managerial positions as supervisory, project, and chief engineers. Engineers with entrepreneurial ambitions can become independent consultants or owners of firms that offer various types of environmental engineering services.

Education and Training

Employers seek candidates who possess at least a bachelor's degree in environmental engineering, civil engineering, chemical engineering, or another related field. Entry-level engineers usually receive on-the-job training, and work under the supervision and direction of experienced engineers.

Air Quality Engineers usually need a master's or doctoral degree to advance to careers in management, consulting, research, or teaching. They must possess a doctorate to teach civil engineering at the college level.

Throughout their careers, Air Quality Engineers enroll in continuing education and training programs to update their skills and keep up with advancements in their fields.

Special Requirements

All engineers who offer engineering services directly to the public or perform work that affects the life, health, or property of the public must be licensed as professional engineers (P.E.) where they practice. Every U.S. state and territory, as well as Washington, D.C., has its own requirements for P.E. licensure. For specific information, contact the board of engineering examiners for the area where you wish to practice. See Appendix I for a list of boards.

Experience, Special Skills, and Personality Traits

Entry-level candidates should have work experience related to the positions for which they apply. They may have gained their experience through internships, work-study programs, student research projects, or summer employment. Applicants should be knowledgeable about basic engineering principles and governmental laws that pertain to air pollution.

Air Quality Engineers need effective writing, computer, communication, analytical, and problem-solving skills for their work. They must also demonstrate strong interpersonal and teamwork skills, as they work with various people from diverse backgrounds. Additionally, these engineers have excellent self-management skills, such as the ability to work independently, handle stressful situations, and handle multiple projects and tasks. Being self-motivated, honest, persistent, detail-oriented, cooperative, and dependable are some personality traits that successful Air Quality Engineers share.

Unions and Associations

Air Quality Engineers can join professional associations at the local, state, and national levels to take advantage of networking opportunities and other professional services and resources. Some national societies include the American Academy of Environmental Engineers, the Air and Waste Management Association, the American Society of Civil Engineers, and the National Society of Professional Engineers. For contact information, see Appendix III.

Tips for Entry

1. To learn about the field of air quality and air pollution control, talk to professionals in the private and public sectors.
2. Many governmental agencies require applicants to be U.S. citizens.
3. Read job application instructions carefully. Employers quickly dismiss job applicants who have not followed directions exactly.
4. Learn as much as you can about a prospective employer. For example, you might check an organization's Web site.
5. Learn more about air quality on the Internet. You might start by visiting these Web sites: Clean Air World, http://www.cleanairworld.org; and U.S. Environmental Protection Agency's Office of Air and Radiation, http://www.epa.gov/air. For more links, see Appendix IV.

WASTEWATER ENGINEER

CAREER PROFILE

Duties: Research, plan, design, and manage wastewater treatment projects and systems; perform duties as required

Alternate Title(s): Environmental Engineer, Civil Engineer, Chemical Engineer, Mechanical Engineer; a title that reflects an engineering function such as Project Engineer

Salary Range: $42,000 to $99,000

Employment Prospects: Good

Advancement Prospects: Good

Prerequisites:

    Education or Training—Bachelor's degree in environmental engineering; on-the-job training

    Experience—Previous work experience generally required

    Special Skills and Personality Traits—Communication, writing, computer, interpersonal, customer service, leadership, analytical, and problem-solving skills; creative, reliable, honest, cooperative, enthusiastic, and self-motivated

    Special Requirements—Professional engineer (P.E.) license may be required

CAREER LADDER

```
┌─────────────────────────────────┐
│   Senior Wastewater Engineer     │
└─────────────────────────────────┘

┌─────────────────────────────────┐
│      Wastewater Engineer         │
└─────────────────────────────────┘

┌─────────────────────────────────┐
│   Junior Wastewater Engineer     │
└─────────────────────────────────┘
```

Position Description

Every day we use water for all sorts of purposes. In our homes, we bathe, wash dishes, water our plants, and flush our toilets. In agriculture, we irrigate croplands and refresh our livestock. In industry, we use water in the manufacturing and construction processes. Most of our water goes down the drain, washes away soil, and flushes out oils and chemicals. It takes solid materials with it. That water is called sewage, or wastewater.

Cities and industries are where most wastewater is produced. That water drains into complex systems of pipes that lead to sewage treatment plants. In rural areas, residential sewage drains into septic tanks, while cropland water flows into nearby bodies of water. Eventually, all wastewater finds its way into rivers, streams, lakes, and oceans. Without control systems, the solid matter content of wastewater would overwhelm natural systems with pollution and result in the death of plants and animals that live in or near water. Our water supplies would be unfit for drinking or other uses. One way or another, wastewater needs to be managed. That engineering job is done by Wastewater Engineers.

Wastewater engineering is the field that studies, designs, and implements the treatment, cleansing, and reuse of wastewater with minimal impact on the environment. Wastewater Engineers employ several methods to treat sewage in treatment plants to convert wastewater into clean water that can be returned to nature, as well as to industries and to drinking water treatment systems. (Drinking water treatment is a separate process.) Wastewater Engineers use certain types of bacteria to digest the solid wastes, as well as a series of filtering and separation systems. These systems include screens, grit chambers, and sedimentation tanks. Next, sewage goes through either an activated sludge or trickling filtration process. The solid matter that remains is called sludge, which is further digested and broken down by bacteria in a sludge digestion tank. In a few locations, a third process involving biological nutrient removal, chemical treatment, microscopic screening, or radiation treatment is employed. Sludge is also treated by various methods to be rendered harmless. Sludge can be used for various purposes or deposited in landfills.

In addition to engineering, chemistry, microbiology, and their physical processes, Wastewater Engineers are knowledgeable about governmental regulations regarding the operation of wastewater treatment facilities. They also have an understanding of the design, planning, construction, and management processes of sewage treatment plants, as well as the materials, equipment, and methods that are employed by such facilities.

Wastewater Engineers work for a variety of organizations, including industries that treat their own wastewater, engineering consulting firms, municipal water treatment agencies, private companies that operate treatment facilities for communities, government regulatory agencies, research and teaching universities, laboratories, and advocacy groups. Some Wastewater Engineers work as self-employed consultants.

In general, Wastewater Engineers:

- evaluate the impact of sewage discharge on groundwater, rivers, lakes, marshlands and oceans
- study corrosion levels in water transport systems, piping, cooling towers, and other systems
- research water treatment technologies
- review local needs for wastewater treatment systems
- evaluate existing systems that need to be improved
- design new facilities and equipment for waste treatment programs, including storage facilities, drainage systems, pumping stations, and erosion control structures
- test designs in laboratories using computer modeling, or in pilot plants
- manage construction of new facilities and oversee their operation
- inspect wastewater facilities for compliance with local, state, and federal regulations as well as with health and safety standards
- recommend corrective measures or equipment modifications to remediate noncompliance issues
- work continuously to improve facility design, construction, and function

Like other engineers, Wastewater Engineers are involved in research, development, design, testing, and various other functions throughout their careers. They perform a multitude of specific tasks in the course of fulfilling their basic functions. Some of their tasks include: preparing accurate drawings, notes, or records; reviewing project plans and designs; proposing regulatory revisions; and performing advanced engineering research, calculations, and analyses of such waste management issues as plant capacity and flow volumes. These engineers also administer contract arrangements for construction, including proposal writing, developing specifications, and documenting the contract process.

Wastewater Engineers continually suggest ways to improve the efficiency, economy, and quality of the performance of wastewater facilities. In addition, they are responsible for ensuring compliance with operational standards and government regulations, as well as for writing comprehensive reports and correspondence. When necessary, Wastewater Engineers consult with government officials, corporate leaders, developers, and construction crews about regulations, business practices, land use, and building concerns. Furthermore, they advise staff and clients about wastewater management issues and facility designs.

Senior engineers may also be responsible for the supervision, direction, and training of junior engineers, technologists, technicians, and other staff.

Wastewater Engineers work in offices, but they often work in the field to survey facility sites, to oversee construction or remediation efforts, and to observe the operations of treatment plants. They work in all types of climates and terrains. Wastewater Engineers work in the proximity of chemicals, sewage, sludge, and other substances. They work with an awareness of safety precautions to avoid injuries to themselves or others. They may be required to wear protective equipment.

Wastewater Engineers usually work a 40-hour week but may put in extra hours when needed to complete tasks or meet deadlines.

Salaries

Salaries for Wastewater Engineers vary, depending on such factors as their education, experience, employer, and geographical location. The U.S. Bureau of Labor Statistics (BLS) reported in its November 2004 *Occupational Employment Statistics* survey that the estimated annual salary for most environmental engineers, including Wastewater Engineers, ranged between $41,570 and $99,120.

Employment Prospects

Opportunities for Wastewater Engineers should remain steady over the next few years. According to the BLS, the job growth for environmental engineers in general is expected to increase by 27 percent or more through 2014. In addition, openings will be created to replace engineers who retire, advance to higher positions, transfer to other occupations, or leave the workforce for various reasons. However, keep in mind that the job market can be affected by downturns in the economy as well as by changes in governmental policies and priorities. For example, when policy makers enact looser environmental regulations, fewer jobs may become available.

Advancement Prospects

Wastewater Engineers may advance in any number of ways, depending on their ambitions and interests. As they gain experience, they receive increasingly greater responsibilities. Additionally, they can become technical specialists or seek opportunities in marketing, finance, or other business areas within an organization. Wastewater Engineers can seek managerial positions, and rise through the ranks to become supervisory, project, and chief engineers, as well as executive officers. Engineers with entrepreneurial ambitions can become independent consultants or owners of firms that offer various types of environmental engineering services.

Education and Training

Minimally, Wastewater Engineers must possess a bachelor's degree in environmental engineering, sanitary engineering, civil engineering, chemical engineering, mechanical engineering, hydrology, or another related field. A master's or doctoral degree is usually required for engineers to advance to careers in management, consulting, research, or teaching. Engineers must hold a doctoral degree to teach civil engineering at the college level.

Employers typically provide entry-level engineers with training programs, which may include both on-the-job and classroom training. New engineers work under the supervision and direction of experienced engineers.

Throughout their careers, Wastewater Engineers enroll in continuing education and training programs to update their skills and keep up with advancements in their fields.

Special Requirements

All engineers who offer engineering services directly to the public or perform work that affects the life, health, or property of the public must be licensed as professional engineers (P.E.) where they practice. Every U.S. state and territory, as well as Washington, D.C., has its particular requirements for licensure. For specific information, contact the board of engineering examiners for the area where you wish to practice. See Appendix II for a list of boards.

Experience, Special Skills, and Personality Traits

Work experience is not necessary for entry-level candidates, but they should have some experience related to the positions for which they apply. They may have gained their experience through internships, work-study programs, student research projects, or summer employment.

Wastewater Engineers need strong communication, writing, and computer skills for their jobs. They must also have effective interpersonal and customer service skills to work well with many people with different backgrounds. In addition, they should have excellent leadership, analytical, and problem-solving skills. Being creative, reliable, honest, cooperative, enthusiastic, and self-motivated are some personality traits that successful Wastewater Engineers share.

Unions and Associations

Many Wastewater Engineers belong to local, state, and national societies to take advantage of networking opportunities, continuing education programs, certification programs, and other professional services and resources. Some national associations include the American Water Works Association, the American Water Resources Association, the American Academy of Environmental Engineers, the American Society of Civil Engineers, and the National Society of Professional Engineers. For contact information for these organizations, see Appendix III.

Tips for Entry

1. As a college student, obtain an internship or part-time job in a wastewater treatment facility or consulting firm to determine if the wastewater field is right for you.
2. Read job announcements carefully. Be sure you meet the minimum qualifications.
3. Many employers allow individuals to apply for vacancies online.
4. Learn more about Wastewater Engineers on the Internet. You might start by visiting these Web sites: American Water Works Association, http://www.awwa.org; and U.S. Environmental Protection Agency's Office of Wastewater Management, http://www.epa.gov/owm. For more links, see Appendix IV.

WASTE MANAGEMENT ENGINEER

CAREER PROFILE

Duties: Study, plan, design, and oversee the management of programs to minimize solid and hazardous wastes; perform duties as required

Alternate Title(s): Solid Waste Engineer, Landfill Engineer, Hazardous Waste Engineer, Environmental Engineer, Civil Engineer

Salary Range: $42,000 to $99,000

Employment Prospects: Good

Advancement Prospects: Good

Prerequisites:

Education or Training—Bachelor's degree in environmental engineering; on-the-job training

Experience—Previous work experience generally required

Special Skills and Personality Traits—Communication, writing, leadership, customer service, interpersonal, and problem-solving skills; self-motivated, detail-oriented, analytical, honest, and creative

Special Requirements—Professional engineer (P.E.) license may be required

CAREER LADDER

```
┌─────────────────────────────────────────┐
│   Senior Waste Management Engineer        │
└─────────────────────────────────────────┘

┌─────────────────────────────────────────┐
│      Waste Management Engineer            │
└─────────────────────────────────────────┘

┌─────────────────────────────────────────┐
│   Junior Waste Management Engineer        │
└─────────────────────────────────────────┘
```

Position Description

Human beings have always discarded unwanted items. For centuries, the things we threw away ended up in dumps that were, for the most part, just large holes in the ground. There, our waste simply sat, was buried, or was burned. The dumps attracted vermin and harbored disease. Whenever hazardous or toxic wastes were placed there or burned, the air, as well as the surrounding soil and water, became contaminated.

Today, much of our solid waste still winds up in large holes, but with a difference: those "holes" are now called landfills, and are characterized by a more sophisticated design and purpose. Landfills are built to prevent toxins from leaching into the ground, and they are designed to be covered and used for other purposes when they become full. The management of our waste has become an engineering concern. More specifically, it is the concern of waste management engineering. The men and women who work in this field are called Waste Management Engineers. They utilize a basic knowledge of design, construction, and maintenance methods to effectively operate solid or hazardous waste management systems.

Waste Management Engineers are environmental engineers with specialized training and experience. Their professional mission is to manage solid wastes in a manner that minimizes the environmental impact of their disposal. In the course of their work, they seek different ways to utilize waste besides throwing it away. Recycling, reusing, and composting are three alternative uses for waste. Solid waste can be used in new products, converted into soil amendments, and used to create energy. Some waste is incinerated. Waste Management Engineers seek ways to reduce the amount of solid waste that we produce. They develop or improve methods to collect, transport, transfer, store, and process waste as well as design the systems that enable these processes to function smoothly and economically.

Modern landfills are the final destination for most of our solid waste. They are lined with nonporous clay or synthetic materials that prevent the seepage of liquids. Over time, solid wastes break down into simpler components. Sometimes that can include substances or liquids that can be hazardous. That is, they can burn, explode, corrode metal, or are toxic. Rainfall drains through waste deposits and collects toxic substances en route. When these liquids seep or leach into soil or groundwater, they contaminate our drinking and agricultural water supplies. Waste Management Engineers design landfill linings to prevent the contamination of soils and waters. They also create drainage systems to handle the flow of extra water and other liquids, as well as systems to deal with the outbreak of underground fires.

Waste Management Engineers also find ways to handle some wastes that are too hazardous to be stored in ordinary landfills. They design systems to dispose of them in ways that protect our air, water, and soil. Such wastes come from industries, laboratories, or hospitals. They can be buried in special double-lined landfills, but other technologies, such as vitrification and encapsulation, are used as well. Other hazardous wastes are sometimes used as raw materials to make new products. Certain hazardous wastes can be consumed by bacteria, which break them down into harmless substances. Hazardous wastes can be burned at very high temperatures until they are rendered harmless.

Waste Management Engineers also apply their expertise to reverse the damage that was caused by older waste management methods. They oversee the remediation of these sites and ensure that the wastes contained therein are treated with more modern methods of disposal.

Waste Management Engineers work for industries as well as local, state, and federal governments. Some are consultants who provide assistance to several organizations. Their tasks vary accordingly. For example, governmental Waste Management Engineers are more closely involved with regulatory processes than are those who work in industry. In general, however, Waste Management Engineers are responsible for performing such duties as:

- studying waste management problems and seeking engineering technology solutions
- conducting environmental studies and preparing the necessary documentation
- analyzing waste in existing waste management projects
- planning, designing, and implementing improvements to new and existing waste management projects
- designing landfills, their linings and covers, and other waste management facilities
- creating new waste management technologies
- devising and implementing waste collection programs, including deciding which equipment is to be used, planning collection routes, and determining transfer station locations
- evaluating proposed projects
- preparing specifications, plans, and cost estimates
- completing design drawings and specifications
- reviewing the design and drafting work performed by other engineers and technicians

- reviewing public concerns about solid waste management activities
- completing construction contract tasks
- inspecting construction sites and ensuring that plans and specifications are followed precisely
- supervising the inspection of waste disposal facilities by engineers and environmental experts
- overseeing emergency cleanup work and providing remedial solutions to problem waste disposal sites or incidents of contamination
- serving as expert witnesses in courts or before government commissions and review boards

Waste Management Engineers are also responsible for ensuring that waste management projects comply with the latest safety and design standards, as well as all local, state, and federal regulations. Senior engineers have the additional duties of supervising, directing, and training junior staff members, which may include engineers, technologists, and technicians.

Waste Management Engineers work in teams comprised of other engineers, microbiologists, geohydrologists, soil scientists, and other professional or technical personnel. They work closely with government officials, landowners, and local waste management corporate leaders.

Waste Management Engineers work a 40-hour week. They sometimes put in additional hours to complete tasks and meet deadlines.

Salaries
Salaries for Waste Management Engineers vary, depending on such factors as their education, experience, position, employer, and geographical location. The U.S. Bureau of Labor Statistics (BLS) reports in its November 2004 *Occupational Employment Statistics* survey that the estimated annual salary for most environmental engineers ranged between $41,570 and $99,120. This occupation also includes Waste Management Engineers.

Employment Prospects
According to the BLS, the job growth for environmental engineers, including Waste Management Engineers, is predicted to increase by 27 percent or more through 2014. Additional openings will be created to replace engineers who retire, advance to higher positions, transfer to other occupations, or leave the workforce for various reasons. However, the job market can be affected by downturns in the economy as well as by changes in governmental policies and priorities. For example, when policy makers loosen environmental regulations, fewer jobs may become available.

Advancement Prospects
Waste Management Engineers may advance in any number of ways, depending on their ambitions and interests. They

can become technical specialists and consultants. They can pursue such management and administrative positions as supervisory, project, and chief engineers, as well as advance to executive officer positions. Waste Management Engineers with entrepreneurial ambitions can become independent consultants or owners of engineering firms that offer waste management engineering services. Some engineers pursue a career in teaching and research at the academic level.

Education and Training

Minimally, Waste Management Engineers must possess a bachelor's degree in environmental engineering, civil engineering, chemical engineering, mechanical engineering or another related field. A master's or doctoral degree is usually required for engineers to advance to careers in management, consulting, research, or teaching. Engineers must possess a doctorate to teach and conduct research at the college and university level.

Employers usually provide entry-level engineers with training programs, which may include both on-the-job training and formal classroom training. New engineers work under the supervision and direction of experienced engineers.

Throughout their careers, Waste Management Engineers enroll in continuing education programs and training programs to update their skills and keep up with advancements in their fields.

Special Requirements

All engineers who offer engineering services directly to the public or perform work that affects the life, health, or property of the public must be licensed as professional engineers (P.E.). Every U.S. state and territory, as well as Washington, D.C., has its own requirements for P.E. licensure. For specific information, contact the board of engineering examiners for the area where you wish to practice. See Appendix II for a list of boards.

Experience, Special Skills, and Personality Traits

Entry-level candidates should have one or more years of work experience related to the positions for which they apply. They may have gained their experience through internships, work-study programs, student research projects, or summer employment. They should also be knowledgeable about pertinent environmental laws and regulations, as well as about processes and methods of waste disposal.

Waste Management Engineers must have effective communication and writing skills, as they need to be able to provide technical information in terms that everyone can understand. In addition, their job requires that they have solid leadership, customer service, interpersonal, and problem-solving skills.

Some personality traits that successful Waste Management Engineers share include being self-motivated, detail-oriented, analytical, honest, and creative.

Unions and Associations

Many Waste Management Engineers belong to professional associations to take advantage of networking opportunities, certification programs, and other professional services and resources. Societies are available at the local, state, and national levels. Some national organizations include the Solid Waste Association of North America, the Air and Waste Management Association, the American Academy of Environmental Engineers, the American Society of Civil Engineers, and the National Society of Professional Engineers. For contact information, see Appendix III.

Tips for Entry

1. Many professional societies offer student memberships. While in college, join an association that interests you. Participate in the various activities that they offer.
2. Check with government agencies, private firms, professional associations, and so forth for job listings. Many organizations have job hot lines or post job listings on their Web sites.
3. Learn more about the waste management field on the Internet. You might start by visiting these Web sites: National Solid Wastes Management Association, http://www.nswma.org; and U.S. Environmental Protection Agency's Office of Solid Waste, http://www.epa.gov/osw. For more links, see Appendix IV.

CHEMICAL ENGINEERING

CHEMICAL ENGINEER

CAREER PROFILE

Duties: Research, design, operate, and maintain equipment and plants for industrial chemical processes; perform duties as required

Alternate Title(s): Process Engineer; a title that reflects a specialty (such as Food Engineer) or an engineering function (such as Development Engineer)

Salary Range: $49,000 to $113,000

Employment Prospects: Good

Advancement Prospects: Good

Prerequisites:

Education or Training—Bachelor's degree in chemical engineering; on-the-job training

Experience—Previous work experience generally required

Special Skills and Personality Traits—Writing, computer, communication, interpersonal, teamwork, leadership, critical thinking, and problem-solving skills; creative, flexible, enthusiastic, detail-oriented, and self-motivated

Special Requirements—Professional engineer (P.E.) license may be required

CAREER LADDER

```
┌─────────────────────────────┐
│   Senior Chemical Engineer   │
└─────────────────────────────┘

┌─────────────────────────────┐
│      Chemical Engineer       │
└─────────────────────────────┘

┌─────────────────────────────┐
│   Junior Chemical Engineer   │
└─────────────────────────────┘
```

Position Description

Each day, our lives are made better by the work done by Chemical Engineers. We marvel at the variety and bounty of the foods we eat and are pleased when new food products hit the market. We put fuel into our cars or trucks and drive for business and pleasure. We wear comfortable clothes made from durable fabrics that require a minimum of care. When we are ill, we take medicines to make us feel better and get well. We read books and magazines printed on glossy paper. We study, work, and play on computers encased in hard shiny plastic.

Chemical engineering is the profession that utilizes the principles of engineering, chemistry, mathematics, physics, and other disciplines to manufacture and use chemicals to produce new products. Food products, vehicle fuels, medicines, and electronics are just a few of the goods that result from the efforts of Chemical Engineers.

Chemical Engineers are not chemists. Chemists understand and work with chemical reactions and interactions.

Chemical Engineers, on the other hand, make such processes work in ways that are practical for the production of manufactured goods. Chemical Engineers use both organic and inorganic chemical compounds to devise better ways to process foods, create synthetic fibers, refine petroleum, develop new medicines, and invent new materials from which a variety of products are made. Many Chemical Engineers are also involved in the design, production, and operation of the equipment and manufacturing facilities needed to use chemical processes to help change raw materials or chemicals into finished products.

Chemical Engineers work in a variety of industries, such as health care, pharmaceuticals, petroleum, plastics, biotechnology, and environmental safety. They are increasingly part of the quest to discover and develop alternative fuels, reduce pollution, and improve the health and well being of all of us. Some Chemical Engineers are engaged in new and emerging technologies such as biotechnology, nanotechnology, and sustainable energy technologies.

Throughout their careers, Chemical Engineers work in different engineering functions. As process design engineers, they specialize in production for various industries that use chemicals to develop new products. In that capacity, they design facilities and equipment, as well as oversee the use of equipment and find ways to improve the production process. They also give advice about obtaining the proper equipment and about how it is to be used.

Chemical Engineers who work in the areas of research and development study ways to create new products and decide how useful they will be. Research and development engineers also work to improve older products and look for more efficient ways to make them.

Some Chemical Engineers are concerned with quality control. They closely observe the manufacturing process to ensure that exacting standards of quality are applied. Quality control engineers test finished products for durability, observe changes in their color, or see how they withstand continued usage in a variety of environmental conditions.

Regulatory affairs engineers study, create, and oversee guidelines for the correct handling of chemicals. These Chemical Engineers research how chemicals impact the environment and devise regulations for their proper use.

Project management, product engineering, test engineering, and consulting are a few other engineering functions in which Chemical Engineers may be engaged. In addition, some Chemical Engineers work in colleges and universities as professors. They teach classes in chemical engineering as well as conduct research to discover new ways to use or produce chemicals. Corporations and government entities use their research findings to develop new and improved products or applications.

Many Chemical Engineers also specialize in an area within chemical engineering, such as:

- petrochemical engineering, the development of better methods of locating and recovering new supplies of oil or natural gas, as well as the improvement of their refinement and production into gasoline, motor oil, or heating fuel
- biochemical engineering, the study of chemical processes in plants and animals, which are used in the agriculture industry to improve food products or develop new ones
- food engineering, which strives to make food crops more resistant to disease and to seek ways to lengthen the shelf life of food products

Some Chemical Engineers choose to devote themselves to a particular industry. For example, some engineers work in the pharmaceuticals industry where they design and develop methods and equipment that serve to produce large quantities of medications at a lower cost. Chemical Engineers may further specialize by working in a particular field, such as environmental control or nuclear decontamination.

There are several levels of expertise within the chemical engineering profession. Junior Chemical engineers typically work under the guidance and supervision of senior engineers. They are given specific directions on their assignments along with clearly defined priorities and goals. As they gain experience and knowledge, they receive more complex assignments and are able to exercise greater levels of authority. They may work as lead persons in certain assignments while directing the activities of other engineers and technicians.

Senior Chemical Engineers are more actively involved with the decision-making process and are more likely to be team leaders. Their decisions are made without direct supervision. Senior engineers are more aware of program needs and work independently in response to those needs. Advanced and executive-level Chemical Engineers are the primary engineers for project divisions or for an entire geographical area. These professionals perform the most difficult engineering tasks. Their level of expertise is wider in scope, and includes other disciplines.

Whatever their specialty, area of concern, or level of expertise, Chemical Engineers perform certain tasks on the job that are similar. For example, they:

- work on new procedures to use chemicals to reach desired results
- study new production processes, or seek ways to improve old ones
- conduct tests in all facets of production to ensure control over such factors as temperature, pressure, specific gravity, and density
- create safety measures for workers to observe when working with chemicals and related equipment
- decide how to arrange the various phases of production for maximum effectiveness
- test the steps of a manufacturing process in laboratory settings on a reduced scale before moving into full-scale production
- devise exacting measurement and control systems for large-scale production facilities
- plan for the layout of equipment in concert with the production stages
- estimate the costs of production and report to their organization's administrators

Chemical Engineers work in offices, laboratories, and factories. They normally work for 40 hours each week but may at times work additional hours when needed.

Salaries

Salaries for Chemical Engineers vary, depending on such factors as their education, experience, job duties, employer, industry, and geographical location. According to the November 2004 *Occupational Employment Statistics* (OES) survey by the U.S. Bureau of Labor Statistics (BLS), the estimated annual salary for most Chemical Engineers ranged between $48,990 and $112,790.

Employment Prospects

The BLS reported in its November 2004 OES survey that an estimated 28,590 Chemical Engineers were employed in the United States. The highest levels of employment for Chemical Engineers were found in the following industries: architectural and engineering services; basic chemical manufacturing; scientific research and development services; resin, rubber, and artificial fibers manufacturing; and petroleum and coal products manufacturing.

Besides chemical process industries (such as specialty chemicals, industrial gases, petrochemicals, and cosmetics), Chemical Engineers are employed in the pharmaceutical, biotechnology, foods and beverages, electronics, design and construction, fuels, aerospace, and environmental safety industries. Chemical Engineers are also employed by government agencies, research institutes, and academic institutions. Some engineers are independent practitioners.

In general, most opportunities will become available as Chemical Engineers advance to higher positions, transfer to other occupations, retire, or leave the workforce for other reasons.

Advancement Prospects

Chemical Engineers may advance in any number of ways, depending on their ambitions and interests. Engineers with management and administrative interests and talents can seek a position as a supervisory, project, or chief engineer. In addition, engineers can advance to executive officer positions within their organization. Engineers with entrepreneurial ambitions can become independent consultants or owners of firms that offer chemical engineering services.

Education and Training

Minimally, a bachelor's degree in chemical engineering, chemistry, or another related field is needed for entry-level positions. A master's or doctoral degree is usually required for Chemical Engineers to advance to careers in management, consulting, research, or teaching. To teach at the college and university level, engineers must possess a doctorate.

Employers typically provide entry-level engineers with training programs, which may include both on-the-job and classroom training. Throughout their careers, Chemical Engineers enroll in continuing education and training programs to update their skills and keep up with advancements in their fields.

Special Requirements

All engineers who offer engineering services directly to the public or perform work that affects the life, health, or property of the public must be licensed as professional engineers (P.E.) in the states where they practice. The licensing process consists of two stages. At the first level, qualifying individuals become licensed as engineers-in-training (E.I.T.). After working several years under the supervision of licensed Chemical Engineers, E.I.T.s become eligible to apply for the P.E. license.

All states, territories, and Washington, D.C., have their own requirements for P.E. licensure. For specific information, contact the board of engineering examiners for the area where you wish to practice. See Appendix II for a list of boards.

Experience, Special Skills, and Personality Traits

Entry-level candidates should have work experience related to the positions for which they apply. They may have gained their experience through internships, work-study programs, student research projects, or summer employment.

Chemical Engineers need strong writing and computer skills for their job. They must also have effective communication, interpersonal, and teamwork skills to work well with many people with different backgrounds. In addition, they should have excellent leadership, critical thinking and problem-solving skills. Being creative, flexible, enthusiastic, detail-oriented, and self-motivated are some personality traits that successful Chemical Engineers share.

Unions and Associations

Many Chemical Engineers belong to local, state, and national societies to take advantage of networking opportunities, continuing education programs, certification programs, and other professional services and resources. Some national societies that serve the general interests of these engineers include the American Institute of Chemical Engineers, the Association of Consulting Chemists and Chemical Engineers, the American Chemical Society, the Society of Women Engineers, and the National Society of Professional Engineers. For contact information, see Appendix III.

Tips for Entry

1. As a high school student, join a student science or engineering club. You might also gain exposure by visiting, and possibly volunteering, at a science or technology museum.
2. In college, get a variety of internships or part-time jobs in different work settings to see which environment suits you the best.
3. Contact employers directly about their job vacancies and selection process.
4. Some Chemical Engineers obtain their P.E. license to enhance their employability.
5. Use the Internet to learn more about Chemical Engineers. You might start by visiting these Web sites: American Institute of Chemical Engineers, http://www.aiche.org; and The World Wide Web Virtual Library: Chemical Engineering (University of Florida), http://www.che.ufl.edu/www-che. For more links, see Appendix IV.

CHEMICAL PROCESS ENGINEER (PETROLEUM AND PETROCHEMICAL INDUSTRIES)

CAREER PROFILE

Duties: Be involved with the research, development, design, or operations of the chemical processing of petroleum and petroleum products; perform duties as required

Alternate Title(s): Chemical Engineer; a title that reflects an engineering function such as Project Engineer or Research Engineer

Salary Range: $49,000 to $113,000

Employment Prospects: Fair

Advancement Prospects: Good

Prerequisites:

 Education or Training—Bachelor's degree in chemical engineering; on-the-job training

 Experience—Previous work experience generally required

 Special Skills and Personality Traits—Computer, writing, communication, presentation, interpersonal, teamwork, leadership, organizational, problem-solving, and time management skills; self-motivated, enthusiastic, respectful, detail-oriented, flexible, and creative

 Special Requirements—Professional engineer (P.E.) license may be required

CAREER LADDER

```
┌─────────────────────────────────────┐
│   Senior Chemical Process Engineer   │
└─────────────────────────────────────┘

┌─────────────────────────────────────┐
│      Chemical Process Engineer       │
└─────────────────────────────────────┘

┌─────────────────────────────────────┐
│   Junior Chemical Process Engineer   │
└─────────────────────────────────────┘
```

Position Description

Petroleum is one of the most important substances used by human beings. Ancient societies as diverse as the Egyptians, the Babylonians, the Chinese, and the Native Americans used petroleum for an equally varied set of purposes. Petroleum pitch was used to seal reed boats, pave roads, and hold buildings together, for example. People throughout the world used petroleum for medical remedies, lamps, and paint. With the advent of the Industrial Revolution, and particularly in mid–19th century America, the modern petroleum industry began in earnest and, along with it, the chemical engineering profession developed and matured.

Chemical Process Engineers in the petroleum and petrochemical industries are concerned with the processing of petroleum. Petroleum, or crude oil, is a substance that is composed mainly of hydrocarbons, which are organic hydrogen and carbon chemical compounds. These hydrocarbons can be gaseous or solid, although most of them are liquid. Through a series of complex refining processes, petroleum is broken down into various mixtures, or fractions. Gasoline is a fraction that can be used without being combined with other substances. Mixing fractions with other substances produces other products. Petroleum can therefore be used to make a variety of everyday items. We are most familiar with such petroleum products as gasoline, motor oil, fertilizers, and plastics. Other products such as fabrics, cosmetics, toothpaste, carpets, and detergents are also made from petroleum or petrochemicals.

Chemical Process Engineers may be involved with research, development, and design. Those engaged with research and development endeavor to introduce new products or improve old ones with an eye toward efficiency or economy, as well as toward environmental concerns. Some engineers concentrate specifically on development to improve established processes and technologies.

Others work with the processes of production. Still others work in the area of design to create the refinery facilities as well as the processes of refining crude oil into new products while concentrating on the issues of customer needs, environmental impacts, and production efficiency. For some Chemical Process Engineers, management and technical sales are areas that require making decisions and offering the expert promotion of new products. They are more concerned with the business aspects of their profession to provide superior products and to maximize profits. They strive to coordinate the activities of their refineries to fulfill their organization's mission and goals.

Some Chemical Process Engineers work in several engineering functions (research, development, design, project management, testing, and so forth) during the course of their careers. These functional specialties can sometimes coincide or overlap. Furthermore, their profession also presents them with opportunities to work in academia as teachers and researchers.

Chemical Process Engineers perform a variety of duties, some of which are generally the same regardless of the role they fulfill. For example, they might:

- explore the world to find and extract new sources of petroleum
- develop new methods of and technologies for exploiting previously overlooked sources of oil
- work to increase yields from petroleum fields
- create new refining processes and systems as well as modify older ones
- test their designs and processes in laboratory and pilot facilities
- develop new products from recycled waste byproducts
- provide advice about plant layout and equipment acquisition
- collect and interpret data to increase their understanding of their organization's day-to-day operations and equipment to facilitate their troubleshooting and documentation of problems
- develop and ensure standards for their operations and the reliability of their equipment
- monitor all facets of their operation and exercise process control over production and quality
- oversee the work of team members and provide schedules
- consult with other organizations in their industry about general or specific concerns

Chemical Process Engineers are expected to be accountable for their industry's safety, efficiency, and impact on the environment. In addition, their job involves solving problems in the areas of operations and business issues, as well as ensuring compliance with governmental laws and regulations.

Chemical Process Engineers work with other engineers, scientists, and specialists, as well as with technicians, staff support personnel, and others within their particular teams or in other areas of concern. Their work also requires them to read journals, books, articles, and industry literature as well as memos and other documents relevant to their particular organization. Reading increases their knowledge and keeps them up-to-date with developments in their industry. They need to be supplied with a continual flow of data to aid in their analyses and decision making. Chemical Process Engineers also write a variety of documents to communicate their expertise and provide new concepts for application in all facets of their work. Many of them use computers to design new refineries as well as to develop their own design software.

Chemical Process Engineers work in offices, laboratories, pilot plants, and refineries. They generally work 40-hour weeks but put in additional hours when needed. They are often required to travel to attend meetings and conferences, or to work on site at pilot plants or refineries. Some of their assignments may require that they work at facilities located in other countries.

Salaries

Salaries for Chemical Process Engineers in the petroleum and petrochemical industries vary. Their earnings depend on such factors as their education, experience, job duties, employer, and geographical location. According to the November 2004 *Occupational Employment Statistics* survey by the U.S. Bureau of Labor Statistics, the estimated annual salary for most chemical engineers ranged between $48,990 and $112,790.

Employment Prospects

Opportunities for Chemical Process Engineers in the petroleum and petrochemical industries exist both nationally and worldwide. They are employed by petroleum and petrochemical companies as well as engineering firms that offer consulting or contracting services to those companies. In general, most openings become available as engineers retire, advance to higher positions, or transfer to other occupations. Some experts in the field believe that the demand for qualified engineers should grow more due to the number of engineers retiring. In addition, the petroleum and petrochemical industry must compete with electronics, pharmaceutical, and other industries for talented candidates. However, the job market can be affected by downturns in the economy.

Advancement Prospects

As engineers gain experience, they are assigned to more complex projects and receive increasingly greater responsibilities.

Engineers with management and administrative interests and talents can seek positions as supervisory, project, and chief engineers, as well as executive officers. Those with entrepreneurial ambitions can become independent consultants or owners of engineering firms that offer consulting or contracting services.

Education and Training

Employers require that Chemical Process Engineers possess at least a bachelor's degree in chemical engineering or another related field. Some employers may prefer to hire candidates who hold an advanced degree.

A master's or doctoral degree is usually required for engineers to advance to careers in management, consulting, research, or teaching. To teach and conduct research in academic institutions, engineers must possess a doctorate.

Employers typically provide entry-level engineers with training programs, which may include both on-the-job and classroom training. Novice engineers work under the supervision and direction of experienced engineers.

Throughout their careers, engineers enroll in continuing education and training programs to update their skills and keep up with advancements in their fields.

Special Requirements

All engineers who offer engineering services directly to the public or perform work that affects the life, health, or property of the public must be licensed as professional engineers (P.E.). Each U.S. state and territory, as well as Washington, D.C., has its own particular requirements for P.E. licensure. For specific information, contact the board of engineering examiners where you wish to practice. See Appendix II for a list of boards.

Experience, Special Skills, and Personality Traits

Entry-level candidates should have work experience related to the positions for which they apply. They may have gained their experience through internships, work-study programs, student research projects, or summer employment.

Computer, writing, communication, and presentation skills are essential for Chemical Process Engineers to be successful in their work. Additionally, they need effective inter-personal and teamwork skills, as they must be able to work well with colleagues, managers, customers, and others from diverse backgrounds. Further, Chemical Process Engineers should have strong leadership, organizational, problem-solving, and time management skills. Being self-motivated, enthusiastic, respectful, detail-oriented, flexible, and creative are some personality traits that successful Chemical Process Engineers have in common.

Unions and Associations

Chemical Process Engineers can join professional associations at the local, state, and national levels to take advantage of networking opportunities and other professional services and resources. Some national societies include the American Institute of Chemical Engineering, the American Chemical Society, the Association of Consulting Chemists and Chemical Engineers, and the National Society of Professional Engineers. For contact information, see Appendix III.

Tips for Entry

1. Talk with professionals in the field about their job. In addition to learning about the types of work they have done, find out what they like about their job and about working in the petroleum or petrochemical industry. Ask them to recommend courses in business and nonchemical engineering fields that would be helpful to your future career.
2. If you think you would like to work abroad, learn one or more foreign languages. Also learn about the culture, geography, economics, and other aspects of countries where you would like to work.
3. Many companies recruit for entry-level positions on college campuses. When you meet with a recruiter, be prepared to be interviewed and have copies of your résumé to hand out.
4. Use the Internet to learn more about chemical process engineering as well as the petroleum and petrochemical industries. You might start by visiting these Web sites: Cheresources.com, http://www.cheresources.com; and Fuels and Petrochemicals Division (American Institute of Chemical Engineers), http://www.missouri.edu/~suppesg/FPD_WEB.htm. For more links, see Appendix IV.

BIOCHEMICAL ENGINEER

CAREER PROFILE

Duties: Be involved in the research, development, design, and operation of the biological processes used in the production of chemicals, medicines, foods, and other products; perform duties as required

Alternate Title(s): Chemical Engineer, Bioengineer; a title that reflects an engineering function such as Project Engineer or Research Engineer

Salary Range: $49,000 to $113,000

Employment Prospects: Good

Advancement Prospects: Good

Prerequisites:

Education or Training—Bachelor's degree in biochemical or chemical engineering; on-the-job training

Experience—Previous work experience generally required

Special Skills and Personality Traits—Writing, computer, communication, problem-solving, critical thinking, leadership, interpersonal, and teamwork skills; inquisitive, innovative, cooperative, enthusiastic, collaborative, self-motivated, and goal-oriented

Special Requirements—Professional engineer (P.E.) license may be required

CAREER LADDER

```
┌─────────────────────────────────┐
│   Senior Biochemical Engineer    │
└─────────────────────────────────┘

┌─────────────────────────────────┐
│      Biochemical Engineer        │
└─────────────────────────────────┘

┌─────────────────────────────────┐
│   Junior Biochemical Engineer    │
└─────────────────────────────────┘
```

Position Description

For the past several years, we have heard more news about developments in medicine that give us hopes for new cures for AIDS, cancer, Alzheimer's, and other diseases. We read reports about new antibiotics and other drugs. The latest discoveries in the realm of genetics and their promises of medical applications reach our eyes and ears with greater frequency. We learn of fuel and plastic products made from corn. We hear about bacteria that can devour oil spills. Many of the professionals involved in bringing all of these wondrous developments to us are Biochemical Engineers.

Biochemical Engineers work in a relatively new profession. Biochemical engineering is a specialty of chemical engineering. This field originated with the development and production of large quantities of antibiotic medicines in the mid-20th century. During the 1980s, a merging of biochemistry and chemical engineering furthered this new field, which applies principals of chemical engineering to biological systems.

Biochemical Engineers use their knowledge of chemistry, biology, and engineering to create new biochemical and biological processes that serve to improve our food supply and environment, treat our illnesses, and develop new consumer products. Some familiar results of their work include medicines such as penicillin, insulin, and new treatments for Parkinson's disease; medical equipment such as heart valves, artificial kidneys, and blood oxygenators; food products such as milk powder, artificial sweeteners, and vitamins; biodegradable plastic cups; cattle feed; and clothing.

New products are created and developed in the science labs. To manufacture finished products, Biochemical Engineers develop and design the chemical processes needed for large-scale production. These specialized chemical engineers can also be engaged in other roles. For example, they may oversee projects while working in the capacity of managers. As project engineers, they develop budgets, manage capital, buy equipment, plan and oversee schedules, and perform other business-oriented tasks.

Many Biochemical Engineers are also involved with basic research in addition to the development of new processes and products. They conduct experiments as well as study the research findings of others. They test their innovative ideas in laboratories on a small scale or under controlled conditions before scaling them up to be used as large-scale processes or to make products.

Biochemical Engineers perform many of the same duties as chemical engineers. For example, they:

- design processes and equipment with particular attention to such factors as heat, transfer, momentum, and mass
- design production units, as well as oversee their installation and use
- use computers to design, model, and simulate processes, products, and manufacturing plants
- ensure that raw materials are available for experiments or production
- monitor the environmental impact of the production processes
- prepare reports and diagrams
- manage schedules and costs
- work closely with other scientists, engineers, technicians, and other organizational personnel that are involved with their projects

Biochemical Engineers work in both office and laboratory settings. Their work occasionally requires them to visit new production facilities. They generally work 40-hour weeks but may need to work extra hours when necessary.

Salaries

Salaries for Biochemical Engineers vary, depending on such factors as their education, experience, employer, and geographical location. The U.S. Bureau of Labor Statistics reports in its November 2004 *Occupational Employment Statistics* survey that the estimated annual salary for most chemical engineers, including Biochemical Engineers, ranged between $48,990 and $112,790.

Employment Prospects

Many Biochemical Engineers are employed by small and large companies in the pharmaceutical, environmental, consulting, food, and waste treatment industries. They also are employed by engineering consulting and contracting firms as well as by government agencies and research institutes. Some engineers are independent practitioners. Many Biochemical Engineers work at universities in teaching or research capacities. Research work is available in government agencies and private sector research organizations.

In general, most opportunities will become available as Biochemical Engineers advance to higher positions, transfer to other occupations, retire, or leave the workforce for other reasons. The job outlook for this occupation has been described by experts in the field as ranging from good to excellent. Many new and experienced Biochemical Engineers have been hired by start-up companies that are concerned with emerging technologies, such as nanotechnology and genetic engineering. However, keep in mind that the job market can be affected by downturns in the economy, which may result in some companies hiring fewer employees as well as laying off personnel.

Advancement Prospects

As Biochemical Engineers gain experience, they are assigned to more complex projects or receive increasingly greater responsibilities. They may advance in any number of ways, depending on their ambitions and interests. They may become technical specialists, or move into the business areas of an organization, such as marketing, technical sales, or finance.

Those with managerial and administrative ambitions may pursue positions as supervisory, project, and chief engineers. In addition, they may advance to executive officer positions within their organization. Engineers with entrepreneurial ambitions can become independent consultants or owners of firms that offer biochemical engineering services.

Education and Training

Employers require that candidates possess at least a bachelor's degree in biochemical engineering, chemical engineering (preferably with an emphasis in biochemical engineering), or another related field. Some employers prefer to hire candidates with advanced degrees. Employers typically provide entry-level engineers with on-the-job training, in which they work under the supervision and direction of experienced engineers. Some employers also provide formal classroom training programs.

A master's or doctoral degree is usually required for careers in management, consulting, research, or teaching. Engineers must hold a doctorate to teach at the college and university level.

Throughout their careers, Biochemical Engineers enroll in continuing education and training programs to update their skills and keep up with advancements in their fields.

Special Requirements

All engineers who offer engineering services directly to the public or perform work that affects the life, health, or property of the public must be licensed as professional engineers (P.E.) where they practice. Every U.S. state and territory, as well as Washington, D.C., has its particular requirements for P.E. licensure. For specific information, contact the board of engineering examiners for the area where you wish to practice. See Appendix II for a list of boards.

Experience, Special Skills, and Personality Traits

Entry-level candidates should have work experience related to the positions for which they apply. They may have gained their experience through internships, work-study programs, academic research projects, or summer employment.

Biochemical Engineers need effective writing, computer, communication, problem-solving and critical thinking skills for their job. In addition, they must possess excellent leadership, interpersonal, and teamwork skills to work well with colleagues, employers, and others from diverse backgrounds. Being inquisitive, innovative, cooperative, enthusiastic, collaborative, self-motivated, and goal-oriented are some personality traits that successful Biochemical Engineers share.

Unions and Associations

Many Biochemical Engineers belong to local, state, and national societies to take advantage of networking opportunities, continuing education programs, and other professional services and resources. Some national societies that serve these engineers are the American Institute of Chemi-

cal Engineers, the American Chemical Society, the Association of Consulting Chemists and Chemical Engineers, and the National Society of Professional Engineers. For contact information, see Appendix III.

Tips for Entry

1. Take advantage of your college career center. It can provide you with information about scholarships, fellowships, internships, work experience programs, job fairs, and so on. The career counselors can also help you develop effective job search skills.
2. A well-presented résumé can make a difference in getting a job interview. Hence, check your résumé and cover letter carefully before giving them to a prospective employer. Be sure all words and names are spelled correctly, and that you have no grammatical, punctuation, or typographical errors.
3. Contact company human resources departments for information about job vacancies and their job selection process.
4. Use the Internet to learn more about biochemical engineering. To get a list of Web sites, enter the keyword *biochemical engineering* in a search engine. To learn about some links, see Appendix IV.

FOOD ENGINEER

CAREER PROFILE

Duties: Be involved in the research, development, design, and operations of the chemical processing of food and food products; perform duties as required

Alternate Title(s): Food Process Engineer, Chemical Engineer; a title that reflects an engineering function such as Project Engineer or Design Engineer

Salary Range: $49,000 to $113,000

Employment Prospects: Good

Advancement Prospects: Good

Prerequisites:

Education or Training—Bachelor's degree in chemical engineering; on-the-job training

Experience—Previous work experience generally required

Special Skills and Personality Traits—Leadership, problem-solving, time management, organizational, communication, interpersonal, teamwork, writing, and computer skills; analytical, curious, creative, self-motivated, dedicated, and practical

Special Requirements—Professional engineer (P.E.) license may be required

CAREER LADDER

```
┌─────────────────────────┐
│   Senior Food Engineer   │
└─────────────────────────┘

┌─────────────────────────┐
│      Food Engineer       │
└─────────────────────────┘

┌─────────────────────────┐
│   Junior Food Engineer   │
└─────────────────────────┘
```

Position Description

Salting, drying, freezing, and canning foods for storage and later consumption are techniques of food processing that humans have developed over the centuries. Just about anyone could process his or her foods through these methods. Today, however, we are more likely to eat foods that are processed by manufacturers. Many of our foods are precooked, preserved, and packaged in large quantities at distant facilities for distribution to our local markets. The profession that studies, develops, and produces food in this manner is food process engineering. The men and women who work in this field are called food process engineers, or Food Engineers.

Food Engineers work with food in a variety of ways. For example, they have developed new techniques to remove caffeine from coffee; they have designed packages for our favorite snack foods; and they have brought microwave ovens into our daily lives. Food Engineers are also involved with new food technologies such as genetic engineering and are concerned about the impact of discarded food packaging on the environment. Food Engineers continually seek ways to make our food more tempting and nutritious.

Food Engineers apply the principles of science and engineering to their work. They face particular challenges because foods are more complex and variable than other substances. Food's chemistry can be broken into basic compounds, which are classified as proteins, fats, enzymes, and so forth. However, within each of these categories, food's compounds exhibit boundless variety, and they often interact with each other in unpredictable ways. Hence, working with food processing is in itself a complex operation.

Like other engineers, Food Engineers may perform any number of engineering functions throughout their careers. In the area of research and development, Food Engineers study the chemical, physical, and flavor properties of food. They use this information to develop new food products. They try different combinations of food to see how they interact with each other and to create new food products or variations on established products. They closely analyze the properties of moisture, observe the interaction of fat with crystalline substances, and pay close attention to the flavors and textures of their products. Food Engineers may, for example, try different amounts of oil, vinegar, honey, spices, or mustard to create a new brand of honey mustard salad dressing. Research and development Food Engineers work in laboratories and approach their work in a carefully controlled fashion.

Many Food Engineers work in the role of designers to create a variety of items for use by the food processing industry. They work with the aid of computer simulation programs to design equipment and facilities for producing food products in quantity. They work with a thorough understanding of the results of research and development. Their job is to ensure that the same biochemical processes and quality established in pilot plants are consistently maintained on a much larger scale for every finished product. In addition to designing or modifying food processing plants and equipment, they also design computerized control systems to efficiently manage the equipment. Once the facilities are completed, other Food Engineers observe the plant functions to ensure their smooth operation.

Some Food Engineers work with facility designs to make sure that food-processing plants are large enough to produce new products in large quantities. They determine where equipment, machinery, and workstations are to be located, and carefully monitor all the stages of construction. By doing so, they work to ensure that products are manufactured and shipped efficiently and economically.

Food Engineers are also engaged in the development of new packaging materials, including new inks for printing product labels on the packages, with an eye toward ensuring their safety and minimal environmental impact. They make their new or improved products in small amounts, which they test at their lab benches or in pilot plants before approving them for large-scale production.

Other Food Engineers perform in the capacity of supervisors or managers. They oversee the activities of teams composed of other Food Engineers, scientists, technicians, construction crews, and others. Still other Food Engineers focus on marketing new or improved products to consumers as well as sell products to companies and institutions. Some Food Engineers provide their services as consultants while working for one or more organizations.

Regardless of their engineering function, Food Engineers perform many of the same duties. For example, they:

- conduct tests during all phases of production to control such variables as temperature and pressure
- implement safety procedures for the use of equipment and materials
- arrange the sequence of production processes for maximum effectiveness

- estimate production costs and prepare progress reports for management review
- develop steps to follow in the laboratory or in production processes
- research new chemical manufacturing processes
- use laboratory data to design measurement and control systems for production facilities

Food Engineers sometimes work independently but more frequently are team members. They work with other engineers but also have dealings with production workers, equipment manufacturers, technical personnel, managers, accountants, and others that are either directly or indirectly involved with food processing.

They use computers for many aspects of their jobs, including designing, analyzing laboratory results, writing reports, and testing production processes. Food Engineers also spend time away from the office or laboratory settings to visit food-processing plants.

Food Engineers usually work 40 hours each week but are occasionally required to work overtime to complete their tasks.

Salaries

Salaries for Food Engineers vary, depending on such factors as their education, experience, job duties, employer, industry and geographical location. According to the November 2004 *Occupational Employment Statistics* survey by the U.S. Bureau of Labor Statistics, the estimated annual salary for most chemical engineers, including Food Engineers, ranged between $48,990 and $112,790.

Employment Prospects

Food processing is one of the largest industries in the United States. Food Engineers are employed by food processing, ingredient manufacturing, food machinery, and packaging companies, as well as instrumentation and control companies. They also find employment with consulting and contracting firms. Other employers include government agencies, pharmaceutical companies, and health-care companies. Some Food Engineers are employed as teachers and researchers in academic institutions. Others are independent practitioners.

Opportunities generally become available as Food Engineers advance to higher positions, transfer to other jobs, retire, or leave the workforce for various reasons. According to some Food Engineers, the job market is steady and slightly increasing for this occupation in the United States. Global opportunities for Food Engineers are expanding in such developing areas as South America, India, and Southeast Asia, where professionals are needed to help build and manage new food plants.

Advancement Prospects

Food Engineers may advance in any number of ways, depending on their ambitions and interests. They can become technical specialists in such areas as process design, plant engineering, equipment design, quality assurance, or research and development. Engineers with management and administrative interests and talents can seek positions as supervisory, project, and chief engineers. To advance to higher positions, engineers are usually required to possess a master's or doctoral degree. Food Engineers with entrepreneurial ambitions can become independent consultants or owners of firms providing food engineering services.

Education and Training

Employers generally hire applicants who possess at least a bachelor's degree in chemical engineering or agricultural engineering, with an emphasis in food process engineering. Some employers prefer to hire candidates who hold an advanced degree in food process engineering or another related field.

Food Engineers who wish to teach and conduct research at the college and university level must possess a doctorate.

Entry-level Food Engineers typically receive on-the-job training, and work under the supervision and guidance of senior engineers. In large companies, they may also receive classroom training.

Throughout their careers, Food Engineers enroll in continuing education and training programs to update their skills and keep up with advancements in their fields.

Special Requirements

All engineers who offer engineering services directly to the public or perform work that affects the life, health, or property of the public must be licensed as professional engineers (P.E.). Every U.S. state and territory, as well as Washington, D.C., has its own specific requirements for P.E. licensure. For specific information, contact the board of engineering examiners for the area where you wish to practice. See Appendix II for a list of boards.

Experience, Special Skills, and Personality Traits

Entry-level candidates should have work experience related to the positions for which they apply. They may have gained their experience through internships, work-study programs, student research projects, or summer employment.

To perform well at their job, Food Engineers need leadership, problem-solving, time management, and organizational skills. Additionally, they must have communication, interpersonal, and teamwork skills, as they must be able to work effectively with different people from diverse backgrounds. Having strong writing and computer skills is essential as well.

Some personality traits that successful Food Engineers share include being analytical, curious, creative, self-motivated, dedicated, and practical.

Unions and Associations

Many Food Engineers join one or more professional societies to take advantage of networking opportunities, continuing education programs, certification programs, and other professional services and resources. These associations are available at the local, state, and national levels. Some national societies that serve the diverse interests of Food Engineers include:

- Institute of Food Technologists
- International Society of Food Engineering
- International Association for Food Protection
- American Institute of Chemical Engineers
- American Society of Agricultural Engineers
- American Association of Cereal Chemistry
- Association of Consulting Chemists and Chemical Engineers
- National Society of Professional Engineers

For contact information for these organizations, see Appendix III.

Tips for Entry

1. During your internship or summer employment, be willing to work with various personnel as well as to learn a variety of tasks. This will help you gain confidence in working in different situations. In addition, you will have gained the valuable experience that future employers desire in candidates.
2. Some food companies send job announcements to many college and university campuses. Check for them at your college career center or student employment office, as well as the food engineering, chemical engineering, or food science department.
3. Maintain a strong network of contacts—fellow students, professors, employers, supervisors, professional society members, and others—whom you can contact during your job searches.
4. Learn more about Food Engineers on the Internet. You might start by visiting these Web sites: FoodProcessing.com, http://www.foodprocessing.com; and Explore Food Engineering (hosted by R. Paul Singh), http://rpaulsingh.com. For more links, see Appendix IV.

MATERIALS ENGINEERING

MATERIALS ENGINEER

CAREER PROFILE

Duties: Be involved in the research, development, design, production, and testing of materials as well as machinery and processes to manufacture materials; perform duties as required

Alternate Title(s): A title that reflects a specialty (such as Ceramic Engineer) or an engineering function (such as Project Engineer)

Salary Range: $45,000 to $103,000

Employment Prospects: Fair

Advancement Prospects: Good

Prerequisites:

Education or Training—Bachelor's degree in materials engineering; on-the-job training

Experience—Previous work experience generally required

Special Skills and Personality Traits—Problem-solving, communication, writing, computer, leadership, interpersonal, teamwork, and self-management skills; analytical, detail-oriented, creative, inquisitive, cooperative, and self-motivated

Special Requirements—Professional engineer (P.E.) license may be required

CAREER LADDER

```
┌─────────────────────────────────┐
│     Senior Materials Engineer    │
└─────────────────────────────────┘

┌─────────────────────────────────┐
│        Materials Engineer        │
└─────────────────────────────────┘

┌─────────────────────────────────┐
│     Junior Materials Engineer    │
└─────────────────────────────────┘
```

Position Description

We live in a world surrounded by things that we make from all types of materials. Some of these materials, such as wood, minerals, or metal, come straight from nature or from the ground. Most of the modern materials that comprise our possessions are human-made. Some of these materials are composites; that is, they are made from several materials. Other human-made materials are synthetic; they are created by the rearrangement of the molecular structure of various materials. Our lives would be very different if many of our newer materials were never engineered to make such products as computers, airplanes, automobiles, buildings, and machines of every description. Materials engineering concentrates on analyzing and designing materials, developing new methods to produce new materials, and finding efficient and economic ways to utilize materials in industry.

Materials Engineers and their work are vital to a variety of modern industries, such as the microelectronics, computer, aerospace, health care, energy, and sports industries. In the general field of engineering, most engineers are concerned with the design, fabrication, and use of equipment or structures. Materials Engineers are concerned with the specific materials that other engineers use to complete their projects. Materials Engineers research, develop, design, extract, produce, process, and test various materials, which are employed to make a vast array of products that we use every day.

Materials Engineers study new ideas or concepts about the behavior of metals; develop new or improved materials; and devise new methods to produce materials. They test and evaluate materials to determine their feasibility for use in new products. They are also involved in standardizing materials formulas and specifications for their production and use, as well as inspecting operating systems and equipment to identify problems with materials.

Materials Engineers apply the principles of engineering, mathematics, chemistry, and physics to study the structure, performance, properties, and synthesis of materials. The materials they work with are varied within specific classes: metals, plastics, ceramics, and semiconductors, as well as the newer classes of materials such as biomaterials and nanomaterials. They examine materials at the microscopic, molecular, and atomic levels in order to devise methods to manipulate or alter materials to create new ones. All materials with which Materials Engineers work must suit the purposes for which they will be used. Materials must be strong or malleable, be able to conduct or resist electrical current, be magnetic or nonmagnetic, be able to reflect or refract light, be resistant to temperature extremes, and be durable, depending on their use.

Materials Engineers have created many of the materials we use in our everyday lives. One example is Teflon, the solid substance that coats many of our cooking utensils. This material was created by freezing and compressing a gas. Another example is fiberglass. It is a composite material made from glass and polymers, from which many automobile bodies are made. A third example is silicon, a common chemical element found in ordinary sand. Our computers process information on chips made from this material.

Materials Engineers perform various engineering functions in the course of their careers, and sometimes carry out several functions simultaneously. They may work as research, design, test, project management, product, or consulting engineers, for example. Some Materials Engineers choose to teach future engineers, as well as conduct research in academic settings.

Most Materials Engineers develop their careers by becoming specialists in a particular aspect of materials engineering. They frequently specialize in particular materials such as optical materials, protective coatings, insulators, papers, or structural materials. Such concentrated fields as biochemical engineering, ceramic engineering, metallurgical engineering, polymer engineering, and electronic engineering are a few of the areas in which Materials Engineers can specialize.

Regardless of their function and specialty, Materials Engineers complete many of the same duties. For example, they:

- conduct studies to solve general, specific, or potential problems with the use of materials
- develop new processes for extracting, refining, and modifying raw materials
- specify processes for testing and producing materials
- plan and design laboratory facilities and equipment for testing and developing materials
- design and implement the use of production facilities and equipment
- oversee all stages of the production processes of new materials in lab settings as well as industrial settings, including the quality testing of finished products

- review information regarding product failure and interpret testing data to uncover the cause for the failure
- solve engineering problems that may arise in the research, development, and production of new materials
- ensure that materials are produced and used according to client specifications and in compliance with regulations
- consult and collaborate with clients as well as other engineers and professionals about the development and use of new materials
- plan new projects and products and recommend the use of appropriate materials and their specifications
- perform a variety of administrative duties, such as preparing budgets, writing reports and correspondence, and estimating project costs

There are several levels of expertise within the materials engineering profession. Junior engineers typically work under the guidance and supervision of senior engineers. Their focus is to develop their skills and their understanding of the rules, regulations, standards, and practices of their area of concern. They are given specific directions on their assignments along with clearly defined priorities and goals.

As Materials Engineers gain experience and knowledge, they receive more complex assignments and are able to exercise greater levels of authority. Some decisions are made at this level. They may work as lead persons in certain assignments while directing the activities of other engineers and technicians.

Senior engineers are more actively involved with the decision-making process and are more likely to be team leaders. They are often responsible for supervising the work of junior engineers, technologists, technicians, and other staff. Senior engineers are more aware of program needs and work independently in response to those needs.

Advanced and executive-level Materials Engineers are the primary engineers for project divisions, or for an entire geographical area. Their level of expertise is wider in scope, and includes other disciplines. They are responsible for making policy decisions and consulting with clients or government agencies at the highest levels.

Materials Engineers work in offices, laboratories, and in such industrial settings as foundries, smelting facilities, and factories. Much of their time is spent alone, particularly in lab settings. However, Materials Engineers are sometimes in contact with other people, most of whom are other engineers. They generally work for 40 hours per week but may work longer hours to meet deadlines and complete their various duties.

Salaries

Salaries for Materials Engineers vary, depending on such factors as their education, experience, job duties, employer, industry, and geographical location. According to the November 2004 *Occupational Employment Statistics* (OES) survey by the U.S. Bureau of Labor Statistics (BLS), the estimated annual salary for most Materials Engineers ranged between $45,130 and $103,210.

Employment Prospects

Materials Engineers are employed in many of the manufacturing industries, as well as in the professional, scientific, and technical services industries. Some work for federal and state government agencies. Materials Engineers also work as researchers and teachers in academic institutions. Some are independent practitioners. An estimated 20,940 Materials Engineers were employed in the United States, as of November 2004, according to the BLS.

The BLS reports that job growth for Materials Engineers is expected to increase by 9 to 17 percent through 2014. The BLS also predicts that the demand for Materials Engineers should increase in the electronics, biotechnology, and plastics industries, as they are needed to develop new materials for products. Additionally, job growth for this occupation is expected to increase among the consulting and contracting firms. Furthermore, opportunities will become available as engineers advance to higher positions, transfer to other occupations, or retire.

Advancement Prospects

Depending on their ambitions and interests, Materials Engineers can advance in any number of ways. They can specialize in specific materials, become technical specialists, or pursue business positions in such areas as marketing, technical sales, or finance.

Those with managerial and administrative ambitions can rise through the ranks as supervisory, project, and chief engineers. In addition, they can advance to executive officer positions within their organization. Engineers with entrepreneurial ambitions can become independent consultants or owners of firms that offer engineering services.

Education and Training

Minimally, Materials Engineers must possess a bachelor's degree in materials engineering or another related field. A master's or doctoral degree is usually required for engineers to advance to careers in research, management, consulting, or teaching. Materials Engineers must possess a doctorate to teach and conduct research at the academic level. Many engineers obtain advanced degrees in a materials engineering specialty that interests them.

Employers typically provide entry-level engineers with training programs, which may include both on-the-job training and classroom training. Throughout their careers, Materials Engineers enroll in continuing education and training programs to update their skills and keep up with advancements in their fields.

Special Requirements

All engineers who offer engineering services directly to the public or perform work that affects the life, health, or property of the public must be licensed as professional engineers (P.E.).

The licensing process consists of two stages. At the first level, qualifying individuals become licensed as engineers-in-training (E.I.T.). After working several years under the supervision of licensed engineers, E.I.T.s become eligible to apply for the P.E. license. Washington, D.C., and every state and territory has its own distinct requirements for P.E. licensure. For specific information, contact the board of engineering examiners for the area where you wish to practice. See Appendix II for a list of boards.

Experience, Special Skills, and Personality Traits

Entry-level candidates should have work experience related to the positions for which they apply. Many recent graduates gained their experience through internships, work-study programs, student research projects, and summer employment.

Materials Engineers need strong problem-solving, communication, writing, and computer skills to perform their various tasks effectively. They must also have strong leadership, interpersonal, and teamwork skills, as they must work well with many people with different backgrounds. In addition, they should have adequate self-management skills, such as the ability to work independently, handle stressful situations, and prioritize multiple tasks. Being analytical, detail-oriented, creative, inquisitive, cooperative, and self-motivated are some personality traits that successful Materials Engineers have in common.

Unions and Associations

Many professional associations at the local, state, and national levels serve the diverse interests of Materials Engineers. By joining one or more societies, engineers can take advantage of professional certification programs, networking opportunities, and other professional resources and services. The following are some national societies for this occupation:

- ASM International
- The Minerals, Metals, and Materials Society
- Materials Research Society
- American Ceramic Society
- Society of Plastics Engineers
- Society for Biomaterials
- NACE International
- Materials Engineering and Sciences Division, American Institute of Chemical Engineers
- Materials Division, ASME International
- National Society of Professional Engineers
- Society of Women Engineers

For contact information, see Appendix III.

Tips for Entry

1. Visit different work settings to determine which environment best fits you.
2. Join a student chapter of a professional society that interests you. Be sure to take advantage of activities that allow you to develop your skills and build up a network of contacts.
3. Check out employment ads in local newspapers. Many large bookstores carry daily or Sunday newspapers from large cities across the country, and sometimes from around the world.
4. Learn more about Materials Engineers on the Internet. You might start by visiting these Web sites: ASM International, http://www.asminternational.org; and Materials Science and Engineering Career Resource Center, http://www.crc4mse.org. For more links, see Appendix IV.

METALLURGICAL ENGINEER

CAREER PROFILE

Duties: Be involved in the research, development, and production of metals and metal products; perform duties as required

Alternate Title(s): Metallurgist, Metal Engineer, Materials Engineer; a title that reflects an engineering function, such as Research Engineer or Consultant

Salary Range: $45,000 to $103,000

Employment Prospects: Good

Advancement Prospects: Good

Prerequisites:

Education or Training—Bachelor's degree in metallurgical engineering; on-the-job training

Experience—Previous work experience generally required

Special Skills and Personality Traits—Writing, communication, leadership, self-management, problem-solving, interpersonal, and teamwork skills; practical, creative, analytical, curious, detail-oriented, and self-motivated

Special Requirements—Professional engineer (P.E.) license may be required

CAREER LADDER

```
┌─────────────────────────────────┐
│  Senior Metallurgical Engineer   │
└─────────────────────────────────┘

┌─────────────────────────────────┐
│      Metallurgical Engineer      │
└─────────────────────────────────┘

┌─────────────────────────────────┐
│   Junior Metallurgical Engineer  │
└─────────────────────────────────┘
```

Position Description

Metals have intrigued the human race for millennia. Prehistoric people used metals for all sorts of purposes, just as we do today. In prehistoric times, people found nuggets of gold, silver, copper, and other pure metals and fashioned them into jewelry, tools, weapons, cooking utensils, and currency. At the dawn of history, our distant ancestors learned that metals could be melted and mixed in various proportions to make alloys. For example, copper and tin were mixed to create bronze, which was stronger than either copper or tin alone. Eventually, people found metals in abundant quantities in mineral or rock deposits, called ores, which they learned to extract and use. They learned to smelt iron and make new alloys. About two hundred years ago, metallurgists began to discover new metallic elements as well as learn more about the properties and behaviors of metals, and thus a new science was born. Great strides were made during the twentieth century with the development of new alloys such as steel or those made with magnesium, as well as with the discovery of aluminum, a strong yet lightweight metal. Today, we enjoy a myriad of metal alloys in our everyday lives, thanks to the work of Metallurgical Engineers.

Metallurgical Engineers work in mines, ore-refining facilities, laboratories, factories, foundries, and offices. They are involved with the research, development, and production of metals and alloys. These engineers use physical or chemical methods to separate metals from ores or waste. They study metals and alloys to better understand their properties and potential for use. They also develop new methods for creating new alloys, and they design the processes, production facilities, machinery, and equipment used to produce metals, alloys, and finished products. Furthermore, they test and analyze samples of metals and alloys from all stages of processing.

Metallurgical Engineers are also involved with the fabrication of a wide variety of metal products, from the small to the large, from coins to bridges. For example, they carefully inspect metal products for defects and corrosion during the manufacturing process, and make recommendations to remediate any problems. In addition, they are engaged in the inspection of large metallic structures, such as water storage tanks, along with their pipes and pumping mechanisms. Corrosion leads to contamination of groundwater supplies. Metallurgical Engineers conduct sampling, testing, failure analysis, and corrosion control efforts to remedy the costly problems associated with aging water supply systems.

In our modern era, many underground sources of metal ore have been depleted. Metallurgical Engineers are increasingly concerned about protecting the environment. Thus, they are involved with the recovery of discarded metals from solid wastes and recycling them for reuse. Metallurgical Engineers also use other recently developed methods of processing metals for new purposes. For example, one method is called powder metallurgy, whereby metal is converted into powder, compressed, and heat-treated. Alloys are made by using this process.

Metallurgical Engineers generally work in one of three categories of metallurgy: *extractive, physical,* and *process.* Extractive metallurgists, or chemical metallurgists, separate metals from ores, or reclaim metals from waste for recycling. They separate small batches in laboratories to analyze them and determine their feasibility for large-scale production. They use a variety of processes to separate metals, including mineral dressing, roasting, sintering, smelting, leaching, electrolysis, and amalgamation. These engineers are also engaged in improving methods for using metals. Additionally, many of them design metal treatment plants and refineries, assess the equipment and processes used in such facilities, and oversee their operations.

Physical metallurgists concentrate on scientifically studying the correlations among the properties and structures of metals. They test metals for impurities. They determine if or how metals can be used, and develop new uses for metals. They research new alloys and seek to improve the strength, performance, and durability of metals. Sometimes, metals can be combined with nonmetallic materials to form composites. Metallurgical Engineers who work in this area process metals, alloys, and composites until they have achieved new characteristics that will fulfill desired purposes.

Process metallurgical engineers, or mechanical metallurgical engineers, produce metals in forms that can be used by industries. They use methods of melting and casting metals as well as such processing procedures as welding, soldering, pressing, extruding, plating, and rolling to make standardized metal components for machines and other manufactured goods.

As they develop their careers, Metallurgical Engineers typically become involved in different engineering functions before settling in a particular area. For example, they may be hired as research, development, design, project, test, or consulting engineers. Some Metallurgical Engineers become academic professors and researchers.

Regardless of their specialty or work setting, Metallurgical Engineers perform many of the same duties. For example, they:

- conduct studies, such as chemical analytical studies or research on the properties and characteristics of metals
- design and develop processes for using metals
- observe metal processing procedures to ensure the use of proper methods and to exercise quality control
- ensure that processing methods are efficient, cost-effective, and are in compliance with environmental regulations
- advise production personnel on processing methods and quality control standards
- conduct investigations to identify failures or the causes of failure
- write technical reports, correspondence, and other documentation
- supervise a staff of other engineers, technicians, and other workers

Metallurgical Engineers work a 40-hour week. They may work the night shifts in industrial settings. On occasion, they may be required to put in extra hours to complete projects or finish research work.

Salaries

Salaries for Metallurgical Engineers vary, depending on such factors as their education, experience, employer, and geographical location. The U.S. Bureau of Labor Statistics reported in its November 2004 *Occupational Employment Statistics* survey that the estimated annual salary for most materials engineers, such as Metallurgical Engineers, ranged between $45,130 and $103,210.

Employment Prospects

Metallurgical Engineers work for small companies and large corporations in many private industries, such as the automobile, electronics, heavy equipment, aerospace, and metals treatment industries. They are also employed by government agencies and research laboratories. For example, the U.S. Mint, the National Aeronautics and Space Administration, and the Federal Aviation Administration are some federal agencies that hire Metallurgical Engineers. In addition, these engineers are employed by engineering firms that offer consulting or contracting services. Some Metallurgical Engineers work as teachers and researchers at academic institutions. Other engineers are independent practitioners.

In general, most opportunities become available as Metallurgical Engineers retire, advance to higher positions, or transfer to other occupations.

Advancement Prospects

Metallurgical Engineers may advance in any number of ways, depending on their ambitions and interests. They may specialize in specific materials, become technical specialists, or seek positions in marketing, technical sales, or other business areas. Engineers with management and administrative interests and talents can seek positions as supervisory, project, and chief engineers. In addition, engineers can advance to executive officer positions within their organization. Those engineers with entrepreneurial ambitions can become independent consultants or owners of engineering firms that offer consulting or contracting services. Some engineers obtain their advanced degrees and seek positions as teachers and researchers at the academic level.

Education and Training

For individuals to enter this field, a bachelor's degree in metallurgical engineering or materials engineering, preferably with an emphasis in metallurgical engineering, is needed. Many Metallurgical Engineers have obtained an advanced degree in metallurgical engineering; they may have earned their undergraduate degree in another engineering field.

Usually, a master's or doctoral degree is required for engineers to advance to careers in management, consulting, research, or teaching. Metallurgical Engineers need a doctorate to teach and conduct research at the college and university level.

Employers typically provide entry-level engineers with training programs, in which new engineers work under the supervision and direction of experienced engineers. Throughout their careers, Metallurgical Engineers enroll in continuing education programs and training programs to update their skills and keep up with advancements in their fields.

Special Requirements

All engineers who offer engineering services directly to the public or perform work that affects the life, health, or property of the public must be licensed as professional engineers (P.E.) where they practice. All states, territories, and Washington, D.C., have their own unique requirements for P.E. licensure. For specific information, contact the board of engineering examiners where you wish to practice. See Appendix II for a list of boards.

Experience, Special Skills, and Personality Traits

Entry-level candidates should have work experience related to the positions for which they apply. They may have gained their experience through internships, work-study programs, student research projects, or summer employment.

Metallurgical Engineers must have excellent writing and communication skills, as they must be able to make clear and comprehensive reports to their colleagues, employers, customers, clients, and others. These engineers also need strong leadership, self-management, problem-solving, interpersonal, and teamwork skills to perform their various tasks well.

Some personality traits that successful Metallurgical Engineers share include being practical, creative, analytical, curious, detail-oriented, and self-motivated.

Unions and Associations

Many Metallurgical Engineers join local, state, and national societies to take advantage of networking opportunities, continuing education programs, and other professional services and resources. Some national societies include the ASM International; the Minerals, Metals, and Materials Society; the ASTM International (formerly the American Society for Testing and Materials); the Materials Engineering and Sciences Division, American Institute of Chemical Engineers; and the National Society of Professional Engineers. For contact information, see Appendix III.

Tips for Entry

1. One option for starting your college career is to complete your freshman and sophomore years at a two-year college, and then transfer to a four-year college or university. Before enrolling at a two-year college, make sure your credits will be accepted by the materials engineering program at the institution where you wish to study.
2. Attend professional conferences. Along with finding out what other professionals and companies are doing, you can learn about new developments and products.
3. Check out publications and Web sites of professional associations for job listings.
4. Use the Internet to learn more about Metallurgical Engineers. You might start by visiting this Web site: Minerals, Metals, and Materials Society, http://www.tms.org. For more links, see Appendix IV.

CERAMIC ENGINEER

CAREER PROFILE

Duties: Be involved in the research, development, design, and production of processes used in creating and combining ceramic materials for products and practical uses; perform duties as required

Alternate Title(s): Materials Engineer; A title that reflects an engineering function, such as Process Engineer

Salary Range: $45,000 to $103,000

Employment Prospects: Fair

Advancement Prospects: Good

Prerequisites:

Education or Training—Bachelor's degree in materials engineering; on-the-job training

Experience—Previous work experience generally required

Special Skills and Personality Traits—Leadership, teamwork, interpersonal, problem-solving, writing, and communications skills; self-motivated, detail-oriented, analytical, creative, and curious

Special Requirements—Professional engineer (P.E.) license may be required

CAREER LADDER

Senior Ceramic Engineer

Ceramic Engineer

Junior Ceramic Engineer

Position Description

Ceramic Engineers are the professionals who design modern ceramics and develop applications for their use. Ceramics are inorganic, nonmetallic materials such as clay, silica, talc, or feldspar that can be molded into useful shapes to fulfill practical functions. Glass, cement, and porcelain are ceramic products, for example. Many modern products are made from a variety of sophisticated ceramic compounds, which are composed of metal and nonmetal materials. The ceramic catalytic converter used in automobile engines is one example.

Modern uses of ceramics include construction, lighting, electrical applications, and sports. Bricks, tiles, cements, and glass are all used in the construction of homes, businesses, office buildings, power plants, and so forth. Glass and other ceramic materials are used in lightbulbs, neon signs, light-emitting diodes, optical fiber networks, and data storage devices. Ceramics are also used in such electronic devices as televisions, computers, and cell phones. The spark plugs that ignite the fuel in our vehicle engines are

partly made with ceramics. New types of baseball bats, snow skis, and even shock absorbers on mountain bikes are made with ceramic materials.

Ceramic engineering is a subdiscipline of materials engineering. Ceramic engineers study the properties of materials they use to produce ceramics. They look for materials that demonstrate electrical, magnetic, and thermal properties. Durable materials are also important. In the absence of appropriate raw materials, Ceramic Engineers use chemical processes to produce the advanced materials that exhibit the properties they need.

Ceramic Engineers are also involved in other areas of research, development, and production. They might foresee new applications for the use of ceramics or generate new concepts for the design of ceramics. Many are involved in the creative design of ceramic materials and products, while others work on the designs of plans for new production equipment as well as implement their use. Still others oversee the production of ceramic materials and product manufacturing. Some Ceramic Engineers are involved in testing samples of proposed ceramics in laboratory settings before approving them for mass production.

There are several categories of ceramics that industries need to manufacture their products. Ceramic Engineers design and create ceramics in every category. Some Ceramic Engineers specialize in working with one category. Structural clay products include bricks, roofing tiles, wall tiles, and sewer pipes. Whiteware is the category that encompasses such products as dinnerware, decorative tiles, and electrical porcelain. Refractories are used in glass, cements, and in certain forms of steel. Glass ceramics are used for windows, bottles, and insulation. Abrasives are used for polishing, grinding, or pressure blasting. Cements are used for paving, buildings, and dams.

Advanced ceramics are categorized as well. Structural ceramics are used in engine parts and cutting tools. Electrical ceramics are used in insulators, capacitors, magnets, integrated circuits, and superconductors. Coatings are used in cutting tools, machine parts, and engine components. Other ceramics are used for chemical or environmental purposes such as for filters and membranes.

Throughout their careers, Ceramic Engineers work in various engineering functions. For example, they may perform as research, development, design, analytical, test, project, and field service engineers. Some Ceramic Engineers are employed as consultants, whereby they provide services for government agencies and private companies.

Some Ceramic Engineers teach at the college and university level. In addition to instructing future engineers, they are involved in basic and applied research. Basic researchers conduct studies to learn and add new knowledge to the ceramics field, while applied researchers use the results of basic research to develop new or improved ceramic products and uses.

Ceramic Engineers complete various duties in the process of fulfilling their functions. For example, they might:

- develop new processes for creating ceramics
- specify processes for testing and producing ceramics
- plan and design laboratory facilities and equipment for testing and developing ceramics
- review information regarding product failure and interpret testing data to uncover the cause for the failure
- oversee all stages of the production processes of new ceramics in lab settings as well as industrial settings, including the quality testing of finished products
- solve engineering problems that may arise
- design and implement the use of production facilities and equipment
- plan new projects and products
- recommend the use of appropriate ceramics and their specifications
- keep up-to-date with new developments in ceramic technologies and production methods

Senior engineers usually have the additional responsibility to supervise and train junior engineers, technologists, technicians, and others on their staff or projects.

Ceramic Engineers work in office settings as well as in academic, laboratory, and industrial settings. They work with other engineers and other people from a wide range of backgrounds and occupations in various industries.

Ceramic Engineers work a 40-hour week but may put in extra hours to complete projects or meet deadlines.

Salaries

Salaries for Ceramic Engineers vary, depending on such factors as their education, experience, job duties, employer, and geographical location. According to the November 2004 *Occupational Employment Statistics* survey by the U.S. Bureau of Labor Statistics, the estimated annual salary for most materials engineers, including Ceramic Engineers, ranged between $45,130 and $103,210.

Employment Prospects

Ceramic Engineers are employed in small companies and large corporations in a variety of industries that manufacture or use ceramics for various products and applications. Some of these industries include the ceramics, glass, bricks, athletic equipment, electronics, automotive, aerospace, telecommunication, energy, nuclear, and medical industries. These engineers also find employment with academic institutions, government agencies, and research institutes, as well as with engineering firms that offer consulting or contracting services.

Most opportunities generally become available as Ceramic Engineers advance to higher positions, transfer to other occupations, retire, or leave the workforce for other reasons. Employers will create additional positions to meet their growing needs, as long as funding is available.

Advancement Prospects

As Ceramic Engineers gain experience, they are assigned to more complex projects and receive increasingly greater responsibilities. They may advance in any number of ways, depending on their ambitions and interests. They may specialize in a particular industry, become technical specialists or consultants, or move into such business functions as marketing, technical sales, or finance.

Those with managerial and administrative ambitions may pursue such positions as supervisory, project, and chief engineers. In addition, they may advance to executive officer positions within their organization. Ceramic Engineers with entrepreneurial ambitions can become independent consultants or owners of engineering firms that offer consulting or contracting services.

Education and Training

Minimally, a bachelor's degree in ceramic engineering, materials engineering, materials science, or another related field is needed for entry-level positions. A master's or doctoral degree is usually required for engineers to advance to careers in management, consulting, research, or teaching. Ceramic Engineers must possess a doctoral degree to teach engineering at the college level.

Employers typically provide entry-level engineers with training programs, which may include both on-the-job and classroom training. Throughout their careers, Ceramic Engineers enroll in continuing education and training programs to update their skills and keep up with advancements in their fields.

Special Requirements

All engineers who offer engineering services directly to the public or perform work that affects the life, health, or property of the public must be licensed as professional engineers (P.E.) where they practice. Each state and territory, as well as Washington, D.C., has its own particular requirements for P.E. licensure. For specific information, contact the board of engineering examiners where you wish to practice. See Appendix II for a list of boards.

Experience, Special Skills, and Personality Traits

Entry-level candidates should have work experience related to the positions for which they apply. They may have gained their experience through internships, work-study programs, student research projects, or summer employment. Along with having ceramic engineering analysis and design experience, applicants should have a background in mathematics, physical sciences, and social sciences.

To perform their job effectively, Ceramic Engineers need strong leadership, teamwork, interpersonal, and problem-solving skills. Excellent writing and communications skills are also important, as they must be able to provide clear and comprehensive reports to both technical and non-technical audiences. Being self-motivated, detail-oriented, analytical, creative, and curious are some personality traits that successful Materials Engineers have in common.

Unions and Associations

Ceramic Engineers can join local, state, and national societies to take advantage of networking opportunities and other professional services and resources. Some national societies include the American Ceramic Society, the ASM International, the Materials Research Society, and the National Society of Professional Engineers. For contact information, see Appendix III.

Tips for Entry

1. In college, talk with professors whose research work interests you. See if you can get involved in a research project.
2. Getting a job requires being persistent. For example: contact employers directly about current job vacancies. If no vacancies are available, ask for the name of the person to whom you can send a résumé for future consideration. Contact that person on a regular basis for an update of job openings.
3. Do you belong to any professional societies? Find out which ones allow their members to post résumés on their Web site.
4. Learn more about Ceramic Engineers on the Internet. You might start by visiting these Web sites: American Ceramic Society, http://www.ceramics.org; and Ceramics.com, http://www.ceramics.com. For more links, see Appendix IV.

MECHANICAL ENGINEERING

MECHANICAL ENGINEER

CAREER PROFILE

Duties: Be involved in the research, development, design, and production of machines, engines, and other mechanical devices; perform duties as required

Alternate Title(s): A title that reflects a specialty (such as Robotics Engineer) or an engineering function (such as Project Engineer or Consultant)

Salary Range: $44,000 to $100,000

Employment Prospects: Good

Advancement Prospects: Good

Prerequisites:

Education or Training—Bachelor's degree in mechanical engineering; on-the-job training

Experience—Previous work experience generally required

Special Skills and Personality Traits—Writing, communication, presentation, leadership, teamwork, interpersonal, analytical, and problem-solving skills; creative, detail-oriented, quick-witted, self-motivated, flexible, cooperative, reliable, and persistent

Special Requirements—Professional engineer (P.E.) license may be required

CAREER LADDER

```
┌─────────────────────────────────┐
│   Senior Mechanical Engineer     │
└─────────────────────────────────┘

┌─────────────────────────────────┐
│      Mechanical Engineer         │
└─────────────────────────────────┘

┌─────────────────────────────────┐
│   Junior Mechanical Engineer     │
└─────────────────────────────────┘
```

Position Description

Our lives are intertwined with machines and devices of every description. Our homes, schools, workplaces, and recreational facilities are filled with labor-saving devices such as dishwashers, refrigerators, computers, copiers, and treadmills. We travel from place to place in motorized vehicles. We ride elevators to the tops of office buildings. Most of our modern amenities, especially those that are mass-produced, are made with the aid of industrial machines. Pencils, candy bars, eyeglasses, photographs, tables, and beds are all made with the use of machines. Even this book was produced by a machine.

Mechanical engineering is the profession involved in the design and manufacture of machines, engines, and other mechanical devices. This discipline, in fact, is one of the oldest and largest engineering branches. The men and women who are engaged in this discipline are known as Mechanical Engineers. They have been involved in the development and creation of almost every modern machine, from the very small to very large.

Mechanical Engineers use their understanding of the fundamentals of engineering science, mathematics, energy, heat, mechanics, design, and manufacturing in their daily work. The particular key to their understanding is in the area of mechanics, which concerns the movement of everything from tiny particles to huge machines and structures. Mechanical Engineers also understand the principles of energy transfer. For example, solar energy is transferred to electrical energy. Energy is also transferred from a battery to the moving parts of a machine.

Their first step toward making a machine is to envision its design and analyze its operation. Mechanical Engineers use computer-aided design (CAD) and computer-aided manufacturing (CAM) systems to model their machine's design and simulate its functions within different design parameters to determine its optimum performance. They factor in the size, shape, and weight of the machine, as well as the materials to be used in its manufacture. The use of power is also taken into consideration. All of these factors are used to create the best virtual prototype of the desired product. When a design incorporates all the essential factors into one cohesive unit, it is called synthesis. Once a design is completed, it is then ready for the production process, which Mechanical Engineers oversee. They are vital to the smooth flow of work in every step of production including testing, quality control, manufacturing, and sales, as well as the maintenance of their finished products.

As Mechanical Engineers gain experience, they typically focus in one or more specialties of mechanical engineering. Some of these areas include computer-aided design and manufacturing; plant engineering and maintenance; automotive engineering; aerospace engineering; laser technology; biomedical applications; electromechanics; robotics; energy systems; pressure vessels and piping; applied mechanics; and heating, refrigeration, and air-conditioning systems.

Additionally, Mechanical Engineers specialize in performing specific engineering functions in the different phases of development and production. They may be employed as researchers, development engineers, designers, production engineers, test engineers, regulatory affairs specialists, sales engineers, consultants, and so on.

Their responsibilities vary, according to their particular function for which they have been employed. For example, design engineers create designs of products that meet customers' requirements and industry standards, and that can be produced economically, while project engineers plan and oversee all the activities that must be completed from start to finish.

Mechanical Engineers also perform many general tasks within the realm of their specific functions. For example, they:

- design instruments and controls, as well as mechanical, heat transfer, hydraulic and thermal systems
- design engineering tools
- plan and oversee the manufacture of testing equipment
- develop testing methods and procedures
- ensure that mechanical systems comply with design and customer specifications
- recommend changes in designs
- estimate the costs of their projects, the materials to be used, and labor
- prepare reports and other documents
- resolve problems, clarify project objectives, and provide technical assistance
- study and evaluate the feasibility of customers' proposals
- investigate system failures and recommend remediation procedures
- attend to the needs of customers and suppliers
- stay up-to-date with new developments in science and technology

Novice engineers typically work under the guidance and supervision of senior engineers. Their focus is to develop their skills and their understanding of the rules, regulations, standards, and practices of their area of concern. As they gain experience and knowledge, they receive more complex assignments and are able to exercise greater levels of authority. They may work as lead persons in certain assignments while directing the activities of other engineers and technicians. Mechanical Engineers gain experience in the areas of testing and fieldwork before moving into more advanced engineering design, production, and management work.

Senior Mechanical Engineers are more actively involved with the decision-making process and are more likely to be team leaders. Their decisions are made without direct supervision. Senior engineers are more aware of program needs and work independently in response to those needs. Advanced to executive-level Mechanical Engineers are the primary engineers for project divisions or for an entire geographical area. These professionals perform the most difficult engineering tasks. They also make policy decisions and consult with clients or government agencies at the highest levels.

Mechanical engineering is a multi-faceted field, involving the input of diverse people from divergent backgrounds, industries, and disciplines. Regardless of their experience, specialty, or function, Mechanical Engineers work with other engineers as well as with technologists, technicians, and scientists. Many of them also interact with government regulators, corporate personnel at all levels, customers, and material suppliers.

Mechanical Engineers generally work for 40 hours per week but occasionally work extra hours to complete tasks or meet deadlines.

Salaries
Salaries for Mechanical Engineers vary, depending on such factors as their education, experience, position, employer, industry, and geographical location. According to the November 2004 *Occupational Employment Statistics* (OES) survey by the U.S. Bureau of Labor Statistics (BLS), the estimated annual salary for most Mechanical Engineers ranged between $44,240 and $100,400.

Employment Prospects
Opportunities for Mechanical Engineers are available in virtually all manufacturing industries. They also find employment with engineering consulting and contracting firms, as well as in government agencies, research institutes, and academic institutions. Mechanical Engineers work all over the world in every country to produce machinery or develop new markets. According to the BLS November 2004 OES survey, about 219,040 Mechanical Engineers were employed in the United States. The highest levels of employment were found in the architectural and engineering services industry, the

aerospace product and parts manufacturing industry, the electronic instrument manufacturing industry, the scientific research and development services industry, and the federal government.

The BLS reports that employment of Mechanical Engineers is expected to grow by 9 to 17 percent through 2014. Many opportunities will be created in emerging technologies, such as biotechnology, nanotechnology, and materials science. In addition to job growth, opportunities will become available as engineers retire, transfer to other occupations, or advance to higher positions.

Because of the versatility of their skills, Mechanical Engineers can also seek positions in other engineering specialties.

Advancement Prospects

Mechanical Engineers may advance in any number of ways, depending on their ambitions and interests. They may specialize in a particular field, such as robotics engineering, or become technical specialists. Some engineers pursue positions in business areas of an organization, such as technical sales or marketing. Engineers with management and administrative interests and talents can seek positions as supervisory, project, and chief engineers. Additionally, they may advance to executive officer positions within their organization. Those with entrepreneurial ambitions can become independent consultants or owners of firms that offer contractual or consulting services. Furthermore, some Mechanical Engineers return to school to pursue careers in law, business, or medicine.

Education and Training

Minimally, a bachelor's degree in mechanical engineering or another related field is needed for applicants seeking entry-level positions. A master's or doctoral degree is usually required for Mechanical Engineers to advance to careers in management, consulting, research, or teaching. To teach and conduct research at the college and university level, engineers need a doctoral degree. Many Mechanical Engineers obtain advanced degrees in a mechanical engineering specialty, such as automotive engineering, that interests them.

Employers typically provide entry-level engineers with training programs, which may include both on-the-job training and formal classroom training. New engineers work under the supervision and direction of experienced engineers.

Throughout their careers, Mechanical Engineers enroll in continuing education programs and training programs to update their skills and keep up with advancements in their fields.

Special Requirements

All engineers who offer engineering services directly to the public or perform work that affects the life, health, or property of the public must be licensed as professional engineers (P.E.) where they practice. The licensing process consists of two stages. At the first level, qualifying individuals become licensed as engineers-in-training (E.I.T.). After working several years under the supervision of licensed Mechanical Engineers, E.I.T.s become eligible to apply for the P.E. license.

Washington, D.C., and every state and territory has its own particular requirements for P.E. licensure. For specific information, contact the board of engineering examiners where you wish to practice. See Appendix II for a list of boards.

Experience, Special Skills, and Personality Traits

Employers usually do not require any previous work experience for entry-level positions. However, many candidates have some work experience, which they gained through student internships, work-study programs, student research projects, or summer employment.

Mechanical Engineers need strong writing, communication, and presentation skills to perform their work effectively. In addition, they must have solid leadership, teamwork, interpersonal, analytical, and problem-solving skills. Being creative, detail-oriented, quick-witted, self-motivated, flexible, cooperative, reliable, and persistent are some personality traits that successful Mechanical Engineers share.

Unions and Associations

Many Mechanical Engineers join professional associations to take advantage of networking opportunities, continuing education programs, certification programs, and other professional services and resources. Societies are available at the local, state, and national levels. Some national societies that serve Mechanical Engineers include: the ASME International (the American Society of Mechanical Engineers), the Society of Manufacturing Engineers, the Society of Women Engineers, and the National Society of Professional Engineers. In addition, Mechanical Engineers join professional associations that serve the different specialties of mechanical engineering, such as the SAE International (the Society of Automotive Engineers) and the American Society of Heating, Refrigerating and Air-Conditioning Engineers. For contact information for the above organizations, see Appendix III.

Tips for Entry

1. Carefully research the different mechanical engineering programs in which you are interested. Which ones offer specialized areas, such as robotics engineering, in which you would like to specialize? Try to visit the various schools as well as talk with professors and students in the mechanical engineering department, to help you determine which school fits your needs the best.
2. Join a student chapter of ASME International or another professional association. Take advantage of

the services and resources that it has to offer its student members.

3. Some employers hire students who have completed internships or work-study programs with them after the students have graduated.

4. Use your college career center to help you conduct your job search. Many centers assist students as well as alumni.

5. Use the Internet to learn more about Mechanical Engineers. You might start by visiting these Web sites: ASME International, http://www.asme.org; and MechEngineer.com, http://www.mechengineer.com. For more links, see Appendix IV.

AUTOMOTIVE ENGINEER

CAREER PROFILE

Duties: Be involved in the development, design, manufacture, and testing of automobiles and other vehicles; perform duties as required

Alternate Title(s): Mechanical Engineer; a title that reflects an engineering function such as Design Engineer

Salary Range: $44,000 to $100,000

Employment Prospects: Fair

Advancement Prospects: Good

Prerequisites:

Education or Training—Bachelor's degree in mechanical engineering; on-the-job training

Experience—Previous work experience generally required

Special Skills and Personality Traits—Leadership, teamwork, analytical, problem-solving, computer, writing, communication, presentation, and self-management skills; self-reliant, motivated, flexible, ethical, creative, and dedicated

Special Requirements—Professional engineer (P.E.) license may be required

CAREER LADDER

```
┌─────────────────────────────────┐
│   Senior Automotive Engineer     │
└─────────────────────────────────┘

┌─────────────────────────────────┐
│      Automotive Engineer         │
└─────────────────────────────────┘

┌─────────────────────────────────┐
│   Junior Automotive Engineer     │
└─────────────────────────────────┘
```

Position Description

It is difficult to imagine our world without motorized vehicles. They have become so much a part of our lives that we almost take them for granted. However, we need them too much to ignore them, and for many of us, they are endlessly fascinating. We approach the yearly introduction of new car models with eager anticipation. We delight in watching freight trucks as they rumble down our highways or as they back into loading docks to bring all manner of goods to enhance our lives. Those of us that cannot drive are thankful for public bus systems that provide us with the mobility to travel to school, work, or shopping destinations. Motorized vehicles would not exist were it not for the important work done by Automotive Engineers to design and improve them.

Automotive Engineers are well versed in the areas of mechanical engineering, vehicle dynamics, stress analysis, and electronics. They apply their understanding of engineering science to researching, designing, developing, producing, and repairing all sorts of light and heavy vehicles including cars, trucks, buses, tractors, rail vehicles, motorcycles, and off-road vehicles. These engineers also work on all kinds of self-propelled vehicles for use in or on the water, in the sky, and in outer space.

Automotive Engineers are actively involved in all phases of the production of vehicles or their various components. In general, they:

- experiment with and test designs and equipment to assess their performance and function
- analyze research data to create new design concepts for new vehicles as well as their various components
- develop prototypes for testing and approval for mass production
- install new factory tooling for assembly lines
- launch new prototype and full-production vehicles at factories
- test finished products, including vehicles as well as their various components, such as engines, brakes, transmissions, other mechanical components, and electrical systems
- maintain or repair vehicles or their components

Many engineers are also involved in conducting research to add new knowledge and understanding about automotive engineering, as well as to develop new and better products and methods for producing them. For example, Automotive Engineers who are concerned with how their industry impacts the environment might devise methods of recycling the materials from old vehicles to make new ones or to use for other purposes.

Many Automotive Engineers specialize in specific aspects of the vehicle industry, such as engine design, body construction engineering, welding, or valve train system design. They may focus particular attention on such aspects of their work as calibration, safety, aerodynamics, electronics, and noise reduction, among others. Many Automotive Engineers further specialize by working on specific types of vehicles or in specific stages of the vehicle production process. For example, some Automotive Engineers are involved in developing new fuel-efficient engines that emit fewer greenhouse gas emissions.

Additionally, Automotive Engineers engage in various engineering functions throughout their careers. For example, they may be involved as designers, researchers, project managers, production engineers, test engineers, or quality engineers. Some engineers choose to specialize in one or more roles.

Regardless of their function or specialty, Automotive Engineers perform a wide range of tasks, such as:

- coordinate engineering activities with other organizational divisions to promote new projects or to assure needed funding
- ensure that all work meets the objectives and mission of their organization
- schedule the progressive stages of the development process
- make sure that parts can be procured from suppliers in time for large-scale production
- coordinate with their manufacturing division to make certain that vehicles and parts are made according to specifications
- confer with production engineers to ensure that the production process flows smoothly and efficiently
- develop new or innovative test methods
- use testing procedures for the specific purpose of finding answers to questions posed by consumers, clients, or other engineers
- analyze research, testing, or technical data and interpret their findings for reports or presentations
- check for systems or engineering problems in finished vehicle or component products
- participate in team meetings to update associates on developments within a project

Senior engineers have the additional responsibility to supervise and direct junior engineers, technologists, technicians, and other personnel.

Automotive Engineers spend a large portion of their working lives on computers. For example, some engineers use computer software and other design methods to plan vehicles and parts from an initial basic concept to a final detailed design. Other engineers create computer simulations to observe or predict product performance in a variety of road or weather conditions. Still others use computerized simulations to verify that each part and component can be built within the specified parameters of cost, safety, and quality requirements.

Their job requires Automotive Engineers to work with a wide range of people on production lines, in design departments, in marketing units, and in management. They confer on a multitude of issues ranging from engineering concerns to costs, quality, and ergonomics, among others. Hence, Automotive Engineers are knowledgeable about other fields of engineering as well as about business practices and more. Automotive Engineers also work with other engineers to design and produce needed components. In addition, they work with their customers to fulfill their design requirements.

Automotive Engineers work in laboratories, offices, and factories. They are sometimes called upon to travel, depending on their position. For instance, Automotive Engineers may be assigned to work overseas in their organizations' design centers. In manufacturing facilities, Automotive Engineers are usually required to wear protective gear, such as steel-toed shoes, hardhats, and safety goggles. Most of them work normal hours. In production environments, shift work or on-call duties may be required. Automotive Engineers generally work between 35 and 40 hours per week. They typically work additional hours to meet deadlines and complete other duties.

Salaries

Salaries for Automotive Engineers vary, depending on such factors as their education, experience, position, and geographical location. According to the U.S. Bureau of Labor Statistics (BLS) in its November 2004 *Occupational Employment Statistics* survey, the estimated annual salary for most mechanical engineers, including Automotive Engineers, ranged between $44,240 and $100,400.

Employment Prospects

Besides working for automotive (automobile, truck, bus, and motorcycle) companies, Automotive Engineers find employment with automotive parts manufacturers, tire companies, fuel companies, and auto racing teams. Research and development organizations hire Automotive Engineers, as do government laboratories that conduct work in the areas of automotive research, development, or regulations. Some Automotive Engineers are self-employed consultants.

Opportunities in the automotive industry are available in the United States as well as worldwide. Those willing to relocate to other localities have better chances of finding the job that most interests them.

According to the BLS, job growth for mechanical engineers (which includes Automotive Engineers) is predicted to increase by 9 to 17 percent during the period between 2004 and 2014. In addition to job growth, openings will become available as Automotive Engineers retire, transfer to other jobs, advance to higher positions, or leave the workforce for various reasons.

Advancement Prospects

Automotive Engineers may advance in any number of ways, depending on their ambitions and interests. Some become technical specialists. Some engineers choose to move into business areas, such as marketing or technical sales. Others pursue managerial and administrative positions, and rise through the ranks as supervisory, project, and chief engineers, and up to executive officer positions. Those with entrepreneurial ambitions can become independent consultants or owners of firms that offer contractual or consulting services.

To advance to management, consulting, research, and teaching positions, engineers need a master's or doctoral degree.

Education and Training

Minimally, Automotive Engineers need a bachelor's degree in mechanical engineering, electrical engineering, or a related field. They may have earned their undergraduate degree with a concentration in automotive engineering. Many Automotive Engineers also possess a master's degree in automotive engineering, mechanical engineering, or another related field. Those engineers who teach and conduct research in academic institutions typically possess a doctoral degree.

Employers typically provide entry-level engineers with training, which may include both on-the-job training and formal classroom training. New engineers work under the supervision and direction of experienced engineers.

Throughout their careers, Automotive Engineers enroll in continuing education programs and training programs to update their skills and keep up with advancements in their fields.

Special Requirements

All engineers who offer engineering services directly to the public or perform work that affects the life, health, or property of the public must be licensed as professional engineers (P.E.) where they practice. Every U.S. state and territory, as well as Washington, D.C., has its own requirements for P.E. licensure. For specific information, contact the board of engineering examiners for the area where you wish to practice. See Appendix II for a list of boards.

Experience, Special Skills, and Personality Traits

Entry-level candidates should have work experience related to the positions for which they apply. They may have gained their experience through internships, work-study programs, student research projects, or summer employment. Having skills in emerging technologies, such as nanotechnology, fuel cells, and gasoline-electric hybrids, may be desirable.

Automotive Engineers need solid leadership, teamwork, analytical, and problem-solving skills to perform their job effectively. Having strong computer, writing, communication, and presentation skills is just as important. In addition, they should have excellent self-management skills, which include the abilities to meet deadlines, organize and prioritize multiple tasks, work independently, and handle stressful situations. Being self-reliant, motivated, flexible, ethical, creative, and dedicated are some personality traits that successful Automotive Engineers share.

Unions and Associations

Automotive Engineers can join local, state, or national societies to take advantage of networking opportunities and other professional services and resources. Societies are available at the local, state, and national levels. Some national societies that serve Automotive Engineers include: the SAE International (the Society of Automotive Engineers), the ASME International (the American Society of Mechanical Engineers), the Society of Manufacturing Engineers, and the National Society of Professional Engineers. For contact information, see Appendix III.

Tips for Entry

1. As a high school student, take advantage of opportunities to tinker with vehicles. For example, you might take an auto shop class if one is available.
2. You can start becoming part of the automotive industry as a college student. For example, you may attend professional conferences, trade shows, seminars on industry-related topics, and other events. Along with learning about new developments, you will have the opportunity to network with professionals.
3. Engineers with skills and experience in both the mechanical and the electronics engineering fields are highly desired by employers.
4. Engineers with international experience are desired by many employers, as they maintain subsidiaries of their operations in other countries. If you have studied, worked, or traveled abroad, be sure to describe your experiences on your job application or résumé.
5. Use the Internet to learn more about automotive engineering and the automotive industry. You might start by visiting the SAE International Web site at http://www.sae.org. For more links, see Appendix IV.

HVAC/R ENGINEER

CAREER PROFILE

Duties: Research, develop, design, and oversee the installation and maintenance of heating, ventilation, air-conditioning, and refrigeration systems; perform duties as required

Alternate Title(s): Mechanical Engineer, HVAC Engineer; a title that reflects an engineering function such as Design Engineer or Research Specialist

Salary Range: $44,000 to $100,000

Employment Prospects: Good

Advancement Prospects: Good

Prerequisites:

Education or Training—Bachelor's degree in mechanical engineering or another related field; on-the-job training

Experience—Previous work experience generally required

Special Skills and Personality Traits—Writing, communication, computer, leadership, interpersonal, teamwork, problem-solving, organizational, and time-management skills; confident, honest, logical, practical, and creative

Special Requirements—Professional engineer (P.E.) license may be required

CAREER LADDER

```
┌─────────────────────────────┐
│    Senior HVAC/R Engineer    │
└─────────────────────────────┘

┌─────────────────────────────┐
│      HVAC/R Engineer         │
└─────────────────────────────┘

┌─────────────────────────────┐
│    Junior HVAC/R Engineer    │
└─────────────────────────────┘
```

Position Description

We live in a world that is vastly different than the one our ancestors inhabited just a few generations ago. One of the amenities that characterize modern life is the comfort we feel in our indoor environments. Whether it is cold or hot outside, we can be assured that the interior of our homes, schools, office buildings, hospitals, shopping malls, and our cars will always be the right temperature because of heating and air-conditioning systems. Ventilating systems constantly circulate the air we breathe indoors. We store our food in refrigerators. Consequently, it stays fresh much longer, and we can eat fruits and vegetable long after their growing season has passed. Heating, ventilation, air-conditioning, and refrigeration (HVAC/R) systems all work on our behalf to make our lives easier. Our demand for interior comfort has become so pervasive that fully one-third of all the energy used in the United States is devoted to operating these systems, according to the American Society of Heating, Refrigerating and Air-Conditioning Engineers, Inc.

An entire discipline of mechanical engineering is involved in designing and overseeing the installation and continual maintenance of these systems. The professionals who work in this field of engineering are heating, ventilation, air-conditioning, and refrigeration (HVAC/R) Engineers.

HVAC/R Engineers design HVAC/R systems for factories, tall buildings, schools, hospitals, and other large facilities. They also plan such systems for aircraft, ships, automobiles, refrigerated cargo boxes on trains or trucks, and space stations. Some HVAC/R Engineers select or design and build customized equipment to install in facilities to meet their specific HVAC/R needs. Some HVAC/R Engineers spend large portions of their careers working in one building to maintain, modify, or repair its HVAC/R systems. Experienced HVAC/R Engineers manage a team of engineers to develop new systems or maintain and repair systems that are already in place.

HVAC/R Engineers are aware of the demand for energy to run the systems they design. Their concern is to create new systems that are energy-efficient but will deliver the level of comfort to which people are accustomed. They incorporate electronic and computerized control devices into new systems to regulate the use of energy. HVAC/R Engineers also seek to protect the outdoor environment. For example, air-conditioning and refrigeration systems are now designed to use coolants that do not harm the atmosphere.

HVAC/R Engineers generally specialize in specific engineering functions within their field. Some HVAC/R Engineers work specifically in the area of design. They use research findings along with engineering methods to design new HVAC/R systems. They calculate appropriate sizes for equipment. They determine the locations of the various components of HVAC/R systems such as ventilation ducts, pipes, wiring, and control mechanisms in buildings. HVAC/R Engineers who design HVAC/R systems use computer programs to make precise calculations to solve engineering problems.

Construction specialists are HVAC/R Engineers who oversee the construction of buildings to ensure that HVAC/R systems are installed properly, meet specifications, and comply with regulations. Facilities engineers work in buildings to manage the use, maintenance, and repair of HVAC/R systems. They supervise a staff of other HVAC/R Engineers, technicians and mechanics. Applications engineers select the necessary equipment, interpret installation plans, and acquire the materials needed to satisfy the provisions of an HVAC/R equipment installation contract.

Project managers supervise the design, materials control, and problem-solving aspects of the use of HVAC/R equipment at a job site. When several companies are involved with these processes, HVAC/R Engineers in the capacity of project managers coordinate the work and communications among those parties.

Some HVAC/R Engineers work as sales engineers. Their function is to provide a relationship among equipment manufacturers, consultants, and contractors to coordinate the process of ordering equipment and having it delivered for installation. Some sales engineers sell equipment and provide service agreements as well as offer technical assistance to their customers.

Consulting engineers ensure that designs, layouts, and specifications for HVAC/R projects are coordinated to meet the requirements of the customer. They direct the application of conservation principles in the use of HVAC/R systems. HVAC/R Engineers in this capacity approve completed projects and ensure that HVAC/R systems are in compliance with environmental health and safety regulations.

Research specialists, who work for private companies as well as university and independent laboratories, develop and test new types of HVAC/R equipment and the control systems that regulate humidity, temperature, atmospheric pressure, and air quality. The information they acquire is used by other HVAC/R Engineers in their work.

Some HVAC/R Engineers are college and university professors. They develop and teach courses in HVAC/R engineering. They also conduct research to develop new HVAC/R technologies and conduct tests on new systems.

HVAC/R Engineers have specific tasks to complete in the course of their day-to-day activities. Many tasks are similar, regardless of their function. For example, they:

- study systems or equipment requirements
- inspect HVAC/R systems and write reports about the results of their investigations
- supervise the setting up of new systems as well as their repair and maintenance
- design new HVAC/R systems
- prepare cost estimates for new HVAC/R systems
- select the necessary equipment for an HVAC/R system
- draw the plans and schematics for systems and the buildings that will use them
- assist in the establishment of safety standards and oversee their implementation
- attend conferences, seminars, and professional society functions, or read books, articles, and journals to stay up-to-date with the latest developments in HVAC/R engineering

HVAC/R Engineers regularly interact with their clients, other engineers, technicians, architects, equipment suppliers, and people who are employed in related trades. Some HVAC/R Engineers supervise a staff of employees.

HVAC/R Engineers mostly work indoors, except when they are needed at outdoor construction sites. They work in their own offices, or meet in the offices of clients or project managers. Research engineers work in laboratories.

Forty-hour weeks are standard for HVAC/R Engineers, but they may occasionally work extra hours to meet deadlines or complete tasks.

Salaries

Salaries for HVAC/R Engineers vary, depending on such factors as their education, experience, employer, and geographical location. According to the November 2004 *Occupational Employment Statistics* survey by the U.S. Bureau of Labor Statistics, the estimated annual salary for most mechanical engineers, including HVAC/R Engineers, ranged between $44,240 and $100,400.

Employment Prospects

Employers of HVAC/R Engineers include HVAC/R equipment manufacturers, service and maintenance firms, and companies that sell HVAC/R merchandise. These engineers also find employment with consulting and contracting firms that offer HVAC/R engineering services, as well as with hospitals, schools, malls, factories, companies, and other organizations where they are needed to manage HVAC/R systems. Other employers include utilities, regulatory agencies, and research institutes. Some HVAC/R Engineers are employed as professors or researchers in colleges and universities.

Some experts in the field report that job prospects for HVAC/R Engineers should remain steady. Numerous opportunities are expected to become available as a large number of professionals will become eligible for retirement over the next several years. In addition, there is a constant demand for improving and developing new systems to be more efficient, cost-effective, and more environmentally safe.

Advancement Prospects

As HVAC/R Engineers gain experience, they are assigned to more complex projects and receive increasingly greater responsibilities. They may advance in any number of ways, depending on their ambitions and interests. They may become technical specialists, or move into the business areas of an organization, such as marketing, technical sales, or finance.

Those with managerial and administrative ambitions may pursue positions as supervisory, project, and chief engineers. In addition, they may advance to executive officer positions within their organization. Engineers with entrepreneurial ambitions can become independent practitioners or owners of firms that offer HVAC/R engineering services.

Education and Training

Minimally, HVAC/R Engineers possess a bachelor's degree in mechanical engineering, architectural engineering, or another related field. A master's degree or doctorate is usually required for engineers to advance to careers in management, consulting, research, or teaching. Engineers need a doctoral degree to teach and conduct research at the college and university level. Many mechanical engineering schools offer an advanced degree in HVAC/R engineering.

Entry-level engineers typically receive on-the job training, in which they work under the supervision and direction of experienced engineers. Some companies also have formal classroom training programs for novice engineers.

Throughout their careers, HVAC/R Engineers enroll in continuing education and training programs to update their skills and keep up with advancements in their fields.

Special Requirements

All engineers who offer engineering services directly to the public or perform work that affects the life, health, or property of the public must be licensed as professional engineers (P.E.) where they practice. Licensure requirements vary in the different states and territories, as well as in Washington, D.C. For specific information, contact the board of engineering examiners where you wish to practice. See Appendix II for a list of boards.

Experience, Special Skills, and Personality Traits

Employers generally do not require previous work experience for entry-level positions. However, applicants should have some experience related to the positions for which they apply. They may have gained their experience through internships, work-study programs, student research projects, or summer employment.

HVAC/R Engineers need strong writing, communication, and computer skills for their work. They also must have solid leadership, interpersonal, teamwork, problem-solving, organizational, and time-management skills. Being confident, honest, logical, practical, and creative are some personality traits that successful HVAC/R Engineers share.

Unions and Associations

Many HVAC/R Engineers join local, state, or national professional associations to take advantage of professional services and resources such as continuing education programs, certification programs, job banks, and networking opportunities. Some national societies that serve HVAC/R Engineers include: the American Society of Heating, Refrigerating and Air-Conditioning Engineers, the ASME International (the American Society of Mechanical Engineers), the Society of Manufacturing Engineers, and the National Society of Professional Engineers. For contact information, see Appendix III.

Tips for Entry

1. Some students take the examination for the engineer-in-training license, the first level of the P.E. licensure, during their senior year in college.
2. Many job interviewers ask candidates about their career goals. Do you know what yours are? Take time to think about what they are and to define them for yourself.
3. Contact employers directly about job vacancies. You might call a company's human resources department or visit the company's Web site.
4. Learn more about HVAC/R Engineers on the Internet. You might start by visiting these Web sites: American Society of Heating, Refrigerating and Air-Conditioning Engineers, http://www.ashrae.org; and HVAC Portal, http://www.hvacportal.com. For more links, see Appendix IV.

ROBOTICS ENGINEER

CAREER PROFILE

Duties: Be involved in the research, design, and production of robots; perform duties as required

Alternate Title(s): Mechanical Engineer; a title that reflects an engineering function such as Design Engineer or Research Engineer

Salary Range: $44,000 to $100,000

Employment Prospects: Good

Advancement Prospects: Good

Prerequisites:

Education or Training—Bachelor's degree in mechanical engineering or another related field; on-the-job training

Experience—Previous work experience generally required

Special Skills and Personality Traits—Writing, communication, leadership, teamwork, interpersonal, and problem-solving skills; enthusiastic, dedicated, self-motivated, honest, creative, innovative, and detail-oriented

Special Requirements—Professional engineer (P.E.) license may be required

CAREER LADDER

```
┌─────────────────────────────┐
│   Senior Robotics Engineer   │
└─────────────────────────────┘

┌─────────────────────────────┐
│      Robotics Engineer       │
└─────────────────────────────┘

┌─────────────────────────────┐
│   Junior Robotics Engineer   │
└─────────────────────────────┘
```

Position Description

Robots are familiar to all of us. We read stories and watch movies that often portray them as monstrous automatons with glowing eyes, or as human-like androids that cheerfully assist space ship pilots. These depictions of robots are fascinating, but what is more interesting is that real robots work behind the scenes to make our lives easier and more prosperous.

Robots are any type of machine that mechanically performs a task or series of tasks by following a computerized program, or by being remotely controlled by a human. Robots rarely look like those portrayed in novels or movies. Some are fixed in place, while others can move about. Many do repetitive work that was formerly done by humans, such as assemble parts to manufacture machines or other goods, lift heavy objects, or paint automobiles. Robots are sent into space to explore the surface of other planets. They also explore the depths of our oceans. They are used by the military to fly over or crawl across hostile terrains to gather information, and by police forces to disarm bombs. In the medical field, robots help physicians perform certain types of surgery. Small robots are now available for use in the home to automatically vacuum the floor. Whatever their purpose, our present-day robots impact all our lives.

Robotics Engineers design all types of robots, keep them maintained, and find new ways to use them. The engineers who design the body and movable parts of a robot, as well as its heat transfer controls, are mechanical engineers. Electrical engineers build the robot's electronic systems, while computer engineers design and program the robot's computing hardware. All of these functions comprise the field of robotics engineering. However, this profile is about the role mechanical engineers play.

Robotics Engineers with mechanical engineering backgrounds use their understanding of the mechanical components in machinery when designing robots. Pneumatic and mechanical power systems, gears, grippers, belts, and bearings are among the moving parts that are used in robotic machines. Robotics Engineers design these parts or modify them to suit the purpose of the proposed machine. They integrate the parts into the whole. They carefully select the materials that make up robotic bodies and parts. They also test robots to ensure that they are working properly.

Some Robotics Engineers are involved in the production of finished robots. They select the equipment, machinery, and facilities to manufacture finished robots. These engineers also ensure the safety, efficiency, and economy of the manufacturing processes.

Other Robotics Engineers are engaged in conducting research. Some perform basic research, usually in academic institutions and research institutes, to learn more about materials, machines, and mechanical systems in order to understand how robots and robotic systems work. Other researchers conduct applied research; they use the results of basic research to solve problems regarding their use and design in the area of robotics, as well as to build new or improved robots.

As they develop their careers, Robotics Engineers perform various engineering functions. Besides being researchers, designers, and production engineers, they can also work as project managers, test engineers, quality engineers, sales engineers, technical service engineers, consultants, and teachers.

Robotics Engineers perform more specific tasks within the realm of their general functions. For example, they:

- design robotic controls and other mechanical systems
- plan and oversee the manufacture of testing equipment
- develop testing methods and procedures
- test scale models or full-size prototype robots to observe their performance under every type of condition
- investigate system failures and recommend remediation procedures
- ensure that robotic mechanical systems comply with design and specifications
- recommend changes in designs
- estimate the costs of their projects, the materials to be used, and labor
- write clear, concise reports and other documents
- read and understand blueprints and schematics
- confer with staff members to resolve problems, clarify project objectives, and provide technical assistance
- coordinate with drafters and technical artists to develop designs
- stay up-to-date with new developments in science, technology, and robotics

Robotics Engineers work in team environments. The development, design, production, operation, and maintenance of robots require input from many engineers and technicians who bring different levels of expertise into these processes. Many Robotics Engineers also work closely with a wide range of personnel in the manufacturing, sales, customer service, and marketing divisions of their corporations.

Robotics Engineers work a 40-hour week. Occasional overtime work may be required to finish projects or to meet deadlines.

Salaries

Salaries for Robotics Engineers vary, depending on such factors as their education, experience, employer, and geographical location. According to the November 2004 *Occupational Employment Statistics* survey by the U.S. Bureau of Labor Statistics, the estimated annual salary for most mechanical engineers, including Robotics Engineers, ranged between $44,240 and $100,400.

Employment Prospects

Many Robotics Engineers are employed in the robotics industry, which includes companies that manufacture and sell robots or parts and systems for the fabrication of robots. In addition, these engineers may find employment in other industries (automotive, aerospace, military, electronics, apparel, and food processing service industries) that use robots and automation systems. Robotics Engineers are also employed by engineering consulting firms, research institutes, and academic institutions.

According to the Robotic Industries Association Web site (http:///www.roboticsonline.com), about 147,000 robots were used in factories in the United States as of May 2005. The society reported that interest in robotics has been increasing over the years. For example, the use of robotics has emerged in the medical, security, and consumer industries.

As practical applications of robotics are found in different industries, new opportunities will become available for Robotics Engineers. In addition to job growth, engineers will be needed to replace those who advance to higher positions, transfer to other occupations, or retire.

Advancement Prospects

As Robotics Engineers gain experience, they are assigned to more complex projects and receive increasingly greater responsibilities. Those with managerial and administrative interests can rise through the ranks as supervisory, project, and chief engineers. Finding jobs with other employers may be required for engineers to obtain a position with greater responsibility and higher pay. Some engineers have entrepreneurial ambitions and pursue careers as independent consultants or owners of firms that offer contractual or consulting services.

Education and Training

Besides mechanical engineering, Robotics Engineers might possess a college degree in electrical engineering, computer science, robotics engineering, physics, or another related field. A bachelor's degree is the minimum requirement for entry-level positions, although some employers may prefer to hire candidates with an advanced degree.

Usually an advanced degree (master's degree or doctorate) is needed for engineers to work in positions in management, research, consulting, and teaching. To teach and conduct research in academic institutions, engineers need a doctoral degree.

Entry-level engineers typically receive on-the-job training, and work under the supervision and direction of senior engineers. In large companies, they may also participate in formal classroom training.

To keep up with advancements in their field as well as update their skills, Robotics Engineers enroll in continuing education programs and training programs throughout their careers.

Special Requirements

All engineers who offer engineering services directly to the public or perform work that affects the life, health, or property of the public must be licensed as professional engineers (P.E.) where they practice. Every U.S. state and territory, as well as Washington, D.C., has its own requirements for P.E. licensure. For specific information, contact the board of engineering examiners for the area where you wish to practice. See Appendix II for a list of boards.

Experience, Special Skills, and Personality Traits

Work experience for entry-level positions is not generally required, but desirable. Many recent graduates have gained practical experience through academic research projects, internships, work-study programs, and part-time employment.

Robotics Engineers need effective writing and communication skills for their job. They must also have strong leadership, teamwork, interpersonal, and problem-solving skills. Some personality traits that successful Robotics Engineers share include being enthusiastic, dedicated, self-motivated, honest, creative, innovative, and detail-oriented.

Unions and Associations

Robotics Engineers can join local, state, and national associations to take advantage of networking opportunities and other professional services and resources. Some national societies that serve the interests of different Robotics Engineers include the ASME International (the American Society of Mechanical Engineers), the Society of Manufacturing Engineers, and the National Society of Professional Engineers. For contact information for the above organizations, see Appendix III.

Tips for Entry

1. You can start preparing for a career in robotics in high school. Enroll in science and mathematics courses. Also take a shop class or two, if you can. Read books and magazines about the field. Check out robotics exhibits at museums. Build your own robots from kits. Join a youth club that offers opportunities to tinker with mechanical devices. These are just a few examples of what you can do.

2. Computer programming experience is highly desirable. Take courses in this area in high school and college.

3. Suppose you did not get a job offer from a company for which you would like to work. Be persistent, and maintain contact with your job interviewer, personnel officer, or other person you may have met while applying for a job. Call or write every so often to ask about job openings as well as to give an update about what you are doing.

4. Use the Internet to learn more about robotics and robotics engineering. You might start by visiting these Web sites: Robotics Online (by the Robotic Industries Association), http://www.roboticsonline.com; and Learn About Robots (by Rich Hooper), http://www.learnaboutrobots.com. For more links, see Appendix IV.

ROLLER-COASTER ENGINEER

CAREER PROFILE

Duties: Plan, design, test, and maintain roller-coaster rides; perform duties as required

Alternate Title(s): Roller-Coaster Designer, Mechanical Engineer; a title that reflects an engineering function such as Project Engineer or Consultant

Salary Range: $44,000 to $100,000

Employment Prospects: Fair

Advancement Prospects: Good

Prerequisites:

Education or Training—Bachelor's degree in mechanical engineering; on-the-job training

Experience—Previous work experience generally required

Special Skills and Personality Traits—Leadership, problem-solving, teamwork, interpersonal, writing, and communication skills; creative, cooperative, flexible, persistent, dependable, composed, and self-motivated

Special Requirements—Professional engineer (P.E.) license may be required

CAREER LADDER

```
┌─────────────────────────────────┐
│   Senior Roller-Coaster Engineer │
└─────────────────────────────────┘

┌─────────────────────────────────┐
│     Roller-Coaster Engineer      │
└─────────────────────────────────┘

┌─────────────────────────────────┐
│   Junior Roller-Coaster Engineer │
└─────────────────────────────────┘
```

Position Description

Roller coasters are fun. They are terrifying. They are both. When we ride them, we feel like we are in mortal peril. We slowly ride uphill with nervous excitement. The cars stop momentarily, just long enough for us to look down at the maze of tracks that awaits us. Suddenly, we plunge down an impossibly steep slope, only to be whipped around sharp corners and head-over-heels through hair-raising loops. It is all over in just a few minutes. We grin from ear to ear and walk away with wobbly knees. Then we get back in line to do it all over again.

Dangerous as roller coasters may look and seem, they are engineered to operate safely. These fun machines are created by teams of different types of engineers. Roller-Coaster Engineers, who possess a mechanical engineering background, develop the technical plans for roller coasters. They work to make preliminary designs into real structures. Civil engineers design the structure of the coaster, while electrical and mechanical engineers design the control and mechanical systems.

Roller coasters are not always the same, as coaster enthusiasts can attest. Some roller coasters are higher than others; some have loops while others do not; some take riders through tunnels or into water; some are built into hillsides or groves of trees; some run two trains of cars simultaneously, or even in opposite directions, on parallel tracks. All roller coasters have one thing in common—they are complicated and require months of careful designing and calculating.

Roller coasters must be able to withstand continual use as well as the forces of nature, such as high winds and earthquakes. They must provide a smooth ride without bumps. The cars must not shake violently from side to side. On some of the newer coaster designs, riders are rapidly propelled to the top of the ride. This rapid ascent imposes a force on the rider's body that should not exceed four times the normal force of gravity.

Roller-Coaster Engineers take these and other factors into account when they work on their designs. The angle of the tracks, the arcs that make up the curves, the shape of the loops, the height of the tracks, the car designs, the wheel and braking systems, and the rider restraints are among the design features that are mathematically calculated to the minutest detail. Roller-Coaster Engineers use computer aided design (CAD) systems to perform these calculations and integrate each factor into the complete design.

Over the years, Roller-Coaster Engineers have developed design and safety standards to follow for the design, construction, and use of all roller coasters. These standards are voluntary, but they are adhered to routinely. In increasingly more areas, these standards are being adopted by government regulatory agencies.

Roller-Coaster Engineers are also concerned with maintaining the rides. They design computerized control systems that continuously monitor the roller coasters. They also ride the coasters to check how they are working. Assisted by technicians, Roller-Coaster Engineers troubleshoot whatever problems arise in the day-to-day operations of the coasters. Rides are inspected during amusement park off-hours. The entire structure, rails, cars, and operating systems are carefully examined for damage. When repair or recalibration is needed, that work is performed before the ride opens again. Trains and cars are taken out of service for repairs if they are functioning improperly.

Roller-Coaster Engineers are experienced in the areas of designing machines as well as electrical and industrial control systems. Their functions and duties are similar to those of other mechanical engineers, except they concentrate specifically on the design, construction, and operation of roller coasters. They perform a wide range of tasks, such as:

• conduct research in laboratories to learn more about materials, machines, and mechanical systems as well as solve problems regarding their use and design for roller coasters
• use research results to build virtual or actual prototypes
• create drawings or equations to express ideas for new coaster designs
• test scale models or computerized models of roller coasters to observe their performance under every type of condition
• select the equipment, machinery, and facilities to manufacture finished products
• ensure the safety, efficiency, and economy of the manufacturing processes
• maintain production equipment on a continual basis
• investigate system failures and recommend remediation procedures
• develop testing methods and procedures
• ensure that mechanical systems comply with design and customer specifications
• recommend changes in designs
• study and evaluate the feasibility of customers' proposals
• estimate the costs of their projects, the materials to be used, and labor
• write clear, concise reports and other documents
• read and understand blueprints and schematics

Roller-Coaster Engineers regularly interact with many types of people—engineers, corporate employees, amuse-ment park personnel, technicians, and manufacturers. For example, their duties may require them to coordinate with drafters and technical artists to develop designs or attend to the needs of customers and suppliers. Roller-Coaster Engineers also confer with staff members to resolve problems, clarify project objectives, and provide technical assistance. Senior engineers may be responsible for supervising, managing, and administering the work of others.

Roller-Coaster Engineers usually work for 40 hours per week but occasionally work overtime to complete projects.

Salaries
Salaries for Roller-Coaster Engineers vary, depending on such factors as their education, experience, employer, and geographical location. According to the U.S. Bureau of Labor Statistics in its November 2004 *Occupational Employment Statistics* survey, the estimated annual salary for most mechanical engineers, which includes Roller-Coaster Engineers, ranged between $44,240 and $100,400.

Employment Prospects
Roller-Coaster Engineers are employed by amusement parks, as well as by consulting and design firms that offer roller coaster engineering services. Some engineers are employed as safety inspectors by state regulatory agencies, as well as by amusement parks and consulting firms.

In general, most opportunities become available as engineers advance to higher positions, transfer to other jobs, retire, or leave the workforce. Employers may create additional positions as their companies grow and the demand for their services increases.

Advancement Prospects
Roller-Coaster Engineers can rise through the ranks as supervisory, project, and chief engineers. Some engineers choose to advance by pursuing careers in technical sales, marketing, finance, or another business area. Other engineers have entrepreneurial ambitions and become independent practitioners or owners of firms that offer contractual or consulting roller coaster engineering services.

Education and Training
Many Roller-Coaster Engineers possess a bachelor's or advanced degree in mechanical engineering. Some hold degrees in civil engineering, structural engineering, electrical engineering, or another related field. Engineers need a bachelor's degree to enter this field. They need a master's or doctoral degree to advance to positions in management, consulting, research, or teaching. Those aspiring to teach or conduct research at the academic level must have a doctorate.

New employees typically receive on-the-job training, and work under the guidance and supervision of senior engineers.

Throughout their careers, Roller-Coaster Engineers enroll in continuing education programs and training programs to update their skills and keep up with advancements in their fields.

Special Requirements

All engineers who offer engineering services directly to the public or perform work that affects the life, health, or property of the public must be licensed as professional engineers (P.E.) where they practice. Every U.S. state and territory, as well as Washington, D.C., has its own particular requirements for P.E. licensure. For specific information, contact the board of engineering examiners for the area where you wish to practice. See Appendix II for a list of boards.

Experience, Special Skills, and Personality Traits

Entry-level candidates should have work experience related to the positions for which they apply. They may have gained their experience through internships, work-study programs, student research projects, or summer employment.

To perform their work well, Roller-Coaster Engineers must have solid leadership, problem-solving, teamwork, and interpersonal skills. They also need strong writing and communication skills. Some personality traits that Roller-Coaster Engineers have in common are being creative, cooperative, flexible, persistent, dependable, composed, and self-motivated.

Unions and Associations

Roller-Coaster Engineers may join professional associations to take advantage of networking opportunities, continuing education programs, certification programs, and other professional services and resources. For example, they are eligible to join such national societies as the ASME International (the American Society of Mechanical Engineers), the Society of Women Engineers, and the National Society of Professional Engineers. For contact information for the above organizations, see Appendix III.

Tips for Entry

1. Gain experience working in the amusement industry. For example, as a high school student you might obtain a summer job at a nearby amusement park. Whether you are a ticket taker, a food server, a game booth operator, or a cartoon character, you are getting an opportunity to see amusement park operations first-hand.

2. It may take several years before you get a job as a Roller-Coaster Engineer. Remember every job provides you with the skills and experience that you need to eventually get to your dream job.

3. Take advantage of professional forums on the Web to network with Roller-Coaster Engineers.

4. Roller-coaster design companies are located throughout the United States and the world. Hence, a willingness to relocate may improve your chances of obtaining a job.

5. You can learn more about roller coaster designing on the Internet. You might start by visiting these Web sites: Coaster Quest.com (hosted by Walt Reiss), http://www.coasterquest.com; and Ultimate Roller Coaster .com, http://www.ultimaterollercoaster.com. For more links, see Appendix IV.

ELECTRICAL, ELECTRONICS, AND COMPUTER ENGINEERING

ELECTRICAL ENGINEER

CAREER PROFILE

Duties: Be involved in the research, design, development, testing, manufacture, and installation of electrical equipment, components, and systems; perform duties as required

Alternate Title(s): A title that reflects a specialty (such as Electronics Engineer or Robotics Specialist) or an engineering function (such as Design Engineer or Project Engineer)

Salary Range: $47,000 to $110,000

Employment Prospects: Fair

Advancement Prospects: Good

Prerequisites:

Education or Training—Bachelor's degree in electrical engineering or a related field; on-the-job training

Experience—Previous work experience generally required

Special Skills and Personality Traits—Communication, teamwork, interpersonal, problem-solving, organizational, and writing skills; detail-oriented, logical, creative, reliable, flexible, cooperative, and trustworthy

Special Requirements—Professional engineer (P.E.) licensure may be required

CAREER LADDER

```
┌─────────────────────────────────┐
│   Senior Electrical Engineer     │
└─────────────────────────────────┘

┌─────────────────────────────────┐
│      Electrical Engineer         │
└─────────────────────────────────┘

┌─────────────────────────────────┐
│   Junior Electrical Engineer     │
└─────────────────────────────────┘
```

Position Description

Electricity is a commodity we use every day. We rarely think about it, unless it suddenly becomes unavailable, and we usually give little thought to how this remarkable power is delivered to our homes and businesses. In some of our newer neighborhoods where electrical lines are underground, we aren't even reminded of the electrical system of poles, towers, wires, transformers, and all the other components that work together to bring electricity to us from miles away. Fortunately, there are men and women who work hard each day to design and maintain our electrical systems. These professionals are called Electrical Engineers.

Electrical engineering is a relatively new field because the widespread use of electricity is a historically recent development. Electrical engineering degree programs were first offered by U.S. educational institutions in the late 1800s. Within the last 150 years, electrical power has become such an indispensable part of our modern life that

electrical engineering is the largest branch of the engineering field.

Electrical Engineers are professionals who use their knowledge of science and mathematics to design, test, and oversee the production of electrical equipment. This equipment is used for a variety of industrial, scientific, military, or commercial purposes. Electrical Engineers also sell and install such equipment. Electrical equipment ranges from the small to the large, from consumer electronics to power generators, such as those found inside enormous hydroelectric dams.

Electrical Engineers also apply electrical, electronic, and magnetic theories to solve the myriad problems they confront in the design, manufacture, and use of electrical machines, control systems, power plants, medical equipment, lighting systems, and communication systems. These engineers play a part in developing the electrical devices with which we are intimately familiar: our electric lights, telephones, computers, televisions, refrigerators, microwave ovens, and other plug-in devices we use each day. Other things that are less familiar, yet vitally important to us, are also developed by Electrical Engineers, such as aircraft navigation systems, industrial robots, and broadcasting stations and communication satellites that beam radio and television signals.

Electrical Engineers specialize in many subfields. One subfield is power engineering. These Electrical Engineers deal with the three major components of our power grid: electricity generation, transmission, and distribution. They design and operate the complex systems that bring electricity from power plants over transmission lines, through transformer substations, and through local electric lines into our homes, offices, and industries.

Another subfield is control systems engineering. That is the discipline that concentrates on designing the circuitry and processors that make certain systems perform in a specified manner. An example of such a control system is an automobile's cruise control, which continually monitors a car's velocity and engine speed to maintain a constant overall rate of speed.

Telecommunications engineering is the subfield that is concerned with electrical information transmission. Such transmissions are carried by cables, fiber optics, or through space from a transmitter to a receiver. Telecommunications engineers design and implement these various communications systems. Electronics engineering is yet another subfield. Electronics engineers develop and produce electrical networks, or circuits, that operate within an enclosed device, such as a radio, computer, or cellular telephone. Some other areas in which Electrical Engineers may specialize include robotic controls, lighting equipment, signal processing, instrumentation, and circuitry.

Throughout their careers, Electrical Engineers work in different engineering functions, or specialties. Research, design, production, testing, and consulting are a few roles in which engineers may be engaged. Some Electrical Engineers teach engineering courses in colleges and universities.

More specifically, Electrical Engineers perform certain tasks that may include:

- studying the principles of electrical theory, which they apply to developing new or improved electrical equipment
- using computer-aided design and computer-aided engineering (CAD/CAE) tools to design all types of electrical equipment, including instruments and components
- evaluating and testing electrical equipment or products
- managing maintenance and testing activities to make sure that all specifications, regulations, and customer needs are met
- inspecting power plant installations and observing their operations
- preparing bidding documents for job contracts or equipment acquisition
- calculating standards and specifications for manufacturing, construction, and installation projects
- meeting with staff and clients to coordinate projects
- keeping up-to-date with new developments in science, engineering, and technology

Electrical Engineers begin their careers by learning their organization's products and design functions before choosing an area in which to specialize. They learn to solve problems, select appropriate materials or equipment, and become acquainted with manufacturing procedures. They perform general tasks in a variety of functions, including design, specification, research, development, testing, or the practical implementation of designs. As they gain experience and knowledge, they receive more complex assignments and are able to exercise greater levels of authority.

Senior Electrical Engineers are more actively involved with the decision-making process and are more likely to be team leaders. They supervise teams composed of other engineers, technicians, and support staff to complete their assigned tasks. Their decisions are made without direct supervision. Senior engineers are more aware of program needs and work independently in response to those needs.

Advanced to executive-level Electrical Engineers are the primary engineers for project divisions and perform the most difficult engineering tasks. They make policy decisions and consult with clients or government agencies at the highest levels. They are responsible for top-level project management and client management, as well as business development and administration.

Electrical Engineers work in office settings. They may work alone or in teams comprised of engineers, technicians, and support staff. They may occasionally be required to work outdoors at installation sites. They work 40 hours per week but may be required to put in extra hours to complete tasks or meet deadlines.

Salaries

Salaries for Electrical Engineers vary, depending on such factors as their education, experience, job, employer, and geographical location. The U.S. Bureau of Labor Statistics (BLS) reported in its November 2004 *Occupational Employment Statistics* (OES) survey that the estimated annual salary for most Electrical Engineers ranged between $47,430 and $110,330.

Employment Prospects

Most Electrical Engineers work for companies that offer engineering, business consultation, scientific, technical, or professional services. Many of them work for computer or electronic equipment manufacturers in such industries as aerospace, medical electronics, and telecommunications. Some Electrical Engineers are employed by government agencies.

According to the BLS's November 2004 OES survey, about 147,120 Electrical Engineers were employed in the United States. The highest levels of employment for Electrical Engineers were in the architectural and engineering services, electronic instrument manufacturing, semiconductor and electronic component manufacturing, and power generation and supply industries.

The BLS reports that the job growth for Electrical Engineers should increase by 9 to 17 percent through 2014. Job vacancies will also result from engineers who advance to higher positions, retire, or transfer to other jobs.

Advancement Prospects

Electrical Engineers may advance in any number of ways, depending on their ambitions and interests. They can become technical specialists and consultants in their areas of interest. Engineers with management and administrative interests and talents can seek positions as supervisory, project, and chief engineers, as well as executive-level managers. To advance to higher positions, engineers are usually required to possess a master's or doctoral degree. Engineers with entrepreneurial ambitions can become independent consultants or owners of engineering consulting firms.

Education and Training

Applicants must have at least a bachelor's degree in electrical engineering or another related field to qualify for entry-level jobs. Engineers usually need a doctorate to teach electrical engineering in colleges and universities. Many Electrical Engineers obtain advanced degrees in an electrical engineering specialty that interests them.

Employers typically give entry-level engineers on-the-job training, and also provide them with formal classroom training programs.

Throughout their careers, Electrical Engineers enroll in continuing education programs and training programs to update their skills and keep up with advancements in their fields.

Special Requirements

All engineers who offer engineering services directly to the public or perform work that affects the life, health, or property of the public must be licensed as professional engineers (P.E.).

The P.E. licensing process consists of two stages. At the first level, qualifying engineers become licensed as engineers-in-training (E.I.T.). After working several years under the supervision of licensed engineers, E.I.T.s become eligible to apply for the P.E. licensure.

Every state and territory, as well as Washington, D.C., has its own licensing requirements. For specific information, contact the board of engineering examiners for the area where you wish to practice. See Appendix II for a list of boards.

Experience, Special Skills, and Personality Traits

Entry-level candidates should have work experience related to the positions for which they apply. They may have gained their experience through internships, work-study programs, student research projects, or part-time employment.

Strong communication, teamwork, and interpersonal skills are essential, as Electrical Engineers must be able to work well with colleagues, managers, clients, and others who come from diverse backgrounds. In addition, Electrical Engineers need effective problem-solving, organizational, and writing skills. Being detail-oriented, logical, creative, reliable, flexible, cooperative, and trustworthy are some personality traits that successful Electrical Engineers share.

Unions and Associations

Many Electrical Engineers belong to local, state, and national societies to take advantage of networking opportunities, continuing education programs, and other professional services and resources. Some national societies that serve the general interests of these engineers include the Institute of Electrical and Electronics Engineers, the National Society of Professional Engineers, the National Society of Black Engineers, and the Society of Women Engineers.

Electrical Engineers also join professional associations that serve their particular specialties, such as the American Association for Artificial Intelligence, the National Association of Radio and Telecommunications Engineers, the Association for Computing Machinery, and the Optical Society of America. For contact information, see Appendix III.

Tips for Entry

1. Some colleges and universities offer cooperative education programs, in which students alternate paid work experiences with their studies. Talk with your college advisor or a college career counselor to find out what is available.
2. One way you can get involved in your field while in college is to join a campus engineering organization or a student branch of a professional organization.
3. Keep up with the latest developments in your field by reading trade and professional publications. You may be able to find free copies at a public or college library.
4. Use the Internet to learn more about electrical engineering. You might start by visiting the Institute of Electrical and Electronics Engineers Web site at http://www.ieee.org. For more links, see Appendix IV.

ELECTRONICS ENGINEER

CAREER PROFILE

Duties: Be involved in the research, design, development, testing, and production of electronic components and systems; perform duties as required

Alternate Title(s): A title that reflects a specialty (such as Telecommunications Engineer) or a particular function (such as Research Engineer)

Salary Range: $49,000 to $114,000

Employment Prospects: Fair

Advancement Prospects: Good

Prerequisites:

Education or Training—Bachelor's degree in electrical engineering or a related field; on-the-job training

Experience—Previous work experience generally required

Special Skills and Personality Traits—Problem-solving, writing, communication, teamwork, interpersonal, and self-management skills; be creative, logical, detail-oriented, persistent, trustworthy, and flexible

Special Requirements—Professional engineer (P.E.) licensure may be required

CAREER LADDER

```
┌─────────────────────────────────┐
│   Senior Electronics Engineer    │
└─────────────────────────────────┘

┌─────────────────────────────────┐
│       Electronics Engineer       │
└─────────────────────────────────┘

┌─────────────────────────────────┐
│   Junior Electronics Engineer    │
└─────────────────────────────────┘
```

Position Description

Electronic devices are part of our everyday lives. They entertain us as well as help us find information and communicate with one another. Consumer electronics are only a small portion of all the electronic devices that touch our lives. Whenever we purchase something, it is scanned by a price code reader, which is also an electronic device. Our homes, schools, and places of business are kept illuminated with electronic lighting systems. Doctors and dentists use electronic devices to examine us. Electronics are used in automobiles, satellites, and ships. Professionals known as Electronics Engineers are involved in the development and production of all the electronic devices in the world.

Electronics engineering is a subfield, or specialty, of electrical engineering. Electrical engineering encompasses everything pertaining to the use of electricity, from large power plants to miniscule electronic components. Electronics Engineers focus their specific attention on enclosed mechanisms or appliances that run on electricity. The science of electronics is a branch of physics that studies the flow of electrons or other electrically charged particles in electrical systems. Electronics Engineers apply the science of electronics to devise and build the circuitry that makes electronic devices work. Additionally, they use a well-rounded body of knowledge in such fields as mathematics, chemistry, optics, electromagnetics, communications, engineering economics, and manufacturing in the course of their work.

Electronics Engineers research, design, develop, test, and produce electronic mechanisms and machinery for various uses in industry, the military, commerce, or science. Electronic products are used in such fields as aerospace guidance, telecommunications, and acoustics, as well as for a variety of instruments and control mechanisms. These electronic products consist of electrical networks, or circuits, that operate within an enclosed device, such as a radio, computer, or cellular telephone. The circuits use the integrated electrical components of resistors, capacitors, inductors, transistors, diodes, and semiconductors to perform a specific function or series of functions.

Electronics Engineers are involved in various engineering functions or specialties. Some engineers use computer-aided design and computer-aided engineering (CAD/CAE) tools to design all types of electronic devices. Many engineers are involved in overseeing and coordinating the manufacturing process. Some manage maintenance and testing activities to make sure that all specifications, regulations, and customer needs are met. Research is also a vital function for Electronics Engineers. They study the principles of electronics, which they apply to new or improved electronic products. Some engineers teach engineering courses in colleges and universities, while others provide consulting services. These are just a few of the engineering specialties in which Electronics Engineers may engage throughout their careers.

Electronics Engineers are responsible for completing specific tasks in the course of their day-to-day activities, such as:

- planning and implementing research procedures within the parameters of the latest electronic theories
- conducting research and incorporating the results into the design of new or improved electronic devices
- analyzing customer needs and costs to decide upon the feasibility of proposed projects
- designing electronic equipment or products according to customer specifications
- preparing documents including drawings and specifications for products as well as their applications and installation
- establishing product performance standards and providing maintenance schedules to ensure those standards are met
- inspecting electronic equipment or systems to ensure safety and performance requirements
- planning and devising modifications to electronic products to improve or enhance their performance
- developing computer programs
- writing technical manuals for new products, as well as installation instructions
- meeting and consulting with other engineers and clients to talk about new or existing projects
- supervising a staff of fellow engineers, technicians, and support personnel

Electronics Engineers find employment in a wide variety of industries, including the high-tech and defense industries. They also work in the areas of manufacturing, industrial and consumer electronics, semiconductors, electronic medical equipment, and optoelectronics. Their jobs are found with firms that specialize in professional and technical services. Some Electronics Engineers are employed by government agencies. Others find employment with communication, wholesale trade, and utility companies. Electronics Engineers are also employed by colleges and universities as researchers and teachers.

Electronics Engineers mainly work in office settings. They may work alone or in teams comprised of engineers, technicians, and support staff. In group settings, Electronics Engineers must be able to interact and communicate effectively with other people from diverse backgrounds. They may occasionally be required to work outdoors at installation sites.

Electronics Engineers work 40 hours per week but occasionally put in extra hours to complete tasks or meet deadlines.

Salaries

Salaries for Electronics Engineers vary, depending on such factors as their education, experience, employer, and geographical location. According to the November 2004 *Occupational Employment Statistics* (OES) survey by the U.S. Bureau of Labor Statistics (BLS), the estimated annual salary for most Electronics Engineers ranged between $49,430 and $113,530.

Employment Prospects

The BLS reports in its November 2004 OES survey that an estimated 133,410 Electronics Engineers were employed in the United States. The highest levels of employment for Electronics Engineers were in the federal government, the semiconductor and electronic component manufacturing industry, the wired telecommunications carriers industry, and the architectural and engineering services industry.

Job opportunities generally become available as Electronics Engineers transfer to other jobs, advance to higher positions, or retire. Employers will create new positions as their business needs expand. According to the BLS, the job growth for electrical engineers (which includes Electronics Engineers) should increase by 9 to 17 percent through 2014. The fastest growth will occur in consulting firms and other service industries.

Advancement Prospects

Electronics Engineers may advance in any number of ways, depending on their ambitions and interests. They can become technical specialists or consultants in a particular field, such as power generation or electrical equipment manufacturing. Engineers with management and administrative interests and talents can seek positions as supervisory, project, and chief engineers, as well as executive-level managers. Those with entrepreneurial ambitions can become independent consultants or owners of technical or consulting firms. A master's or doctoral degree is usually required for engineers to advance to careers in management, consulting, research, or teaching.

Education and Training

Entry-level applicants must possess at least a bachelor's degree in electrical engineering or another related field.

Novice engineers typically receive on-the-job training. Their employers may also provide them with formal classroom training programs.

Throughout their careers, Electronics Engineers enroll in continuing education programs and training programs to update their skills and keep up with advancements in their fields.

Special Requirements

All engineers who offer engineering services directly to the public or perform work that affects the life, health, or property of the public must be licensed as professional engineers (P.E.). Every state and territory, as well as Washington, D.C., has its own requirements for P.E. licensure. For specific information, contact the board of engineering examiners for the area where you wish to practice. See Appendix II for a list of boards.

Experience, Special Skills, and Personality Traits

Entry-level candidates should have work experience related to the positions for which they apply. They may have gained their experience through internships, work-study programs, student research projects, or part-time employment.

Electronics Engineers need strong problem-solving, writing, communication, teamwork, and interpersonal skills to perform effectively at their jobs. They also need good self-management skills, such as the ability to work independently, meet deadlines, handle stressful situations, and prioritize multiple tasks.

Some personality traits that successful Electronics Engineers share include being creative, logical, detail-oriented, persistent, trustworthy, and flexible.

Unions and Associations

Professional associations are available at the local, state, and national levels. By joining one or more societies, Electronics Engineers can take advantage of networking opportunities, publications, continuing education programs, and other professional services and resources. The Institute of Electrical and Electronics Engineers, the Society of Women Engineers, and the National Society of Professional Engineers are a few professional associations at the national level that serve the general interests of Electronics Engineers.

Electronics Engineers might also belong to societies that serve their particular interests, such as the Association for Computing Machinery, the American Institute of Aeronautics and Astronautics, or the Society of Manufacturing Engineers. For contact information, see Appendix III.

Tips for Entry

1. Carefully research the academic programs in which you are interested. Are an engineering program's mission and philosophy compatible with yours? Does it offer the courses that you need and want? Are there professors under whom you want to study? Does the program offer any practical training opportunities?
2. Contact prospective employers directly to learn about internships as well as job vacancies. Be sure to also learn about their selection process.
3. Learn more about Electronics Engineers on the Internet. You might start by visiting the following Web site: The EE Compendium (by Randy Rasa), http://ee.cleversoul.com.

TELECOMMUNICATIONS ENGINEER

CAREER PROFILE

Duties: Research, design, develop, test, maintain, and administer telecommunication systems; perform duties as required

Alternate Title(s): Electrical Engineer; a title that reflects an engineering function such as Test Engineer or Sales Engineer

Salary Range: $47,000 to $114,000

Employment Prospects: Fair

Advancement Prospects: Good

Prerequisites:

Education or Training—Bachelor's degree in electrical engineering or a related field; on-the-job training

Experience—Previous work experience generally required

Special Skills and Personality Traits—Problem-solving, time-management, organizational, writing, presentation, interpersonal, teamwork, and communication skills; curious, creative, persistent, disciplined, patient, responsible, honest, and courteous

Special Requirements—Professional engineer (P.E.) licensure and/or FCC license may be required

CAREER LADDER

Senior Telecommunications Engineer

Telecommunications Engineer

Junior Telecommunications Engineer

Position Description

Humans have always endeavored to speak with each other over long distances. Our ancestors devised many methods of long-distance communication, such as lighting fires at night, sending smoke signals by day, playing drums, or waving flags. Messengers traveled great distances overland by foot or horseback, or overseas by ship, as messages were relayed from one person to the next until the message could be delivered to its final destination.

The nineteenth century ushered in a new era of communications with the invention of the telegraph. This device enabled people to instantly send messages back and forth over unprecedented distances by using a code transmitted over electrical wires. Subsequent inventions, such as the telephone, radio, television, and computer, have expanded upon the use of wired or wireless electrical systems to transmit information around the globe. These various modern systems that are used for speaking or sending video, data, text, and pictures through electronic means are collec-

tively called telecommunications. The professionals who research, plan, analyze, design, install, test, maintain, and administer these systems are known as Telecommunications Engineers.

Telecommunications Engineers are specialists within the field of electrical engineering. They work with a wide range of communications devices and networks that serve a variety of purposes. Telecommunication systems can range in size and complexity. For example, a telephone system can be used within a building as well as be used for communicating outside the building. The system allows its users to dial private numbers to reach each other without using the main telephone company's switchboard. Likewise, computer networks can be similarly localized. Local access networks (LANs) permit computer users to communicate with each other within a building or cluster of buildings. Wide area networks (WANs) permit computer users to communicate with each other at greater distances, such as in a corporation composed of a headquarters and several branch offices located in different cities. Some of these telecommunication systems make use of satellite technology.

Telecommunications Engineers may specialize in one or more of these types of networks. They may work within an organization to implement and manage the systems, as well as to coordinate different networks to work in harmony with each other, according to the needs of the organization. Their work includes evaluating equipment requirements, ordering appropriate circuitry, overseeing the installation of networks, testing the equipment, troubleshooting problems, analyzing network performance, and updating systems by developing and introducing new products.

Telecommunications as an industry serves to develop the equipment and network technologies that are utilized in the various telecommunication systems. Within the telecommunications industry, Telecommunications Engineers work in the areas of research and development, as well as the production, implementation, maintenance, selling, and management of telecommunication devices and systems. Each engineer within a company performs a unique engineering function, but all the areas of concern operate together in a unified fashion to meet project goals.

Telecommunications Engineers work in teams with other engineers, software designers, graphic designers, and support personnel to complete projects. They work closely with clients to ensure that the systems they design meet the clients' specifications. They keep abreast with new technologies, such as wireless systems, with an eye toward upgrading existing systems as well as toward developing new ones.

Depending upon their engineering function or area of expertise, Telecommunications Engineers perform a variety of duties. They might:

- develop and put fiber-optic systems into operation
- provide accurate and thorough project designs
- keep records of network or systems designs, the facilities in which they are installed, and their client's bandwidth requirements
- design and install direct current (DC) power plants
- respond to requests for service, maintenance, or repair of networks and systems, as well as schedule the needed work
- inspect wiring systems for quality, as well as for compliance with plans, government standards, easements, and permits
- coordinate the activities of clients, engineers, and contractors to install systems
- review construction plans and bidding documents
- build and test prototype equipment
- advise on materials and cost requirements needed for projects
- maintain good relationships with staff and clients
- provide technical assistance and management to staff members and clients
- train new staff members

Telecommunications Engineers find work in a variety of industries, including the financial, transportation, hospitality, services, and defense industries. They work in government or private research and development laboratories, as well as in regulatory agencies. Telecommunications Engineers work for companies that manufacture broadcasting equipment, televisions, radios, computers, satellites, and telephones. They also work for hardware and software development firms.

Telecommunications Engineers work independently or in teams with other engineers, technicians, and support staff. They are in frequent contact with people from a wide spectrum of trades, professions, or other career backgrounds, including marketing, computer, technical, construction, and sales personnel.

Telecommunications Engineers work mainly in such indoor locations as offices, laboratories, and installation sites. Some engineers are occasionally required to travel locally, or even to other countries. Some problems at distant locations may require return trips, as system difficulties can only be resolved by reproducing the problem in a laboratory at their home office.

Telecommunications Engineers generally work 40 hour per week. They sometimes work overtime to complete tasks or meet deadlines. Some engineers work on an on-call basis, depending on the needs of their employer.

Salaries

Salaries for Telecommunications Engineers vary, depending on such factors as their education, experience, employer, and geographical location. Specific salary information for this occupation is unavailable, but these engineers generally earn salaries similar to electrical and electronics engineers. The U.S. Bureau of Labor Statistics reported in its November 2004 *Occupational Employment Statistics* survey that the estimated annual salary for most electrical engineers ranged between $47,430 and $110,330, and for most electronics engineers, between $49,430 and $113,530.

Employment Prospects

Opportunities should remain favorable for Telecommunications Engineers in the coming years, partly due to the continuing development of new technologies and the growing demand by personal consumers and businesses for cellular telephones, cable, palm-pilots, and other technologies. Most job openings become available as Telecommunications Engineers are promoted, retire, or transfer to other jobs. Employers will create additional positions as their companies expand.

Advancement Prospects

Telecommunications Engineers may advance in any number of ways, depending on their ambitions and interests. They can become technical specialists as well as pursue engineering management positions. In addition, engineers can advance to executive officer positions within their organization. Engineers with entrepreneurial ambitions can become independent consultants or owners of technical or consulting firms.

Education and Training
Minimally, a bachelor's degree in electrical engineering, communications engineering, or another related field is needed for entry-level positions. A master's degree or doctorate is usually required for engineers to advance to careers in management, consulting, research, or teaching.

Novice engineers typically receive on-the-job training while working under the guidance and supervision of senior engineers. Some employers also provide entry-level engineers with formal classroom training.

Throughout their careers, Telecommunications Engineers enroll in continuing education and training programs to update their skills and keep up with advancements in their fields.

Special Requirements
All engineers who offer engineering services directly to the public or perform work that affects the life, health, or property of the public must be licensed as professional engineers (P.E.). The requirements for licensure vary with each state and territory, as well as Washington, D.C. For specific information, contact the board of engineering examiners for the area where you wish to practice. See Appendix II for a list of boards.

Telecommunications Engineers may also be required to possess appropriate Federal Communications Commission (FCC) licenses. For example, engineers who repair and maintain aircraft stations and aeronautical ground stations that are used to communicate with aircraft must hold a commercial radio operator license, granted by the FCC.

Experience, Special Skills, and Personality Traits
Entry-level candidates should have work experience related to the positions for which they apply. They may have gained their experience through internships, work-study programs,

student research projects, or employment. Employers also seek candidates who are familiar with broadcasting and telecommunication rules and standards.

To be effective at their work, Telecommunications Engineers must have excellent problem-solving, time-management, organizational, writing, and presentation skills. They also need strong interpersonal, teamwork, and communication skills, as they must be able to work well with various people from diverse backgrounds. Being curious, creative, persistent, disciplined, patient, responsible, honest, and courteous are some personality traits that successful Telecommunications Engineers share.

Unions and Associations
Telecommunications Engineers can join professional associations to take advantage of professional services and resources such as publications, continuing education programs, certification, and networking opportunities. Some national societies that serve the interests of these engineers are:

- Institute of Electrical and Electronics Engineers
- Society of Cable Telecommunications Engineers
- National Association of Radio and Telecommunications Engineers
- National Society of Professional Engineers

For contact information, see Appendix III.

Tips for Entry
1. Stay up-to-date with the latest issues and trends in the telecommunications industry by reading trade and professional publications, both in print and online.
2. Do your research on companies in which you are interested. Ask a reference librarian for help in finding business journals and other materials that can provide relevant information.
3. Use the Internet to learn more about Telecommunications Engineers, as well as the telecommunications industry. To get a list of Web sites, enter the keywords *telecommunications engineers, telecommunications engineering,* or *telecommunications industry* in a search engine. To learn about some links, see Appendix IV.

CONTROL ENGINEER

CAREER PROFILE

Duties: Research, develop, design, test, and manufacture control mechanisms and systems; perform duties as required

Alternate Title(s): Control Systems Engineer, Automatic Control Engineer, Automation Engineer, Electrical Engineer; a title that reflects an engineering function, such as Project Engineer

Salary Range: $47,000 to $110,000

Employment Prospects: Fair

Advancement Prospects: Good

Prerequisites:

Education or Training—Bachelor's degree in electrical engineering, control systems engineering, or a related field; on-the-job training

Experience—Previous work experience generally required

Special Skills and Personality Traits—Computer, programming, leadership, interpersonal, teamwork, communication, writing, presentation, organizational, and planning skills; ethical, collaborative, energetic, detail-oriented, flexible

Special Requirements—Professional engineer (P.E.) licensure may be required

CAREER LADDER

```
┌─────────────────────────────┐
│   Senior Control Engineer   │
└─────────────────────────────┘

┌─────────────────────────────┐
│      Control Engineer       │
└─────────────────────────────┘

┌─────────────────────────────┐
│   Junior Control Engineer   │
└─────────────────────────────┘
```

Position Description

In the field of control engineering, "control" refers to a mechanical means to regulate or optimize the performance of machines or systems. Many of us are familiar with one sort of control: the thermostat. Whenever our interior room temperature reaches a specific level, a thermostat detects the temperature and automatically starts the furnace or air conditioner to restore the room to a desired level of comfort. This convenient device is one type of control that was designed by Control Engineers.

Electrical Control Engineers, also known as automatic control engineers, automation engineers, or control systems engineers, are specialists within the field of electrical engineering. Their professional mission is to design automated control systems for a wide range of machines and mechanical system operations. Control Engineers draw upon mathematical and engineering methods to study and design control systems, which are also known as control loops. All automatic control systems are composed of three components: sensors, responders, and actuators. These components work together in a continuous, coordinated loop of feedback and control functions to detect or sense changes in a system's operational environment, respond to such changes, and put into motion the necessary adjustments for the system to work properly. For example, an automobile's cruise control system detects an incline and responds by increasing fuel to the engine so the car accelerates to its preset velocity.

Control Engineers seek to optimize the performance of mechanized systems through the use of control systems such as those found in aircraft autopilots, automated manufacturing assembly lines, household appliances, robots, computers, and space vehicles. Regardless of the simplicity or complexity of these control systems, they all utilize the same basic feedback principles.

Depending upon their level of expertise or years of experience, electrical Control Engineers fulfill a variety of engineering functions. They work in the areas of research, design, testing, planning, and production of control mechanisms. Some of them investigate and devise new developments in automated control system technology. These new developments are taken into consideration and integrated into new control system designs. Some Control Engineers use computer-aided design (CAD) programs to generate their designs.

Many Control Engineers are involved in testing new designs before approving their large-scale production. Senior engineers who are project managers oversee groups of other engineers, technicians, and support personnel to work on large or complex projects. They are responsible for ensuring that schematics and wiring diagrams are properly prepared, as well as that the proper equipment is used for the assembly of control systems. Other Control Engineers work closely with clients to assure that specifications for their control systems are met and that projects are completed within appropriate time and cost parameters. They also work with suppliers to procure the appropriate materials or equipment to complete the preparation of control systems. Some Control Engineers work in academic settings where they teach and conduct research.

Electrical Control Engineers complete specific tasks in the course of their work. They may:

- meet with staff and clients to coordinate projects
- evaluate and test control equipment or products
- calculate standards and specifications for manufacturing, construction, and installation projects
- inspect control installations and observe their operations
- develop and organize appropriate documents that outline or identify plans, schematics, specifications, and standards for their projects
- prepare reports and studies
- prepare bidding documents for job contracts or equipment acquisition

Control Engineers work for firms that offer control systems engineering services on a contractual basis, as well as in a wide range of industries that manufacture or utilize automated control systems.

They work in offices as well as in manufacturing environments. Control Engineers work in group settings that collaborate on projects and are results-oriented. Travel may be required for engineers to interact with clients or to attend meetings.

Control Engineers generally work for 40 hours per week. Additional hours are occasionally required for them to complete tasks or meet deadlines.

Salaries

Salaries for electrical Control Engineers vary, depending on such factors as their education, experience, employer, industry, and geographical location. Specific salary information for these engineers is unavailable, but they generally earn salaries similar to electrical engineers. According to the November 2004 *Occupational Employment Statistics* survey by the U.S. Bureau of Labor Statistics, the estimated annual salary for most electrical engineers ranged between $47,430 and $110,330.

Employment Prospects

Opportunities vary in the different industries. In general, they become available as Control Engineers are promoted, transfer to other jobs, or retire. Companies will create additional positions as they grow and expand.

Advancement Prospects

As Control Engineers gain experience, they are assigned to more complex projects as well as receive increasingly greater responsibilities. Senior engineers can become technical specialists, consultants, and managers. Those with entrepreneurial ambitions can become independent consultants or owners of technical or consulting firms.

Education and Training

Minimally, applicants need a bachelor's degree in electrical engineering, control systems engineering, mechanical engineering, or another related field for entry-level positions. A master's or doctoral degree is usually required for engineers to advance to careers in management, consulting, research, or teaching.

Entry-level engineers usually receive on-the-job training while working under the guidance of senior staff members. In some companies, they are required to complete formal classroom training programs.

Throughout their careers, electrical Control Engineers enroll in continuing education and training programs to update their skills and keep up with advancements in their fields.

Special Requirements

Engineers who offer engineering services directly to the public or perform work that affects the life, health, or property of the public must be licensed as professional engineers (P.E.). Every U.S. state and territory, as well as Washington D.C., has its own unique licensing requirements. For specific information, contact the board of engineering examiners for the area where you wish to practice. See Appendix II for a list of boards.

Experience, Special Skills, and Personality Traits

Entry-level candidates should have work experience related to the positions for which they apply. They may have gained

their experience through internships, work-study programs, student research projects, postdoctoral training, or part-time employment.

Electrical Control Engineers must be computer literate with strong programming skills. They also need effective leadership, interpersonal, teamwork, communication, writing, and presentation skills. Having excellent organizational and planning skills is essential too. Being ethical, collaborative, energetic, detail-oriented and flexible are some personality traits that successful Control Engineers have in common.

Unions and Associations

Electrical Control Engineers can join professional societies to take advantage of networking opportunities, continuing education programs, and other professional services and resources. Some national societies that serve their diverse interests are the Instrumentation, Systems, and Automation Society, the IEEE Control Systems Society, and the Guid-

ance Navigation and Control Technical Committee, part of the American Institute of Aeronautics and Astronautics. For contact information, see Appendix III.

Tips for Entry

1. In high school, take courses in mathematics as well as physics and chemistry to help you prepare for an engineering program in college.
2. Read questions carefully on a job application. Your answers need to directly relate to the questions being asked. You might first draft and revise your answers on another piece of paper before copying them to your application.
3. Use the Internet to learn more about control systems engineering. You might start by visiting the following Web site: Instrumentation, Systems, and Automation Society, http://www.isa.org. For more links, see Appendix IV.

COMPUTER HARDWARE ENGINEER

CAREER PROFILE

Duties: Research, develop, design, test, and manufacture computers and computer-related equipment; perform duties as required

Alternate Title(s): Computer Engineer, Electrical Engineer; a title that reflects a specialty (such as Computer Chip Designer) or engineering function (such as Research Engineer)

Salary Range: $51,000 to $126,000

Employment Prospects: Fair

Advancement Prospects: Good

Prerequisites:

Education or Training—Bachelor's or advanced degree in computer or electrical engineering; on-the-job training

Experience—Previous work experience generally required

Special Skills and Personality Traits—Communication, writing, problem-solving, analytical, interpersonal, and teamwork skills; detail-oriented, persistent, innovative, and curious

Special Requirements—Professional engineer (P.E.) licensure may be required

CAREER LADDER

```
┌─────────────────────────────────────┐
│  Senior Computer Hardware Engineer   │
└─────────────────────────────────────┘

┌─────────────────────────────────────┐
│    Computer Hardware Engineer        │
└─────────────────────────────────────┘

┌─────────────────────────────────────┐
│  Junior Computer Hardware Engineer   │
└─────────────────────────────────────┘
```

Position Description

Computers impact each of our lives, even when we are not using our personal computers. Computers manage all of our financial accounts. They control traffic signals. Our subway and elevated railway systems are monitored and controlled by computers. Computers record our supermarket transactions. Some of our everyday consumer electronics contain imbedded computers, as do automobiles, automated robotic systems, aircraft, and spacecraft. Large mainframe computers predict weather patterns or simulate military maneuvers. Men and women called Computer Hardware Engineers design all of these machines, from hand-held calculators to large supercomputers.

The term *computer hardware* refers to the chips, circuit boards, keyboards, and all the other physical parts of a computer, as well as to modems, printers, scanners, and other computer accessories.

Computer Hardware Engineers are involved with areas of research that they anticipate will lead to more powerful computer systems. Additionally, they are involved in the development and manufacturing of computers and computer-related products.

Before designing a computer hardware project, these engineers analyze current market trends and their client's needs to determine the new product's specifications and which technology will be implemented in the product. With that information, they can then design the hardware architecture of the computer system, while considering how the equipment's components will integrate and interface with each other. They also consider how the equipment's operating system will interface with the software. Computer Hardware Engineers work on computer-aided design (CAD) systems to create their design.

The design is then used to simulate a theoretical model of their computer product, from which they build and test a physical prototype to verify its reliability and feasibility for economical mass production. Before moving into the production phase, they determine and correct errors or faults in the systems. Prototypes are also tested at outside pilot sites for the further diagnosis of errors or faults, which will be corrected before production proceeds. Once mass production of the product begins, Computer Hardware Engineers test the product again to ensure that it has no flaws before being released into the marketplace.

Computer Hardware Engineers usually work in teams composed of engineers, computer scientists, systems analysts, marketing specialists, and others.

Throughout their careers, Computer Hardware Engineers work in different engineering specialties or functions. Product development engineer, design engineer, applications engineer, project engineer, test engineer, production engineer, sales engineer, and consultant are a few of these engineering specialists.

Other Computer Hardware Engineers work in the field of education as instructors or as researchers. They teach academic courses in computer engineering, electrical engineering, or computer science. Those involved with research seek to develop new theories, methodologies, and technologies as well as to find practical uses for computers in a wide variety of fields.

Computer Hardware Engineers work in office, classroom, laboratory, or manufacturing environments. They usually work a 40-hour week but may occasionally work overtime to complete projects or meet deadlines. Extra hours may also be spent keeping up-to-date with the latest developments in their field by reading journals, attending seminars, or taking training courses.

Salaries

Salaries for Computer Hardware Engineers vary, depending on such factors as their education, experience, employer, and geographical location. According to the November 2004 *Occupational Employment Statistics* (OES) survey by the U.S. Bureau of Labor Statistics (BLS), the estimated annual salary for most Computer Hardware Engineers ranged between $51,190 and $125,800.

Employment Prospects

The BLS reported in its November 2004 OES survey that an estimated 79,670 Computer Hardware Engineers were employed in the United States. They mostly work for computer and electronic product manufacturers, scientific or technical service firms, or in the telecommunications industry. Some engineers also find employment in educational institutions and government agencies. Some Computer Hardware Engineers are self-employed consultants.

Competition for jobs is strong. Many opportunities will become available as engineers transfer to other jobs, advance to higher positions, or retire. Employers will create new positions as their needs expand. The BLS predicts the job growth for Computer Hardware Engineers should

increase by 9 to 17 percent through 2014, partly due to foreign competition in the manufacturing of computer hardware and American companies utilizing computer hardware engineering services in other countries.

Advancement Prospects

Engineers can rise through the supervisory and managerial ranks as project managers, departmental managers, and executive-level managers. Those with entrepreneurial ambitions can become independent consultants or start up their own technical or consulting companies.

Education and Training

Minimally, a bachelor's degree in computer engineering, electrical engineering, or another related field is needed for entry-level positions. A master's or doctorate degree is usually required for engineers to advance to careers in management, consulting, research, or teaching.

Novice engineers typically receive on-the-job training while working under the supervision and guidance of experienced personnel. Some companies also provide employees with formal classroom training programs.

Throughout their careers, Computer Hardware Engineers enroll in continuing education and training programs to update their skills and keep up with advancements in their fields.

Special Requirements

Computer Hardware Engineers may be required to be licensed professional engineers (P.E.) in the states where they practice. The requirements for P.E. licensure differ in each state, as well as in each territory and Washington, D.C. For specific information, contact the board of engineering examiners for the area where you wish to practice. See Appendix II for a list of boards.

Experience, Special Skills, and Personality Traits

Entry-level candidates should have work experience related to the positions for which they apply. They may have gained their experience through internships, work-study programs, student research projects, postdoctoral training, or part-time employment.

Computer Hardware Engineers must have strong communication, writing, problem-solving, and analytical skills. They also need effective interpersonal and teamwork skills to work well with many people with different backgrounds. Being detail-oriented, persistent, innovative, and curious are some personality traits that successful Computer Hardware Engineers share.

Unions and Associations

Computer Hardware Engineers can join professional associations at the local, state, or national level to take advantage of continuing education programs, publications, networking opportunities, and other professional resources and services. Two national societies are the Association for Computing Machinery and the Institute of Electrical and Electronics Engineers. Professional engineers are eligible to join the National Society of Professional Engineers. For contact information, see Appendix III.

Tips for Entry

1. Companies sometimes offer full-time jobs to graduates who have completed internships or work-study programs with them.

2. When seeking a job, take advantage of the resources at your college career center. Most college career centers also help alumni with job searches.

3. You can learn more about computer hardware engineering on the Internet. To get a list of Web sites, enter the keywords *computer hardware engineers* or *computer engineering* in a search engine. To learn about some links, see Appendix IV.

SOFTWARE ENGINEER

CAREER PROFILE

Duties: Be involved in the research, development, design, testing, production, and maintenance of software products and systems; perform duties as required

Alternate Title(s): Software Developer, Research Software Engineer

Salary Range: $47,000 to $120,000

Employment Prospects: Excellent

Advancement Prospects: Good

Prerequisites:

Education or Training—Bachelor's degree in software engineering or a related field; on-the-job training

Experience—Be knowledgeable about a variety of computer systems and technologies; previous work experience generally required

Special Skills and Personality Traits—Problem-solving, self-management, writing, communication, interpersonal, and teamwork skills; creative, detail-oriented, analytical, persistent, goal-oriented, enthusiastic, and self-motivated

Special Requirements—Professional engineer (P.E.) licensure may be required

CAREER LADDER

```
┌─────────────────────────────┐
│   Senior Software Engineer   │
└─────────────────────────────┘

┌─────────────────────────────┐
│      Software Engineer       │
└─────────────────────────────┘

┌─────────────────────────────┐
│   Junior Software Engineer   │
└─────────────────────────────┘
```

Position Description

Software is a term that is familiar to most of us. We use it in our computers, our cell phones, and our video games. We can visit any office supply store and choose from hundreds of software titles that allow us to create documents, spreadsheets, multimedia presentations, Web sites, and various other projects for our work as well as personal pleasure. The professionals who prepare these programs are Software Engineers.

Software Engineers research, create, produce, and maintain computer software products. They develop software for use in all types of computer systems used in scientific research, businesses, government operations, protective services, legal systems, education, banking, financial services, utilities, telecommunications, transportation, manufacturing, and other areas of human endeavor. There are two basic types of software: operating system software, which provides the instructions that allow computers to operate automatically, and application software, which performs the various tasks (such as word processing) required by computer users.

Software Engineers are responsible for ensuring that software products perform in a predictable and reliable manner and that they are cost-effective and of high quality. These engineers apply their knowledge about computer science, engineering, and mathematics to designing, developing, testing, evaluating, and maintaining their software products. They possess programming skills and occasionally use those skills in the course of their work. However, they are more concerned with analyzing and solving problems with the programming than actually writing the lines of code that instruct the computer how to perform a function or operation.

Software Engineers work in a number of settings. Most of these engineers work for firms that specialize in computer system design and associated services, as well as with computer and electronic equipment manufacturers.

Software Engineers set up the specifications, or algorithms, for what a particular application should do, which are given to a computer programmer to use to write the code in a computer language such as Java. Hence, their work is part of a team effort. The software development team also includes other computer engineers, marketing specialists, manufacturing personnel, graphic designers, and others. Together, they work through the stages of research and development, software design, and programming, as well as quality assurance and testing, to bring a new software product to market. Software Engineers may be involved with one or all stages of this process. They may also be involved with writing user manuals or other documentation associated with the software product. Software Engineers are oftentimes the project managers who oversee the activities of their team. In that capacity, they plan projects, write proposals, administer budgets, and coordinate schedules. They also provide training and supervision for other staff members.

Virtually every organization—businesses, manufacturers, government agencies, hospitals, schools, nonprofit groups, and so on—has processes that require specialized software systems and applications to operate more efficiently and economically. Software Engineers who work in organizations design and coordinate the construction of computer software systems for their employers. They also oversee the specific software needs of different departments, revise and enhance software systems, plan for future software systems, and troubleshoot problems, among other tasks.

Software Engineers also work as consultants. They may be self-employed as independent consultants, or work for technical or management consulting firms. These are usually experienced engineers who may specialize in particular areas of software development, such as design or testing, or in providing services to specific industries.

Some Software Engineers are employed as instructors or professors in colleges and universities, where they teach software engineering courses to students at the undergraduate or graduate levels. Many of them are also involved in conducting basic research. Their research leads to new theories, methodologies, and tools for use in the software development field. Other Software Engineers do research as their primary function, working in laboratories situated on college campuses as well as within government agencies or industrial facilities.

Most Software Engineers work in office settings or computer laboratories. They work at least 40 hours per week but frequently work evenings or weekends to meet deadlines or complete projects. Some engineers travel often to meet with clients.

Salaries

Salaries for Software Engineers vary, depending on such factors as their education, experience, employer, and geographical location. The U.S. Bureau of Labor Statistics (BLS) reported the following ranges of estimated wages in its November 2004 *Occupational Employment Statistics* survey: $47,340 to $114,690 for Software Engineers who work on general computer applications software or specialized utility programs and $51,380 to $119,750 for Software Engineers who work on systems software.

Employment Prospects

Businesses, government agencies, and other organizations continually need Software Engineers for maintaining and improving their computer systems as well as to implement new and more complex, sophisticated technologies. According to the BLS, job growth for Software Engineers is expected to increase by 27 percent or more through 2014. In addition to job growth, opportunities will become available as Software Engineers retire, advance to higher positions, or transfer to other jobs. Keep in mind that job opportunities can decrease as more companies decide to outsource software engineering jobs to firms in other countries.

Growth areas in which there have been an increasing demand for Software Engineers to design and develop software systems and applications include information security, electronic commerce, wireless networks, and hand-held computers.

Advancement Prospects

Software Engineers who have supervisory and managerial ambitions can advance to such positions as project managers, departmental managers, and chief information officers. After becoming experts in their specialties, entrepreneurial engineers might become independent consultants or start their own technical or consulting businesses.

Education and Training

Minimally, a bachelor's degree in software engineering, computer engineering, computer science, or another related field is the general requirement for entry-level positions. A master's or doctoral degree is usually required for engineers to advance to careers in management, consulting, research, or teaching. Engineers must possess a doctorate to teach engineering at the college level.

Entry-level engineers typically receive on-the-job training while working under the guidance and supervision of senior engineers. Some companies provide their employees with formal classroom training programs.

Throughout their careers, Software Engineers enroll in continuing education and training programs to update their skills and keep up with advancements in their fields.

Special Requirements

Software Engineers may be required to obtain professional engineer (P.E.) licensure if their work affects the public safety and welfare or if they offer their services directly to the public. The requirements for licensing differ in each state and territory, as well as in Washington, D.C. For specific information, contact the board of engineering examiners for the area where you wish to practice. See Appendix II for a list of boards.

Experience, Special Skills, and Personality Traits
Employers typically seek entry-level candidates who have knowledge of a variety of computer systems and technologies. Having work experience is preferred. Recent graduates may have gained relevant experience through internships, work-study program student research projects, postdoctoral training, or part-time employment.

Software Engineers must have strong problem-solving, self-management, writing, communication, interpersonal, and teamwork skills to be effective at their work. Being creative, detail-oriented, analytical, persistent, goal-oriented, enthusiastic, and self-motivated are some personality traits that successful Software Engineers have in common.

Unions and Associations
Software Engineers can join professional associations at the local, state, or national level to take advantage of networking opportunities, continuing education programs, and other professional services and resources. Two national societies that serve the interests of these engineers are the Technical Council on Software Engineering (part of the IEEE Computer Society) and the Special Interest Group on Software Engineering (part of the Association for Computing Machinery). For contact information, see Appendix III.

Tips for Entry
1. Many educational institutions offer software certification programs that are aimed at programmers and other computer specialists who are interested in switching to a software engineering career.
2. Some Software Engineers obtain professional certification to enhance their employability.
3. Job titles for Software Engineers vary from company to company. Be sure to read job vacancy announcements carefully.
4. Use the Internet to learn more about software engineering. To get a list of Web sites, enter the keywords *software engineering* or *software engineers* in a search engine. To learn about some links, see Appendix IV.

INFORMATION TECHNOLOGY (IT) ENGINEER

CAREER PROFILE

Duties: Design and manage an organization's information systems; perform duties as required

Alternate Title(s): IT Specialist, IT Manager, System Administrator, Network Architect, Network Administrator

Salary Range: $37,000 to $92,000

Employment Prospects: Good

Advancement Prospects: Fair

Prerequisites:

    Education or Training—Associate or bachelor's degree in computer science or a related field; on-the-job training

    Experience—Previous work experience generally required

    Special Skills and Personality Traits—Writing, problem-solving, analytical, communication, interpersonal, customer service, and leadership skills; organized, energetic, self-motivated, creative, resourceful, reliable, flexible, and detail-oriented

CAREER LADDER

```
┌─────────────────────────────────────────────┐
│ Senior Information Technology Engineer        │
└─────────────────────────────────────────────┘

┌─────────────────────────────────────────────┐
│ Information Technology                         │
└─────────────────────────────────────────────┘

┌─────────────────────────────────────────────┐
│ Junior Information Technology Engineer         │
└─────────────────────────────────────────────┘
```

Position Description

Today's business and office environments are distinguished from those of just a few decades ago in one major way: digital connectedness. Organizations—companies, law firms, hospitals, schools, nonprofit groups, government agencies, and so on—offer information instantly and freely to anyone who visits their Web sites. Meetings are conducted via video conferencing among business personnel who sit in offices hundreds or thousands of miles apart from each other. They present their concepts with multimedia programs that they deliver over computer networks. Employees write memos or letters with their desktop computers and send them to each other by e-mail over their organization's intranet, or to other interested parties by way of the Internet. Today, most organizations cannot function without these digital information technologies and their software components.

Information technology is an important area of concern for a certain category of engineers who design, implement, and manage the networked systems that characterize our modern business environments. These professionals are called Information Technology (IT) Engineers. They apply the disciplines of computer science and communication science in combination with the fields of social science, mathematics, and engineering to improve the functionality of organizations through the use of computers and telecommunications devices. These engineers differ from computer scientists and engineers in that they do not design or build such equipment. Rather, IT Engineers focus primarily on the use of these technologies within and among organizations. They confer with people in the organizations about how they need to use information technologies and then work to implement their use.

IT Engineers analyze an organization's needs for the establishment of and connection to the company intranets, extranets, and local or wide area networks (LANs and WANs) as well as to the Internet. They design or configure the network or networks and install the needed hardware and software. Further, IT Engineers maintain the system hardware and software, monitor the network's performance, analyze problems that may arise, and work to resolve those problems. They ensure that the systems and networks are user friendly—that is to say that everyone in the organization can easily work with and understand the equipment and software, as well as readily access the various networks.

IT Engineers fulfill various responsibilities, depending on their level of expertise, their years of experience, and the size of their organizations. Senior IT Engineers possess a more thorough understanding of telecommunications, computers, their various hardware and software components, and how they may interconnect through networks. They are well versed in the use of various programming languages and computer operating systems (such as Windows or Unix platforms). They keep up with new developments in telecommunications and computer technologies. They understand what their organizations need to maintain up-to-date information systems or networks. Hence, senior IT Engineers anticipate the need for modifications, improvements, new equipment acquisitions, and new software developments. They serve as group leaders who oversee a staff of engineering and technical personnel who provide maintenance services, assist employees with hardware or software problems, and install new equipment where it is needed.

IT Engineers complete specific tasks in the course of their work. For example, they might:

- assist the organization's administrative and management personnel to plan, design, and implement information technology systems and networks
- set priorities for the completion of projects involving system or network design, installation, maintenance, and operation
- research and implement new technologies and software while concurrently maintaining an older system
- analyze, identify, and implement system and network security for the protection of hardware, software, and data
- set standards for organization-wide use of hardware and software
- operate master consoles to remotely monitor the performance of or troubleshoot problems in the use of systems and networks
- maintain written records and manage budgets
- develop work plans and schedule completion times
- write and maintain technical documents pertinent to networks and systems
- maintain relationships with hardware and software vendors
- provide technical support to employees within the organization
- lead and motivate a staff of engineers and technical personnel

IT Engineers often work longer hours than the standard 40-hour week. Some are required to be available at all times during working hours; some may be on call 24 hours, usually on a rotating basis. Some IT Engineers travel to complete their assignments.

Salaries

Salaries for IT Engineers vary, depending on such factors as their education, experience, job duties, employer, industry, and geographical location. Specific salary information for IT Engineers is unavailable, but a general idea of their earnings can be gained by looking at similar occupations. According to the November 2004 *Occupational Employment Statistics* survey by the U.S. Bureau of Labor Statistics (BLS), the estimated annual salary for most network and computer systems administrators ranged between $37,470 and $92,130.

Employment Prospects

IT Engineers work for all sorts of organizations and industries in both the public and private sectors. They are employed by private companies, hospitals, schools, libraries, government agencies, nonprofit organizations, research institutes, consulting firms, engineering services, computer hardware vendors, and other establishments.

Job opportunities are widely available due to the continuing development in new and more complex applications and technologies and the need of businesses, governmental agencies, and other organizations to maintain and upgrade safe and secure information systems. Because many organizations do not have the resources to employ permanent staff, they hire IT Engineers on a temporary basis for part-time or full-time work, as well as use freelancers or independent consultants. According to an expert in the field, there is a fair amount of competition for positions. Experienced IT Engineers with the specific skills sought by employers have the best opportunities.

Advancement Prospects

As engineers gain experience, they are assigned to more complex projects as well as receive increasingly greater responsibilities.

IT Engineers may advance in any number of ways, depending on their ambitions and interests. They might become technical specialists and consultants. They might pursue engineering management positions. Those with entrepreneurial ambitions can become independent contractors or owners of companies that offer technical or consulting services.

Education and Training

Educational requirements vary from employer to employer. Minimally, some employers require an associate degree, while others prefer a bachelor's degree. College degrees may have been earned in computer science, information science, information technology, or another related field. Employers sometimes hire applicants with a high school diploma, if they have qualifying work experience.

Novice IT Engineers usually receive on-the-job training while working under the guidance and supervision of experienced engineers. Some companies also provide formal classroom training programs.

Throughout their careers, IT Engineers enroll in continuing education and training programs to update their skills and keep up with advancements in their fields.

Experience, Special Skills, and Personality Traits

Entry-level candidates should have work experience related to the positions for which they apply. They may have gained their experience through internships, work-study programs, student research projects, postdoctoral training, or part-time employment. Candidates who have experience in customer support, computer operations, or system administration are desired by employers.

To perform well at their job, IT Engineers must have strong writing, problem-solving, and analytical skills. They also need effective communication, interpersonal, customer service, and leadership skills, as they must work well with various people from different backgrounds. Being organized, energetic, self-motivated, creative, resourceful, reliable, flexible, and detail-oriented are some personality traits that successful IT Engineers share.

Unions and Associations

IT Engineers can join professional associations to take advantage of networking opportunities, continuing education programs, and other professional services and resources. Societies available at the national level are the Association of Information Technology Professionals, Association for Computing Machinery, IEEE Computer Society, and SAGE (a USENIX Association Special Interest Group). For contact information, see Appendix III.

Tips for Entry

1. How well-rounded are you? Employers also look at the general interests of prospective applicants. While in high school or college, you might participate in one or more intramural sports, school clubs, or community organizations.
2. Many employers prefer to hire applicants who have work experience within their industry.
3. Some employers have a selection process that includes the ability to pass a background investigation and a drug screening.
4. Many IT Engineers obtain professional or technical certifications on a voluntary basis to enhance their employability.
5. Use the Internet to learn more about IT Engineers. You might start by visiting these Web sites: SAGE, http://sage-web.sage.org; and Earth Web.com: The IT Industry Portal, http://www.earthweb.com. For more links, see Appendix IV.

AEROSPACE ENGINEERING

AEROSPACE ENGINEER

CAREER PROFILE

Duties: Research, design, develop, test, manufacture, and maintain aircraft, spacecraft, rockets, and missiles as well as their engines, parts, components, and systems; perform duties as required

Alternate Title(s): Aeronautical Engineer, Astronautical Engineer; a title that reflects a specialty (such as Avionics Engineer) or an engineering function (such as Design Engineer)

Salary Range: $56,000 to $115,000

Employment Prospects: Fair

Advancement Prospects: Good

Prerequisites:

Education or Training—Bachelor's degree in aerospace engineering or a related field; on-the-job training

Experience—Previous work experience generally required

Special Skills and Personality Traits—Teamwork, interpersonal, communication, writing, problem-solving, and analytical skills; curious, logical, creative, detail-oriented, flexible, and dedicated

Special Requirements—Professional engineer (P.E.) licensure may be required

CAREER LADDER

```
┌─────────────────────────────────┐
│   Senior Aerospace Engineer     │
└─────────────────────────────────┘

┌─────────────────────────────────┐
│      Aerospace Engineer         │
└─────────────────────────────────┘

┌─────────────────────────────────┐
│   Junior Aerospace Engineer     │
└─────────────────────────────────┘
```

Position Description

Human beings have always been fascinated by the power of flight. Our ancestors gazed into the sky and longingly watched birds soar among the clouds. They told myths and fables about angels and about magical people who could fly or attempted to fly by constructing wings that strapped onto their arms. It was not until the late 18th century, however, that humans actually took flight in balloons. During ensuing decades, balloons became more sophisticated and pervasive as a means for human flight. Meanwhile, people began to experiment with gliders, which allowed them to fly short distances, but without engines. They also designed and tried to fly airplanes, but it was not until 1903 that Orville and Wilbur Wright made the first successful airplane flight.

In just a little over one hundred years, human beings have been flying as if it were second nature. Travelers routinely fly great distances in commercial airliners. Astronauts have flown into outer space and to the moon and back. The machines that enable us to travel to such magnificent heights are increasingly safe and sophisticated, thanks to the men and women who design them—Aerospace Engineers.

Aerospace engineering is a field that is both diverse and specialized. Aerospace Engineers are involved in the research, design, development, testing, and manufacturing of aircraft, spacecraft, rockets, and missile systems as well as of their engines, parts, components, and systems. They also assist with the design and implementation of space missions, including selecting the appropriate launch vehicle, scheduling the launch time, analyzing and plotting missile trajectories and spacecraft routes, and determining which equipment and personnel are the best to complete the mission.

Aerospace Engineers apply the principles of aerodynamics, aeroacoustics, astrodynamics, fluid dynamics, flight dynamics and structures, thermodynamics, propulsion, and energy conversion to their work. With this knowledge, they are able to design improved aircraft and propel spacecraft beyond Earth's orbit. For example, they improve aircraft landing systems and select engine materials that withstand extreme temperature. They also apply this specialized knowledge to such earthbound activities as studying the impact of wind on buildings or researching new designs for artificial hearts. In addition, these engineers help doctors to understand how blood circulation is affected by gravity-free space flights. Furthermore, Aerospace Engineers help develop aviation and aerospace safety standards.

Aerospace engineering consists of two basic divisions: aeronautics and astronautics. Aeronautical engineering is concerned particularly with aircraft and systems that operate within the Earth's atmosphere. Aerospace Engineers who work in this field design and analyze the internal structure of aircraft, create autopilot systems, build and test rocket or jet engines, conduct wind tunnel tests, and so forth. The aircraft that they design are for both military and civilian applications.

Astronautical engineering, on the other hand, is specifically involved with designing missiles or launch vehicles as well as manned or unmanned spacecraft, such as the space shuttle or satellites. Aerospace Engineers in this area of concern calculate the orbits that spacecraft will take around the Earth, design satellite components, plan for future space missions, work toward improving propulsion and power systems, design communication systems, and so on.

Further, Aerospace Engineers specialize by focusing their expertise in a particular specialty of aerospace engineering. Some of these areas include stress analysis, aerodynamics, propulsion, fluid mechanics, structural design, celestial mechanics, navigational systems, flight tests, cost analysis, instrumentation, and guidance and control systems. They also specialize in a specific kind of aircraft or spacecraft, such as commercial airliners, helicopters, fighter jets, satellites, or missiles and rockets.

Aerospace Engineers also specialize in performing specific engineering functions in the process of designing and producing aerospace products. The following are just a few of the various types of positions that they might fill.

- Research engineers use their understanding of science, mathematics, and engineering to develop new or improved products or manufacturing methods.
- Analytical engineers conduct in-depth assessments of proposed products and evaluate whether the design of each product meets customer requirements, or will withstand a variety of stress factors.
- Design engineers take the concept or working model of a product and create a design that meets production requirements in addition to such specifications as aerodynamics or astrodynamics, structure, and weight.
- Test engineers design, conduct, oversee, and review the testing of aircraft in wind tunnels, as well as in actual flights, from which they may determine the performance of propulsion, aerodynamics, stability, and other factors.

- Project engineers plan, direct, and coordinate activities of aerospace projects.
- Sales engineers contact customers and make sales presentations to demonstrate how products or services can fulfill their immediate or future needs.
- Field service engineers examine performance reports on products and make recommendations to solve problems.

Aerospace Engineers use computer-aided design (CAD) systems, robotics, advanced optics, and laser technologies in the course of their work. The technologies that they develop are used throughout the aerospace and aviation industries, but are also used in everyday products such as Teflon, Velcro, hand-held calculators, and freeze-dried foods.

Most Aerospace Engineers work for large aerospace companies such as Boeing, Lockheed Martin, or Pratt and Whitney, as well as for government agencies like the National Aeronautics and Space Administration (NASA) or for the military. Others find work in companies that provide such services as mechanical engineering, electrical engineering, ship design, or civil engineering, as well as in the automotive and computer industries. Some work in the areas of building design, robotics, power plant design, weapons design, or aerospace products and parts. Still others find work in academic environments as university professors or researchers.

Many of the tasks that Aerospace Engineers perform are specific to their particular functions. Engineers commonly perform other general duties. For example, they might:

- develop plans, procedures, and systems
- review and evaluate data, plans, designs, documentation, specifications, or procedures
- troubleshoot problems
- provide estimates of cost, time, quantities, materials, and so on
- prepare correspondence, reports, proposals, and other documents
- prepare blueprints and mathematical calculations for plans or designs
- attend project and departmental meetings
- provide advice and consultation to others
- supervise technicians and other staff members

There are several levels of expertise within the aerospace engineering profession. Junior engineers typically work under the guidance and supervision of senior engineers. Their focus is to develop their skills and their understanding of the rules, regulations, standards, and practices of their area of concern. As engineers gain experience and knowledge, they receive more complex assignments and are able to exercise greater levels of authority.

Senior engineers are more actively involved with the decision-making process and are more likely to be team leaders. They are more aware of program needs and work independently in response to those needs. Advanced to executive-level engineers are the primary engineers for project divisions. They are responsible for top-level project management, client management, and business development and administration. They also make policy decisions and consult with clients or government agencies.

Aerospace Engineers mostly work with other engineers within their organization or at other similar workplaces. They also interact regularly with other people in a wide range of occupations. Aerospace Engineers work in offices and laboratories as well as in machine shops and manufacturing plants. They usually work a 40-hour week but put in additional hours to complete tasks or to meet deadlines. Engineers sometimes travel to attend training sessions or professional conferences.

Salaries

Salaries for Aerospace Engineers vary, depending on such factors as their education, experience, job, employer, and geographical location. According to the November 2004 *Occupational Employment Statistics* (OES) survey by the U.S. Bureau of Labor Statistics (BLS), the estimated annual salary for most Aerospace Engineers ranged between $56,190 and $114,950.

Employment Prospects

The BLS reported in its November 2004 OES survey that about 79,730 Aerospace Engineers were employed in the United States. Almost 50 percent of them were employed by the aerospace industry. The four other major industries that employed Aerospace Engineers included the federal government; the architectural and engineering services industry; the scientific research and development services industry; and the communications equipment manufacturing industry.

Although the job growth for Aerospace Engineers is predicted to decline through 2014, according to the BLS, opportunities should still be favorable. Aerospace Engineers will be needed to replace those who retire, advance to higher positions, or transfer to other jobs. The BLS further reports that the number of students graduating in aerospace has declined in recent years, which may lead to an increasing demand for Aerospace Engineers, especially since a large number of Aerospace Engineers are expected to retire within the coming years.

Keep in mind that the job market for Aerospace Engineers is dependent on such factors as the state of the economy, and the demand for products by the military and the federal government as well as by the airlines, corporations, private pilots, and other civilian consumers.

Advancement Prospects

Aerospace Engineers can advance in any number of ways, depending on their ambitions and interests. They can become technical specialists, consultants, engineering managers, and executive officers. Engineers with entrepreneurial ambitions can become independent consultants or owners of technical or consulting firms.

Education and Training

Entry-level applicants need at least a bachelor's degree in aerospace engineering, mechanical engineering, electrical engineering, or another related field. Some employers prefer to hire applicants who have a master's or doctoral degree. An advanced degree is usually required for engineers to advance to careers in management, consulting, research, or teaching. Engineers must possess a doctoral degree to teach aerospace engineering at the college level.

Employers typically provide new employees with training programs, which may include on-the-job training and formal classroom training programs. Entry-level engineers usually work under the supervision and guidance of senior engineers.

Throughout their careers, Aerospace Engineers enroll in continuing education programs and training programs to update their skills and keep up with advancements in their fields.

Special Requirements

Aerospace Engineers who offer their services directly to the public or perform work that affects the life, health, or property of the public must be licensed as professional engineers (P.E.). Every state and territory, as well as Washington, D.C., has its own licensing requirements. For specific information, contact the board of engineering examiners for the area where you wish to practice. See Appendix II for a list of boards.

Experience, Special Skills, and Personality Traits

Entry-level candidates should have work experience related to the positions for which they apply. Having experience in the aerospace industry is desirable. They may have gained their experience through internships, work-study programs, student research projects, postdoctoral training, or part-time employment.

Because they must work well with colleagues, managers, and others, Aerospace Engineers must have effective teamwork, interpersonal, and communication skills. Additionally, they need strong writing, problem-solving, and analytical skills. Being curious, logical, creative, detail-oriented, flexible, and dedicated are some personality traits that successful Aerospace Engineers share.

Unions and Associations

At some aerospace plants, Aerospace Engineers are members of a labor union that represents them in negotiations with employers. The union seeks the best contractual terms relating to wages, benefits, and working conditions.

Many Aerospace Engineers join professional associations to take advantage of networking opportunities, continuing education programs, and other professional services and resources. Some of the national societies that serve the diverse interests of these engineers include:

- American Institute of Aeronautics and Astronautics
- American Astronautical Society
- Institute of Electrical and Electronics Engineers
- ASME International
- Society of Flight Test Engineers
- Society of Women Engineers
- National Society of Professional Engineers

For contact information, see Appendix III.

Tips for Entry

1. In high school, start learning about aerospace and engineering. You might take up model rocketry, remote-controlled aircraft, or flying as a hobby. You can read books, magazines, and Web sites related to aerospace, as well as visit aerospace museums and participate in summer youth programs related to aerospace or engineering.

2. Some aerospace companies recruit for entry-level jobs on campus. Even if you won't be graduating soon, talk with the recruiters. Learn about the companies. Also ask about internship or work-study opportunities that they might have.

3. To learn about available jobs with the U.S. government, visit USAJOBS on the Internet (which is part of the Office of Personnel and Management Web site) at http://www.usajobs.opm.gov.

4. Learn more about Aerospace Engineers on the Internet. You might start by visiting these Web sites: Aerospace Industries Association, http://www.aia-aerospace.org; and American Institute of Aeronautics and Astronautics, http://www.aiaa.org. For more links, see Appendix IV.

AVIONICS ENGINEER

CAREER PROFILE

Duties: Research, develop, design, test, produce, and install electronics and electro-mechanical and computer systems on board aircraft, spacecraft, missiles, and rockets; perform duties as required

Alternate Title(s): A title that reflects a specialty (such as Avionics Software Engineer or Acoustica Engineer) or an engineering function (such as Design Engineer or Test Engineer)

Salary Range: $49,000 to $114,000

Employment Prospects: Good

Advancement Prospects: Good

Prerequisites:

Education or Training—Bachelor's degree in electrical engineering or another related field; on-the-job training

Experience—Previous work experience generally required

Special Skills and Personality Traits—Interpersonal, teamwork, writing, communication, and presentation skills; persistent, flexible, creative, innovative, and self-motivated

Special Requirements—Professional engineer (P.E.) licensure may be required

CAREER LADDER

```
┌─────────────────────────────┐
│   Senior Avionics Engineer   │
└─────────────────────────────┘

┌─────────────────────────────┐
│      Avionics Engineer       │
└─────────────────────────────┘

┌─────────────────────────────┐
│   Junior Avionics Engineer   │
└─────────────────────────────┘
```

Position Description

When entering an airplane, we sometimes get a glimpse of the interior of the cockpit, where the pilot sits. Whether the plane is a large commercial jetliner or a small single-engine private plane, the electronic gadgetry within looks formidably complicated. The dials, gauges, buttons, and switches are all significant to the pilot. These electronic devices keep track of everything that is happening on the aircraft. The electronic systems on board aircraft are called avionics. More specifically, avionics refers to all of the electronic systems and imbedded computer devices that check and control an aircraft's mechanical and electrical systems. These include communication, navigation and identification systems, autopilot systems, flight control systems, engine control systems, and power distribution systems, as well as the electronic flight management systems. On military aircraft, avionics also includes systems for weapons delivery and reconnaissance. Sometimes an aircraft's other electronic systems that are not used by pilots, such as passenger video terminals, are also considered to be avionics. Avionics systems include both hardware and software components, and are designed and installed by professionals called Avionics Engineers.

Avionics Engineers are involved in researching, developing, designing, testing, manufacturing, and installing all avionics systems on aircraft, spacecraft, missiles, rockets, and satellites. There are several areas in which these engineers may specialize. They may be engaged in a particular engineering discipline, such as acoustica engineering, mechanical engineering, reliability engineering, hardware design engineering, or software engineering. They may specialize according to their area of work—commercial aviation, general aviation, military aviation, etc.—or type of aircraft such as single-engine airplanes, helicopters, fighter jets, and spacecraft.

Avionics Engineers may also specialize in the types of units on which they work, such as distance measuring equipment or, in particular, such avionics systems as navigation, flight control, or communications systems. Further, Avionics Engineers may be involved in specific engineering functions, such as research, design, testing, or project management. For example, test engineers are involved in the testing and evaluation of systems to make sure that they adhere to manufacturer specifications and meet Federal Aviation Administration (FAA) requirements.

Avionics Engineers are responsible for performing certain tasks on a regular basis. For example, they might:

- play a part in the planning, developing, coordination, and directing of large or small engineering projects of varying complexity
- participate in evaluating designs, conducting trade studies, and reviewing design development projects
- prepare diagrams for electrical installation
- perform concept and cost studies in coordination with materials vendors and clients
- ensure that projects and associated contractors provide avionics products that meet requirements within cost, and schedule them accordingly
- make sure that the work performed meets with federal aviation regulations (FAR) requirements
- develop software that recognizes in-flight anomalies or failures
- identify the need for safety improvements
- provide technical assistance to other engineers or technicians
- keep up-to-date with the latest developments in the field of avionics or other aircraft fields to recommend innovations or improvements

Avionics Engineers generally work in groups comprised of other engineers, scientists, technicians, and other personnel. Their working environment is typically within an office setting, although their duties may require that they complete tasks in laboratories, factories, or on test flights. Some Avionics Engineers may be required to travel to complete their duties. They usually work for 40 hours per week but may occasionally put in additional hours to complete duties and projects.

Salaries

Salaries for Avionics Engineers vary, depending on such factors as their education, experience, employer, and geographical location. Specific salary information for Avionics Engineers is unavailable, but they earn salaries similar to electronics engineers. The estimated annual salary for most electronics engineers ranged between $49,430 and $113,530, according to the November 2004 *Occupational Employment Statistics* survey by the U.S. Bureau of Labor Statistics.

Employment Prospects

Most Avionics Engineers work for large avionics companies, such as Rockwell Collins, Honeywell, and Motorola.

Some find employment in companies that manufacture airframes or subassemblies; some work in repair shops. Many of these engineers are employed by government agencies such as the National Aeronautics and Space Administration (NASA), the FAA, and the Department of Transportation, as well as by the military. Still others find work as researchers in academic institutions or government research centers.

Opportunities for Avionics Engineers are favorable, and should remain good for the next several years, partly due to the many engineers who are approaching retirement age. Keep in mind that the job market for avionics specialists is generally driven by the development of new airplanes and defense spending in which the military requires new or updated aircraft and weapon systems.

Advancement Prospects

As Avionics Engineers gain experience, they are assigned to more complex projects as well as receive increasingly greater responsibilities. Their advancement prospects vary, depending on their ambitions and interests. They can become technical specialists or consultants. Engineers with management and administrative interests and talents can seek positions as supervisory, project, and chief engineers. In addition, Avionics Engineers can advance to executive officer positions within their organization. Engineers with entrepreneurial ambitions can become independent consultants or owners of technical or consulting firms. They can also pursue careers as teachers in academic institutions.

Education and Training

Minimally, applicants for entry-level positions must possess a bachelor's degree in electrical engineering, electrical engineering technology, aeronautical engineering, mechanical engineering, computer science, or another related field. A master's or doctoral degree is usually required for engineers to pursue careers in management, consulting, research, or teaching.

Employers typically provide new employees with training programs, which may include on-the-job training and formal classroom training programs. Entry-level engineers usually work under the supervision and guidance of senior engineers.

Throughout their careers, Avionics Engineers enroll in continuing education programs and training programs to update their skills and keep up with advancements in their fields.

Special Requirements

Avionics Engineers who offer their services directly to the public or perform work that affects the life, health, or property of the public must be licensed as professional engineers (P.E.). Every state and territory, as well as Washington, D.C., has its own requirements for P.E. licensure. For specific information, contact the board of engineering examiners for the area where you wish to practice. See Appendix II for a list of boards.

Experience, Special Skills, and Personality Traits

Entry-level candidates should have work experience related to the positions for which they apply. Having experience in the aerospace industry is desirable. They may have gained their experience through internships, work-study programs, student research projects, or part-time employment.

Avionics Engineers require effective interpersonal and teamwork skills, as they must work well with colleagues, managers, and others from diverse backgrounds. Their job also requires that they have strong writing, communication, and presentation skills. Being persistent, flexible, creative, innovative, and self-motivated are some personality traits that successful Avionics Engineers have in common.

Unions and Associations

Avionics Engineers can join local, state, and national societies to take advantage of networking opportunities, continuing education programs, and other professional services and resources. For example, they are eligible to join such national engineering societies as the Institute of Electrical and Electronics Engineers, the American Institute of Aeronautics and Astronautics, or the Society of Women Engineers. Professional engineers can belong to the National Society of Professional engineers. For contact information, see Appendix III.

Tips for Entry

1. Before filling in a job application, go over the job description for the position you are seeking. How do your work experience, skills, and knowledge match the job description? When you fill out your application, be sure your descriptions clearly demonstrate how you are qualified for the job.
2. Being computer literate is essential. You should be knowledgeable about word processing, spreadsheet, and presentation applications as well as software modeling tools.
3. Some companies hire only candidates who can obtain and maintain a security clearance.
4. You can learn more about avionics engineering on the Internet. To get a list of Web sites, enter the keywords *avionics engineering or avionics engineers* in a search engine. To learn about some links, see Appendix IV.

FLIGHT TEST ENGINEER

CAREER PROFILE

Duties: Conduct flight tests and evaluations of aircraft characteristics, performance, and systems; perform duties as required

Alternate Title(s): Test Operations Engineer

Salary Range: $56,000 to $115,000

Employment Prospects: Fair

Advancement Prospects: Good

Prerequisites:

  Education or Training—Bachelor's degree in aerospace engineering or a related field; on-the-job training

  Experience—Previous work experience generally required

  Special Skills and Personality Traits—Teamwork, interpersonal, communication, writing, problem-solving, and critical thinking skills; logical, detail-oriented, persistent, flexible, and cooperative

CAREER LADDER

```
┌─────────────────────────────────┐
│   Senior Flight Test Engineer    │
└─────────────────────────────────┘

┌─────────────────────────────────┐
│      Flight Test Engineer        │
└─────────────────────────────────┘

┌─────────────────────────────────┐
│   Junior Flight Test Engineer    │
└─────────────────────────────────┘
```

Position Description

When we fly—whether in a large airliner, a military troop transport plane, a single-engine airplane, or a helicopter—it is with the expectation and assurance that the flight will be smooth and free of hazards. The pilot will be able to keep the aircraft on a steady course and all the aircraft's equipment, components, and instruments are in working order. Perhaps we fly with the realization that the aircraft was thoroughly tested before it was brought into service, and we know that a qualified pilot tested it in flight. What we may not realize, however, is that other professionals known as Flight Test Engineers had a hand in the testing process.

Flight Test Engineers test and evaluate newly designed or updated aircraft. They help determine if an aircraft is capable of flight, and they examine the aircraft's handling capabilities and performance.

These engineers are responsible for planning each test according to standard formats. They must obtain the appropriate testing gear and write a plan for the test before conducting the test. Once the testing procedures are completed, they must write a clear, concise report that describes and comments about the test procedures and results.

They work in teams that include other Flight Test Engineers and test pilots. Flight testing is conducted in various stages and in several locales because a variety of factors such as weather conditions must be taken into consideration. For example, some tests are conducted during takeoff, while others are conducted mid-flight or during landing. Takeoff testing is generally completed in calm conditions, but other phases of testing are conducted in turbulent conditions. Some testing is done with certain types of runways, and at varying ground or air speeds. Contingency tests are arranged in case the required conditions cannot be met. Hence, the aircraft must be taken to wherever conditions are favorable. Flight Test Engineers are therefore required to travel frequently. Testing an aircraft may take several weeks, while each phase of the test may take several hours to complete.

Aircraft are tested thoroughly. Every part is monitored and evaluated, including the airframe, the engine and landing gear, and the units that receive data from the flight deck to control the aircraft's systems. The testing equipment is very complex, and allows the Flight Test Engineers to record precise measurements at any given point in time during the test flight. Different tests focus on an aircraft's maneuverability and acceleration capabilities, fuel efficiency, structural stresses, avionics (electronic equipment) performance, and so on.

Flight Test Engineers are present for onboard testing of large aircraft, but much of their testing, particularly for smaller aircraft, is done in wind tunnels or in control rooms on the ground. In those settings, they monitor banks of computer monitors and other electronic equipment to observe the streams of data that are recorded while the aircraft is in flight.

When these engineers do have occasion to fly, they do so as passengers and conduct hardware and software tests or collect other data while the aircraft is flying. They also make sure that the aircraft works according to specifications. Onboard tests include the tracking of fuel usage, checking the landing gear positions, and monitoring ballast for shifts in the center of gravity.

Gathering, interpreting, and reporting all the data that is recorded during flight tests are important duties that Flight Test Engineers perform. They use electronic data recorded by their equipment as well as spoken or written reports provided by the test pilots. In addition, the equipment that is used on board during the testing must be readily available for use. Hence, these engineers maintain a stock of such calibrated anad sensitive instruments as transducers, sensors, probes, air data booms, portable weather stations, and position measuring equipment.

Flight Test Engineers have specific tasks that they perform, such as:

- compile test documents for each flight or test point
- make sure that flight test data has been recovered and made ready for inputting to the test database
- coordinate test requests for authorization and implementation
- assist in organizing test pilots and other engineers and with implementing instrumentation to make sure that the aircraft is properly set up to satisfy testing goals
- ensure that aircraft is ready to be flown and tested on schedule
- review evacuation plans and each crew member's responsibilities before each test
- write procedures manuals for test pilots
- prepare presentations for meetings and conferences

Because flight testing is a high-risk venture, Flight Test Engineers are trained in first aid, CPR, and firefighting.

Depending on the size of the aircraft, or the size of their organization, some of these engineers specialize in flying in aircraft for in-flight testing. They may also be assigned to specific activities, such as conducting tests on specific types of aircraft, setting up the instrumentation, performing certain tests, planning or scheduling tests, analyzing data, or preparing reports.

Flight Test Engineers work long hours, and travel to various locations as required.

Salaries

Salaries for Flight Test Engineers vary, depending on such factors as their education, experience, employer, and geo-

graphical location. Specific salary information for these engineers is unavailable, but they generally earn salaries similar to aerospace engineers. According to the November 2004 *Occupational Employment Statistics* survey by the U.S. Bureau of Labor Statistics, the estimated annual salary for most Aerospace Engineers ranged between $56,190 and $114,950.

Employment Prospects

The U.S. government is the largest employer of Flight Test Engineers. Most of them work as military and civilian Flight Test Engineers in the U.S. Department of Defense. Some Flight Test Engineers are employed by the National Aeronautics and Space Administration (NASA) and the Federal Aviation Administration (FAA). These engineers can also find employment with private companies; some of the larger private employers are Boeing, Lockheed Martin, and Northrop Grumman.

According to some experts in the field, the job market is generally good, especially for experienced Flight Test Engineers. The federal government usually offers more opportunities for recent graduates. Keep in mind that the job market in the aerospace industry is dependent on such factors as the state of the economy and the demand for products by the military and the federal government as well as by the airlines, corporations, private pilots, and other civilian consumers.

Advancement Prospects

Flight Test Engineers may advance in any number of ways, depending on their ambitions and interests. They can become technical specialists and consultants as well as pursue supervisory and management positions, such as lead engineer, project manager, and chief engineer. As they become highly experienced, entrepreneurial engineers can become independent consultants or owners of technical or consulting firms.

Education and Training

Minimally, a bachelor's degree in aerospace engineering, electrical engineering, mechanical engineering, or another engineering field is needed for candidates seeking entry-level positions. Employers typically provide novice Flight Test Engineers with training, which can involve on-the-job training and formal classroom training programs.

Throughout their careers, Flight Test Engineers enroll in training and continuing education programs to update their skills and keep up with advancements in their fields.

Experience, Special Skills, and Personality Traits

Entry-level candidates should have work experience related to the positions for which they apply. They may have gained

their experience through internships, work-study programs, student research projects, or employment.

To perform well at their job, these engineers need excellent teamwork, interpersonal, communication, writing, problem-solving, and critical thinking skills. Being logical, detail-oriented, persistent, flexible, and cooperative are some personality traits that successful Flight Test Engineers share.

Unions and Associations

The Society of Flight Test Engineers and the American Institute of Aeronautics and Astronautics are two national societies that serve the interests of Flight Test Engineers. By joining a professional association, engineers can take advantage of various professional services and resources, such as continuing education programs, publications, and networking opportunities. For contact information for the above organizations, see Appendix III.

Tips for Entry

1. Talk with Flight Test Engineers to learn more about their work and how they got their jobs.
2. When doing a job search, be sure to contact people with whom you have worked during your internships or work study programs. Also talk with your professors and peers.
3. Contact prospective employers directly for information about job vacancies and their selection process.
4. Learn more about flight test engineering on the Internet. You might start by visiting the Society of Flight Test Engineers Web site at http://www.sfte.org. For more links, see Appendix IV.

NASA ENGINEER

CAREER PROFILE

Duties: Conduct basic or applied research in aeronautics, space phenomena, or another area; perform duties as required

Alternate Title(s): Aerospace Technologist; a title that reflects a specialty such as Aerospace Engineer or Mechanical Engineer

Salary Range: $31,000 to $119,000

Employment Prospects: Fair

Advancement Prospects: Good

Prerequisites:

Education or Training—Bachelor's degree in an engineering, science, or mathematics field

Experience—One year of work experience

Special Skills and Personality Traits—Teamwork, interpersonal, communication, research, writing, organizational, and problem-solving skills; enthusiastic, creative, innovative, persistent, and hard working

CAREER LADDER

```
┌─────────────────────────┐
│     Senior Engineer     │
└─────────────────────────┘

┌─────────────────────────┐
│        Engineer         │
└─────────────────────────┘

┌─────────────────────────┐
│     Junior Engineer     │
└─────────────────────────┘
```

Position Description

We live in what is commonly called the space age. Since the middle of the 20th century, humans have rocketed man-made objects, animals, and human beings beyond the confines of the Earth's atmosphere and gravity field. Many of those objects continue to orbit the Earth, while others have probed the far reaches of our solar system and beyond. We have sent men to walk on the moon and brought them safely back to Earth. Robotic devices crawl along the surface of Mars and beam photographs and other data back to Earth. Satellites orbit the Earth on a continuing basis to monitor our weather, transmit television broadcasts, and gather all sorts of information. The International Space Station, on which crews of men and women conduct experiments, orbits the Earth. Many of these projects have been made possible through the auspices of the National Aeronautics and Space Administration (NASA), the U.S. government agency responsible for space exploration. More specifically, these space faring projects and technologies were designed by NASA Engineers.

Engineers and scientists comprise more than half the professional workforce at NASA and are generally referred to as aerospace technologists. They hold backgrounds in the various fields of science, engineering, and mathematics.

NASA Engineers may be engaged in conducting basic or applied research. They conduct basic research to gain further understanding and knowledge about space phenomena and the science of aeronautics. For example, they investigate the behavior of materials and structures in different environments and propulsion systems. Those NASA Engineers involved in applied research are concerned with applying scientific knowledge to develop and design new or improved space vehicles, devices, instrumentation, products, and processes. In addition, many of the technologies and products that NASA Engineers and scientists have invented are now being used in medicine, construction, transportation, food manufacturing, firefighting, and other areas to make lives on Earth healthier and safer.

Aerospace research and development at NASA is generally divided into different subject areas, which are further subdivided into specialties. The following are a few of the subject areas in which NASA Engineers work:

• Aerospace engineering: Engineers specialize in creating new or improved technologies for aircraft, spacecraft, missiles, and related parts.

- Electrical and electronic systems: Engineers work on the various electrical components and systems that run aircraft, spacecraft, missiles, and rockets.
- Fluid and flight mechanics: Engineers investigate, develop, test, and evaluate the fluid and flight mechanics that pertain to aircraft and space vehicles.
- Materials and structures: Engineers research, develop, design, manufacture, fabricate, process, test, and evaluate the many kinds of metallic and nonmetallic materials that may be used in aircraft and space vehicles, as well as the structures that are used in all phases of ground support for space travel.
- Propulsion and power: Engineers are concerned with studying, developing, designing, testing, and evaluating various propulsion systems (such as liquid, solid, chemical, nuclear, and antimatter) and aerospace power generation systems, along with their parts and subsystems.
- Data systems: Engineers research, design, develop, test, and evaluate computer hardware and software systems for aerospace and aeronautical purposes, including onboard computer and ground control computer systems.

NASA Engineers collaborate on research projects with other engineers, scientists, mathematicians, technicians, research assistants, and other personnel. Their work varies each day, as they perform various tasks. For example, NASA Engineers might conduct experiments, analyze and interpret data, conduct research on the World Wide Web, read scientific journals and other research literature, plan and organize their work schedules, meet with colleagues to discuss projects, and prepare written reports. Many of them also supervise research assistants and technicians who provide administrative and research support.

NASA Engineers are expected to stay up-to-date with developments and technologies in their disciplines. This involves various activities, such as reading professional journals and books, attending professional conferences, enrolling in educational or training programs, and networking with colleagues.

These engineers work in full-time, permanent, or temporary positions. They mostly work indoors in offices and laboratories. They generally work 40 hours a week but put in additional hours whenever necessary to complete various tasks. On occasion, they may be required to travel to various NASA locations to perform their duties.

Salaries
Wages for NASA Engineers vary, depending on such factors as their education, experience, pay rank, and geographical location. Their salaries are based on the federal pay schedule called the general schedule (GS). Depending on their qualifications, new NASA Engineers usually receive starting salaries ranging from the GS-7 to GS-11 levels. They can advance up to the GS-15 level. In 2006, the annual basic pay for the GS-7 to GS-15 levels ranged from $31,209 to $118,957. Employees in metropolitan areas earn additional pay for living in an area with a higher cost of living.

To qualify for entry-level positions at a higher salary, job candidates generally need a master's or doctoral degree if they do not have the required minimum number of years of work experience.

Employment Prospects
As of 2005, NASA employed over 19,000 workers, of which more than half were engineers and scientists. NASA Engineers work throughout the United States. They work mostly in NASA centers and facilities, such as the Johnson Space Center in Houston, Texas, the Marshall Space Flight Center in Huntsville, Alabama, or the Ames Research Center in Mountain View, California.

Opportunities generally become available as NASA Engineers retire, advance to higher positions, or transfer to other jobs. Job prospects are expected to be good in the coming years due to the large number of employees who will soon become eligible for retirement. The number of engineering graduates in the last few years has declined; thus, NASA must compete with the private sector, educational institutions, and other employers for the best job candidates.

NASA hires only U.S. citizens for permanent positions.

Advancement Prospects
As NASA Engineers gain experience, they can seek transfers to positions that interest them. Senior engineers can advance to lead, supervisory, and managerial positions. Those with entrepreneurial interests might pursue careers as independent consultants or owners of firms that offer technical or consulting services to NASA and other clients.

Education and Training
Minimally, applicants for entry-level positions must possess a bachelor's degree in an appropriate field of engineering, science, or mathematics. Degrees in engineering technology are unacceptable. A master's or doctoral degree may be required for engineers to qualify for some research positions.

Entry-level engineers typically receive on-the-job training while working under the supervision and guidance of experienced engineers.

Throughout their careers, NASA Engineers enroll in continuing education and training programs to update their skills and keep up with advancements in their fields.

Experience, Special Skills, and Personality Traits
To enter at the GS-7 level, applicants must have at least one year of professional work experience related to the positions for which they apply. They may have gained their work experience through summer employment, internships, work-study

programs, or research assistantships. They may substitute a master's degree for the work experience requirement.

NASA Engineers need excellent teamwork, interpersonal, and communication skills, as they must work well with colleagues, managers, and others from diverse backgrounds. In addition, their jobs require that they have effective research, writing, organizational, and problem-solving skills.

Some personality traits that successful NASA Engineers share include being enthusiastic, creative, innovative, persistent, and hard working.

Unions and Associations

Many NASA Engineers belong to professional associations to take advantage of networking opportunities, continuing education programs, publications, and other professional services and resources. They join societies that serve their particular fields and interests. For example, some of the various national engineering societies are:

- American Institute of Aeronautics and Astronautics
- American Association for Artificial Intelligence
- Association for Computing Machinery
- ASME International
- Institute of Electrical and Electronics Engineers
- Society of Women Engineers
- Society of Hispanic Professional Engineers

For contact information, see Appendix III.

Tips for Entry

1. NASA offers several types of employment and work study programs for students. For information visit the NASA Student Employment webpage at http://www.nasajobs.nasa.gov/studentopps/employment/default.htm.
2. When you are looking for job vacancies, remember that NASA engineering positions are under the job title *Aerospace Technologist*.
3. NASA visits some colleges and universities to recruit for entry-level positions. Contact your college career center to find out if and when NASA may be coming to your school. If it is not, a counselor should be able to help you find out which nearby schools NASA is visiting.
4. For specific information about NASA employment, visit the NASA Jobs webpage at http://nasajobs.nasa.gov.
5. Explore the world of NASA at its Web site by going to http://www.nasa.gov.

AGRICULTURAL AND BIOLOGICAL ENGINEERING

AGRICULTURAL ENGINEER

CAREER PROFILE

Duties: Research, develop, design, test, and produce solutions to problems concerning agriculture, food systems, and other biological systems; perform duties as required

Alternate Title(s): Biological Systems Engineer, Bioprocess Engineer; a title that reflects a specialty (such as Farm Machinery Engineer) or an engineering function (such as Design Engineer)

Salary Range: $39,000 to $91,000

Employment Prospects: Fair

Advancement Prospects: Good

Prerequisites:

Education or Training—Bachelor's degree in agricultural engineering or a related field; on-the-job training

Experience—Previous work experience generally required

Special Skills and Personality Traits—Leadership, analytical, problem-solving, writing, communication, interpersonal, and teamwork skills; curious, detail-oriented, creative, precise, clever, and enthusiastic

Special Requirements—Professional engineer (P.E.) licensure may be required

CAREER LADDER

```
┌─────────────────────────────────────┐
│     Senior Agricultural Engineer     │
└─────────────────────────────────────┘

┌─────────────────────────────────────┐
│        Agricultural Engineer         │
└─────────────────────────────────────┘

┌─────────────────────────────────────┐
│     Junior Agricultural Engineer     │
└─────────────────────────────────────┘
```

Position Description

Most of us in today's society live in urban or suburban areas. We may travel through rural areas on occasion. We know that our food and other agricultural products are raised and harvested in these locations. What we often overlook, however, is that the processes of growing crops and managing the land are complicated. Fortunately, Agricultural Engineers are professionals who develop solutions to the problems that confront farmers, ranchers, agribusinesses, conservation workers, horticulturists, groundskeepers, and others.

Agricultural Engineers use knowledge of engineering technology, as well as the biological and physical sciences, to research, analyze, and find solutions to agricultural problems. They also utilize relevant knowledge from such fields as mechanical, electrical, environmental, and civil engineering, as well as from construction technology, hydraulics, and soil mechanics. These engineers focus on problems that arise in the use and conservation of soil, water, and forest resources. In addition, they come up with new methods and technologies to improve crop yields, develop new or improved food processing methods, or lengthen the shelf life of foods and other agricultural products. They conduct research on seeds, fertilizers, and pesticides, as well as devise methods to control plant or animal diseases.

These engineers also design and install irrigation and drainage systems, as well as greenhouses, thereby contributing to the efficient use of water and the better management of soil. They oversee conservation procedures. They devise new methods of harvesting crops, and use computers to improve the processing and distribution of agricultural products. Furthermore, Agricultural Engineers design, improve, and test agricultural machinery, vehicles, and equipment, as well as plan and construct farm buildings, rural power systems, flood control projects, and pollution control projects.

One relatively new area of concern for Agricultural Engineers is precision farming, or site-specific farming. They assist farmers to focus their attention on specific sections of acreage to monitor and control the needs for soil amendments, pest controls, or irrigation by using such technologies as Global Positioning Systems (GPS), remote sensing, and instantaneous yield monitors. These technologies help farmers maximize the potential of their land while reducing production costs. At the same time, these technologies have the effect of improving the quality of the environment through decreased usage of chemical fertilizers and pesticides.

Throughout their careers, Agricultural Engineers work in different engineering functions or specialties. Design engineer, product engineer, test engineer, sales engineer, and engineering manager are a few roles in which Agricultural Engineers may be engaged. In addition, some engineers work in colleges and universities as instructors. They teach classes in agricultural engineering as well as conduct research.

Most Agricultural Engineers specialize in the specific areas of agricultural or food processing equipment, soil and water engineering, waste management, new crop development, production and distribution of food or other agricultural products, environmental quality concerns, soil analysis, building farm structures, or aquaculture. Some of these engineers are involved with bioengineering, or biological engineering. For example, they use applied enzymes to convert fats into new substances that are less harmful and that result in healthier food products.

There are several levels of expertise within the agricultural engineering profession. Junior engineers typically work under the guidance and supervision of senior engineers. Their focus is to develop their skills and their understanding of the rules, regulations, standards, and practices of their area of concern. As engineers gain experience and knowledge, they receive more complex assignments and are able to exercise greater levels of authority.

Senior engineers are more actively involved with the decision-making process and are more likely to be team leaders. Their decisions are made without direct supervision. Advanced to executive-level Agricultural Engineers are the primary engineers for project divisions, or for an entire geographical area. These professionals perform the most difficult engineering tasks. They make policy decisions and consult with clients or government agencies at the highest levels. They are also responsible for top-level project management and client management, as well as business development and administration.

Agricultural Engineers work with other people, particularly farmers, scientists, and other engineers. They frequently work with computers, as well as with other equipment and technologies pertinent to their agricultural work, such as lasers, hydraulics, and even robotics. Increasingly, Agricultural Engineers work with GPS and other guidance systems.

They work both indoors and outdoors. Their indoor work is conducted in offices, manufacturing plants, and laboratories. They work at such outdoor locations as farms, construction sites, or in wilderness areas or fish hatcheries. Exposure to some hazardous equipment or substances can be expected, but injury rates are low for these engineers.

Agricultural Engineers usually work a 40-hour week, but longer hours are sometimes required for the completion of projects or for meeting deadlines. Travel to manufacturing facilities, farms, or other locations to attend meetings is a regular part of the life of many Agricultural Engineers.

Salaries

Salaries for Agricultural Engineers vary, depending on such factors as their education, experience, occupation, employer, and geographical location. According to the November 2004 *Occupational Employment Statistics* survey by the U.S. Bureau of Labor Statistics (BLS), the estimated annual salary for most Agricultural Engineers ranged between $38,840 and $91,000.

Employment Prospects

Although much of the work of Agricultural Engineers is directly tied to farming, many of them find work in a wide range of locales, from urban industrial parks to wilderness areas.

Many Agricultural Engineers are employed with local, state, and federal government agencies such as those concerned with soil, water, agriculture, or fisheries. Many of these engineers work for agricultural companies, farm equipment manufacturers, food products companies, engineering firms, management consulting firms, and research and testing services. Some engineers find employment with cooperative extension services, which are nonformal education programs that are sponsored by the U.S. Department of Agriculture and based at land-grant universities. Others are employed as faculty in colleges and universities. In addition, some Agricultural Engineers are self-employed as independent consultants.

In the United States, agricultural engineering is a small field compared to other engineering disciplines. However, opportunities should remain continuously favorable due to the continuing global demand for food supplies at affordable prices. The BLS predicts that job growth for Agricultural Engineers should increase by 9 to 17 percent through 2014. In addition to job growth, opportunities will become available as Agricultural Engineers retire, advance to higher positions, or transfer to other jobs.

Advancement Prospects

Agricultural Engineers may advance in any number of ways, depending on their ambitions and interests. They can become technical specialists and consultants in a particular field, such as agricultural waste management, food safety, or agricultural equipment design. They can pursue career paths in marketing, sales, or other business areas. Engineers with management and administrative interests and talents can seek positions as supervisory, project, and chief engineers, as well as executive officers within their organization. To advance to higher positions, engineers are usually required to possess a master's or doctoral degree. Agricultural Engineers with entrepreneurial ambitions can become independent consultants or owners of technical or consulting firms.

Education and Training

Agricultural Engineers must possess at least a bachelor's degree in agricultural engineering or another engineering discipline. A master's or doctoral degree is usually required to pursue careers in management, consulting, research, or teaching.

Agricultural engineering programs are mostly offered at state colleges and universities that are designated as U.S. land-grant schools. Many programs are changing their names to reflect their particular areas of interest. For example, a program may now be called Agricultural and Biological Engineering or Agricultural and Environmental Engineering.

Employers typically provide entry-level engineers with training programs, which may include both on-the-job training and formal classroom training. New engineers work under the supervision and direction of experienced engineers.

Throughout their careers, Agricultural Engineers enroll in continuing education programs and training programs to update their skills and keep up with advancements in their fields.

Special Requirements

Agricultural Engineers who offer their services directly to the general public or perform work that affects the public safety and welfare must be licensed professional engineers (P.E.). The requirements for P.E. licensure differ in each state and territory, as well as in Washington, D.C. For specific information, contact the board of engineering examiners for the area where you wish to practice. See Appendix II for a list of boards.

Experience, Special Skills, and Personality Traits

Entry-level candidates should have work experience related to the positions for which they apply. They may have gained their experience through internships, work-study programs, student research projects, postdoctoral training, or part-time employment.

To perform well at their various responsibilities, Agricultural Engineers need strong leadership, analytical, problem-solving, writing, and communication skills. And because they must work well with many people from diverse backgrounds, they must have effective interpersonal and teamwork skills.

Some personality traits that successful Agricultural Engineers share are being curious, detail-oriented, creative, precise, clever, and enthusiastic.

Unions and Associations

Agricultural Engineers can join professional societies to take advantage of networking opportunities, continuing education programs, certification, publications, and other professional services and resources. The American Society of Agricultural and Biological Engineers is the major society that serves the interests of Agricultural Engineers. Professional engineers might join the National Society of Professional Engineers. For contact information, see Appendix III.

Tips for Entry

1. While in high school, gain exposure to the agricultural world. For example, you might join the 4-H or the Future Farmers of America.
2. Build up strong writing skills. You want to be able to write technical descriptions that are clear, logical, and easy to understand, particularly by non-technical readers.
3. Obtain an internship or summer employment with a company for which you would like to work after graduation. Many companies offer full-time jobs to graduates who impress them.
4. Learn more about agricultural engineering on the Internet. You might start by visiting the American Society of Agricultural and Biological Engineers at http://www.asabe.org.

BIOSYSTEMS ENGINEER

CAREER PROFILE

Duties: Be involved in the research, development, design, testing, manufacture, and implementation of solutions to problems regarding living systems and to the management of land and water resources; perform duties as required

Alternate Title(s): Biological Engineer, Biological Systems Engineer; a title that reflects a specialty (such as Environmental Engineer) or an engineering function (such as Test Engineer or Product Development Engineer)

Salary Range: $39,000 to $91,000

Employment Prospects: Fair

Advancement Prospects: Good

Prerequisites:

Education or Training—Bachelor's degree in biological engineering, agricultural engineering, or a related field; on-the-job training

Experience—Previous work experience generally required

Special Skills and Personality Traits—Leadership, problem-solving, analytical, writing, communication, interpersonal, and teamwork skills; helpful, creative, innovative, flexible, and detail-oriented

Special Requirements—Professional engineer (P.E.) licensure may be required

CAREER LADDER

```
┌─────────────────────────────────┐
│   Senior Biosystems Engineer    │
└─────────────────────────────────┘

┌─────────────────────────────────┐
│      Biosystems Engineer        │
└─────────────────────────────────┘

┌─────────────────────────────────┐
│   Junior Biosystems Engineer    │
└─────────────────────────────────┘
```

Position Description

Modern industries and new technologies are found just about everywhere in the world, and with them have come tremendous changes in our environment and social structure. Our industrial and technological advances have resulted in a great shift in population from farms to cities. As a result, fewer people are involved with food or fiber production, and yet productivity in those areas has increased within the last century. The environment has been negatively impacted, however. We see the results in the increased levels of pollutants in our atmosphere, soil, and water. These are emitted each year by our electrical power stations as well as by the other industrial mechanisms that consume our finite natural resources at an ever-accelerating rate. A new profession, biosystems engineering, is at the forefront of seeking solutions to address these concerns.

(This discipline is also known as bioengineering and biological engineering.)

The biosystem, or biosphere, is the combined system of land, water, and air that work together to support life and produce food. Biosystems Engineers analyze biological systems and design products by using the knowledge they obtain through the study of bio-molecular and molecular processes. Biosystems engineering may include the food and agricultural engineering disciplines but encompasses all engineering fields that are applied to living organisms.

Biosystems Engineers use their knowledge of science, mathematics, technology and engineering practices in the course of their daily work. They employ the traditional facets of engineering, such as research, design, manufacturing, implementation, function, maintenance, repair, and the upgrading of systems or products. They thereby work to protect the environment, control pollution and pests, efficiently use natural resources, ensure a sufficient and healthful food supply, safely handle biomaterials, develop renewable energy resources, and improve the processing of food and nonfood agricultural products. These engineers work with structures, land, water, energy, and waste products.

Biosystems Engineers may develop new processes for making antibiotics, or research how microscopic organisms can be used to devour oil spills. They may find new uses for plant fibers, contribute to the development of new pharmaceuticals, look for ways to convert organic materials into fuel, and invent sensors that interface with the Global Positioning System (GPS) satellites to identify the mineral content of cropland soil. They may design new agricultural, food processing, and construction equipment, as well as waste-treatment systems.

Biosystems Engineers specialize in various areas of engineering expertise. Some of their specialties include:

- environmental permitting and remediation—the investigation and cleanup of mining, construction, or other sites
- food and process engineering, which involves work in all phases of food production and distribution as well as with pharmaceuticals and waste treatment
- biofuels, which concerns the conversion of biomass such as lawn clippings, wood chips, or solid wastes into fuel
- forest engineering—the management of forest resources through balanced planting and harvesting, as well as through the planning of roadways and the designing of equipment that minimizes environmental impact
- information and electronic technologies, which includes the development and implementation of detection sensors that monitor crops and test soils
- power and machinery—the design of new biologically sensitive machines that perform agricultural tasks with minimal damage to the ecosystem
- natural resources and environmental engineering—the design and evaluation of agricultural, mining, construction, transportation, and forestry industry management practices
- irrigation and drainage, which involves seeking ways to assist with efficient crop production while ensuring water quality and reduced soil erosion
- aquaculture—the safe and efficient production of seafood in controlled environments
- standards and safety engineering—the development of universal standards for the design of machines and systems
- safety and health, which involves analyzing injury information, as well as studying the proper use of machines and compliance standards with the goal to improve safety practices

Throughout their careers, Biosystems Engineers work in different engineering functions, or specialties. For example, they may perform such functions as research, design, testing, production, quality control, sales, or technical services. Some of them teach part-time or full-time in colleges and universities as professors. Along with teaching classes, many conduct research within their areas of interest.

Biosystems Engineers generally work for 40 hours per week but may occasionally put in extra hours to complete tasks or meet deadlines.

Salaries
Salaries for Biosystems Engineers vary, depending on such factors as their education, experience, position, employer, and geographical location. According to the November 2004 *Occupational Employment Statistics* survey by the U.S. Bureau of Labor Statistics, the estimated annual salary for most agricultural engineers (which includes biosystems engineers) ranged between $38,840 and $91,000.

Employment Prospects
Biosystems Engineers are employed in many industries and fields. Some employers include food processing companies, pharmaceutical manufacturers, biotechnological companies, environmental consulting firms, greenhouse manufacturers, research institutes, regulatory agencies, and academic institutions. These engineers also find employment with cooperative extension services, which are nonformal education programs that are sponsored by the U.S. Department of Agriculture and based at land-grant universities. Some of these engineers are self-employed as consultants or head their own engineering services companies.

Biosystems engineering is a relatively young profession, but some experts in the field believe opportunities should continue to grow because of the global demand for safe and affordable food supplies as well as the need to conserve natural resources and protect the environment. Employers will create new positions as their organizations' needs grow and expand. In addition, openings will become available as Biosystems Engineers advance to higher positions, transfer to other jobs, or retire.

Advancement Prospects
Biosystems Engineers may advance in any number of ways, depending on their ambitions and interests. They can become technical specialists as well as pursue careers in engineering management or corporate management. They can also pursue career paths in marketing, sales, or other business areas. Engineers with entrepreneurial ambitions can become independent consultants or owners of technical or consulting firms.

Education and Training
Minimally, entry-level applicants must possess a bachelor's degree in biological engineering, agricultural engineering,

or another related field. A master's or doctoral degree is usually required for engineers to advance to careers in management, consulting, research, or teaching.

Entry-level engineers typically receive on-the-job training while working under the guidance of experienced engineers. Some companies also provide their employees with formal classroom training programs.

Throughout their careers, Biosystems Engineers enroll in continuing education programs and training programs to update their skills and keep up with advancements in their fields.

Special Requirements

Biosystems Engineers who offer their services directly to the general public or perform work that affects the public safety and welfare must be licensed professional engineers (P.E.). The licensing requirements differ in each state and territory, as well as in Washington, D.C. For specific information, contact the board of engineering examiners for the area where you wish to practice. See Appendix II for a list of boards.

Experience, Special Skills, and Personality Traits

Entry-level candidates should have work experience related to the positions for which they apply. They may have gained their experience through internships, work-study programs, student research projects, postdoctoral training, or part-time employment.

Biosystems Engineers need excellent leadership, problem-solving, analytical, writing, and communication skills for their job. Having effective interpersonal and teamwork skills is also important, as they must work well with colleagues, managers, and others from different backgrounds. Being helpful, creative, innovative, flexible, and detail-oriented are some personality traits that successful Biosystems Engineers share.

Unions and Associations

Many Biosystems Engineers are members of local, state, or national professional associations that provide a variety of professional services and resources such as networking opportunities and continuing education programs. Some national societies that serve the diverse interests of this profession include the American Society of Agricultural and Biological Engineers, the American Academy of Environmental Engineers, and the Society of Women Engineers. Professional engineers are eligible to join the National Society of Professional Engineers. For contact information, see Appendix III.

Tips for Entry

1. Talk with different professionals in biosystems engineering to learn more about their work. Also ask them for advice about courses in engineering and other disciplines that they think might be helpful.

2. Obtain internships or part-time employment in different work settings to get an idea of the work environment you prefer.

3. Check out job banks on the Internet for job listings. Also visit Web sites of employers for whom you would like to work. They sometimes post job listings as well as accept job applications and résumés online.

4. Use the Internet to learn more about the biosystems engineering field. To get a list of Web sites, enter the keywords *biosystems engineering, biological engineering,* or *biosystems engineers* in a search engine. To learn about some links, see Appendix IV.

AQUACULTURAL ENGINEER

CAREER PROFILE

Duties: Research, design, construct, and manage equipment and systems for producing aquatic plants and animals; perform duties as required

Alternate Title(s): Biological Engineer, Water Systems Engineer; a title that reflects an engineering function such as Research Engineer

Salary Range: $39,000 to $91,000

Employment Prospects: Poor

Advancement Prospects: Good

Prerequisites:

    Education or Training—Bachelor's degree in biological engineering, agricultural engineering, or a related field; on-the-job training

    Experience—Previous work experience generally required

    Special Skills and Personality Traits—Analytical, problem-solving, writing, communication, interpersonal, and teamwork skills; detail-oriented, logical, creative, innovative, and flexible

    Special Requirements—Professional engineer (P.E.) licensure may be required

CAREER LADDER

```
┌─────────────────────────────────┐
│   Senior Aquacultural Engineer   │
└─────────────────────────────────┘

┌─────────────────────────────────┐
│     Aquacultural Engineer        │
└─────────────────────────────────┘

┌─────────────────────────────────┐
│   Junior Aquacultural Engineer   │
└─────────────────────────────────┘
```

Position Description

We have always derived part of our nutritional needs from plants and animals that inhabit our oceans, rivers, and lakes. Seaweed, finfish, and shellfish bring special flavors and nutrients to our tables. Over recent decades, our expanding population has increased demand for seafood to such an extent that commercial fisheries must sail farther into the oceans to catch sufficient quantities of our favorite seafood species. Sources of unpolluted water are also diminishing, which further compounds the problem of providing our populations with enough seafood. As a result, a new area of agriculture was developed to help meet the increased demand—aquaculture.

Aquaculture involves the cultivation and harvest of aquatic plants and animals from freshwater or seawater farms. (Ocean aquaculture is called mariculture.) Hence, when we visit our fish markets, we may now choose to purchase either wild or farmed seafood products. Everything from seaweed to salmon to trout, from crayfish to oysters, and even alligators, is raised in farms. Seafood species may be raised in net cages or pens in the sea or in freshwater ponds that can be either natural or human-made. Aquaculture is also more than raising fish for food. Ornamental fish and baitfish are raised in aquacultural farms, and fish hatcheries are a part of aquaculture, too.

Aquacultural engineering is a relatively new subset of agricultural engineering. Aquacultural Engineers are knowledgeable about biology, physiology, and economics, and also have backgrounds in such fields as chemical, environmental, or agricultural engineering. These engineers are concerned with solving various problems associated with farming aquatic plants and animals. They work to design or improve fish rearing systems. They look for ways to increase production while keeping costs low and sustaining a healthy environment. Aquaculture produces waste byproducts that Aquacultural Engineers seek to reduce, along with reducing excessive use of water. They also participate in raising fish, as well as in harvesting, sorting, and processing procedures.

In addition, Aquacultural Engineers study ways to raise and feed fish stocks. Fish convert food efficiently, but some fish require live prey, while other fish thrive on artificially produced food pellets. Some species do well in pens or cages, while others need to swim freely in open bodies of water.

Aquacultural Engineers also design the various types of facilities and equipment needed for successful fish farming. They solve the problems presented by the introduction of diseases or parasites to farmed species by designing oxygenation, filtration, and disinfecting equipment. These engineers conduct research and design small-scale systems that are tested and operated in laboratory settings before being scaled up to full-sized facilities. They oversee the construction of these facilities, including the selection and installation of materials and equipment. As aquaculture expands, the farming facilities increase in size, and are adapted for each species' habitat and growth patterns. Large sea cages are designed to withstand water pressure, storms, and strong currents. These engineers also develop instruments for measuring these variables. Some fish farming systems are situated indoors or in human-made ponds. Aquacultural Engineers utilize all their engineering skills to design and construct these facilities to fit the location, species, and production capacities as required. Their work may require them to call upon their expertise in many fields that can vary from acoustics to robotics.

Aquacultural Engineers may perform one or more engineering functions, or specialties, throughout their careers. They may be engaged as designers, project managers, researchers, test engineers, quality control engineers, sales engineers, engineering managers, or teachers.

These engineers perform a variety of tasks in the course of their work. For example, they might:

- design ponds, cages, or tanks, which includes calculating water flow, material strength, and adequate room for a particular species
- repair, adapt, or maintain equipment
- develop and install systems to regulate water quality, energy supplies, and security
- conduct assessments of sea- and land-based aquaculture production facilities
- design and maintain fish and shellfish processing machines and equipment
- organize the work of farm facility staff
- collaborate with other engineers in the areas of research, development, design, and construction
- manage aquaculture facilities

Aquacultural Engineers generally work 40-hour weeks but may be required to put in extra hours to complete tasks or meet deadlines.

Salaries

Salaries for Aquacultural Engineers vary, depending on such factors as their education, experience, employer, and geographical location. Specific salary information for this profession is unavailable, but these engineers generally earn salaries similar to agricultural engineers. The estimated annual salary for most agricultural engineers ranged between $38,840 and $91,000, according to the November 2004 *Occupational Employment Statistics* survey by the U.S. Bureau of Labor Statistics.

Employment Prospects

Although engineers have engaged in aquacultural engineering since the 1970s, the discipline has formally been around since 1990; hence it is still a young and very small profession. Job opportunities overall are limited. Aquacultural Engineers can find employment with consulting companies, although only a few companies in the United States offer aquacultural engineering services. Other sources of employment are government agencies, such as the U.S. Department of Agriculture and state fish and game agencies, as well as colleges and universities.

According to an expert in the field, most of the engineers who practice aquaculture typically get jobs with engineering firms while working as civil, biological, or environment engineers. When projects require aquacultural experience, they will usually be assigned.

The aquaculture industry is expected to grow through the coming decades, because of the worldwide demand for fish and the decreasing rate of natural fish supplies. Job opportunities for Aquacultural Engineers should increase as employers need their expertise in research, design, development, and so on.

Advancement Prospects

As engineers gain experience, they are assigned to more complex projects as well as receive increasingly greater responsibilities. Senior engineers can become technical specialists or pursue careers in management, consulting, or teaching. Engineers with entrepreneurial ambitions can become independent consultants or owners of engineering consulting firms.

Education and Training

Employers may require Aquacultural Engineers to hold a degree in biological engineering, agricultural engineering, environmental engineering, or another related field. A bachelor's degree is the minimum requirement for jobs with private companies, while a master's or doctoral degree is usually needed for research and teaching jobs.

Recent graduates typically receive on-the-job training while working under the supervision and guidance of senior engineers.

Throughout their careers, Aquacultural Engineers enroll in continuing education programs and training programs to update their skills and keep up with advancements in their fields.

Special Requirements

All engineers who offer engineering services directly to the public or perform work that affects the life, health, or property of the public must be licensed as professional engineers (P.E.). Every state and territory, as well as Washington, D.C., has its own licensing requirements. For specific information, contact the board of engineering examiners for the area where you wish to practice. See Appendix II for a list of boards.

Experience, Special Skills, and Personality Traits

Entry-level candidates should have work experience related to the positions for which they apply. They may have gained their experience through internships, work-study programs, student research projects, postdoctoral training, or employment.

Like other agricultural and biological engineers, Aquacultural Engineers need strong analytical, problem-solving, writing, and communication skills. Because they must work well with many people from diverse backgrounds, they also need effective interpersonal and teamwork skills. Being detail-oriented, logical, creative, innovative, and flexible are some personality traits that successful Aquacultural Engineers have in common.

Unions and Associations

Many Aquacultural Engineers are members of professional associations that offer various professional services and resources, such as publications, professional certification, and networking opportunities. Some national societies which they can join are the Aquacultural Engineering Society, the World Aquaculture Society, the American Fisheries Society, and the American Society of Agricultural and Biological Engineers. For contact information, see Appendix III.

Tips for Entry

1. If you are in high school, you can start learning about aquaculture. For example, read books and magazines about the subject, and visit a fish farm or hatchery, if one is nearby.
2. While in college, take advantage of research assistantships that are available with aquacultural professors.
3. The more practical experience you have, the greater your chances are for obtaining a position.
4. Join a professional association and get involved with its activities. Go to its conferences to learn about new developments as well as to network with your peers.
5. You can learn more about aquaculture and aquacultural engineering on the Internet. To get a list of Web sites, enter the keywords *aquaculture, aquaculture research center,* or *aquacultural engineering* in a search engine. To learn about some links, see Appendix IV.

FOREST ENGINEER

CAREER PROFILE

Duties: Develop and carry out forest management plans; design and supervise timber harvests; plan and oversee road construction; may conduct research; perform duties as required

Alternate Title(s): Agricultural Engineer; a title that reflects a particular job (such as Timber Manager or Watershed Specialist) or an engineering function (such as Research Engineer)

Salary Range: a $39,000 to $91,000

Employment Prospects: Fair

Advancement Prospects: Good

Prerequisites:

Education or Training—Bachelor's degree in agricultural engineering or a related field; on-the-job training

Experience—Previous work experience generally required

Special Skills and Personality Traits—Critical thinking, problem-solving, conflict resolution, communication, writing, computer, interpersonal and teamwork skills; self-motivated, diplomatic, trustworthy, flexible, creative, innovative, and energetic

Special Requirements—Professional engineer (P.E.) licensure may be required

CAREER LADDER

```
┌─────────────────────────────┐
│   Senior Forest Engineer    │
└─────────────────────────────┘

┌─────────────────────────────┐
│      Forest Engineer        │
└─────────────────────────────┘

┌─────────────────────────────┐
│   Junior Forest Engineer    │
└─────────────────────────────┘
```

Position Description

Whether we live in, near, or far from them, forests impact our daily lives in many ways. Forests provide the atmosphere with oxygen. Our houses are made largely from the wood that is harvested from forests, as is much of our furniture and most of our paper products. Many of us enjoy hiking and camping in forests and access our favorite getaway spots via current or former logging roads. Our forests are maintained in near-pristine conditions for the most part. Some of the professionals who contribute to the management of our forests are called Forest Engineers. These engineers utilize expertise from such other engineering fields as geotechnical, foundation, and structural engineering as well as from the areas of hydraulics, stream morphology, and slope stability.

Forest Engineers solve various problems that arise in the process of managing forestlands. In times past, the field of forestry management mainly emphasized the production of wood. This emphasis has progressed to incorporate other uses of our forest resources as well as to managing and sustaining diverse ecosystems. To these ends, Forest Engineers help develop methods and equipment for planning and implementing roads and recreational facilities in addition to reforestation, harvesting, and waste management. They design and oversee the construction, putting in place, and utilization of the buildings and equipment that forest management personnel need to perform all their activities.

Roads are needed for loggers and the public to access each area of the forest. In the United States, these roads traverse more miles than the entire interstate highway system. They are designed by Forest Engineers to minimize soil erosion and degradation. Furthermore, bridges over streams are designed to protect fish and other wildlife. Forest Engineers plan the location of each road, culvert, and bridge while calculating the risks to the environment.

Forest Engineers evaluate the physical and economic implications of new or alternative harvesting methods. These methods are implemented only with the assurance that their use will minimize negative impacts on wildlife, soil, and water quality, as well as on the beauty of the forest. Forest Engineers design and implement remediation projects where environmental damage has occurred. In steep or sensitive areas where access roads are infeasible, other harvesting equipment or methods such as forwarders, skyline cable logging systems, and helicopters are utilized. Forest Engineers plan for and implement the use of these harvesting techniques.

These engineers have a unique responsibility in that their engineering work is applied to vast areas of land and to living systems that have a life cycle spanning decades. They consequently design construction projects and establish harvest work schedules that anticipate events to occur several years in the future. As a result, they solve problems that are immensely complex in terms of time and area constraints but endeavor to keep the solutions simple.

Forest Engineers conduct research into harvesting techniques and transportation planning, but also direct their research efforts to such areas as water control and mapping techniques. They seek ways to manage forests in a manner that is environmentally, politically, and legally responsible as well as economically feasible and physically possible.

These engineers perform a variety of tasks in the course of their careers. They might:

- survey timber land and draw topographical maps
- survey road and bridge locations
- determine the location of storage facilities and loading areas
- choose appropriate methods and equipment for harvesting trees and handling logs
- design and oversee the construction of roads or rail networks
- plan and manage the building of campsites, equipment storage structures, and water and sewage systems
- inspect roads, culverts, and bridges, rate their condition, and recommend repairs
- develop plans for quarries for producing road surfacing materials
- assess roads for compliance to environmental regulations make hydrologic and hydraulic calculations for designing and placing bridges and culverts
- analyze the costs of timber sales, harvesting methods, and the treatment of timber stands
- investigate timber stands to evaluate their condition of readiness for timber sales and incorporate this information along with environmental assessments, contracts, and other reports into a contract package
- prepare documents, graphs, maps, and references for reports or sales packages
- direct and manage timber sales, road construction, and road maintenance as well as supervise contract and pricing negotiations
- supervise and train a staff of employees

Forest Engineers work for federal government agencies such as the USDA Forest Service, the Bureau of Land Management, or the Bureau of Indian Affairs as well as state and regional government forestry agencies. They also work for logging companies and others in the forestry industry. Additionally, many work for consulting firms and equipment manufacturers. Companies that hire Forest Engineers range in size from family-operated firms to large multinational corporations. Some Forest Engineers are self-employed consultants.

These engineers occasionally work outdoors, and thus are exposed to a variety of weather conditions and work with many natural resources. They work with other people as well as with computers and very complicated machines. Forest Engineers work 40 hours per week but may occasionally put in extra hours to meet deadlines or complete projects.

Salaries

Salaries for Forest Engineers vary, depending on such factors as their education, experience, occupation, employer, and geographical location. Specific salary information for Forest Engineers is unavailable, but they generally earn salaries similar to agricultural engineers. According to the November 2004 *Occupational Employment Statistics* survey by the U.S. Bureau of Labor Statistics, the estimated annual salary for most agricultural engineers ranged between $38,840 and $91,000.

The College of Forestry at Oregon State University stated on its Web site (http://www.cof.orst.edu) in 2005 that the average starting salaries for their graduates ranged between $35,000 and $40,000.

Employment Prospects

The forest engineering profession is small, with opportunities generally becoming available as Forest Engineers transfer to other jobs, advance to higher positions, or retire. Jobs are available throughout the United States, as well as worldwide.

Advancement Prospects

Depending on their interests and ambitions, Forest Engineers can seek advancement by becoming technical specialists, consultants, engineering managers, or corporate managers. Those with entrepreneurial ambitions can become independent consultants or owners of technical or consulting firms. To advance to higher positions, they may be required to obtain a master's or doctoral degree.

Education and Training

Many employers prefer to hire entry-level candidates who possess a bachelor's degree in forest engineering, forestry, or another related field.

Novice engineers typically receive on-the-job training while working under the supervision and guidance of senior engineers.

Throughout their careers, Forest Engineers enroll in continuing education and training programs to update their skills and keep up with advancements in their fields.

Special Requirements

All engineers who offer engineering services directly to the public or perform work that affects the life, health, or property of the public must be licensed as professional engineers (P.E.). Licensing requirements vary in the different states and territories, as well as in Washington, D.C. For specific information, contact the board of engineering examiners for the area where you wish to practice. See Appendix II for a list of boards.

In Oregon and Washington, Forest Engineers are registered as professional logging engineers, while in most other states they are licensed as agricultural engineers.

Experience, Special Skills, and Personality Traits

Entry-level candidates should have work experience related to the positions for which they apply. They may have gained their experience through internships, work-study programs, student research projects, or past employment.

To be effective at their job, Forest Engineers need strong critical thinking, problem-solving, conflict resolution, communication, and writing skills. They should also have adequate computer skills, including the ability to use word processing, database, spreadsheet, and other software applications. In addition, they need excellent interpersonal and teamwork skills, as they must be able to work well with colleagues, managers, government representatives, and others. Being self-motivated, diplomatic, trustworthy, flexible, creative, innovative, and energetic are some personality traits that successful Forest Engineers share.

Unions and Associations

Many Forest Engineers belong to one or more professional associations to take advantage of networking opportunities, continuing education programs, publications, and other professional services and resources. Some national engineering societies that serve the interests of this profession include the Council on Forest Engineering, the Society of American Foresters, and the American Society of Agricultural and Biological Engineers. For contact information, see Appendix III.

Tips for Entry

1. To gain forestry experience, you might obtain a summer job with a forest agency, park system, private company, or conservation group. Many organizations hire high school students as well as college students for summer work.
2. Learn how to use GIS (geographic information systems) and GPS (Global Positioning System) technology to enhance your employability. GIS is a computer system that collects, stores, manipulates, and displays spatial data about geographical locations, while GPS is a satellite-based navigation system.
3. You may have greater chances of obtaining the job you want by being willing to relocate to another city, state, or even country.
4. Use the Internet to learn more about Forest Engineers. To get a list of Web sites, enter the keywords *forest engineers or forest engineering* in a search engine. To learn about some links, see Appendix IV.

MACHINERY SYSTEMS ENGINEER

CAREER PROFILE

Duties: Research, develop, design, test, and manufacture agricultural, forestry, construction, and industrial equipment and machinery; perform duties as required

Alternate Title(s): Farm Equipment Systems Engineer, Agricultural Engineer; a title that reflects an engineering function such as Design Engineer, Product Planner, or Engineering Manager

Salary Range: $39,000 to $91,000

Employment Prospects: Fair

Advancement Prospects: Good

Prerequisites:

Education or Training—Bachelor's degree in agricultural engineering or a related field; on-the-job training

Experience—Previous work experience generally required

Special Skills and Personality Traits—Analytical, problem-solving, teamwork, communication, and writing skills; creative, innovative, detail-oriented, curious, and self-motivated

Special Requirements—Professional engineer (P.E.) licensure may be required

CAREER LADDER

```
┌─────────────────────────────────────┐
│  Senior Machinery Systems Engineer   │
└─────────────────────────────────────┘

┌─────────────────────────────────────┐
│     Machinery Systems Engineer       │
└─────────────────────────────────────┘

┌─────────────────────────────────────┐
│  Junior Machinery Systems Engineer   │
└─────────────────────────────────────┘
```

Position Description

Throughout history, people have endeavored to devise ways to make the work of cultivating crops and livestock less labor-intensive. Some of the earliest farm implements were spades, rakes, wedges, axes, scythes, and plows. In more modern times, plows were attached to tractors. Various planting, harvesting, and processing machines replaced the hand tools and horse- or oxen-drawn implements of our forebears. Today farmers use even more complicated and sophisticated machines in their work. The agricultural engineers who specialize in the development and manufacture of these machines are called Machinery Systems Engineers.

Agricultural Machinery Systems Engineers use electronics, sensors, and the latest in engineering design techniques to research, develop, and test machinery for every aspect of the processing of food and other agricultural products. These machines are used to prepare soil, plant seeds, apply fertilizer or pesticides, harvest crops, bale hay, milk cows, and feed livestock as well as perform some of the gardening tasks we do at home.

Agricultural Machinery Systems Engineers have backgrounds in the areas of biology, mechanical design, electronics, instrumentation and control, manufacturing and assembly methods, and quality control, which they apply to their work. In addition to the machines used in agriculture and food processing, these engineers create systems and machinery that are used in lawn and garden care as well as in the construction, mining, forestry, paper manufacturing, and materials handling industries. These engineers use such tools and techniques as computer-aided design and manufacturing (CAD/CAM) technologies, solid modeling, and dynamic simulation to design these machines.

Machinery Systems Engineers design, improve, and manufacture machines that will precisely spray crops, transport agricultural products and waste, irrigate croplands, and harvest many different types of food or fiber crops. They research new developments in this field, and apply their findings to new designs. They also test new or improved designs to make sure that the machines will perform as anticipated.

These engineers are concerned with how the machines impact the environment, and they strive to conserve energy, improve efficiency, and reduce the costs associated with purchasing and running the machines. Some of them design equipment to be used specifically in other countries to manage the types of crops that are grown there.

Machinery Systems Engineers are involved with current trends in precision farming. They develop machines that can distinguish between crops and unwanted weeds, which the machine then sprays selectively with herbicides. In addition, they design the devices that track soil conditions in sections of fields, which enable farmers to treat each section of their crops appropriately to effect maximum yields.

Many Machinery Systems Engineers conduct their research at universities, where they focus on basic or applied research in their areas of interest. For example, basic researchers might search for new knowledge about how equipment interacts with soil or plants, while those involved in applied research might study the various needs for farm production in their immediate area or around the world. Their university research is often devoted to fulfilling farm equipment needs that private-sector firms are unable to meet.

These engineers work in large or small companies within the food and equipment industries that manufacture machines and systems for farm equipment, food or fiber processing, and grounds keeping. They also work in industries that produce machines used in forestry and the mining occupations. Agricultural Machinery Systems Engineers find employment in engineering management, marketing, or sales or form their own farm equipment companies. Many are consultants. Some teach agricultural engineering courses in colleges and universities. Others work for government agencies and for cooperative extension services, which are non-formal education programs that are sponsored by the U.S. Department of Agriculture and based at land-grant universities.

Agricultural Machinery Systems Engineers generally work 40 hours per week, but may occasionally work extra hours as needed to complete tasks and meet deadlines.

Salaries

Salaries for Machinery Systems Engineers vary, depending on such factors as their education, experience, employer, and geographical location. Specific salary information for these engineers is unavailable, but they generally earn salaries similar to agricultural engineers. According to the November 2004 *Occupational Employment Statistics* survey by the U.S. Bureau of Labor Statistics, the estimated annual salary for most agricultural engineers ranged between $38,840 and $91,000.

Employment Prospects

Job openings typically become available as agricultural Machinery Systems Engineers retire, advance to higher positions, or transfer to other jobs. The job market in general remains good, according to an expert in the field. Bear in mind that the job market fluctuates with the farm economy. When the market is strong, companies usually have need for more engineers. There are a few major equipment manufacturers in the United States, mostly located in the Midwest. Small manufacturers are found throughout the country.

Advancement Prospects

Agricultural Machinery Systems Engineers may advance in any number of ways, depending on their ambitions and interests. They can become technical specialists as well as seek positions in engineering management or corporate management. Some pursue career paths in product planning, marketing, sales, or other areas. Engineers with entrepreneurial ambitions can become independent consultants or start up their own consulting or technical firms or small manufacturing companies.

Education and Training

Minimally, entry-level applicants must possess a bachelor's degree in agricultural engineering, mechanical engineering, or a related field. A master's or doctoral degree is usually required for engineers to advance to careers in management, consulting, research, or teaching. Engineers must possess a doctorate to teach at the college level.

Entry-level engineers typically receive on-the-job training while working under the supervision and guidance of senior engineers. Some companies also provide formal classroom training programs.

Throughout their careers, Machinery Systems Engineers enroll in continuing education programs and training programs to update their skills and keep up with advancements in their fields.

Special Requirements

All engineers who offer engineering services directly to the public or perform work that affects the life, health, or property of the public must be licensed as professional engineers (P.E.). Every U.S. state and territory, as well as Washington, D.C., has its own requirements for P.E. licensure. For specific information, contact the board of engineering examiners for the area where you wish to practice. See Appendix II for a list of boards.

Experience, Special Skills, and Personality Traits

Entry-level candidates should have work experience related to the positions for which they apply. They may have gained

their experience through internships, work-study programs, student research projects, postdoctoral training, or summer employment.

Machinery Systems Engineers must have effective analytical, problem-solving, teamwork, communication, and writing skills to perform well at their job. Being creative, innovative, detail-oriented, curious, and self-motivated are some personality traits that successful engineers have in common.

Unions and Associations

Machinery Systems Engineers might join one or more professional associations to take advantage of networking opportunities, continuing education programs, publications, and other professional services and resources. At the national level, for example, they might belong to the American Society of Agricultural and Biological Engineers. For contact information, see Appendix III.

Tips for Entry

1. Growing up on a farm or working on one provides valuable work experience that can count on your résumé.
2. Contact employers directly for information about job vacancies.
3. Use the Internet to learn more about agricultural Machinery Systems Engineers and their area of work. To get a list of Web sites, enter the keywords *agricultural machinery, agricultural machinery systems, or agricultural machinery systems engineers* in a search engine. To learn about some links, see Appendix IV.

BIOMEDICAL ENGINEERING

BIOMEDICAL ENGINEER

CAREER PROFILE

Duties: Be involved in the research, development, and design of medical technology to help improve the diagnosis and treatment of patients; perform duties as required

Alternate Title(s): A title that reflects a specialty (such as Clinical Engineer) or an engineering function (such as Designer or Project Engineer)

Salary Range: $43,000 to $113,000

Employment Prospects: Good

Advancement Prospects: Good

Prerequisites:

Education or Training—Bachelor's degree in biomedical engineering or a related field; on-the-job-training

Experience—Previous work experience generally required

Special Skills and Personality Traits—Problem-solving, analytical, writing, communication, presentation, interpersonal, teamwork, and leadership skills; curious, detail-oriented, open-minded, determined, and creative

Special Requirements—Professional engineer (P.E.) licensure may be required

CAREER LADDER

```
┌─────────────────────────────────┐
│   Senior Biomedical Engineer    │
└─────────────────────────────────┘

┌─────────────────────────────────┐
│      Biomedical Engineer        │
└─────────────────────────────────┘

┌─────────────────────────────────┐
│   Junior Biomedical Engineer    │
└─────────────────────────────────┘
```

Position Description

Medical problems are complex, and Biomedical Engineers provide their unique perspective and talents to help solve them. Their profession, biomedical engineering, combines engineering and the life sciences. As in other engineering disciplines, Biomedical Engineers use engineering principles, scientific theories, and knowledge from such diverse fields as physics, mathematics, chemistry, and the social sciences. They integrate this knowledge with their understanding of the life sciences and physiology to study disease processes and to develop new products, tools, or techniques for health care professionals to use in the treatment of medical conditions. Many of these engineers have additional training in medicine and other fields.

Biomedical Engineers conduct research; design instruments, medical apparatuses, and software; and develop new medical procedures. They simulate procedures and test prototype devices under extreme conditions before approving them for clinical use or placing them on the market. Bio-

medical Engineers work with physicians, nurses, physical therapists, and other medical professionals. They work in hospitals, government agencies, corporations, research laboratories, and academic institutions.

The following are a few examples of developments in medicine that biomedical engineering makes possible. Biomedical Engineers develop new computer applications such as neural nets that perform in similar fashion to the human nervous system. They create computerized models of human physiological systems. They design computerized monitoring machines, artificial organs, and new technologies for the automatic delivery of medicines. They invent machines that help disabled people be mobile or accomplish tasks. They develop laser eye surgery systems, cardiac pacemakers, and defibrillators, as well as artificial blood vessels and joints.

These engineers also design hospital units such as clinical laboratories that make use of advanced technologies. They create imaging technologies such as computed tomography

(CT) and magnetic resonance imaging (MRI) machines. They develop new biomaterials that are used to make non-rejecting implants. Additionally, Biomedical Engineers investigate the biomechanics of injury and wound healing, as well as develop wheelchairs, prostheses, or other therapeutic devices and adapt them to individual specifications to better enhance patients' lives.

Many Biomedical Engineers are involved with conducting studies in academic, government, industrial, or other research laboratories. Some of them perform basic research to gain further knowledge and understanding of biological systems. Others perform applied research wherein they seek solutions to specific medical and health-care problems. Still others are involved in the research, development, and design of new medical devices and instrumentation for commercial purposes.

Biomedical engineering is a wide-ranging field, and many engineers focus on special areas of interest. Some of these specialties are:

- bioinstrumentation—the application of electronics, computers, and measurement methods to create instruments and equipment, such as heart monitors, glucose monitors, and X-rays, for diagnostic or treatment purposes
- biomaterials—the use of both living tissue and artificial materials, including metal alloys, ceramics, polymers, and composites to make implants such as artificial bones or joints, heart valves, and artificial organs, as well as such substances as dental adhesives and bone cement
- systems physiology—the use of science and engineering to predict the behavior of the human body, specific organs, or organ systems as well as to understand their function
- medical imaging—the combination of knowledge about sound or radiation with the use of electronic MRI, ultrasound, or CT devices to display images of internal organs
- biomechanics—the application of classic mechanics (such as fluid mechanics and transport phenomenon) to study motion, material deformation, and the flow of chemicals across membranes in organisms or devices that lead to the development of such things as artificial hearts, heart valves, or hip replacements
- rehabilitation engineering—the development of personalized prosthetic or transport devices, as well as procedures to use in the home or workplace, to help patients with disabilities move more freely and live independently
- clinical engineering—the use of technology to support patient care in hospitals and other clinical settings, which includes the development and maintenance of databases containing medical instrumentation and equipment records as well as the procurement and use of medical instruments
- cellular, tissue, and genetic engineering—the use of biochemistry and anatomy to study cells and subcellular structures to understand illnesses or diseases and develop cures at the microscopic level

- orthopedic bioengineering—the application of engineering and computational mechanics to understand bone, joint, and muscle functions as well as to design artificial joint replacements made from biomaterials.

Specialists within biomedical engineering often work in combination with one another. For example, Biomedical Engineers who design artificial joints work with other engineers who study biomechanics. Biomedical Engineers who design electronic muscle stimulation devices collaborate with specialists in the area of biomaterials. This cooperative effort is essential to the continuing rapid development of new technologies as well as the growth of the biomedical engineering profession.

There are several levels of expertise within the biomedical engineering profession. Junior engineers typically work under the guidance and supervision of senior engineers. Their focus is to develop their skills and their understanding of the rules, regulations, standards, and practices of their area of concern. They are given specific directions on their assignments along with clearly defined priorities and goals. As they gain experience and knowledge, they receive more complex assignments and are able to exercise greater levels of authority.

Senior engineers are more actively involved with the decision-making process and are more likely to be team leaders. Their decisions are made without direct supervision. These engineers are more aware of program needs and work independently in response to those needs. They are expected to implement departmental customer service and partnership concepts, for example.

Advanced to executive-level Biomedical Engineers are the primary engineers for project divisions. They perform the most difficult engineering tasks. They make policy decisions and consult with clients or government agencies at the highest levels. They are also responsible for top-level project management, client management, and business development and administration.

Biomedical Engineers usually work for 40 hours per week but may put in additional hours to meet deadlines or complete projects.

Salaries

Salaries for Biomedical Engineers vary, depending on such factors as their education, experience, job duties, employer, and geographical location. The estimated annual salary for most Biomedical Engineers ranged between $43,490 and $113,070, according to the November 2004 *Occupational Employment Statistics* (OES) survey by the U.S. Bureau of Labor Statistics (BLS).

Employment Prospects

The BLS reported in its November 2004 OES survey that an estimated 10,050 Biomedical Engineers were employed in the United States. The highest levels of employment were in scientific research and development services, pharmaceutical and medicine manufacturing, medical equipment and supplies manufacturing, general medical and surgical hospitals, and electronic instrument manufacturing.

Many experts in the field describe the general job market for Biomedical Engineers as being quite favorable. According to the BLS, job growth for Biomedical Engineers should increase by 27 percent or more through 2014. The aging of the population and the increasing interest in personal health and healthcare in the United States are contributing factors to the demand for Biomedical Engineers to design and develop technologies for new and better diagnostic products, medical devices and equipment, and medical procedures. Several specialties, such as rehabilitation engineering, orthopedic engineering, and tissue engineering are steadily growing which also contributes to the need for Biomedical Engineers.

In addition to job growth, opportunities will become available as Biomedical Engineers transfer to other jobs, advance to higher positions, or retire.

Advancement Prospects

Biomedical Engineers may advance in any number of ways, depending on their ambitions and interests. They can become technical specialists as well as pursue such managerial positions as supervisory, project, and chief engineers. Some engineers choose to move into positions in marketing, technical sales, and other business areas. Some enter medical school and go on to pursue a career in medicine. Engineers with entrepreneurial ambitions can become independent practitioners or owners of firms that offer various types of environmental engineering services.

Education and Training

Minimum educational requirements vary for entry-level positions. For some positions, applicants may need only a bachelor's degree in biomedical engineering, chemical engineering, or another related field. For other positions, employers may prefer to hire candidates with a master's or doctoral degree. Usually an advanced degree is required for engineers to advance to careers in management, consulting, research, and teaching. Many Biomedical Engineers have obtained advanced training in other fields; for example, some engineers have earned a doctor of medicine (M.D.) degree.

Employers typically provide entry-level engineers with training programs, which may include both on-the-job training and formal classroom training. New engineers work under the supervision and direction of experienced engineers.

Throughout their careers, Biomedical Engineers enroll in continuing education and training programs to update their skills and keep up with advancements in their fields.

Special Requirements

All engineers who offer engineering services directly to the public or perform work that affects the life, health, or property of the public must be licensed as professional engineers (P.E.). Every state and territory, as well as Washington, D.C., has its own licensing requirements. For specific information, contact the board of engineering examiners for the area where you wish to practice. See Appendix II for a list of boards.

Experience, Special Skills, and Personality Traits

Entry-level candidates should have work experience related to the positions for which they apply. They may have gained their experience through internships, work-study programs, student research projects, postdoctoral training, or employment.

Having strong problem-solving, analytical, writing, communication, and presentation skills is essential for Biomedical Engineers. Additionally, they need effective interpersonal, teamwork, and leadership skills, as they must work well with colleagues, managers, technicians, medical doctors, and others from diverse backgrounds. Being curious, detail-oriented, open-minded, determined, and creative are a few personality traits that successful Biomedical Engineers share.

Unions and Associations

Many Biomedical Engineers belong to local, state, and national societies to take advantage of professional services and resources, such as publications, continuing education programs, and networking opportunities. Some national societies that serve the diverse interests of Biomedical Engineers include:

- Biomedical Engineering Society
- IEEE Engineering in Medicine and Biology Society
- American Institute for Medical and Biological Engineering
- American College of Clinical Engineering
- Rehabilitation Engineering and Assistive Technology Society of North America
- American Society of Biomechanics
- Tissue Engineering and Regenerative Medicine International Society
- American Association for the Advancement of Science
- American Institute of Chemical Engineers

For contact information, see Appendix III.

Tips for Entry

1. While in high school, take life science courses to help you prepare for a career in biomedical engineering.
2. Every biomedical program has its own philosophy and academic focus. Carefully research your choices

to find one that is compatible with your academic and career goals.

3. Obtain a research assistantship job (or volunteer) with a professor whose research work interests you.

4. Construct your résumé so that it points out clearly how your engineering skills, student research projects, and field work apply to the biomedical field.

5. Use the Internet to learn more about Biomedical Engineers. You might start by visiting the Biomedical Engineering Society Web site at http://www.bmes. org. For more links, see Appendix IV.

CLINICAL ENGINEER

CAREER PROFILE

Duties: Manage medical technology in hospitals or other clinical settings; be involved in the research, design, development, and production of medical instruments and equipment; perform duties as required

Alternate Title(s): Biomedical Engineer, Clinical Manager; a title that reflects an engineering function such as Design Engineer or Project Engineer

Salary Range: $43,000 to $113,000

Employment Prospects: Good

Advancement Prospects: Good

Prerequisites:

    Education or Training—Bachelor's degree in clinical engineering or another related field; on-the-job training

    Experience—Previous work experience generally required

    Special Skills and Personality Traits—Leadership, interpersonal, teamwork, communication, analytical, problem-solving, and writing skills; meticulous, self-motivated, curious, flexible, and creative

    Special Requirements—Professional engineer (P.E.) licensure may be required

CAREER LADDER

```
┌─────────────────────────────────┐
│     Senior Clinical Engineer     │
└─────────────────────────────────┘

┌─────────────────────────────────┐
│        Clinical Engineer         │
└─────────────────────────────────┘

┌─────────────────────────────────┐
│   Associate Clinical Engineer    │
└─────────────────────────────────┘
```

Position Description

A visit to a hospital today reveals a world that is more high-tech than ever before. Lab technicians take blood samples and use machines to analyze their chemical composition. A patient may be asked to walk on a treadmill while being hooked up to monitors via wires pasted to the body. Other patients may be fed intravenously or have vital signs monitored by complicated-looking machines. More complex diagnostic and surgical equipment is also found in special sections of hospitals. These and many more medical devices are managed by professional men and women known as Clinical Engineers. They also participate in the design of diagnostic, treatment, and monitoring instruments and equipment as well as those used in research or rehabilitation.

Clinical engineering is a specialty of biomedical engineering. Clinical Engineers are problem solvers who are equally adept at working with both human and technological systems. In addition to their engineering expertise, they approach their careers with an understanding of such subjects as the physical sciences, physiology, systems analysis, medical terminology, instrumentation, and measurement, along with an experiential background in hospital operations, procedures, and ethics. This expertise and set of skills enable Clinical Engineers to manage and solve problems with the use of highly sophisticated medical technologies.

Clinical Engineers fulfill engineering roles in various settings. Many Clinical Engineers work in clinical settings as technology managers. (These workplaces include hospitals and such companies as shared service or asset management firms.) They are on board to ensure that medical instruments and equipment work safely and effectively. These engineers are responsible for managing and coordinating budgets and service contracts with regard to the purchase of medical equipment systems used by medical professionals. They may supervise a staff of personnel called biomedical equipment technicians who work to maintain that equipment. These engineers ensure that projects are completed in a timely fashion to meet deadlines. They may also assist with the collection of patient data, such as performing blood pressure measurements.

In clinical settings, they participate in the planning process by learning about new technologies and recommending how they can be used. Clinical Engineers ensure that medical equipment complies with regulations while looking into problems that occur with its use. They also work closely with doctors, nurses, and other hospital professionals to evaluate new product designs or prototypes during clinical trials. In addition, they train technical and medical staff to use the instruments or equipment properly. Their leadership efforts in these areas of concern contribute greatly toward better patient safety by helping to reduce medical errors.

Clinical Engineers also work for industries that develop and market new medical technology products. They attend to all stages of product development from research to design to testing to sales and technical support. These engineers attend to a variety of tasks in the course of their work. Depending on their engineering function, they may:

- support and lead product development projects and provide customer support
- perform and administer data collection and analysis, as well as clinical trials and testing, and document the results
- test and evaluate prototypes
- ensure that products meet regulatory or market requirements
- manage and ensure the quality of all facets of project planning, including schedules, cost analysis, charts, and documentation
- coordinate the work of staff or contract personnel

Some Clinical Engineers work as instructors in academic institutions, where they develop and teach courses in instrument and equipment technology. Full-time faculty are also involved in conducting basic or applied research in their areas of interest. Other Clinical Engineers work in private practice as consultants or expert witnesses. Some Clinical Engineers are also employed by governmental regulatory agencies and research centers.

All Clinical Engineers are expected to keep up-to-date with new developments in their field by reading technical literature, attending professional conferences, and networking with their peers.

Clinical Engineers usually work 40 hours per week but may be required to put in extra hours to complete projects or meet deadlines.

Salaries

Salaries for Clinical Engineers vary, depending on such factors as their education, experience, job duties, employer, and geographical location. Specific salary information for these engineers is unavailable, but they generally earn salaries similar to biomedical engineers. According to the November 2004 *Occupational Employment Statistics* survey by the U.S. Bureau of Labor Statistics (BLS), the estimated annual salary for most biomedical engineers ranged between $43,400 and $113,070.

Employment Prospects

In general, opportunities become available as Clinical Engineers transfer to other jobs, advance to higher positions, or retire. Employers will create additional positions as their organizations grow and expand. The BLS reports that the biomedical engineering profession, which includes Clinical Engineers, is expected to grow by 27 percent or more through 2014.

According to an expert in the field, opportunities should be favorable for Clinical Engineers in the future. As medical technologies become more integrated, there will be a continuing need for experts to handle their management in clinical settings.

Advancement Prospects

Clinical Engineers with management and administrative ambitions can become project leaders, program managers, directors, and executive officers. Those with entrepreneurial ambitions can become independent consultants or owners of technical or consulting firms. Some engineers choose to move into teaching and research positions in academic institutions or go to medical school and pursue a career in medicine.

Education and Training

In general, applicants need at least a bachelor's degree in biomedical engineering or another related field to qualify for entry-level positions. Many employers prefer to hire candidates with at least a master's degree because they have more academic training. Usually a master's or doctoral degree is required for engineers to advance to careers in management, consulting, research, and teaching.

Employers typically provide entry-level engineers with training programs, which may include both on-the-job training and formal classroom training.

Throughout their careers, Biomedical Engineers enroll in continuing education and training programs to update their skills and keep up with advancements in their fields.

Special Requirements

All engineers who offer engineering services directly to the public or perform work that affects the life, health, or property of the public must be licensed as professional engineers (P.E.). Licensing requirements vary with each state and territory, as well as Washington, D.C. For specific information, contact the board of engineering examiners for the area where you wish to practice. See Appendix II for a list of boards.

Experience, Special Skills, and Personality Traits

Entry-level candidates should have work experience related to the positions for which they apply. They may have gained their experience through internships, work-study programs, student research projects, postdoctoral training, or part-time employment.

Clinical Engineers must have excellent leadership, interpersonal, teamwork, and communication skills, as they must be able to work well with technical and medical professionals from diverse backgrounds. In addition, they need strong analytical, problem-solving, and writing skills to perform their various duties.

Some personality traits that successful Clinical Engineers share include being meticulous, self-motivated, curious, flexible, and creative.

Unions and Associations

Clinical Engineers can join professional associations to take advantage of publications, certification, continuing education programs, networking opportunities, and other professional services and resources. Some national societies include the American College of Clinical Engineering, the Association for the Advancement of Medical Instrumentation, the Biomedical Engineering Society, and the American Institute For Medical and Biological Engineering. For contact information, see Appendix III.

Tips for Entry

1. Take advantage of the programs and services offered by your college career center. Career counselors can help you find internships, employment, scholarships, and fellowships. They can also help you develop strong job search skills.
2. Get experience in the medical device industry through an internship or employment.
3. When you do a job search, be sure to contact current and former colleagues, instructors, and others whom you know for job leads.
4. Use the Internet to learn more about Clinical Engineers. You might start by visiting the American College of Clinical Engineering Web site at http://www.accenet.org. For more links, see Appendix IV.

REHABILITATION ENGINEER

CAREER PROFILE

Duties: Provide direct service delivery of technological solutions to problems facing people with physical disabilities; may be involved in the research and development of technological solutions; perform duties as required

Alternate Title(s): Rehabilitation Technology Specialist, Biomedical Engineer; a title that reflects an engineering function, such as Project Manager or Research Engineer

Salary Range: $43,000 to $113,000

Employment Prospects: Fair

Advancement Prospects: Good

Prerequisites:

Education or Training—Bachelor's degree in biomedical engineering or a related field; on-the-job training

Experience—Previous work experience generally required

Special Skills and Personality Traits—Analytical, problem-solving, teamwork, writing, communication, interpersonal, and self-management skills; logical, self-motivated, flexible, friendly, and creative

Special Requirements—Professional engineer (P.E.) licensure may be required

CAREER LADDER

```
┌─────────────────────────────────────┐
│   Senior Rehabilitation Engineer     │
└─────────────────────────────────────┘

┌─────────────────────────────────────┐
│      Rehabilitation Engineer         │
└─────────────────────────────────────┘

┌─────────────────────────────────────┐
│   Junior Rehabilitation Engineer     │
└─────────────────────────────────────┘
```

Position Description

Today, technology and medicine are introducing devices and therapies that increasingly provide individuals with physical disabilities with the ability and opportunity to live independently and enjoy more active, mobile lives. Men and women who work in the field of rehabilitation engineering, a specialty of the biomedical engineering profession, are specifically involved in designing and developing technological solutions to the problems that people with disabilities face each day.

Rehabilitation Engineers possess a comprehensive understanding of the human body. They are also adept in the fields of mechanical engineering, biomedical engineering, rehabilitation science, and industrial design as well as mathematics, the physical and life sciences, analysis, and logic. They are experts in the areas of disability, resources, laws, and technology.

Many Rehabilitation Engineers are involved in providing direct service delivery and work closely with occupational therapists, physical therapists, and medical professionals. These engineers' responsibility is to modify existing devices or design new ones to fulfill the client's requirements. The engineers evaluate the needs of their clients. They apply their analyses to design, make, and test devices or equipment that allow their clients to overcome or compensate for their disabilities. For example, Rehabilitation Engineers adjust wheelchairs or scooters to be more comfortable or to allow the user to sit in a position that optimizes their ability to be mobile and complete their daily tasks. They design computer hardware devices and their attendant software programs that enable people to communicate. They also develop sophisticated prosthetics, modify home and workplace environments, and design steering wheel, accelerator, and brake pedal enhancement for automobiles.

These engineers are responsible for completing a variety of tasks. For example, they may:

- process technology referrals
- consult with clients
- supply evaluations specifically tailored for their clients' job-related requirements
- recommend special equipment to meet the needs of clients
- install equipment for work or home, as well as orient and provide follow-up consultation to clients in the use of the equipment
- troubleshoot equipment function difficulties and provide modification or repairs
- maintain records of activities
- train clients and employees to operate adaptive equipment
- apply for funding and prepare documentation that justifies clients' needs for equipment
- keep up-to-date with the latest technologies for assistive or prosthetic equipment
- evaluate equipment for future recommendation to clients

Rehabilitation Engineers are also involved in research and development and work for equipment manufacturers, government agencies, hospitals, medical institutions, and universities. For example, they may be engaged in developing new materials for strength, endurance, or malleability to optimize the lifespan and usability of medical devices. Some engineers assist in the design of buildings and thoroughfares to accommodate the disabled. Others create methods of preventing repetitive injuries and design courses for adaptive training programs that employers may use in the workplace.

Rehabilitation Engineers may specialize in one or more areas. These specialties include: seating and mobility; computer technology and its accessibility; augmentative and alternative communications; assistive devices for the deaf or blind; prosthetics; vehicle modification; environmental control; and modifications for homes, jobsites, or farms.

Rehabilitation Engineers work for 40 hours per week but may be required to put in extra hours to complete tasks or meet deadlines.

Salaries

Salaries for Rehabilitation Engineers vary, depending on such factors as their education, experience, job duties, employer, and geographical location. Specific salary information for these engineers is unavailable, but they generally earn salaries similar to biomedical engineers. According to the November 2004 *Occupational Employment Statistics* survey by the U.S. Bureau of Labor Statistics (BLS), the estimated annual salary for most biomedical engineers ranged between $43,490 and $113,070.

Employment Prospects

Rehabilitation engineering is relatively a young and very small profession compared to other engineering disciplines such as civil engineering. The BLS reports that rehabilitation engineering is one of the biomedical engineering specialties that is growing quickly, thus increasing a demand for engineers. In general, the job growth for biomedical engineers, which includes Rehabilitation Engineers, should increase by 27 percent or more through 2014.

Advancement Prospects

Depending on their interests and ambitions, Rehabilitation Engineers can advance in various ways. Those with management and administrative ambitions can become project leaders, program managers, directors, and executive officers. Engineers with entrepreneurial ambitions can become independent consultants or owners of technical or consulting firms. Some engineers choose to move into teaching and research positions in academic institutions or go to medical school and pursue a career in medicine.

Education and Training

Applicants for entry-level positions need at least a bachelor's degree in biomedical engineering, mechanical engineering, or another related field. Many Rehabilitation Engineers possess a master's degree in rehabilitation engineering.

Entry-level engineers typically receive on-the-job training while working under the supervision and guidance of experienced engineers. Some employers also provide formal classroom training programs.

Throughout their careers, Rehabilitation Engineers enroll in continuing education programs and training programs to update their skills and keep up with advancements in their fields.

Special Requirements

All engineers who offer engineering services directly to the public or perform work that affects the life, health, or property of the public must be licensed as professional engineers (P.E.). Every state and territory, as well as Washington, D.C., has its own requirements for P.E. licensure. For specific information, contact the board of engineering examiners for the area where you wish to practice. See Appendix II for a list of boards.

Experience, Special Skills, and Personality Traits

Entry-level candidates should have work experience related to the positions for which they apply. They may have gained their experience through internships, work-study programs, student research projects, or summer employment. For positions in which engineers would be working directly with consumers, having basic knowledge of physiology and the medical aspects of disability, as well as knowledge of the rehabilitation and the assistive technology evaluation processes, is essential.

To be effective at their work, Rehabilitation Engineers need strong analytical, problem-solving, teamwork, writing, and communication skills. They also need excellent interpersonal skills to work well with colleagues, managers, consumers, and others. Having good self-management skills, such as the ability to handle stressful situations, meet deadlines, and prioritize multiple tasks, is also important. Being logical, self-motivated, flexible, friendly, and creative are a few personality traits that successful Rehabilitation Engineers share.

Unions and Associations

Many Rehabilitation Engineers join professional associations to take advantage of professional certification, continuing education programs, networking opportunities, and other professional services and resources. Some national societies that serve the interests of these engineers include the Rehabilitation Engineering and Assistive Technology Society of North America, the Biomedical Engineering Society, and the American Institute for Medical and Biological Engineering. For contact information, see Appendix III.

Tips for Entry

1. A willingness to relocate can improve your job opportunities.
2. An expert in the field says that more opportunities are found in such large metropolitan areas as Chicago, Los Angeles, and New York.
3. Learn more about Rehabilitation Engineers on the Internet. You might start by visiting these Web sites: Rehabilitation Engineering and Assistive Technology Society of North America, http://www.resna.org; and Rehab Engineer, http://rehabengineer.homestead.com. For more links, see Appendix IV.

TISSUE ENGINEER

CAREER PROFILE

Duties: Conduct basic or applied research; design and conduct research projects; may teach engineering courses; perform duties as required

Alternate Title(s): Cell and Tissue Engineer, Biomedical Engineer; a title that reflects an engineering function such as Research Engineer

Salary Range: $39,000 to $124,000

Employment Prospects: Poor

Advancement Prospects: Good

Prerequisites:

Education or Training—Master's degree in biomedical engineering or a related field

Experience—Previous work experience generally required

Special Skills and Personality Traits—Problem-solving, analytical, writing, communication, presentation, teamwork, and interpersonal skills; curious, detail-oriented, creative, dedicated, flexible, and self-motivated

CAREER LADDER

```
┌─────────────────────────────┐
│   Senior Tissue Engineer    │
└─────────────────────────────┘

┌─────────────────────────────┐
│      Tissue Engineer        │
└─────────────────────────────┘

┌─────────────────────────────┐
│   Junior Tissue Engineer    │
└─────────────────────────────┘
```

Position Description

Throughout recorded history, human beings have endeavored to heal diseases and injuries, but it has only been in the last few decades that medical professionals have tried to replace diseased body parts via transplants. Without meticulous care and special medications, transplanted organs are rejected by the recipient's immune system. This, coupled with the difficulty with finding suitable donor organs, leaves many injured or sick patients with few or no options for recovery. The future, on the other hand, holds promise through the efforts of a profession called tissue engineering.

Tissue engineering is a young but growing specialty of biomedical engineering. In a very real sense, people have been practicing a form of tissue engineering for centuries, through the practice of breeding new strains of crops or animals. This breeding, which served to achieve the desired tissue function, physical form, traits, or behavior in plants and animals, provided a rudimentary platform for the development of modern tissue engineering.

Tissue Engineers, also known as biomedical engineers, are engaged in basic and applied research. They conduct research to further their understanding of molecular and cellular components of tissue and how they behave or interact. They also seek to understand such things as how to grow tissues or organs in the laboratory for implantation, how to stimulate cellular growth in the body to stop or reverse tumor growth, and how stimulating cells through mechanical or electrical means will affect their functions. They investigate the potential for cloning and stem cell techniques to further their efforts.

Additionally, they are involved in developing new methods of tissue generation, which one day may result in growing entire organs to replace diseased hearts, lungs, kidneys, or livers. Currently, bone, cartilage, and skin can be grown within or outside the body and implanted to replace hips, knees, or burned skin. Four major types of clinical therapies are being used to replace tissues or organs. Tissues may be harvested from one part of a patient's body and be transplanted into another location within the patient's body. Tissues may be taken from another person and transplanted. Some tissues from certain animals may also be used for transplanting into human patients. Lastly, human-made devices such as artificial hearts or hips may be implanted. Tissue Engineers are building upon these traditional clinical therapies to create new therapies.

Tissue engineering is a multidisciplinary field wherein Tissue Engineers collaborate with such professionals as molecular biologists, cell biologists, biomaterials engineers, robotics engineers, advanced imaging specialists, and bioreactor equipment developers. They combine knowledge from biology and chemistry, as well as electrical, mechanical, and chemical engineering to research and develop methods to control the growth and function of cells and tissues.

Most Tissue Engineers work as faculty at the university level. As teachers, they are responsible for teaching courses that are part of a prescribed curriculum within their department. Their teaching duties include preparing course outlines, class lectures, and lab work; creating examinations and grading student papers; supervising student research projects; and advising students about school and career matters.

Research professors are responsible for seeking funding for their projects, which covers overhead costs, staff salaries, and buying equipment and supplies. This involves such tasks as identifying funding sources (such as government agencies and private corporations) and preparing grant proposals. In addition, their research tasks include designing experiments, performing tests, gathering and analyzing data, preparing reports, planning work schedules, attending meetings, and supervising research and lab assistants. They are also expected to publish the results of their research through scholarly journals, books, or electronic media.

Tissue Engineers are expected to stay up-to-date with developments in their field. They network with colleagues; read current books, journals, and other publications; and participate in professional conferences.

Tissue Engineers, as professors, have a flexible work schedule. They typically work more than 40 hours a week and often work evenings and weekends to perform their various teaching and research duties.

Salaries

Salaries for Tissue Engineers vary, depending on such factors as their education, experience, employer, and geographical location. Specific salary information for these engineers is unavailable, but they generally earn salaries similar to biomedical engineers. The estimated annual salary for most biomedical engineers ranged between $43,490 and $113,070 according to the November 2004 *Occupational Employment Statistics* survey by the U.S. Bureau of Labor Statistics. Most engineering professors earned an estimated annual salary that ranged between $39,430 and $124,140.

Employment Prospects

Because tissue engineering is still a young field, opportunities in the private sector are currently limited, but they are expected to expand in the years to come. Some Tissue Engineers find work in companies that provide tissue products such as artificial skin or cartilage. Most Tissue Engineers are employed as professors in biomedical engineering departments at four-year colleges and universities.

Job openings generally become available as engineers retire, transfer to other jobs, or advance to higher positions. Employers may create additional positions as long as funding is available.

Advancement Prospects

In private settings, Tissue Engineers can become technical specialists as well as pursue such managerial positions as supervisory, project, and chief engineers.

Tenure-track faculty begin their careers as instructors or assistant professors. After serving a specific number of years, their academic, research, and service records are reviewed to determine if they should be granted tenure. When professors are granted tenure, they cannot be fired without just cause and due process. With tenure, assistant professors can rise through the ranks as associate professors and professors. Those with managerial and administrative ambitions can seek academic positions as department chairs, academic deans, administrative directors, provosts, and presidents.

Education and Training

Depending on the employer and job position, applicants must possess either a master's or doctoral degree in biomedical engineering, bioengineering, chemical engineering, or another related field. A doctorate is usually required for engineers to teach in colleges and universities. Some Tissue Engineers possess a medical degree along with a doctorate in engineering or science.

Many doctoral candidates spend two or more years completing postdoctoral training before accepting a permanent position.

Throughout their careers, Tissue Engineers enroll in continuing education and training programs to update their skills and keep up with advancements in their fields.

Experience, Special Skills, and Personality Traits

Academic institutions seek applicants who show they have the capability to be both excellent teachers and researchers. Applicants should have previous teaching experience, which they may have gained as graduate teaching assistants, lecturers, or adjunct instructors. Many employers prefer that candidates have several years of postdoctoral training.

To perform well at their work, Tissue Engineers need strong problem-solving, analytical, writing, communication, and presentation skills. They also need excellent teamwork and interpersonal skills, as they must work effectively with colleagues, students, administrators, and others. Being curious, detail-oriented, creative, dedicated, flexible, and self-motivated are some personality traits that successful Tissue Engineers share.

Unions and Associations

Many Tissue Engineers are members of professional associations to take advantage of professional services and resources, such as publications and networking opportunities. Some national societies that Tissue Engineers might join include the Tissue Engineering and Regenerative Medicine International Society, the Biomedical Engineering Society, the American Institute for Medical and Biological Engineering, and the American Association for the Advancement of Science. Faculty members may join such academic societies as the National Association of Scholars and the American Association of University Professors.

For contact information for the above organizations, see Appendix III.

Tips for Entry

1. While in high school, you can start learning about tissue engineering research. For example, you might read books and professional journals, as well as visit relevant Web sites.

2. Talk with your college advisor, along with other professors, to help you develop an educational program that reflects your interests and ambitions.

3. Many professional associations post job listings at their Web site, which nonmembers are allowed to access.

4. Use the Internet to learn more about Tissue Engineers. You might start by visiting these Web sites: Tissue Engineering and Regenerative Medicine International Society, http://www.tesinternational.org; and Pittsburgh Tissue Engineering Initiative, http://www.ptei.org. For more links, see Appendix IV.

INDUSTRIAL, MANUFACTURING, AND SYSTEMS ENGINEERING

INDUSTRIAL ENGINEER

CAREER PROFILE

Duties: Design, improve, and install systems that help organizations increase their efficiency and cut costs; perform duties as required

Alternate Title(s): A title that reflects a specialty (such as Human Factors Engineer) or an engineering function (such as Project Engineer)

Salary Range: $43,000 to $96,000

Employment Prospects: Good

Advancement Prospects: Good

Prerequisites:

Education or Training—Bachelor's degree in industrial engineering or a related field

Experience—Previous work experience generally required

Special Skills and Personality Traits—Communication, interpersonal, teamwork, leadership, time management, problem-solving, and negotiation skills; creative, curious, analytical, detail-oriented, adaptive, resourceful, diplomatic, ethical, and patient

Special Requirements—Professional engineer (P.E.) licensure may be required

CAREER LADDER

```
┌─────────────────────────────────┐
│   Senior Industrial Engineer     │
└─────────────────────────────────┘

┌─────────────────────────────────┐
│      Industrial Engineer         │
└─────────────────────────────────┘

┌─────────────────────────────────┐
│   Junior Industrial Engineer     │
└─────────────────────────────────┘
```

Position Description

Our modern society is a productive one. We generate goods and services in great quantities and in an efficient manner. We may hear of a new product that is being developed and, not long afterwards, that product can be found in retail stores in just about every community. Likewise, we enjoy quick response when we need some sort of service assistance. For example, when we visit a bank, a teller helps us after a short wait and our business is accomplished on a timely basis. Certainly, much of our productivity is achieved through the conscientious efforts of employees who work efficiently. Nevertheless, the efficiencies of our service and manufacturing economic sectors are carefully planned for and implemented by professionals called Industrial Engineers.

Industrial Engineers are sometimes known as systems integrators because they help organizations optimize their combined production of goods and services. They design, improve, and install systems that combine people, information, energy, equipment, and materials. Their emphasis is on the human component of these systems. Their goal is to save money for their organizations while increasing their efficiency.

Most of these engineers work in manufacturing industries. More of them are increasingly finding employment with business organizations, government agencies, and in the service industries where they are concerned with office automation, devising methods for cutting costs, and consolidating office functions. Their skills and expertise are widely used and they find employment in more industries than do any other type of engineer. Furthermore, some Industrial Engineers teach future generations of engineers in colleges and universities.

Industrial Engineers differ from those who work in other engineering professions in that they design work methods or procedures rather than machines or structures. Their job entails such undertakings as laying out work areas, analyzing and planning workers' job duties, and the handling of materials through all phases of production, storage, and distribution. In nonmanufacturing industries, they are responsible for organizing the implementation and delivering of services.

Industrial Engineers use their knowledge of mathematics and the sciences (physical, engineering, and behavioral) to innovate, change, and coordinate systems, as well as to solve problems pertaining to organization and production within work environments. In addition, they draw upon their expertise in such areas as statistics, stochastic processes, mathematical modeling, and computer science. It is this body of knowledge and its practical applications that further set these engineers apart from other engineers. Rather than deal with set formulas and precise designs, Industrial Engineers work with the many variables inherent with human behavior. This inspires flexibility with their approach to designing production systems.

These engineers may specialize in several areas. For example:

- Human factors engineers apply their knowledge about perception, mental processes, and body movements to their designs for equipment and the workplace to augment their usability for workers.
- Manufacturing systems engineers are involved with the analysis, design, and planning of manufacturing systems, processes, and methods.
- Operations research engineers study and develop new principles and procedures for evaluating, identifying, analyzing, organizing, and designing coordinated physical and operational systems.
- Production and management systems engineers plan, schedule, allocate, and control the measures that are needed to improve productivity and to use available physical, economic, and human resources in the production and distribution of goods and services.

Industrial Engineers conduct research, analyze data, design systems, plan processes, solve problems, manage changes, and coordinate the implementation of new systems, methods, and processes. They may be involved in a variety of projects, such as:

- finding new ways to manufacture products in a manner that will prevent worker injury
- designing or improving hospital admissions procedures
- converting facilities to utilize just-in-time production systems
- putting efficient manufacturing methods into practice
- devising and implementing material handling systems for a warehouse facility
- conceiving the layout of a ship repair facility
- working on a design project to make medical devices
- inputting their concerns about manufacturing and purchasing to construction processes
- studying, devising, and implementing efficiency measures in government

Industrial Engineers review production steps that lead to the completion of manufactured products or services. They are actively engaged in working with and communicating with other people. They ask many questions about work processes. They speak to production personnel, technicians, clerical staff, and administrators. They observe how workers perform their duties, how their equipment is set up, and how they use it to determine more efficient methods of completing the work.

These engineers use computers to analyze their observations as well as simulate work processes and control assembly lines. They then write reports and create charts or diagrams about how to more efficiently design the workplace. Their reports may offer recommendations for altering production steps or rearranging equipment. They may calculate some of these changes mathematically.

Industrial Engineers often concern themselves with several projects at a time. Each of their projects must be accurately completed. Their recommendations impact the profitability and costs of an organization's endeavors. Their decisions also affect the lives of workers as well as relations between labor and management. These factors occasionally contribute to a heightened level of stress for these engineers.

There are several levels of expertise within the industrial engineering profession. Junior engineers typically work under the guidance and supervision of senior engineers. Their focus is to develop their skills and their understanding of the rules, regulations, standards, and practices of their area of concern. They are given specific directions on their assignments along with clearly defined priorities and goals. As Industrial Engineers gain experience and knowledge, they receive more complex assignments and are able to exercise greater levels of authority.

Senior Industrial Engineers are more actively involved with the decision-making process and are more likely to be team leaders. They are more aware of program needs and work independently in response to those needs. Advanced to executive-level engineers are the primary engineers for project divisions. These professionals perform the most difficult engineering tasks. They make policy decisions and consult with clients or government agencies at the highest levels. They are responsible for top-level project management and client management, as well as business development and administration. They oversee all of the aspects of planning, design, and consultation.

Industrial Engineers work in office settings, but they are often required to visit other work areas, including manufacturing facilities. They generally work 40-hour weeks but occasionally put in extra hours to complete tasks or meet deadlines.

Salaries

Salaries for Industrial Engineers vary, depending on such factors as their education, experience, job duties, employer, industry, and geographical location. The U.S. Bureau of

Labor Statistics (BLS) reported in its November 2004 *Occupational Employment Statistics* (OES) survey that the estimated annual salary for most Industrial Engineers ranged between $43,220 and $95,690.

Employment Prospects

According to the BLS's November 2004 OES survey, an estimated 184,900 Industrial Engineers were employed in the United States. Opportunities are available in almost all industries. The BLS reported the highest levels of employment for Industrial Engineers in these industries: motor vehicle parts manufacturing, aerospace product and parts manufacturing, semiconductor and electronic component manufacturing, electronic instrument manufacturing, and architectural and engineering services.

In general, the demand for Industrial Engineers should continue to be favorable because organizations, particularly manufacturers, constantly seek ways to improve productivity and quality while reducing their costs. The BLS predicts that job growth for Industrial Engineers should increase by 9 to 17 percent through 2014. Opportunities will also become available as these engineers advance to higher positions, retire, or transfer to other jobs.

Advancement Prospects

Industrial Engineers may advance in any number of ways, depending on their ambitions and interests. They can become technical specialists as well as pursue project management or production supervision positions. Some Industrial Engineers move into positions in marketing, technical sales, and other business areas, while others become researchers and teachers. Engineers with entrepreneurial ambitions can become independent practitioners or owners of firms that offer technical or management consulting services.

Education and Training

Entry-level applicants must possess at least a bachelor's degree in industrial engineering or another related field. A master's or doctoral degree is usually required for engineers to pursue careers in management, consulting, research, or teaching. Engineers must possess a doctoral degree to teach industrial engineering at the college level. Many Industrial Engineers obtain advanced degrees in an industrial engineering specialty that interests them.

Employers typically provide entry-level engineers with on-the-job training while working under the supervision and guidance of experienced engineers. Many companies also have formal classroom training programs for their employees.

Throughout their careers, Industrial Engineers enroll in continuing education and training programs to update their skills and keep up with advancements in their fields.

Special Requirements

All engineers who offer engineering services directly to the public or perform work that affects the life, health, or prop-erty of the public must be licensed as professional engineers (P.E.) where they practice. Every state and territory, as well as Washington, D.C., has its own licensing requirements. For specific information, contact the board of engineering examiners for the area where you wish to practice. See Appendix II for a list of boards.

Experience, Special Skills, and Personality Traits

Entry-level candidates should have work experience related to the positions for which they apply. They may have gained their experience through internships, work-study programs, student research projects, postdoctoral training, or part-time employment. Employers generally prefer to hire candidates who have experience within their particular industry.

Having strong communication, interpersonal, and teamwork skills is essential for Industrial Engineers as they work with various people—colleagues, managers, vendors, and customers—from diverse backgrounds. In addition, these engineers need effective leadership, time management, problem-solving, and negotiation skills. Successful Industrial Engineers share such personality traits as being creative, curious, analytical, detail-oriented, adaptive, resourceful, diplomatic, ethical, and patient.

Unions and Associations

Many Industrial Engineers belong to local, state, and national societies to take advantage of networking opportunities, continuing education programs, certification, and other professional services and resources. Two national societies that serve the interests of these engineers are the Institute of Industrial Engineers and the Human Factors and Ergonomics Society. Professional engineers can join the National Society of Professional Engineers. For contact information, see Appendix III.

Tips for Entry

1. Courses in drafting, drawing, business administration, computer science, and electronics can help you prepare for a career in industrial engineering. Talk with professionals, teachers, or a counselor to determine which classes would be the best ones to take.
2. To enhance your employability, consider obtaining a master's degree in industrial engineering, business, or another related field. Some graduate students complete their studies while working full-time.
3. Along with looking at professional and trade journals for job announcements, check out opportunities that may be posted with your local unemployment office.
4. Use the Internet to learn more about industrial engineering. You might start by visiting these Web sites: Institute of Industrial Engineers, http://www.iienet.org; and The World-Wide Web Virtual Library: Industrial Engineering, http://www.isye.gatech.edu/www-ie. For more links, see Appendix IV.

MANUFACTURING ENGINEER

CAREER PROFILE

Duties: Develop, design, install, and monitor all the systems involved in the manufacturing process; perform duties as required

Alternate Title(s): Manufacturing Systems Engineer; a title that reflects a specialty (such as Quality Engineer) or an engineering function (such as Applications Engineer or Project Manager)

Salary Range: $44,000 to $113,000

Employment Prospects: Fair

Advancement Prospects: Good

Prerequisites:

Education or Training—Bachelor's degree in manufacturing engineering or another related field

Experience—Previous work experience generally required

Special Skills and Personality Traits—Leadership, problem-solving, organizational, writing, communication, interpersonal, teamwork, and self-management skills; creative, curious, ethical, persistent, calm, patient, and logical

Special Requirements—Professional engineer (P.E.) licensure may be required

CAREER LADDER

```
┌─────────────────────────────────────┐
│    Senior Manufacturing Engineer     │
└─────────────────────────────────────┘

┌─────────────────────────────────────┐
│       Manufacturing Engineer         │
└─────────────────────────────────────┘

┌─────────────────────────────────────┐
│    Junior Manufacturing Engineer     │
└─────────────────────────────────────┘
```

Position Description

It is easy for us to think about manufacturing in terms of big factories with belching smokestacks that churn out products around the clock. We may envision factory workers toiling at their assembly line stations while performing repetitive tasks. Not long ago, that was indeed the predominant manufacturing system, but that was just one stage in the long history of manufacturing. In the preindustrial world, one person, such as a candle maker or blacksmith, made each item by hand or with his or her own equipment. As societies expanded, such craftspeople could not make enough products to meet demand. Hence, small factories were built to produce several identical products simultaneously in batches or lots. With increased demand, larger factories with assembly lines began to produce each product singly, one step at a time. In today's manufacturing environment, products are produced in small quantities on demand for just-in-time delivery, and computerized machines increasingly do most of the work rather than armies of assembly line workers. Whichever system is used, in order for any modern manufacturing concern to function optimally or profitably, it must be meticulously engineered—designed, organized, and managed. Professionals known as Manufacturing Engineers perform that work.

These engineers are instrumental in creating every manufactured product, from processed foods to furniture to automobiles. They help manufacturing companies stay competitive in the modern marketplace. Manufacturing Engineers assist companies to shorten their product development and production lead times as well as to maximize their companies' production efficiency. These engineers also respond to changes in consumer demand as well as ensure product variety, quality, and competitive pricing. In addition, they help companies provide their workers with safe working environments.

Manufacturing Engineers are knowledgeable about engineering science, mathematics, chemistry, physics, computer science, statistics, and current manufacturing technologies and processes. They use this knowledge to create or study designs for products and plan how to manufacture them. They create appropriate manufacturing systems, design the necessary tools, and develop the plans for production. They are well versed in the latest computer-controlled manufacturing technologies, such as computer-aided design (CAD) and computer-aided manufacturing (CAM) systems; they design or evaluate new materials and are able to adapt the technologies and materials for use in producing finished goods.

These engineers plan new production facilities. They also use computers to design and create models for new products. They decide how products will be made, direct production processes, and test products. In addition, they observe and test output levels and recommend measures to optimize productivity. Furthermore, these engineers solve problems that may arise during manufacturing.

Manufacturing Engineers may specialize in certain technologies such as new materials, or in computer and robotic manufacturing systems. They may also specialize in specific industries, such as the aerospace, automobile, or household goods industries. Some of these engineers specialize in a particular area of work, such as in process engineering where they direct their attention to how tools and work pieces interact with each other. Others work as production engineers to integrate all the processes, parts, and systems of manufacturing a product. Some are concerned with the entire manufacturing process from product design to distribution, financing, and sales. Others are involved in conducting research or teaching engineering classes in colleges and universities.

Today's manufacturing environment is a challenge for these engineers as they must learn about and utilize new ideas and tactics for manufacturing to reduce costs and improve productivity in the increasingly competitive manufacturing economic sector. Consequently, Manufacturing Engineers are responsible for developing winning strategies for planning the best production methods and systems for their companies, including making decisions about where to locate production facilities.

These engineers are engaged in a variety of activities or tasks in the course of their work. They might:

- automate factories through the use of computers or robotic technologies
- analyze production operations to find ways to improve productivity
- develop work assignments for machines, equipment, and personnel
- devise and implement quality-control procedures
- design plant layouts
- create management information systems
- design workstations and plant control systems
- take part in meetings to discuss production improvements and estimate the requirements and costs of upgrading technology and systems

- determine the most efficient use of staff, equipment, and materials
- install manufacturing equipment
- inspect equipment systems for problems or failures, discuss the problems with staff, and initiate or manage repair procedures
- train and supervise other engineers and support staff
- look into environmental hazards
- identify and utilize new equipment suppliers
- conduct safety tests and remove hazards
- keep up-to-date with current developments in manufacturing and engineering by reading books and journals as well as by attending meetings or taking courses

Manufacturing industries as diverse as the farm machinery, automobile, industrial equipment, household goods, and electronics industries employ Manufacturing Engineers. Government agencies and educational institutions also employ these engineers. Some Manufacturing Engineers own consulting companies.

These engineers usually work for 40 hours each week but put in additional hours as needed. They may work evening or night shifts. They work in offices, laboratories, and plant floors. Working conditions in production areas may be noisy and dirty.

Salaries

Salaries for Manufacturing Engineers vary, depending on such factors as their education, experience, job duties, employer, and geographical location. Specific salary information for this occupation is unavailable, but an idea can be obtained by looking at the salaries for engineers in general. According to the November 2004 *Occupational Employment Statistics* survey by the U.S. Bureau of Labor Statistics, the estimated annual salary for most engineers not listed separately in the survey ranged between $44,040 and $113,000.

Employment Prospects

Job openings become available as Manufacturing Engineers are promoted, transfer to other occupations, or retire. Employers will create additional positions as their needs grow. In general, opportunities should be favorable for experienced engineers in this specialty due to the constant need to improve and update manufacturing systems. Keep in mind that employment is influenced by the health of the economy. During economic downturns, for example, fewer jobs become available.

Advancement Prospects

Manufacturing Engineers may advance in any number of ways, depending on their ambitions and interests. As they gain experience, they are assigned to more complex projects as well as receive increasingly greater responsibilities. Senior engineers can become technical specialists, consultants, and engineering managers. Some engineers move into positions in marketing, technical sales, or another business area, while others pursue careers in research or teaching. Engineers with entrepreneurial ambitions can become independent consultants or owners of technical or consulting firms.

Education and Training

Minimally, a bachelor's degree in manufacturing engineering, industrial engineering, or another related field is needed for applicants to qualify for entry-level positions. A master's or doctoral degree is usually required to pursue careers in management, consulting, or research. Engineers must possess a doctorate to teach civil engineering at the college level.

Entry-level engineers receive on-the-job training while working under the supervision and guidance of experienced engineers. Many of them also receive formal classroom training.

Throughout their careers, Manufacturing Engineers enroll in continuing education and training programs to update their skills and keep up with advancements in their fields.

Special Requirements

All engineers who offer engineering services directly to the public or perform work that affects the life, health, or property of the public must be licensed as professional engineers (P.E.). Licensing requirements differ in each state and territory, as well as in Washington, D.C. For specific information, contact the board of engineering examiners for the area where you wish to practice. See Appendix II for a list of boards.

Experience, Special Skills, and Personality Traits

Entry-level candidates should have work experience related to the positions for which they apply. They may have gained their experience through internships, work-study programs, student research projects, postdoctoral training, or employment. Employers generally prefer to hire candidates who have experience within their particular industry.

To perform well at their work, Manufacturing Engineers need effective leadership, problem-solving, organizational, writing, and communication skills. They also must have strong interpersonal and teamwork skills to be able to work well with many people from diverse backgrounds. In addition, they need excellent self-management skills, such as the ability to work independently, handle stressful situations, meet deadlines, and prioritize multiple tasks. Being creative, curious, ethical, persistent, calm, patient, and logical are some personality traits that successful Manufacturing Engineers share.

Unions and Associations

Manufacturing Engineers belong to local, state, and national societies to take advantage of networking opportunities, continuing education programs, and other professional services and resources. The Society of Manufacturing Engineers is a professional association that serves the interests of this profession at the national level. For contact information, see Appendix III.

Tips for Entry

1. While you are in college, you can gain valuable experience by participating in a cooperative education program that allows you to work in an industrial setting. Students usually alternate semesters of paid work experience and academic studies in these work-study programs.
2. Job ads and job announcements usually give brief details about a vacancy. Contact a company's human resources department for obtaining a complete job description.
3. Many professional and trade manufacturing associations have job banks on their Web sites that allow access to nonmembers.
4. Use the Internet to learn more about Manufacturing Engineers and manufacturing industries. You might start by visiting these Web sites: Society of Manufacturing Engineers, http://www.sme.org; and National Association of Manufacturers, http://www.nam.org. For more links, see Appendix IV.

SYSTEMS ENGINEER

CAREER PROFILE

Duties: Define, develop, and consolidate entire systems, from their conception to their operation; perform duties as required

Alternate Title(s): Systems Architect; a title that reflects a specialty (such as Quality Engineer) or an engineering function (such as Product Engineer)

Salary Range: $44,000 to $113,000

Employment Prospects: Good

Advancement Prospects: Good

Prerequisites:

Education or Training—Bachelor's degree in systems engineering or another engineering field

Experience—Previous work experience generally required

Special Skills and Personality Traits—Leadership, negotiation, time management, problem-solving, communication, and writing skills; analytical, resourceful, creative, diplomatic, patient, inquisitive, adaptable, and ethical

Special Requirements—Professional engineer (P.E.) licensure may be required

CAREER LADDER

```
┌─────────────────────────────┐
│   Senior Systems Engineer    │
└─────────────────────────────┘

┌─────────────────────────────┐
│      Systems Engineer        │
└─────────────────────────────┘

┌─────────────────────────────┐
│  Associate Systems Engineer  │
└─────────────────────────────┘
```

Position Description

We are all familiar with systems. Some of us enjoy home entertainment systems consisting of DVD players, CD players, amplifiers, screens, and speakers. Our bodies are systems, and they contain such subsystems as our nervous, endocrine, and cardiovascular systems. Our automobiles are systems composed of wheels, engines, and transmissions, as well as braking and steering systems. We drive our automobiles on a system of streets, roads, and highways. Our society itself is a system of governments, industries, communities, and so on. Systems can be composed of people, facilities, machines, data, services, methodologies, or a combination of all these components. In our complex modern world, systems are increasingly complicated and range in size from the miniscule to the tremendous.

Systems engineering is a relatively new field in which large engineering projects are administered by the use of several interrelated engineering endeavors. Systems Engineers define, develop, and consolidate high-caliber systems. Unlike other engineers, who focus on individual facets of a system, Systems Engineers concern themselves with entire systems. Their job is to see the big picture. They give consideration to what the various components of a system will do or how they should perform before they think about what such entities will be.

These engineers are adept at grasping the complexity of systems. They know how to use appropriate methods and tools to configure and solve systems engineering problems. Their work is interdisciplinary; that is, several engineering approaches are used to solve problems with the design and implementation of systems. These engineers work in teams composed of engineers from different disciplines, as well as scientists, technicians, business people, and others.

Systems Engineers' mission is to form and guide a process for the development and sustainment of systems from concept to production to operation. They give consideration to both the business and technical needs of their clients. Hence, they pay attention to such details of a project as cost, scheduling considerations, and social issues that may arise in addition to the design and functionality of the system in question. Systems Engineers are also concerned with the testing, manufacturing, and disposal of systems as well as with training and providing support to clients in the use of systems.

Systems Engineers are trained in a multiplicity of academic disciplines, including physics, mathematics, biology, chemistry, computer science, business ethics, and management as well as such engineering fields as civil engineering and materials engineering. They utilize their training and expertise to offer work that focuses on such important aspects of systems engineering as:

- designing compatibility
- defining systems requirements
- managing projects
- analyzing costs
- scheduling
- providing for maintenance needs
- ensuring ease of operations
- looking ahead toward necessary system upgrades
- keeping the lines of communication open among engineers, suppliers, managers, and clients

These engineers work with systems in a variety of industries. They work in the petroleum industry wherein they are involved with all the activities of oil companies. They manage drilling, processing, and the maintenance of equipment. Industrial Systems Engineers work toward making production safer and more efficient. They understand the scientific principles that make machines work. They design solutions to the myriad problems that arise in keeping industrial systems running smoothly.

In the area of environmental concerns, Systems Engineers work in the fields of waste disposal, wastewater treatment, water purification, and others. Software Systems Engineers design software that will work on multiple computer operating systems. They also create software that enables industries to more efficiently control such complex systems as assembly lines or quality control facilities. Electronics Systems Engineers work in the robotics, telecommunications, and microelectronic industries to design, put in place, operate, and maintain such systems as information networks and automated production systems.

Systems Engineers may specialize in any one or more of the following specialty areas: requirements engineering; risk and opportunity management; baseline control (or configuration management); technical planning and effort assessment; systems architecture; design development; verification and validation; process definition; tool support; systems integration; and integrated logistics support.

Each member of a systems engineering team has a specific function or role to play, such as designer, planner, verifier, or analyzer. Their involvement with the life of a system can be summarized with seven basic tasks, which are: stating the problem, investigating alternatives, modeling the

system, integrating system elements, launching the system, assessing the system's performance, and re-evaluating the system on a continuous basis.

Systems Engineers are responsible for carefully and accurately documenting their work activities. Their team efforts place them in situations where they must communicate clearly and work effectively with other people from a wide range of backgrounds and careers. They may be involved with marketing and sales concerns. As managers, they maintain a balance of project elements and ensure that all personnel work together toward a common goal.

These engineers are largely employed with industries or government agencies that perform work that advances technology and its uses for business purposes. Their work is mostly in defense industries, as well as in such arenas as manufacturing, consulting, construction, biomedical systems, instrumentation, telecommunications, computer engineering, and aerospace, among others. Some Systems Engineers are engaged in teaching courses and conducting research at the college and university level.

Systems Engineers work in office settings, but they are often required to visit other work areas, including manufacturing facilities. They generally work 40-hour weeks but may occasionally put in extra hours to complete tasks or meet deadlines.

Salaries

Salaries for Systems Engineers vary, depending on such factors as their education, experience, position, employer, industry, and geographical location. Specific salary information for this occupation is unavailable, but an idea can be obtained by looking at the salaries for engineers in general. According to the November 2004 *Occupational Employment Statistics* survey by the U.S. Bureau of Labor Statistics, the estimated annual salary for most engineers not listed separately in the survey ranged between $44,040 and $113,000.

Employment Prospects

Because of the increasing complexity of systems, the demand for Systems Engineers in both the public and private sectors is expected to grow through the years. In general, most opportunities become available as engineers are promoted, transfer to other jobs, or retire. Organizations create additional positions to fit their growing needs, as long as funding is available.

Advancement Prospects

Systems Engineers may advance in any number of ways, depending on their ambitions and interests. They can become technical specialists as well as pursue engineering management and executive-level positions. Some Industrial Engineers move into positions in marketing, technical sales, and other business areas, while others become researchers and teachers. Engineers with entrepreneurial ambitions can become independent practitioners or owners of firms that offer consulting services.

Education and Training

Minimally, applicants for entry-level positions need a bachelor's degree in systems engineering or in another related field. A master's or doctoral degree is usually required for engineers to pursue careers in management, consulting, research, or teaching. Engineers must possess a doctorate to teach systems engineering at the college level.

Employers typically provide entry-level engineers with training programs, which may include both on-the-job training and formal classroom training. New engineers work under the supervision and direction of experienced engineers.

Throughout their careers, Systems Engineers enroll in continuing education programs and training programs to update their skills and keep up with advancements in their fields.

Special Requirements

All engineers who offer engineering services directly to the public or perform work that affects the life, health, or property of the public must be licensed as professional engineers (P.E.) where they practice. Every state and territory, as well as Washington, D.C., has its own licensing requirements. For specific information, contact the board of engineering examiners for the area where you wish to practice. See Appendix II for a list of boards.

Experience, Special Skills, and Personality Traits

Requirements for entry-level positions vary from employer to employer. In general, entry-level candidates should have work experience related to the positions for which they apply. They may have gained their experience through internships, work-study programs, student research projects, postdoctoral training, or employment. Having experience within an employer's industry is also preferable.

To perform well at their job, Systems Engineers must have strong leadership, negotiation, time management, problem-solving, communication, and writing skills. Being analytical, resourceful, creative, diplomatic, patient, inquisitive, adaptable, and ethical are some personality traits that successful Systems Engineers share.

Unions and Associations

Systems Engineers may join local, state, and national societies to take advantage of networking opportunities, continuing education programs, and other professional services and resources. Some national societies include the International Council on Systems Engineering, the Institute of Industrial Engineers, and the IEEE Systems, Man, and Cybernetics Society. For contact information, see Appendix III.

Tips for Entry

1. In high school, you can prepare for a career in systems engineering by taking courses in advanced mathematics, physics, and computer science.
2. Some engineers enhance their employability by obtaining appropriate professional certification from recognized organizations such as the International Council on Systems Engineering.
3. Learn more about Systems Engineers on the Internet. You might start by visiting the International Council on Systems Engineering Web site, http://www.incose. org. For more links, see Appendix IV.

HUMAN FACTORS ENGINEER

CAREER PROFILE

Duties: Design, develop, implement, and improve integrated systems so that people can use machines or systems more effectively and easily; perform duties as required

Alternate Title(s): Human Factors Specialist, Engineering Psychologist; a title that reflects a specialty (such as Ergonomics Engineer or Usability Engineer) or an engineering function (such as Research Engineer)

Salary Range: $39,000 to $124,000

Employment Prospects: Good

Advancement Prospects: Good

Prerequisites:

Education or Training—Master's or doctoral degree in human factors or a related field

Experience—Previous work experience generally required

Special Skills and Personality Traits—Project management, problem-solving, presentation, writing, communication, interpersonal, and teamwork skills; enthusiastic, flexible, creative, analytical, and detail-oriented

Special Requirements—Professional engineer (P.E.) licensure may be required

CAREER LADDER

> **Senior Human Factors Engineer**

> **Human Factors Engineer**

> **Associate Human Factors Engineer**

Position Description

Imagine driving an automobile in which the steering mechanism was a stick-shaped device rather than a steering wheel. What if you piloted an airplane in which the wing flap and landing gear controls looked so much alike that it was easy to confuse them? Suppose you had to work with a computer without a mouse or "dropdown" menu options. All these unwieldy devices were in common usage at one time. Automobiles, airplanes, computers, and many other common machines and systems are much easier and more comfortable to use today because of the efforts of professionals who work in the field of human factors engineering.

Human Factors Engineers strive to maximize the performance of people in their use of products, processes, and systems, particularly in the workplace. They do so by studying and modifying how people interact with certain types of devices, equipment, machines, and their work environment. People cannot use machines or systems effectively without ease of use, a minimum of errors, and a low level of physical or psychological stress. Hence, their mental and physical needs, capabilities, and expectations are considered when Human Factors Engineers design such systems.

When systems are difficult to use, or when their use causes injury, production declines. Human Factor Engineers approach this issue from various specialties that draw upon their knowledge of physiology, psychology, and sociology in addition to their training in engineering design and research methodologies. Some of these areas in which Human Factors Engineers specialize are ergonomics, user interface design, and human-computer interaction (HCI).

Ergonomics engineers are engaged in the design and layout of equipment that enables people to interact or interface with it comfortably and safely, as in adjustable desks that can be raised and lowered by the user. They also adapt objects to conform to people's body shapes, correct their postures, or help them avoid injury, as in ergonomic chairs and computer keyboards.

User interface design engineers are involved in the development of the features of equipment systems or computer hardware and software that are used by a person to control its operation, as in the accelerator, brakes, and steering wheel of an automobile or a computer's keyboard and mouse. The ease of utility for such designs is often called user friendly.

HCI engineers study how people and computers interact. These engineers use there findings to determine which information is presented to a computer user and how it is presented, as well as how computer applications may be improved.

Human Factors Engineers may also specialize in the area of error prevention. In this specialty, engineers study the phenomenon of human error and determine where it can be predicted in order to design systems that will help prevent or minimize error.

Human Factors Engineers are involved in such engineering functions as project management, technical services, forensics, design, testing, regulatory affairs, or research at various stages of their careers. They may teach at colleges and universities, conduct research, publish their findings, and provide service to their communities.

These engineers are responsible for performing a variety of tasks, which vary each day. They may:

- manage programs for government or industry clients
- be involved with projects that confront the issue of worker fatigue
- work with clients to better understand their problems with using systems
- develop tools and processes specifically appropriate to human factors
- test developmental prototypes of new products
- coordinate with equipment designers, producers, and suppliers to ensure product compliance with ergonomic design specifications
- assist clients to test new ergonomic systems

A wide range of private sector industries including the aviation, aerospace, automotive, energy, computer, communications, manufacturing, and medical devices industries hire Human Factors Engineers. They work in industries that need their services in the areas of usability testing, interface design, or software development. A few of these engineers work in the area of research. Some engineers are employed by government agencies and the military.

Human Factors Engineers work in office settings. They may be required to travel to other locations to complete some of their tasks. They generally work for 40 hours each week but may put in extra hours to finish projects.

Salaries

Salaries for Human Factors Engineers vary, depending on such factors as their education, experience, employer, and geographical location. The U.S. Bureau of Labor Statistics (BLS) reported in its November 2004 *Occupational Employment Statistics* (OES) survey that the estimated annual salary for most industrial engineers, which includes Human Factors Engineers, ranged between $43,220 and $95,690. The estimated annual salary for most postsecondary engineering teachers ranged between $39,430 and $124,140.

Employment Prospects

According to some experts in the field, opportunities for Human Factors Engineers should be favorable in the coming years, as this profession is needed to ensure that products are usable and efficient for consumers and employees.

Job openings generally become available as engineers transfer to other jobs, advance to higher positions, or retire. Employers will create additional positions as their companies grow and expand.

Advancement Prospects

Human Factors Engineers may advance in any number of ways, depending on their ambitions and interests as well as their work setting. For example, in industry, they can become technical specialists or pursue engineering management positions, while academic instructors can rise through the ranks as assistant, associate, and full professors. Engineers with entrepreneurial ambitions can become independent practitioners or owners of firms that offer technical or consulting services.

Education and Training

Most employers prefer to hire candidates who possess at least a master's degree in human factors, industrial engineering, engineering psychology, or another related field for entry-level positions. Some employers, such as colleges and universities, prefer that candidates hold a doctorate.

Entry-level engineers typically receive on-the-job training while working under the supervision and guidance of experienced engineers. Some companies also provide novice engineers with formal classroom training as well.

Throughout their careers, Human Factors Engineers enroll in continuing education and training programs to update their skills and keep up with advancements in their fields.

Special Requirements

Engineers who offer engineering services directly to the public or perform work that affects the life, health, or property of the public must be licensed as professional engineers

(P.E.) where they practice. Every state and territory, as well as Washington, D.C., has its own requirements for P.E. licensure. For specific information, contact the board of engineering examiners for the area where you wish to practice. See Appendix II for a list of boards.

Experience, Special Skills, and Personality Traits

Employers generally prefer to hire candidates for entry-level positions who have work experience related to the positions for which they apply. They may have gained their experience through internships, work-study programs, student research projects, postdoctoral training, or employment. Candidates should also have some experience with or be knowledgeable about the industry of a prospective employer.

Human Factors Engineers need strong project management, problem-solving, presentation, and writing skills for their job. They also must have effective communication, interpersonal, and teamwork skills as they work with many people from diverse backgrounds. Being enthusiastic, flexible, creative, analytical, and detail-oriented are some personality traits that successful Human Factors Engineers share.

Unions and Associations

Human Factors Engineers can join professional associations to take advantage of networking opportunities, certification, continuing education programs, job banks, and other professional services and resources. Some national societies that serve the diverse interests of these engineers include:

- Human Factors and Ergonomics Society
- Aerospace Human Factors Association
- Special Interest Group on Computer-Human Interaction (part of the Association for Computer Machinery)
- Institute of Industrial Engineers
- International Society for Performance Improvement

For contact information for the above organizations, see Appendix III.

Tips for Entry

1. Mentors can help you develop your career. Find a professor or a professional in the field who is interested in your work and willing to be your mentor.
2. While completing your studies, maintain a portfolio of your accomplishments, which may include student papers, research studies, presentations, publications, job performance evaluations, and so on. Be sure to bring your portfolio to your job interviews.
3. Thoroughly research the graduate schools in which you are interested. Does a program match your interests? Are there instructors with whom you want to study? If you decide later to obtain a doctorate, can you complete the program at a school or will you need to transfer?
4. Contact alumni who work in companies or industries that interest you. They may be able to tell you about current or future job openings as well as whom to contact in their organization.
5. Use the Internet to learn more about Human Factors Engineers. You might start by visiting these Web sites: Human Factors and Ergonomics Society, http://www.hfes.org; and Usernomics, http://www.usernomics.com. For more links, see Appendix IV.

QUALITY ENGINEER

CAREER PROFILE

Duties: Develop quality programs that ensure that raw materials, products, and manufacturing processes meet company and industrial standards; perform duties as required

Alternate Title(s): Quality Control Engineer, Quality Assurance Engineer, Quality Specialist

Salary Range: $44,000 to $113,000

Employment Prospects: Good

Advancement Prospects: Good

Prerequisites:

    Education or Training—Bachelor's degree in an engineering or science field

    Experience—One to two years of work experience

    Special Skills and Personality Traits—Leadership, problem-solving, self-management, teamwork, interpersonal, computer and writing skills; self-motivated, flexible, detail-oriented, observant, and responsible

    Special Requirements—Professional engineer (P.E.) licensure may be required

CAREER LADDER

```
┌─────────────────────────────┐
│   Senior Quality Engineer    │
└─────────────────────────────┘

┌─────────────────────────────┐
│      Quality Engineer        │
└─────────────────────────────┘

┌─────────────────────────────┐
│   Junior Quality Engineer    │
└─────────────────────────────┘
```

Position Description

People have striven for quality of production throughout history. With the onset of the Industrial Revolution and the mass production of goods, quality became increasingly important. Production began to involve many people who used sophisticated equipment, rather than solitary craftspersons. More people in the production process led to greater potential for mistakes. Hence, quality needed to be assured for every step of production and for every component of a product, just as much as for the finished product. Today, quality is an imperative facet of our increasingly competitive manufacturing economic sector. Our technologically sophisticated consumer products and advanced manufacturing techniques, combined with internationally agreed-upon quality standards, have created a need for quality control and assurance in every manufacturing process. Quality Engineers are the professionals who fill this very need.

In manufacturing, the term *quality* refers to products having all the characteristics required to meet customer satisfaction and to products being free of any defects or deficiencies. Quality is also a desired characteristic of services, information systems, and training programs that are provided by a wide spectrum of enterprises. Quality is basic for any organization to sustain a record of success. Industry, government, educational institutions, healthcare organizations, and businesses constantly seek improvement. Through their activities of inspection, testing, analysis, and corrective action, Quality Engineers oversee continuous improvement in such aspects of enterprise as documentation systems, statistical methods, testing systems, reliability programs, and failure-analysis techniques.

Quality Engineers are responsible for developing standards, policies, procedures, and programs that ensure that quality requirements are fulfilled. They check for unsatisfactory performance and can request that work be redone, materials or products thrown out, or even stop production until corrections have been made. They analyze which factors impact quality. They understand and apply various tools and the latest methodologies to effect quality improvements, reduced costs, increased productivity, and improved responsiveness.

These engineers are involved with designing and evaluating products or services. They may specialize in such areas as design and sales, or work with marketing professionals to evaluate customer feedback about product or service performance. They ensure that materials and equipment used in work processes also meet quality requirements. They oversee staffs of quality technicians, inspectors, specialists, and other personnel. Some Quality Engineers conduct research at institutions of higher learning or industrial research facilities. Some of them also teach courses in colleges and universities.

They often work closely with manufacturing engineers and technicians. Their duties vary, depending on their experience, position, and other factors. Some duties that Quality Engineers might perform include:

- applying quality control standards
- inspecting, testing, and evaluating the precision and accuracy of production equipment and quality testing and inspection tools
- developing quality control standards for processing raw materials into products
- conducting audits to confirm that processes are in compliance with company specifications and industrial standards
- preparing documentation, reports, and accurate, detailed records
- performing statistical analyses
- training other quality staff personnel
- staying up-to-date with laws and industry standards that regulate the quality of products or services their companies provide

Industries, government agencies, educational institutions, and service industries employ Quality Engineers. Many of them work in manufacturing plants. They perform most of their assignments indoors and may be required to do some light lifting (up to twenty pounds). Their work may occasionally be repetitive.

In industrial settings, most Quality Engineers have offices apart from production areas, but they spend a large portion of their time on the production floor. Some of these engineers work where conditions may be noisy, dirty, or hot, particularly in such places as steel plants. Others work in cleaner environments, such as in the production facilities of electronics or pharmaceutical industries. Those who are involved with analysis or testing work in laboratory settings may be exposed to fumes or toxic substances.

These engineers generally work for 40 hours per week. Many of them work evening or night shifts, which may include weekends.

Salaries

Salaries for Quality Engineers vary, depending on such factors as their education, experience, position, employer, industry, and geographical location. Specific salary information for this occupation is unavailable, but an idea can be obtained by looking at the salaries for engineers in general. According to the November 2004 *Occupational Employment Statistics* survey by the U.S. Bureau of Labor Statistics, the estimated annual salary for most engineers not listed separately in the survey ranged between $44,040 and $113,000.

Employment Prospects

Opportunities for experienced Quality Engineers should be favorable in the coming years because quality is so vital to the success of all manufacturing and service industries. Openings generally become available as engineers are promoted, transfer to other jobs, or retire. Employers will create additional positions as their organizations grow and expand.

Advancement Prospects

Quality Engineers may advance in any number of ways, depending on their ambitions and interests. They can become technical specialists or move into positions in human resources, marketing, or another business area. Those with managerial and administrative ambitions can pursue either engineering management or nontechnical management positions. Engineers with entrepreneurial ambitions can become independent practitioners or owners of firms that offer consulting services.

Education and Training

Minimally, applicants for entry-level positions need a bachelor's degree in an engineering or science discipline. Some employers prefer to hire candidates who hold an advanced degree. Many Quality Engineers obtain a master's or doctoral degree in industrial engineering with a concentration in quality engineering.

A master's or doctoral degree is usually required for engineers to advance to careers in management, consulting, or research. Engineers must possess a doctorate to teach engineering at the college level.

Entry-level engineers usually receive on-the-job training while working under the supervision and guidance of experienced engineers. In some companies, they are also given formal classroom training.

Throughout their careers, Quality Engineers enroll in continuing education and training programs to update their skills and keep up with advancements in their field.

Special Requirements

All engineers who offer engineering services directly to the public or perform work that affects the life, health, or property of the public must be licensed as professional engineers (P.E.) where they practice. Every state and territory, as well as Washington, D.C., has its own requirements for P.E.

licensure. For specific information, contact the board of engineering examiners for the area where you wish to practice. See Appendix II for a list of boards.

Experience, Special Skills, and Personality Traits

Many employers require that applicants for entry-level positions have one to two years of work experience in quality. They may have gained their experience through internships, work experience programs, or employment. Employers also prefer to hire candidates who have experience working in their industry.

Quality Engineers need excellent leadership, problem-solving, self-management, teamwork, and interpersonal skills for their line of work. Having strong computer and writing skills is also essential. Some personality traits that successful Quality Engineers share include being self-motivated, flexible, detail-oriented, observant, and responsible.

Unions and Associations

Many Quality Engineers join a professional society to take advantage of networking opportunities, continuing education programs, certification, job bank, and other professional services and resources. The American Society for Quality is a national society that serves the interests of this profession. For contact information, see Appendix III.

Tips for Entry

1. Be sure to read job announcements carefully as job titles and duties for Quality Engineers vary from one company to the next.
2. To enhance their employability, some Quality Engineers obtain professional certification from recognized organizations such as the American Society for Quality.
3. Take advantage of job banks on the Internet, such as Monster, Inc. (http://www.monster.com), to learn about job openings.
4. Learn more about the field of quality on the Internet. You might start by visiting the American Society for Quality Web site, http://www.asq.org. For more links, see Appendix IV.

MORE ENGINEERING DISCIPLINES

ACOUSTICAL ENGINEER

CAREER PROFILE

Duties: Research, develop, design, and test acoustical systems for various purposes; perform duties as required

Alternate Title(s): A title that reflects a specialty (such as Audio Engineer or Noise Control Engineer) or an engineering function (such as Project Engineer)

Salary Range: $44,000 to $113,000

Employment Prospects: Good

Advancement Prospects: Good

Prerequisites:

Education or Training—Bachelor's or master's degree in acoustical engineering or a related field; on-the-job training

Experience—Previous work experience generally required

Special Skills and Personality Traits—Problem-solving, writing, communication, interpersonal, and teamwork skills; analytical, cooperative, creative, resourceful, and flexible

Special Requirements—Professional engineer (P.E.) licensure may be required

CAREER LADDER

```
┌─────────────────────────────────┐
│     Senior Acoustical Engineer   │
└─────────────────────────────────┘

┌─────────────────────────────────┐
│       Acoustical Engineer        │
└─────────────────────────────────┘

┌─────────────────────────────────┐
│    Junior Acoustical Engineer    │
└─────────────────────────────────┘
```

Position Description

Sounds are important to just about everyone. It is easier for us to communicate with one another when we can hear well. We enjoy the sounds of nature, the soft murmuring of a baby, and music. Sometimes, however, sounds can be annoying or harmful to us. The science of acoustics is the study of how sound travels, how it can be detected, and how it behaves in various environments. Acoustical engineering is linked to the science of acoustics.

Acoustical Engineers are concerned with the generation of sounds and how they interact with objects. They are engaged in seeking solutions to problems regarding the creation of useful sounds or how to reduce unpleasant and unwanted sounds. In addition, Acoustical Engineers are involved in finding practical applications for using sound in a wide range of technologies. For example, sound is used in technologies for such purposes as testing industrial materials, diagnosing medical conditions, locating fish for commercial fishermen, mapping underwater land features,

eliminating vibrations in structures, seismic surveying, and finding oil-bearing rocks underground, among others.

The field of acoustical engineering covers so many areas of interest that Acoustical Engineers usually specialize in a particular area. One major area is audio engineering, or electroacoustics. Audio engineers are concerned with problems related to recording and reproducing sound. They also work with microphones, loudspeakers, and other devices that convert sound energy into a different kind of energy, and vice versa. Some of these engineers find work as recording directors or technical directors.

Architectural acoustics is another major area in which Acoustical Engineers work. These engineers are involved in the design of office buildings, auditoriums, recording studios, churches, factories, homes, and other structures. They ensure that buildings are designed so that pleasing sound is efficiently distributed and unwanted noises are minimized.

Another major area is noise control. These Acoustical Engineers are involved in solving problems caused by noise pollution by controlling noise at its source and along its path as well as constructing noise barriers.

Many Acoustical Engineers are engaged in the area of bioengineering. They apply their research about how sounds interact with biological tissues to find technological solutions for preventing or improving hearing loss, as well as enabling the speech and hearing impaired to communicate.

Still another major specialty is musical acoustics. Engineers in this area are knowledgeable about the structure and qualities of music, such as melody and pitch, which they use to design musical instruments. Further, some Acoustical Engineers are engaged in lesser-known acoustical specialties such as underwater acoustics, aeroacoustics (or aerodynamic sound), structural acoustics, or physical acoustics (how sounds travel through gas, liquid, or other substance).

Acoustical Engineers are involved with all the engineering functions of research, design, development, testing, consulting, and project management. Their duties vary according to their specific areas of concern. In general, they might:

- use sound level meters, recorders, and data analysis equipment to measure and analyze sounds produced by various sources in a variety of environments
- oversee sound and vibration test programs
- develop sound improvement or noise reduction techniques and technologies
- identify noise sources and implement controls
- conduct acoustic research in laboratory settings
- prepare lab proposals and research reports
- work with or supervise a staff of engineers to complete projects
- administer community sound-level measurement programs
- collaborate with manufacturing and marketing personnel to complete projects within specified guidelines
- keep up-to-date with current testing standards, building codes, construction practices, and developments in the acoustic science and engineering disciplines

Most of these engineers work in lab or office settings, but often visit other locations to complete tests, measurements, and other field assignments. They basically work for 40 hours per week but may put in extra hours during evenings. Some Acoustical Engineers must travel to perform fieldwork.

Salaries

Salaries for Acoustical Engineers vary, depending on such factors as their education, experience, employer, and geographical location. Specific salary information for this occupation is unavailable, but an idea can be obtained by looking at the salaries for engineers in general. According to November 2004 *Occupational Employment Statistics* survey by the U.S. Bureau of Labor Statistics, the estimated annual salary for most engineers not listed separately in the survey ranged between $44,040 and $113,000.

Employment Prospects

Acoustical Engineers work in a wide range of occupational environments. Their expertise is in demand with the architecture and construction industries, defense contractors, and manufacturers of such items as musical instruments, audio equipment, hearing aids, automobile mufflers, and jet engines.

Job opportunities should continuously be favorable for experienced Acoustical Engineers. According to the Acoustical Society of America, there is a demand for Acoustical Engineers in many of the acoustical specialties. In general, most opportunities become available as Acoustical Engineers advance to higher positions, transfer to other occupations, or retire. Employers will create additional positions as their needs grow.

Advancement Prospects

Acoustical Engineers may advance in any number of ways, depending on their ambitions and interests. They may become technical specialists, or move into the business areas of an organization, such as marketing, technical sales, or finance. Those with managerial and administrative ambitions may pursue engineering management positions as well as executive officer positions within their organization. Engineers with entrepreneurial ambitions can become independent consultants or owners of firms that offer acoustical engineering services. Furthermore, Acoustical Engineers can pursue careers as academic teachers and researchers.

Education and Training

Educational requirements vary among employers but, in general, they prefer to hire applicants who have completed formal coursework in acoustics. Depending on the employer, individuals who are seeking an entry-level position may need a bachelor's or master's degree in acoustical engineering, mechanical engineering, electrical engineering, aeronautical engineering, physics, or another related field. A master's or doctoral degree is usually required for engineers to fill positions in management, consulting, or research. Engineers must possess a doctorate to teach in colleges and universities.

Entry-level engineers normally receive on-the-job training while working under the supervision and guidance of experienced engineers. In some companies, they also participate in formal classroom instruction.

Throughout their careers, Acoustical Engineers enroll in continuing education programs and training programs to update their skills and keep up with advancements in their fields.

Special Requirements

All engineers who offer engineering services directly to the public or perform work that affects the life, health, or property of the public must be licensed as professional engineers (P.E.). Every U.S. state and territory, as well as Washington, D.C., has its own licensing requirements. For specific information, contact the board of engineering examiners for the area where you wish to practice. See Appendix II for a list of boards.

Experience, Special Skills, and Personality Traits

Entry-level candidates should have work experience related to the positions for which they apply. They may have gained their experience through internships, work-study programs, student research projects, postdoctoral training, or employment. Most employers prefer to hire applicants who have experience working in their industry.

To perform well at their work, Acoustical Engineers need strong problem-solving, writing, communication, interpersonal, and teamwork skills. Being analytical, cooperative, creative, resourceful, and flexible are some personality traits that successful engineers share.

Unions and Associations

Many Acoustical Engineers join local, state, or national professional associations to take advantage of such professional services and resources as networking opportunities, continuing education programs, publications, and job listings. Some national societies that serve the diverse interests of these engineers include:

- Acoustical Society of America
- Institute of Noise Control Engineering of the USA
- National Council of Acoustical Consultants
- Audio Engineering Society
- International Institute of Acoustics and Vibration
- Society of Women Engineers
- National Society of Professional Engineers

For contact information, see Appendix III.

Tips for Entry

1. Talk with several Acoustical Engineers to learn about their jobs as well as their career paths.
2. While you are in college, intern with an acoustical consulting firm to gain work experience.
3. Join a professional association. Participate in its activities and network with your colleagues.
4. Learn more about Acoustical Engineers and the field of acoustics on the Internet. You might start by visiting these Web sites: Acoustical Society of America, http://asa.aip.org; and Acoustics.org, http://www.acoustics.org. See Appendix IV for more links.

ARCHITECTURAL ENGINEER

CAREER PROFILE

Duties: Be involved in the research, planning, design, implementing, and managing of engineered systems in buildings; perform duties as required

Alternate Title(s): A title that reflects a specialty (such as Structural Engineer or Fire Protection Engineer) or a particular function (such as Project Engineer or Consultant)

Salary Range: $44,000 to $98,000

Employment Prospects: Good

Advancement Prospects: Good

Prerequisites:

Education or Training—Bachelor's degree in architectural engineering or related field; on-the-job training

Experience—Previous work experience generally required

Special Skills and Personality Traits—Leadership, analytical, problem-solving, writing, communication, interpersonal, and teamwork skills; creative, detail-oriented, honest, flexible, and curious

Special Requirements—Professional engineer (P.E.) licensure usually required

CAREER LADDER

```
┌─────────────────────────────────┐
│   Senior Architectural Engineer  │
└─────────────────────────────────┘

┌─────────────────────────────────┐
│     Architectural Engineer       │
└─────────────────────────────────┘

┌─────────────────────────────────┐
│   Junior Architectural Engineer  │
└─────────────────────────────────┘
```

Position Description

Architecture, or building design, impacts all our lives. We shelter ourselves in buildings of all descriptions—homes, schools, churches, office buildings, and retail stores, to name a few. We sometimes take these structures for granted, but some buildings fill us with a sense of awe and wonder. Their exterior and interior features are designed by architects to heighten their beauty and aesthetics as much as their usefulness. Architecture is indeed an art as much as it is a science. However, when we use our buildings, we also need to benefit from acceptable air circulation, electricity, and plumbing systems, as well as sound structural design. Architects do not design and install these functional features, but professionals called Architectural Engineers do.

Architectural engineering involves researching, planning, designing, implementing, and managing engineered systems in our modern buildings. Architectural Engineers provide practical aspects to building projects to complement the creative aspects provided by architects, with whom they work. They may be engaged in residential, commercial, or industrial construction.

These engineers use their knowledge of mathematics, science, and engineering principles to solve problems about building construction as well as about the placement and integration of various systems in buildings to fit within their design parameters. These systems include structural, mechanical, electrical, lighting, plumbing, HVAC (heating, ventilating, and air-conditioning), communications, and fire protection systems. Such systems are needed in newly constructed buildings as well as in older buildings that require system upgrades, and Architectural Engineers are involved in both types of projects.

They consult with architects about the design for a building. These engineers keep certain factors in mind when studying the architects' work, such as how to incorporate the materials and engineered systems into the building's interior while maintaining its design integrity and aesthetic appeal.

The work that they perform is a team effort that involves architects, other engineers, technicians, contractors, and others. Architectural Engineers become involved once a construction project has been approved and contracted. They conduct tests and study project feasibility. They perform structural analyses, obtain and provide seismic studies, prepare detailed system plans, diagrams, and drawings, and estimate the costs of constructing and maintaining the systems. Furthermore, they manage the construction projects in part or in whole. They design the various building systems with consideration to environmental concerns, in accordance with regulations, and within cost restraints.

Many building projects are immense, and require the installation and management of several complex engineered systems. In such large projects, each engineer involved needs to focus on a particular engineering concern. Architectural Engineers specialize in four basic areas:

- structural engineering—the analysis and design of buildings with particular focus on such factors as the loads carried, and the forces exerted by structural components and structural materials
- construction engineering—the management of the construction process through finishing projects safely, on time, within budget, and according to quality guidelines
- mechanical engineering—the design and implementation of various mechanical systems such as HVAC and fire protection systems throughout the structure
- electrical engineering—the installation and operation of electrical power equipment and lines as well as lighting, communication, and acoustic systems

All Architectural Engineers understand structural design for all types of buildings and materials. They are well-versed in architectural design principles and have an appreciation for the aesthetics of architectural design. Their work requires them to keep up-to-date with building codes.

These engineers usually handle several projects at the same time. Their tasks often involve making mathematical and financial calculations. They use such computer programs as Word, Excel, CAD (computer-aided design), and other architectural and design software to assist them with their duties. They may develop computer simulations to help them devise appropriate solutions to structural problems. For example, an Architectural Engineer might create a computer model to determine how a structure would respond to earthquakes. These engineers also write technical reports as well as make presentations to project teams, clients, and others. Senior engineers may be assigned to supervise a staff of engineers, technicians, and other support personnel.

Architectural Engineers generally work in office settings, but spend time out of the office to visit building sites or to inspect and manage engineered systems. They work 40 hours per week and put in additional hours when needed.

Salaries

Salaries for Architectural Engineers vary, depending on such factors as their education, experience, job duties, employer, and geographical location. According to the November 2004 *Occupational Employment Statistics* survey by the U.S. Bureau of Labor Statistics, the estimated annual salary for most civil engineers, which includes Architectural Engineers, ranged between $43,530 and $97,650.

Employment Prospects

Employers of Architectural Engineers include architectural and engineering firms, construction companies, building materials companies, research institutes, and testing laboratories. They also find employment with government agencies and academic institutions. Some are self-employed practitioners.

Architectural engineering is a young and growing discipline, and opportunities continue to increase each year. Many architectural engineering programs in universities report a high demand for their graduates. According to some experts in their field, employment prospects are favorable for Architectural Engineers and should remain strong and stable for the coming years.

Advancement Prospects

As engineers gain experience, they are assigned to more complex projects as well as receive increasingly greater responsibilities.

Architectural Engineers may advance in any number of ways, depending on their ambitions and interests. They can become technical specialists or consultants; they can move into nontechnical areas (such as human resources or marketing) of their organizations; and they can seek positions in engineering management. In addition, these engineers can pursue research and teaching careers. Engineers with entrepreneurial ambitions can become independent consultants or owners of consulting firms.

Education and Training

Minimally, a bachelor's degree in architectural engineering or another related field is needed for individuals to obtain entry-level positions. A master's or doctoral degree is usually required for them to advance to careers in management, consulting, or research. Engineers must hold a doctorate to teach in colleges and universities.

Undergraduate programs in architectural engineering may be four or five years long, depending on the school. Five-year programs usually consist of general engineering, architectural design, and architectural engineering coursework.

Employers typically provide entry-level engineers with training programs, which may include both on-the-job training and formal classroom instruction. New engineers work under the supervision and direction of experienced engineers.

Throughout their careers, Architectural Engineers enroll in continuing education and training programs to update their skills and keep up with advancements in their fields.

Special Requirements

Because their work affects the public safety and welfare, Architectural Engineers must be licensed as professional engineers (P.E.) where they practice. The P.E. licensing process consists of two stages. At the first level, qualifying engineers become licensed as engineers-in-training (E.I.T.). After working several years under the supervision of licensed Architectural Engineers, E.I.T.s become eligible to apply for the P.E. license.

Licensing requirements differ in each state and territory, as well as in Washington, D.C. For specific information, contact the board of engineering examiners for the area where you wish to practice. See Appendix II for a list of boards.

Experience, Special Skills, and Personality Traits

Entry-level candidates should have work experience related to the positions for which they apply. They may have gained their experience through internships, work-study programs, student research projects, or part-time employment.

Architectural Engineers need excellent leadership, analytical, problem-solving, writing, and communication skills. They also need effective interpersonal and teamwork skills to work well with various people from different backgrounds. Being creative, detail-oriented, honest, flexible, and curious are some personality traits that successful Architectural Engineers share.

Unions and Associations

Many Architectural Engineers belong to professional associations to take advantage of networking opportunities, continuing education programs, certification, and other professional services and resources. Some national societies that serve the diverse interests of Architectural Engineers are:

- American Society of Heating, Refrigerating and Air-Conditioning Engineers
- Architectural Engineering Institute
- Illuminating Engineering Society of North America
- National Society of Black Engineers
- National Society of Professional Engineers
- Society of Fire Protection Engineers
- Society of Women Engineers
- Structural Engineering Institute

For contact information, see Appendix III.

Tips for Entry

1. Some courses that may help prepare you for a career in architectural engineering are drawing (freehand sketching), computer-aided drafting, word processing, and computer programming.
2. Some experts recommend that students get experience in construction to gain a practical understanding of issues that they would face while making designs as Architectural Engineers.
3. Many employers prefer to hire candidates for entry-level positions who already have their engineer-in-training license.
4. Check out job listings that are posted at professional associations.
5. You can learn more about architectural engineering on the Internet. To get a list of Web sites, enter the keywords *architectural engineering* or *architectural engineers* in a search engine. To learn about some links, see Appendix IV.

FIRE PROTECTION ENGINEER

CAREER PROFILE

Duties: Be involved in the research, design, testing, installation, and maintenance of fire detection and suppression systems; perform duties as required

Alternate Title(s): None

Salary Range: $44,000 to $113,000

Employment Prospects: Excellent

Advancement Prospects: Good

Prerequisites:

Education or Training—Bachelor's degree in fire protection engineering or another related field; on-the-job training

Experience—Previous work experience generally required

Special Skills and Personality Traits—Problem-solving, communication, teamwork, interpersonal, computer, math, and writing skills; curious, creative, innovative, honest, impartial, determined, and patient

Special Requirements—Professional engineer (P.E.) licensure usually required

CAREER LADDER

```
┌─────────────────────────────────────┐
│  Senior Fire Protection Engineer     │
└─────────────────────────────────────┘

┌─────────────────────────────────────┐
│     Fire Protection Engineer         │
└─────────────────────────────────────┘

┌─────────────────────────────────────┐
│  Junior Fire Protection Engineer     │
└─────────────────────────────────────┘
```

Position Description

Fire is important to us for heat, food preparation, and many other purposes. When it is controlled, it is indispensable. Unfortunately, fire can be a destructive force and cost us dearly in lost lives, injuries, and property damage. We rely on firefighters to control and extinguish fires, but there is another group of professional men and women who work hard to prevent and limit fires. These professionals are known as Fire Protection Engineers.

These engineers specialize in limiting the destruction of fire on lives and property. Their profession builds on other engineering fields such as mechanical, electrical, chemical, and civil engineering to analyze fire hazards and work to prevent them. These engineers work to lessen the damage caused by fires through the design of buildings, post-fire investigations and analyses, research, and other functions. Fire Protection Engineers apply scientific, mathematical, and engineering principles to protect communities and their surroundings from the devastation caused by fires.

Fire Protection Engineers are familiar with how fires start and spread inside and outside of buildings and how

they can be detected, managed, and put out. They use this knowledge to help plan the design of buildings to reduce the risk of fire damage while working with building owners, architects, other engineers, and fire marshals. Fire Protection Engineers recommend materials and structures that are more fire resistant. They design building features that can act as fire barriers to block the spread of fire within and between buildings. They plan for the placement of emergency lighting and alarm systems as well as fire escapes, fire stairs, and fire exits.

Fire Protection Engineers fulfill a wide range of functions. They solve fire prevention problems in many environments, such as industrial complexes, schools, office buildings, hospitals, hotels, and even submarines, spacecraft, and aircraft. They conduct research on the causes of fire, how fires behave, and how to control fires. Fire Protection Engineers also work on research projects for a variety of government, academic, and corporate institutions. These projects involve developing new fire suppression methods, analyzing how fire impacts various materials, estimating evacuation times, and determining the risk of fire in the use of consumer products. Additionally, many consumer products are tested by these engineers for their ability to resist or retard fire.

Some Fire Protection Engineers are involved in designing fire detection systems that detect smoke, flames, or excess heat, as well as trigger warning systems. They design or improve fire suppression systems, such as automatic sprinkler systems, that extinguish fires by using water, foam, dry chemical, or other agents. They create emergency lighting, communication, and exit systems. These engineers also inspect, test, and maintain these systems. They are involved in risk assessment and management of fire prevention systems and programs for all types of facilities. They investigate fires or explosions, write technical reports, and serve as expert witnesses in court cases involving fire incidents.

Fire Protection Engineers also find challenges in outdoor environments, as the numbers of wildfires increase at the edge of expanding cities and suburbs. They look into new methods of preventing and fighting such fires. They conduct research into new materials that may work better than water to prevent the spread of fires. This research is also beneficial to local and regional regulators who use the data provided by Fire Protection Engineers to adopt new protective fire standards. Insurance companies seeking to reduce financial losses incurred in fire incidents also use their research. In addition, these engineers conduct tests involving real fires to confirm the results of laboratory research.

Fire Protection Engineers' duties vary with their particular position. They may:

- determine the cause of fires and develop prevention methods
- research new fire retardants and the safety of materials, devices, and products
- study buildings and building complexes to evaluate fire prevention systems
- advise clients about their use of fire detection and extinguishing systems
- train company staffs to organize and implement fire protection programs
- evaluate local fire departments
- use computer modeling to predict the growth and behavior of fire and smoke
- provide expert testimony at court hearings
- keep up-to-date with developments in their field as well as with current governmental fire codes and standards

Fire Protection Engineers work with engineers from other disciplines, as well as with architects, building owners, firefighters, attorneys, government regulatory committees, and others to develop fire prevention programs and design and construct buildings that are safe from the threat of fire.

These engineers work for 40 hours per week. Occasionally, they work overtime to meet deadlines and complete their assorted tasks.

Salaries

Salaries for Fire Protection Engineers vary, depending on such factors as their education, experience, employer, and geographical location. Specific salary information for this occupation is unavailable, but an idea can be obtained by looking at the salaries for engineers in general. According to the November 2004 *Occupational Employment Statistics* survey by the U.S. Bureau of Labor Statistics, the estimated annual salary for most engineers not listed separately in the survey ranged between $44,040 and $113,000.

Employment Prospects

Fire Protection Engineers work in a variety of settings, both nationwide and globally. They find opportunities in most businesses and industries as well as in many government agencies at the local, state, and federal levels, including all branches of the military. Some of them work for consulting companies that specialize in fire protection engineering. Others work for trade associations, testing laboratories, research facilities, architectural firms, and academic institutions.

Employment in general is favorable for experienced Fire Protection Engineers. According to the Worcester Polytechnic Institute Fire Protection Engineering Program Web site, the demand for Fire Protection Engineers exceeds the number of graduates in this field each year.

Advancement Prospects

Fire Protection Engineers can advance in any number of ways, depending on their ambitions and interests. They can become technical specialists as well as advance to managerial positions as supervisory, project, and chief engineers. Some engineers move into positions in marketing, technical sales, or another business area. Engineers with entrepreneurial ambitions can become independent practitioners or owners of firms that offer various types of fire protection engineering services. Furthermore, some engineers pursue research and teaching careers in colleges and universities.

Education and Training

Minimally, individuals need a bachelor's degree to obtain entry-level positions. They may have earned their degree in fire protection engineering, architectural engineering, mechanical engineering, electrical engineering, or another related field. A master's or doctoral degree is usually required for them to advance to careers in management, consulting, research, or teaching.

Entry-level engineers usually receive on-the-job training while working under the guidance and supervision of experienced engineers. They may also receive formal classroom instruction.

Throughout their careers, Fire Protection Engineers enroll in continuing education and training programs to update their skills and to stay current with advancements in their field.

Special Requirements

All engineers who offer engineering services directly to the public or perform work that affects the life, health, or property of the public must be licensed as professional engineers (P.E.). Licensure requirements vary in the different states and territories, as well as in Washington, D.C. For specific information, contact the board of engineering examiners for the area where you wish to practice. See Appendix II for a list of boards.

Experience, Special Skills, and Personality Traits

Entry-level candidates should have work experience related to the positions for which they apply. They may have gained their experience through internships, work-study programs, student research projects, or part-time employment.

To perform well at their work, Fire Protection Engineers need excellent problem-solving, communication, teamwork, and interpersonal skills. Having strong computer, math, and writing skills is also essential. Being curious, creative, innovative, honest, impartial, determined, and patient are some personality traits that successful Fire Protection Engineers share.

Unions and Associations

Fire Protection Engineers can join professional associations to take advantage of various professional resources and services such as networking opportunities, continuing education programs, publications, and research findings. Some national societies that serve their interests are:

- American Society of Safety Engineers
- Architectural Engineering Institute
- National Fire Protection Association
- National Society of Professional Engineers
- Society of Fire Protection Engineers
- Society of Women Engineers

For contact information, see Appendix III.

Tips for Entry

1. Become a volunteer firefighter to gain practical knowledge about how fires spread as well as how they can be put out.
2. Talk with Fire Protection Engineers to learn more about their work. Ask if you can follow and watch an engineer at work for a few hours.
3. Use the Internet to learn more about Fire Protection Engineers. You might start by visiting the Society of Fire Protection Engineers Web site, http://www.sfpe. org. Also check out this organization's Web site about Fire Protection Engineering careers at http://www. careersinfireprotectionengineering.com. See Appendix IV for more links.

GEOLOGICAL ENGINEER

CAREER PROFILE

Duties: Investigate, develop, design, implement, and manage solutions for problems relating to the earth and earth systems; perform duties as required

Alternate Title(s): Geophysical Engineer, Hydrogeological Engineer; a title that reflects an engineering function such as Project Engineer

Salary Range: $42,000 to $119,000

Employment Prospects: Good

Advancement Prospects: Good

Prerequisites:

Education or Training—Bachelor's degree in geological engineering or a related field; on-the-job training

Experience—Previous work experience generally required

Special Skills and Personality Traits—Teamwork, interpersonal, leadership, problem-solving, writing, and communication skills; logical, creative, trustworthy, flexible, and self-motivated

Special Requirements—Professional engineer (P.E.) licensure may be required

CAREER LADDER

```
┌─────────────────────────────────┐
│   Senior Geological Engineer     │
└─────────────────────────────────┘

┌─────────────────────────────────┐
│      Geological Engineer         │
└─────────────────────────────────┘

┌─────────────────────────────────┐
│   Junior Geological Engineer     │
└─────────────────────────────────┘
```

Position Description

We use geological materials in everyday life. We put oil and gasoline in our automobiles. We use metals to make such common objects as jewelry, computers, kitchen utensils, and the like. Our buildings, highways, and bridges sit upon solid foundations made from rocks and other earth materials. We travel through tunnels that are carved through solid rock. All these things are made possible through the efforts of men and women who work in the field of geological engineering.

Geological Engineers explore, manage, and use materials, especially minerals, that are found on or under the Earth's surface. Theirs is a relatively new engineering field that arose from both geotechnical engineering and the science of geology. These engineers perform such engineering activities as surveying and developing fossil fuel deposits, classifying and planning environmental sites, studying and engineering groundwater resources, investigating natural and human-made hazardous sites, and studying such phenomena as rock and slope stability. They also apply engineering principles to the use of geological materials for such purposes as designing tunnels, mines, and roads used for and in relation to the extraction of minerals.

Besides geology, Geological Engineers have a background in physics, chemistry, mathematics, and engineering mechanics. They also have a background in the social sciences and economics. Their skills are similar to those of geologists, environmental engineers, and civil engineers. In fact, Geological Engineers work with these other professionals to study the interactions that take place between the earth and such engineered structures as buildings, tunnels, and roads. Geological Engineers analyze, design, and plan the foundations for these structures, as well as assist in their construction and operation. They also help other engineers to design foundations for large structures such as dams, port facilities, bridges, and waste storage systems.

To help plan for the construction of structures, Geological Engineers examine geological factors such as rocks and rock formations on and below the surface of construction sites and consider how structures will impact the environment.

They give consideration to how the structural design will relate to the site's geology and how much of a structural load the site can bear. They analyze sloped areas for their stability, and where needed, design ways to remedy instability in such areas. They investigate the water resources of the area and work to protect them from the contaminating effects of construction activity. In addition, they study and recommend how the area's geological resources can be used as materials in the construction design and process.

Many Geological Engineers are concerned with finding and removing oil, natural gas, coal, minerals, and metals from the earth. These engineers design both open pit and underground mines. They also oversee the construction of underground tunnels and shafts, as well as create methods for transporting the extracted materials to processing centers. Some Geological Engineers are involved in taking mineral samples or locating groundwater prior to construction. Others explore and evaluate the conditions that are to be found in deep excavations. They detonate explosives and measure the impact of the shock waves underground. They also give consideration to the presence of earthquake faults and how mining activity will impact their movement.

Geological Engineers may specialize in specific areas within their field, such as hydrology, environmental concerns, geomechanics and geotechnics, petroleum and minerals, and geological science. Within these specialties, these engineers may focus on:

- searching for and developing groundwater sources, including the design of facilities to control groundwater
- identifying, managing, and disposing of groundwater contamination and solid waste
- designing excavations above and below the ground
- investigating geological engineering sites
- evaluating natural geologic hazards
- locating mineral, metal, petroleum, and coal deposits and facilitating their extraction
- working in such areas as global climate change, planetary science, and sedimentary rock sequence simulation

Geological Engineers are responsible for performing general duties in the course of their careers. They conduct studies and surveys. They plan and coordinate data collection programs. They analyze the results of these information gathering activities and map the studied areas to assist in their development for civil engineering, mining, waste management, and petroleum projects. These engineers prepare reports and correspondence as well as complete required paperwork. They also develop budgets and schedules. Senior engineers may be assigned to supervise a staff of other engineers, scientists, technicians, and support staff.

Geological Engineers work in a variety of employment environments. In the private sector, their most common occupation is as consulting engineers in firms that specialize in that service. They may also work for environmental firms as specialists, as well as for electric utility companies, construction firms, mining companies, and academic or private research institutes. In the public sector, these engineers work for government agencies at all levels where they are involved in such areas as research, environmental protection, natural resources conservation, and energy generation. Some of them conduct research and teach courses in colleges and universities.

Most of these engineers work in office settings and put in a standard 40-hour workweek. They also must spend time working in outdoor settings at remote field locations. Their trips to these locations may last for several days or weeks. When they work on their field assignments, Geological Engineers may be required to perform physically demanding tasks in all weather conditions. At many sites, these engineers wear such protective gear as hard hats and steel-toed boots.

Salaries

Salaries for Geological Engineers vary, depending on such factors as their education, experience, job duties, employer, and geographical location. The estimated annual salary for most Geological Engineers ranged between $42,150 and $119,110, according to the November 2004 *Occupational Employment Statistics* survey by the U.S. Bureau of Labor Statistics.

Employment Prospects

Major employers of Geological Engineers include engineering and consulting firms, state regulatory agencies, federal government agencies (such as the U.S. Geological Survey and the U.S. Environmental Protection Agency), petroleum companies, petroleum services companies, and mining companies.

In general, job opportunities become available as Geological Engineers transfer to other occupations, advance to higher positions, or retire. Employers will create additional positions to meet the needs of their growing organizations.

According to some experts in their field, the job market for Geological Engineers is favorable. It should remain strong for the coming years, as groundwater usage and energy consumption in the United States continue to grow.

Advancement Prospects

Geological Engineers can advance in any number of ways, depending on their ambitions and interests. They can become technical specialists and consultants. They can pursue engineering management positions. They can also move into positions in marketing, technical sales, or another business area. Engineers with entrepreneurial ambitions can become independent practitioners or owners of firms that offer various types of environmental engineering services. These engineers can also pursue research and teaching careers in academic settings.

Education and Training

Minimally, a bachelor's degree in geological engineering or another related field is needed for individuals to obtain entry-level positions. A master's or doctoral degree is usually required for them to advance to careers in management, consulting, and research. Engineers must possess a doctorate to teach at the college level.

Employers typically provide entry-level engineers with training programs, which may include both on-the-job training and formal classroom instruction. New engineers work under the supervision and direction of experienced engineers.

Throughout their careers, Geological Engineers enroll in continuing education programs and training programs to update their skills and keep up with advancements in their fields.

Special Requirements

All engineers who offer engineering services directly to the public or perform work that affects the life, health, or property of the public must be licensed as professional engineers (P.E.). Licensing requirements vary in the different states and territories, as well as in Washington, D.C. For specific information, contact the board of engineering examiners for the area where you wish to practice. See Appendix II for a list of boards.

Experience, Special Skills, and Personality Traits

Entry-level candidates should have work experience related to the positions for which they apply. They may have gained their experience through internships, work-study programs, student research projects, postdoctoral training, or part-time employment.

Geological Engineers need effective teamwork and interpersonal skills, as they must work well with colleagues, managers, and others from diverse backgrounds. Their job also requires that they have strong leadership, problem-solving, writing, and communication skills. Being logical, creative, trustworthy, flexible, and self-motivated are some personality traits that successful engineers share.

Unions and Associations

Many Geological Engineers belong to local, state, or national societies to take advantage of networking opportunities, continuing education programs, research findings, publications, and other professional services and resources. Some national societies that serve the diverse interests of these engineers include:

- American Geological Institute
- Association of Environmental and Engineering Geologists
- Environmental and Engineering Geophysical Society
- Geological Society of America
- International Society of Explosives Engineers
- National Society of Professional Engineers
- Society for Mining, Metallurgy, and Exploration
- Society of Petroleum Engineers
- Society of Women Engineers

Tips for Entry

1. Make sure geological engineering is the field in which you want to work. For example, you can read books and periodicals about the field. Talk with professionals. Get summer or part-time jobs with geological engineering firms or other organizations.
2. Some individuals earn a bachelor's degree in another field and then obtain a master's degree in geological engineering in order to enter this field.
3. Take advantage of your college career center as you prepare to do your job search. Career counselors can help you find job openings as well as assist you to improve your job search skills.
4. Learn new technologies to enhance your employability.
5. Learn more about Geological Engineers on the Internet. You might start by visiting the Association of Environmental and Engineering Geologists Web site, http://www.aegweb.org. For more links, see Appendix IV.

MINING ENGINEER

CAREER PROFILE

Duties: Plan, design, oversee the construction of, and direct mining operations; perform duties as required

Alternate Title(s): A title that reflects an engineering function such as Project Engineer

Salary Range: $42,000 to $119,000

Employment Prospects: Good

Advancement Prospects: Good

Prerequisites:

Education or Training—Bachelor's degree in mining engineering or another related field; on-the-job training

Experience—Previous work experience generally required

Special Skills and Personality Traits—Leadership, analytical, problem-solving, organizational, communication, interpersonal, and teamwork skills; have spatial ability; resourceful, creative, detail-oriented, flexible and versatile

Special Requirements—Professional engineer (P.E.) licensure may be required

CAREER LADDER

```
+-----------------------------+
|   Senior Mining Engineer    |
+-----------------------------+

+-----------------------------+
|      Mining Engineer        |
+-----------------------------+

+-----------------------------+
|   Junior Mining Engineer    |
+-----------------------------+
```

Position Description

The mining industry is vital to our economy and to our way of life. Mining is our sole source for the metals and minerals that we need for everyday purposes, such as for making automobiles and computers, constructing buildings, and conducting electricity. Our society has many uses for every metal and mineral that miners extract from the earth.

Human beings of all cultures have been extracting minerals and metals from out of the ground for thousands of years. As we have progressed through the centuries, mining techniques have also progressed from the digging of shallow holes to the excavation of large open pit mines and elaborate deep underground mines that extend for miles under the Earth's surface. In early civilizations, engineers found rudimentary ways to avoid tunnel collapses and flooding as well as to maintain the flow of fresh air into deep mine shafts. In our modern age, Mining Engineers continue in this tradition to design and operate highly sophisticated mines in a safe and environmentally beneficial manner. Mining Engineers work at mine sites all around the world. Some mines are located underneath the ocean.

Mining Engineers design and construct both open pit quarries and underground mines after surveying their sites for mineral deposits and ascertaining the economic and regulatory feasibility of the mines' operation. These engineers do much of their design work on computers. They design underground tunnels, shafts, and galleries, as well as create methods for transporting the extracted materials to processing centers. They also oversee the construction of these facilities, which can be enormous.

Some of them work with geologists or metallurgists to find and evaluate sources for ore. Others design mining equipment and develop ore extraction methods. They manage the processes that separate metals or minerals from the soil and the rock that are all extracted together.

Mining Engineers are entrusted to ensure the safe and efficient operations of mines while minimizing the environmental impact of the surrounding area. They work on the reclamation of the land and resolve water and air pollution issues. They develop and utilize the latest technologies for environmental remediation purposes. In addition, they design mine facilities with an eye toward worker safety in compliance with accepted safety standards and by adhering to governmental safety regulations. For example, they develop ventilating systems and roof supports and construct access roads that lead to mine sites. Mining Engineers also examine mine walls and gallery ceilings, test air samples, and inspect mining equipment.

Many of these engineers are involved in research. They work at universities or research institutions. They experiment with new mining techniques and equipment, as well as develop new designs for mining facilities. Some Mining Engineers work as consultants. Consultants may work in cities and travel to mining locations to offer their services on a wide range of projects and technical areas. Mining Engineers are also involved in the areas of mine production, ore processing, equipment testing, and machinery installation. Some of them are investment analysts and advisors, while others manage mine companies.

Mining Engineers often specialize in mining a particular metal or mineral. They may also specialize in particular types of mining, such as open pit or underground mining. These engineers work in other specific areas of the mining engineering profession, such as equipment design, rock mechanics, mine design, environmental remediation, and hydrothermal studies.

These engineers have a multiplicity of specific tasks to perform in fulfilling their functions. They may:

- ascertain the depth, extent, and quality of mineral deposits
- develop plans for mine shafts, tunnels, or pits including their dimensions and depth
- plan for the location of future mines, the type of equipment to be used, and methods of post-operation site restoration
- design and manage the construction of infrastructure such as water supply and drainage systems, energy supplies, access roads, and materials processing facilities
- supervise such projects as cost estimates; mine construction; extraction, processing, and refining systems development; tailings and other waste management; and environmental projects
- analyze employee safety and health issues
- review mine plans, permit applications, and mine restoration plans
- prepare environmental impact statements
- look into property damage claims
- write or read technical reports
- perform engineering calculations
- draw or review preliminary design sketches
- meet with the public to discuss pertinent laws and policies, as well as field complaints about accidents, hazards, and emergencies

Mining Engineers work in and near all types of mines as well as adjoining construction sites. Many of these sites are located in isolated regions of the world. Their work may be physically demanding. When they are performing such tasks as research, consulting, designing, and administration, they work in offices or laboratories.

These engineers work for private mining concerns. They may also find career opportunities with engineering consulting companies, state and federal government agencies, and with the construction and finance industries.

Mining Engineers generally work regular 40-hour workweeks. They may occasionally put in extra hours to complete tasks. Some mining concerns require their staff to work around the clock in shifts.

Salaries

Salaries for Mining Engineers vary, depending on such factors as their education, experience, job duties, employer, and geographical location. According to the November 2004 *Occupational Employment Statistics* (OES) survey by the U.S. Bureau of Labor Statistics (BLS), the estimated annual salary for most Mining Engineers ranged between $42,150 and $119,110.

Employment Prospects

Mining engineering is a small occupation. The BLS reported in its November 2004 OES survey that about 5,480 mining and geological engineers were employed in the United States.

The job growth for this occupation is expected to decline through 2014, according to the BLS. However, job opportunities should be favorable because a large number of Mining Engineers are becoming eligible for retirement in these coming years. In addition, fewer schools are offering mining engineering programs. Job opportunities are available worldwide.

Advancement Prospects

Mining Engineers may advance in any number of ways, depending on their ambitions and interests. They can become technical specialists as well as pursue engineering management positions. Some engineers choose to move into positions in marketing, technical sales, and other business areas. Engineers with entrepreneurial ambitions can become independent practitioners or owners of technical or consulting firms.

Education and Training

Applicants for entry-level positions must possess at least a bachelor's degree in mining engineering, civil engineering, geological engineering, or another related field. A master's or doctoral degree is usually required for them to pursue careers in management, consulting, research, or teaching.

Employers typically provide entry-level engineers with training programs, which may include both on-the-job training and formal classroom instruction. New engineers work under the supervision and direction of experienced engineers.

Throughout their careers, Mining Engineers enroll in continuing education programs and training programs to update their skills and keep up with technological advancements.

Special Requirements

All engineers who offer engineering services directly to the public or perform work that affects the life, health, or property of the public must be licensed as professional engineers (P.E.) where they practice. Every state and territory, as well as Washington, D.C., has its own licensing requirements. For specific information, contact the board of engineering examiners for the area where you wish to practice. See Appendix II for a list of boards.

Experience, Special Skills, and Personality Traits

Prior work experience is not needed for individuals to obtain entry-level positions, but it is preferred by employers. Many recent graduates have gained practical experience through internships, work-study programs, student research projects, or part-time employment.

Mining Engineers need strong leadership, analytical, problem-solving, organizational, and communication skills to succeed in their work. In addition, these engineers need effective interpersonal and teamwork skills, as they must be able to work with various people from diverse backgrounds. They must also have excellent spatial ability. Being resourceful, creative, detail-oriented, flexible, and versatile are some personality traits that successful Mining Engineers share.

Unions and Associations

Many Mining Engineers belong to professional associations to take advantage of networking opportunities, continuing education programs, and other professional services and resources. Some national societies include:

- American Institute of Mining, Metallurgical, and Petroleum Engineers
- International Society of Explosives Engineers
- Mining and Metallurgical Society of America
- National Society of Professional Engineers
- Society for Mining, Metallurgy, and Exploration
- Women in Mining

For contact information, see Appendix III.

Tips for Entry

1. As a college student, get a summer mining job to gain experience.
2. Talk with professionals to learn about their job and career path.
3. Professors, work supervisors, and colleagues are some resources you might contact for leads to current and upcoming job vacancies.
4. You can learn more about mining engineering on the Internet. To get a list of Web sites, enter any of these keywords into a search engine: *mining engineering, mining engineers,* or *mining industry.* To learn about some links, see Appendix IV.

NAVAL ENGINEER

CAREER PROFILE

Duties: Be involved in the research, design, construction, operation, and maintenance of waterborne vehicles and ocean structures; perform duties as required

Alternate Title(s): Naval Architect, Marine Engineer, Ocean Engineer; a title that reflects an engineering function, such as Design Engineer

Salary Range: $41,000 to $110,000

Employment Prospects: Good

Advancement Prospects: Good

Prerequisites:

Education or Training—Bachelor's degree in naval engineering, marine engineering, or another related field; on-the-job training

Experience—Previous work experience generally required

Special Skills and Personality Traits—Leadership, problem-solving, communication, writing, interpersonal, and teamwork skills; cooperative, trustworthy, creative, flexible, and dedicated

Special Requirements—Professional engineer (P.E.) licensure may be required

CAREER LADDER

```
┌─────────────────────────────┐
│   Senior Naval Engineer      │
└─────────────────────────────┘

┌─────────────────────────────┐
│      Naval Engineer          │
└─────────────────────────────┘

┌─────────────────────────────┐
│   Junior Naval Engineer      │
└─────────────────────────────┘
```

Position Description

Rivers, lakes, seas, and oceans cover more of the Earth's surface than does land. These bodies of water have always provided a means for mobility and trade for all cultures. For much of our known history, oceans in particular were a formidable barrier to long-distance travel to all but the most hardy of navigators and sailors. Today, waterborne vessels of all descriptions are used as a means of transportation, national defense, exploration, and commerce. Well-designed and technologically advanced vessels and their crews ensure that our manufactured and food products are distributed economically among all the nations, that troops and equipment are transported to combat zones, that sea lanes are protected, and that travelers are provided with a safe and comfortable experience.

Naval Engineers are engaged in the design, construction, operation, and maintenance of all types of waterborne vessels, including naval ships, cruise ships, aircraft carriers, oil rigs, tankers, Coast Guard cutters, submarines, yachts, sail-boats, fishing boats, ferry boats, and so on. These engineers are also concerned with the design, building, and operation of a wide range of ocean structures, from offshore platforms that are used for the exploration and production of oil and gas to engineered structures that deal with erosion of coastlines and the movement of pollution in freshwater and saltwater bodies. In addition, Naval Engineers work on the development and production of various instruments, equipment, and systems that can be used in bodies of water, such as underwater welding and drilling equipment, computerized buoys, underwater video equipment, and underwater robots.

Naval engineering is a discipline that encompasses naval architecture, marine engineering, and ocean engineering. These subdisciplines are interrelated and often overlap, but each has a specific function in the general field of naval engineering.

Naval architects are the engineers who design ships, yachts, or other craft. They establish a vessel's size and shape, determine the form of the hull, and design the structure while accounting for such factors as the vessel's stability and weight distribution as well as the location of various internal sections including living quarters. They work to ensure that the vessels they design can withstand harsh environments and extreme climatic conditions.

Marine engineers work with shipboard systems as well as those on ocean structures. They design or choose the machinery and mechanical, electrical, fluid, and control systems that are used to provide functionality to ships. These engineers also design, operate, and maintain engines, turbines, gears, propellers, and steam boilers. They may work aboard vessels or offshore platforms to deal with these systems as well as provide fresh water and electrical services.

Ocean engineers are concerned with surface and subsurface ocean environments and how they impact ships and structures. They also investigate the movement of ocean waters and seismic faults. These engineers design submersible vehicles to use in such operations as submarine rescue, shipwreck recovery, and studying the ocean floor. They design these vessels to withstand tremendous pressure, cold temperatures, extreme tidal conditions, and to be propelled at great depths. In addition, ocean engineers design coastal structures such as deep-water ports or computerized buoys and ocean environmental engineering systems, as well as assist with oceanographic research.

Naval Engineers specialize by focusing on one of the subdisciplines within their particular interest. For example, they may specialize in designing offshore oil platforms or working with ocean environmental systems. They might focus on ship production and management, designing yachts or combat ships, or working with shipboard power plants. As engineers gain experience, they might specialize in one or more particular engineering functions, such as design, research, testing, management, or consulting. Some of them teach engineering courses at colleges, universities, and military academies.

These engineers apply mathematics, science, and engineering principles and methods to their work. In addition, Naval Engineers are well versed in the areas of design economics, production methods, and the design of electrical systems.

They perform a variety of specific tasks to fulfill their functional requirements. For example, they may:

- prepare and review designs with consideration toward budgeting and allocating appropriate funds
- convert vessels for other purposes, such as transforming an oil tanker into a crane ship
- modify piping, electrical, ventilation, or other structural systems of a vessel
- upgrade a dry dock facility
- prepare repair specifications and operating manuals for shipboard operating systems

- supervise an engineering staff in all aspects of ship design, maintenance, and operation
- develop maintenance plans for ships, offshore platforms, and their operating systems
- coordinate inspection routines
- analyze and design deep water ports
- plan new uses for waterways
- develop methods to protect marine wildlife
- research the behavior of ocean environments through the use of such equipment as wave tanks and towing tanks
- serve as an expert witness for various court and other legal proceedings

Naval Engineers work in a variety of settings from offices to laboratories to ships to offshore oil platforms. They may travel extensively, particularly if they are employed on board ocean-going vessels. These engineers work 40 hours per week but may be required to put in extra hours to complete projects or meet deadlines.

Salaries

Salaries for Naval Engineers vary, depending on such factors as their education, experience, employer, and geographical location. According to the November 2004 *Occupational Employment Statistics* survey by the U.S. Bureau of Labor Statistics, the estimated annual salary for most marine engineers and naval architects ranged between $41,280 and $109,690.

Employment Prospects

Naval Engineers find employment in government agencies (such as the U.S. Army Corps of Engineers and the National Oceanic and Atmospheric Administration) and in the shipbuilding and ship design industries. Some of them work for offshore oil companies and for architectural and engineering firms. Naval Engineers also work for research institutes and academic institutions. Some of these engineers are employed in the automotive industry. The two major employers are the U.S. Navy and the major U.S. shipbuilding companies.

Some experts in the field report that job opportunities for Naval Engineers are generally plentiful and should remain favorable in the coming years. Growing concerns about international trade, maritime security, and national defense, as well as environmental protection and security, will likely increase the demand for Naval Engineers.

Advancement Prospects

Naval Engineers can advance in any number of ways, depending on their ambitions and interests. They can become technical specialists or consultants. Those with management and administrative interests and talents can seek positions as supervisory, project, and chief engineers.

In addition, they can advance to executive officer positions within their organization.

These engineers can also pursue opportunities in business areas of their organizations, such as human resources, marketing, or sales. Engineers with entrepreneurial ambitions can become independent consultants or owners of technical or consulting firms. Furthermore, Naval Engineers can pursue research and teaching careers in colleges and universities.

Education and Training

Applicants for entry-level positions must possess at least a bachelor's degree in naval engineering, naval architecture, marine engineering, ocean engineering, or another related discipline. For engineers to advance to careers in management, consulting, research, or teaching, a master's or doctoral degree is normally required.

Entry-level engineers usually receive on-the-job training while working under the supervision and guidance of experienced engineers. Some of them are also given formal classroom instruction.

Throughout their careers, Naval Engineers enroll in continuing education programs and training programs to update their skills and keep up with advancements in their fields.

Special Requirements

All engineers who offer engineering services directly to the public or perform work that affects the life, health, or property of the public must be licensed as professional engineers (P.E.). Every U.S. state and territory, as well as Washington, D.C., has its own requirements for licensure. For specific information, contact the board of engineering examiners for the area where you wish to practice. See Appendix II for a list of boards.

Experience, Special Skills, and Personality Traits

Entry-level candidates should have work experience related to the positions for which they apply. They may have gained their experience through internships, work-study programs, student research projects, or part-time employment.

To perform well at their work, Naval Engineers must have strong leadership, problem-solving, communication, and writing skills. Additionally, they need excellent interpersonal and teamwork skills, as they work with colleagues, managers, and others from diverse backgrounds.

Some personality traits that successful Naval Engineers share include being cooperative, trustworthy, creative, flexible, and dedicated.

Unions and Associations

Many Naval Engineers join professional associations to take advantage of networking opportunities, continuing education programs, and other professional services and resources. Some national societies that serve the interests of these engineers include the American Society of Naval Engineers, the Society of Naval Architects and Marine Engineers, and the Marine Technology Society. For contact information, see Appendix III.

Tips for Entry

1. Along with mathematics, physics, science, and English, courses in mechanical drawing and shop can help prepare you for a career in naval engineering.
2. Talk with professionals as well as with your college advisor and professors for guidance in selecting courses that match your interests and ambitions.
3. Depending on the school, its naval engineering program may be called marine engineering; naval architecture and marine engineering; naval architecture and ocean engineering; or another name.
4. Contact employers directly to learn about internships or job openings.
5. Use the Internet to learn more about Naval Engineers. To get a list of Web sites, enter the keywords *naval engineers, naval architects, marine engineers, naval engineering,* or *marine engineering* into a search engine. To learn about some links, see Appendix IV.

OCEAN ENGINEER

CAREER PROFILE

Duties: Research, design, construct, operate, and maintain instrumentation, equipment, vessels, and structures for oceanographic research and work operations; may perform consulting, teaching, or administration duties; perform duties as required

Alternate Title(s): Marine Engineer; Coastal Engineer, Civil Engineer, Naval Architect or other title that reflects a specialty or a position

Salary Range: $41,000 to $110,000

Employment Prospects: Good

Advancement Prospects: Good

Prerequisites:

Education or Training—Bachelor's degree in ocean engineering or related field

Experience—Oceanography and/or engineering experience required

Special Skills and Personality Traits—Analysis, design, computer, problem-solving, writing, communication, interpersonal, and teamwork skills; creative, adaptive, trustworthy, dedicated, competent, persistent

Special Requirements—Professional engineer (P.E.) license may be required

CAREER LADDER

```
┌─────────────────────────────┐
│   Senior Ocean Engineer     │
└─────────────────────────────┘

┌─────────────────────────────┐
│      Ocean Engineer         │
└─────────────────────────────┘

┌─────────────────────────────┐
│   Junior Ocean Engineer     │
└─────────────────────────────┘
```

Position Description

Ocean Engineering is an engineering specialty that is part of naval engineering and oceanography, the geoscience that deals with the study of ocean and coastal environments. Ocean Engineers combine their engineering skills and knowledge of oceanography to develop complex engineering systems for oceanographic research, marine transportation, mineral exploration, oil production, commercial fishing, coastline protection, ocean resources management, and other oceanographic operations.

Ocean Engineers design and build various instrumentation, equipment, vessels, and structures that can function in the ocean waters. Their designs must be able to withstand cold temperatures, currents, tides, waves, severe storms, saltwater corrosion, marine fouling (buildup of barnacles or other marine growth on structures), and other conditions of the ocean environment. Some examples of their inventions are computerized buoys; underwater video equipment; seismometers (which record earthquakes under the ocean floors); acoustical devices for detecting objects under the ocean; remote-controlled submersibles; drilling equipment; underwater welding equipment; oil tankers; submarines; navy ships; recreational boats; and platforms for oil exploration and production.

In addition, Ocean Engineers are involved with various types of oceanographic operations, and work closely with ocean scientists, technicians, and other engineers. For example, Ocean Engineers might:

- develop new products, such as measuring instrumentation, automatic underwater vehicles, drilling equipment, or stationary platforms for oil exploration
- provide technical support to ocean scientists on research expeditions
- be involved in all phases of oil exploration and production—discovering, producing, and delivering offshore petroleum resources

- develop new methods of oil production that can protect marine wildlife and coastal regions from the undesirable side effects of offshore oil production
- improve the design and construction of oil tankers, recreational boats, submarines, and other ships so that they are safer, faster, sounder, yet less expensive
- design deepwater ports, ports, and breakwaters
- design coastal recreational facilities
- solve coastline problems such as natural shoreline erosion or coastal development
- create ways to lessen the impact of storms and other natural shoreline processes
- plan new uses of waterways for marine transportation
- participate in managing ocean resources to ensure the survival of marine species and continuing supplies of food for the world

Many Ocean Engineers work on basic and applied research projects for industry, academic institutions, government agencies, and research institutes. They might specialize in particular aspects of ocean engineering, such as acoustics, robotics, naval architecture, coastal engineering, chemical engineering, or civil engineering. Typically, academic researchers have the ability to choose topics of interest while Ocean Engineers in other settings conduct research that fits their employers' objectives and missions.

Most Ocean Engineers have a combination of research, consulting, teaching, and/or administration responsibilities. Their duties vary, depending on their specialty, work setting, and position. Those working in nonprofit or academic sectors might be involved with writing grant proposals to fund their research projects. Those working in the private sector might perform various types of services for customers, such as inspecting installations, scouting potential sites for building structures, or making presentations about their employers' products.

Ocean Engineers work in offices and laboratories as well as in the field. Their field assignments may involve traveling to other countries to provide service, train customers, or operate equipment and systems. Researchers often conduct field expeditions that require working and living on research ships for weeks or months at a time. Some Ocean Engineers go undersea to conduct experiments, install ocean pipes, or perform other tasks.

All Ocean Engineers are expected to keep up with technologies and developments in their specialties. They network with colleagues, read professional journals, attend professional meetings, and so forth.

Salaries

Salaries vary, depending on such factors as their education, experience, employer, and job responsibilities. According to the November 2004 *Occupational Employment Statistics* survey by the U.S. Bureau of Labor Statistics, the estimated annual salary for most marine engineers and naval architects, including Ocean Engineers, ranged between $41,280 and $109,690.

Employment Prospects

Ocean Engineers work for businesses, such as ocean engineering firms, and for the oil, shipbuilding, marine transportation, and other industries. They are also employed by research institutes, government agencies, colleges, and universities.

Job opportunities usually become available as engineers retire, advance to higher positions, or transfer to other jobs.

Advancement Prospects

Ocean Engineers advance in any number of ways, depending on their positions, ambitions, and interests. Those interested in management and administrative work may find opportunities in any work setting.

Education and Training

To enter this field, candidates are required to hold a bachelor's degree in ocean engineering, oceanography, or another engineering discipline (such as civil engineering or mechanical engineering). They would need a master's or a doctoral degree to conduct research or to advance to top management positions. A doctoral degree is usually required for these engineers to obtain teaching positions in universities and four-year colleges.

Special Requirements

Ocean Engineers may by required to have a professional engineer (P.E.) license, depending on the employer or position. For example, Ocean Engineers must be licensed P.E.s if they provide consulting services or prepare engineering plans that will be submitted to public authorities for approval. Licensure requirements vary from state as well as in the District of Columbia and the U.S. territories. For specific information, contact the board of engineering examiners for the area in which you wish to practice. See Appendix II for a list of boards.

Experience, Skills, and Personality Traits

Many Ocean Engineers enter this field with experience as oceanographers, civil engineers, marine environmentalists, naval architects, or marine engineers, or with experience from other marine-related technical fields.

For entry-level positions, employers generally choose candidates who have related work experience, which may have been gained through research projects, internships, employment, postdoctoral training, and so on. They should have developed skills in such areas as analysis and design.

To do well in their jobs, Ocean Engineers need strong computer, problem-solving, writing, and communication skills. Additionally, they need superior interpersonal and teamwork skills, as they work with various people from diverse backgrounds. Some personality traits that successful Ocean Engineers share are being creative, adaptive, trustworthy, dedicated, competent, and persistent.

Unions and Associations

Ocean Engineers can join professional associations to take advantage of professional services and resources, such as education programs and networking opportunities. Many are members of societies that specifically serve the ocean engineering field, such as the Society of Naval Architects and Marine Engineers, the Oceanic Engineering Society, and the Marine Technology Society. Ocean Engineers are also eligible to join other engineering societies, such as the Institute of Electrical and Electronic Engineers or the the ASME International. See Appendix III for contact information.

Tips for Entry

1. While you are an undergraduate student, talk with your professors, college adviser, or college career counselor for suggestions about internships, work experience, or research assistantships that may be available.
2. Contact employers directly to learn about internships and job openings.
3. Learn more about ocean engineering on the Internet. To get a list of relevant Web sites to read, enter the keywords *ocean engineering* or *ocean engineers* in any search engine. For some links, see Appendix IV.

NUCLEAR ENGINEER

CAREER PROFILE

Duties: Research, design, develop, test, and implement nuclear technologies for energy, chemical processing, space exploration, and other purposes; perform duties as required

Alternate Title(s): A title that reflects an engineering function such as Project Engineer or Plant Engineer

Salary Range: $63,000 to $119,000

Employment Prospects: Good

Advancement Prospects: Good

Prerequisites:

Education or Training—Bachelor's degree in nuclear engineering or a related field; on-the-job training

Experience—Previous work experience generally required

Special Skills and Personality Traits—Analytical, problem-solving, writing, communication, teamwork, and interpersonal skills; curious, creative, detail-oriented, patient, precise, dedicated, and trustworthy

Special Requirements—Professional engineer (P.E.) licensure may be required

CAREER LADDER

```
┌─────────────────────────────────┐
│     Senior Nuclear Engineer      │
└─────────────────────────────────┘

┌─────────────────────────────────┐
│        Nuclear Engineer          │
└─────────────────────────────────┘

┌─────────────────────────────────┐
│    Associate Nuclear Engineer    │
└─────────────────────────────────┘
```

Position Description

The atom contains a tremendous amount of energy, particularly considering its infinitesimal size. Ancient societies such as the Greeks and Romans developed theories of the existence of atoms, but it was only in more recent centuries that atoms were closely studied. In the 1940s, the power of the atom was harnessed and released with the development of the atom bomb and nuclear bombs. After the war, scientists and engineers turned their attention to more peaceful applications for this source of energy. Today, nuclear technologies have a variety of useful purposes. Perhaps most well known is the use of nuclear energy to run power plants that generate electricity. Nuclear technology is also used in medicine, food processing, chemical processing, space exploration, manufacturing, and waste disposal, as well as in scientific and environmental research. These products, systems, and processes are developed and implemented by professionals called Nuclear Engineers.

Nuclear engineering is a field that is concerned with nuclear physics and how radiation and matter interrelate.

Nuclear fission and nuclear fusion are the two most important principles of nuclear physics with which Nuclear Engineers work. Fission refers to the energy that is released when an atom is split. Fusion refers to the energy that is released when two light atoms combine to form a heavier atom. Nuclear Engineers also work with radiation, which is energy emitted by certain types of substances whose atoms are unstable and are decaying.

Nuclear Engineers find practical applications for these principles of nuclear physics. They design, develop, test, analyze, operate, and maintain such nuclear fission technologies as reactors and weapons. They also develop the fuels and components that make nuclear power plants run. In addition, Nuclear Engineers design and manage nuclear propulsion systems for aircraft carriers and submarines as well as design power systems for satellites and long-range space probes.

Nuclear Engineers also create various types of instruments that are used in industry and by research institutions. Semiconductor and advanced materials companies use

190   CAREER OPPORTUNITIES IN ENGINEERING

plasma-processing technologies that are designed by Nuclear Engineers. Some of these engineers work on the development of cancer therapy treatments. Some work with X-ray machines and other imaging equipment for use in medical centers, airports, and other places. Others find ways to produce and use radioisotopes for medical and oil industry purposes. In addition, Nuclear Engineers develop techniques to use radiation to pasteurize and preserve foods.

Others develop technologies called tracers that help them to find leaks in oil pipelines and determine how underground water sources travel. Some of these engineers help to develop various industrial products such as radiation-treated insulation for computer wiring, or radiation thickness gauges that are used to precisely produce certain thicknesses of such materials as paper or aluminum. Nuclear Engineers also research methods for using waste fuel from nuclear reactors. Some of them work in the areas of arms control and nuclear weapon non-proliferation as well as develop regulations governing the safe use of radioactive materials and nuclear power systems.

Nuclear engineering projects are team efforts. Nuclear Engineers work with other engineers, scientists, and technicians to research, analyze and solve problems, create designs, construct and inspect facilities, and manage systems and facilities. They are sometimes the supervisors of their work teams. They use engineering principles and practices as well as economics and mathematics, in addition to their knowledge of nuclear physics, to work to develop beneficial technologies and systems.

Nuclear Engineers specialize in several ways. They may work in specific industries or certain technologies. As they gain experience, these engineers may specialize in performing a particular engineering function or specialty such as research, design, analysis, testing, facilities management, engineering management, consulting, or teaching.

Those who work in the area of fission are largely employed in laboratories within the nuclear power industry or for the government. In industrial laboratories, they conduct research to develop new designs for reactors with improved safety features. Those who work in government laboratories conduct similar research but also look into other concerns, such as nuclear weapons design and the study of nuclear fuels and their cycles.

These engineers may specialize in fusion research, in which they study such things as plasmas and electrodynamics. They also investigate how various materials resist radiation or high temperatures. They design and build special facilities, such as tokamaks, which are ring-shaped nuclear reactors for producing fusion. Some engineers are concerned with methods of handling stockpiles of nuclear materials.

Nuclear Engineers are responsible for attending to duties that are specific to their profession. For example, they might:

- research, design, and develop the instruments, equipment, systems, and processes used in nuclear energy and radiation applications
- oversee the processes and upkeep of nuclear facilities
- monitor and inspect facilities and equipment
- seek and identify problems as well as suggest remediation methods
- develop and implement safety or emergency procedures
- analyze mishaps and apply preventative measures
- conduct research on the latest developments in nuclear physics and engineering
- investigate methods for the use and disposal of nuclear material

In the course of their work, Nuclear Engineers review project proposals and estimate the costs of their implementation. They also write documents pertaining to procedures, research results, recommendations, and other aspects of their daily activities. They use computers as aids in their research, to make calculations, create designs, analyze data, prepare budgets, and write pertinent documents. These engineers are expected to keep up-to-date with new developments in their field by reading books, papers, and journals as well as by conducting research. Some serve on government commissions that monitor and regulate the nuclear industry.

Nuclear Engineers spend most of their working lives in office or laboratory settings but are also required to travel to other facilities such as reactor, laboratory, or testing installations. Those engineers who specialize in construction usually work outdoors or in mobile offices near their construction sites.

Nuclear Engineers who work with reactor fuels or radioisotopes wear precautionary equipment—such as radiation measuring and recording devices—and protective clothing, including radiation protection suits, hardhats, and work boots. They need to be continuously alert and attend to very exacting details, as well as be able to work in stressful situations.

These engineers generally work for 40 hours per week but may work as long as 50 hours to meet production schedules or deadlines.

Salaries

Salaries for Nuclear Engineers vary, depending on such factors as their education, experience, employer, and geographical location. According to the November 2004 *Occupational Employment Statistics* (OES) survey by the U.S. Bureau of Labor Statistics (BLS), the estimated annual salary for most Nuclear Engineers ranged between $62,870 and $119,080.

Entry-level Nuclear Engineers who work for the federal government start at either the GS-5 or GS-7 level of the general schedule (GS), the pay schedule for most federal employees. Engineers with several years of experience may be hired at the GS-12 or GS-13 level. In 2006, the annual basic pay for the GS-5 to GS-13 levels ranged from $25,195 to $85,578.

Employment Prospects

The BLS reported in its November 2004 OES survey that an estimated 15,870 Nuclear Engineers were employed in the United States. About 40 percent of these engineers were employed by the power generation and supply industry. Other large employers included the scientific research and development services industry, the federal government, and the architectural and engineering services industry.

Most job openings become available as Nuclear Engineers are promoted, transfer to other jobs, or retire. Although there is predicted to be little growth for this occupation through 2014 (as reported by the BLS), opportunities should continue to be favorable. According to the American Nuclear Society, a large number of Nuclear Engineers are now, or soon will be, eligible for retirement, and qualified applicants are needed to take their place. Furthermore, in recent years, fewer students have been enrolling in and graduating from nuclear engineering programs.

Nuclear Engineers are needed to keep nuclear plants in operation, as well as to perform research and development for future power sources. Some engineers also find a demand for their expertise in such areas as defense, medical technology, and the environment. The demand for Nuclear Engineers may also increase in the future as new nuclear plants are approved for construction.

Advancement Prospects

Nuclear Engineers may advance in any number of ways, depending on their ambitions and interests. They can become technical specialists or consultants, as well as pursue such managerial positions as supervisory, project, and chief engineer. Some engineers seek teaching and research positions at colleges and universities. Engineers with entrepreneurial goals may become independent practitioners or owners of technical or consulting firms.

Education and Training

Many Nuclear Engineers possess an advanced degree, which may be a master's or doctoral degree. Minimally, a bachelor's degree in nuclear engineering or another related field is needed for individuals to obtain entry-level positions. A master's or doctoral degree is usually required for them to advance to careers in management, consulting, research, or teaching.

Employers typically provide entry-level engineers with training programs, which may include both on-the-job training and formal classroom training. New engineers work under the supervision and direction of experienced engineers.

Throughout their careers, Nuclear Engineers enroll in continuing education programs and training programs to update their skills and keep up with the latest advancements in their field.

Special Requirements

Some employers require that Nuclear Engineers be licensed professional engineers (P.E.) or engineers-in-training (E.I.T.).

All states and territories, as well as Washington, D.C., require engineers who provide work directly to the public or perform work that affects the public safety and welfare to be licensed in their jurisdiction. For specific information about P.E. licensure, contact the board of engineering examiners for the area where you wish to practice. See Appendix II for a list of boards.

Experience, Special Skills, and Personality Traits

Entry-level candidates should have work experience related to the positions for which they apply. They may have gained their experience through internships, work-study programs, student research projects, postdoctoral training, or part-time employment.

Nuclear Engineers need excellent analytical, problem-solving, writing, and communication skills for their line of work. Additionally, they need strong teamwork and interpersonal skills, as they must work well with various people from diverse backgrounds. Some personality traits that successful Nuclear Engineers share include being curious, creative, detail-oriented, patient, precise, dedicated, and trustworthy.

Unions and Associations

Many Nuclear Engineers are members of the American Nuclear Society, the national professional association that serves the general interests of this profession. (For contact information, see Appendix III.) By joining this or other societies, Nuclear Engineers can take advantage of networking opportunities, publications, continuing education programs, and other professional services and resources.

Tips for Entry

1. Some employers recruit for entry-level positions on college campuses. Contact your college career center or engineering department for information about recruiting events.
2. To be hired for some positions, individuals must be able to obtain security clearance. This generally involves an employer performing a thorough background check.
3. To learn about job openings with the federal government, visit the U.S. Office of Personnel Management Web site at USAJOBS, http://www.usajobs.opm.gov.
4. Use the Internet to learn more about Nuclear Engineers. You might start by visiting the American Nuclear Society Web site, http://www.ans.org. For more links, see Appendix IV.

PETROLEUM ENGINEER

CAREER PROFILE

Duties: Locate potential sites for oil and natural gas; oversee the production of oil and gas fields; perform other duties as required

Alternate Title(s): A title that reflects a specialty (such as Reservoir Engineer) or an engineering function (such as Project Engineer)

Salary Range: $49,000 to $141,000

Employment Prospects: Good

Advancement Prospects: Good

Prerequisites:

Education or Training—Bachelor's degree in petroleum engineering or another related field

Experience—Previous work experience generally required

Special Skills and Personality Traits—Self-management, problem-solving, writing, communication, teamwork, and interpersonal skills; detail-oriented, analytical, creative, self-motivated, curious, tactful, and ethical

Special Requirements—Professional Engineer (P.E.) licensure may be required

CAREER LADDER

```
┌─────────────────────────────────┐
│   Senior Petroleum Engineer      │
└─────────────────────────────────┘

┌─────────────────────────────────┐
│      Petroleum Engineer          │
└─────────────────────────────────┘

┌─────────────────────────────────┐
│   Junior Petroleum Engineer      │
└─────────────────────────────────┘
```

Position Description

Petroleum and natural gas have become our major sources for energy. We use them as fuels to power our vehicles, aircraft, ships, and trains, as well as our equipment and machinery. We also use these fuels to generate heat and electricity for our homes, businesses, factories, schools, hospitals, and institutions. In addition, the chemicals (known as petrochemicals) from petroleum and natural gas are used for fabricating a wide range of products—including drugs, cosmetics, detergents, synthetic fibers, carpets, food packaging materials, fertilizers, paints, plastics, and synthetic rubber.

Petroleum engineering is the discipline involved with the production, storage, and transportation of petroleum (or oil) and natural gas. Petroleum Engineers are the men and women who are responsible for finding and producing oil and natural gas supplies, which are located thousands of feet under the earth's surface in rock and sand. Most of these engineers work in remote areas around the world, including locations in deserts, on mountains, and on oil platforms in oceans.

Their major duties include exploring potential sites for reservoirs of oil or gas, making plans for drilling exploratory wells, and determining if potential sites would be cost-effective and profitable for their companies. Petroleum Engineers are responsible for overseeing the construction and operation of oil fields and gas fields. They also monitor the performance of individual wells and develop better recovery methods to increase their production of oil or gas. In addition, they design wells, storage tanks, and transportation systems. Furthermore, these engineers oversee the dismantling of wells or fields after they are exhausted as well as the removal of hazardous and other waste from the sites.

Petroleum Engineers use sophisticated, complex technologies to assist them with their exploration and production tasks. For example, Petroleum Engineers use seismic technology, which is the reflection of sound waves off of underground formations, to locate possible oil or gas deposits. Another example is drilling technology that embeds computers in the drilling equipment, which allows engineers to accurately target a specific area more than a mile under the earth's surface. Petroleum Engineers also depend on computer models to simulate their drilling options for exploratory wells, the performance of individual wells, and other matters.

These engineers usually specialize in different areas such as drilling, production operations, reservoir characteristics, and environmental remediation. Their job titles reflect their specialties. For example:

- petrophysical engineers examine the rock that holds oil deposits to determine how much is there and how easily it may flow through the rock.
- drilling engineers plan and oversee the construction operations of wells
- production engineers are responsible for the development of wells and the oversight of daily field operations
- reservoir engineers use mathematical models to predict, evaluate, and estimate the amount of oil or gas that is in a reservoir

Petroleum Engineers work in interdisciplinary teams that include geological engineers and other engineers, technologists, technicians, and other support personnel.

Petroleum Engineers perform a variety of tasks that vary each day. For example, they may be engaged in conducting studies to improve operations, developing work plans, analyzing and interpreting data, developing budgets or work schedules, preparing technical reports, conferring with colleagues to troubleshoot design or production problems, inspecting wells, or testing machinery to ensure that it is working properly. These engineers are also responsible for ensuring that operations are in compliance with company policies and procedures as well as appropriate laws and regulations.

Senior engineers may be responsible for supervising and directing teams of junior engineers, technicians, and other support personnel. They give work assignments to their staff members, monitor their work, and make corrective actions as needed.

Petroleum Engineers are involved in other specialties besides field work. Many work in refineries where they are engaged in the different phases of product development and manufacturing. Some are sales engineers who sell drilling and other types of equipment to customers, while others work as field service engineers who provide technical services for that equipment. Other Petroleum Engineers are engaged as researchers. They may be involved in basic research—seeking new knowledge and understanding—or applied research—using basic research to develop new or improved technologies for oil production. Some Petroleum Engineers are full-time or part-time instructors who teach engineering courses in colleges and universities.

Petroleum Engineers find employment with major oil companies as well as smaller, independent petroleum exploration, production, and service companies. They are also employed by engineering consulting firms, government agencies, and equipment suppliers. Some engineers are independent consultants.

Most oil companies are global enterprises, hence Petroleum Engineers may be assigned to branch offices and field operations anywhere in the world. They work outdoors in drilling sites and oil fields, as well as indoors in offices and laboratories.

Petroleum Engineers usually work a 40-hour week but put in additional hours as needed to complete their tasks. Engineers who are assigned to drill sites sometimes work seven days a week; they are also on-call 24 hours a day in case of emergencies or when changes occur in drilling conditions. Field engineers are exposed to loud noises and hazardous equipment, which requires wearing hard hats, work boots, or other protective clothing.

Salaries

Salaries for Petroleum Engineers vary, depending on such factors as their education, experience, and employer. The estimated annual salary for most of these engineers ranged between $49,240 and $140,850, according to the U.S. Bureau of Labor Statistics (BLS) in its November 2004 *Occupational Employment Statistics* (OES) survey.

Employment Prospects

The BLS reported in its November 2004 OES survey that an estimated 14,790 Petroleum Engineers were employed in the United States. Nearly 50 percent were employed in the oil and gas extraction industry. The architectural and engineering services industry employed about 2,000 Petroleum Engineers, and about 1,400 of these engineers were engaged in support activities for mining companies.

According to the BLS, the job growth for this occupation is predicted to decline through 2014. However, opportunities should still continue to be favorable because the number of openings is expected to be greater than the number of students graduating in the petroleum engineering field. Most job opportunities for Petroleum Engineers become available as individuals retire, advance to higher positions, or transfer to other occupations.

Job opportunities are also available worldwide. Many American companies employ Petroleum Engineers to work in their overseas facilities; additionally, many foreign oil companies hire American Petroleum Engineers.

Advancement Prospects

As Petroleum Engineers gain experience, they are assigned to more complex projects as well as receive increasingly greater responsibilities. They may advance in any number of ways, depending on their ambitions and interests. They may become technical specialists, or move into the business areas of an organization, such as marketing, sales, or finance.

Those with managerial and administrative ambitions may pursue such positions as supervisory, project, and chief engineers. In addition, they may advance to executive officer positions within their organization. Engineers with entrepreneurial ambitions can become independent practitioners or owners of firms that offer consulting services.

Education and Training

Petroleum Engineers possess at least a bachelor's degree in petroleum engineering, chemical engineering, civil engineering, or another engineering discipline. Some engineers have a bachelor's degree in an earth science discipline such as geology or geophysics. Many Petroleum Engineers also hold a master's or doctoral degree in their field.

Minimally, individuals need a bachelor's degree for entry-level positions. A master's or doctoral degree is usually required for them to advance to careers in management, consulting, or research. Engineers who wish to teach courses at the college level must hold a doctorate.

Entry-level engineers receive on-the-job training while working under the supervision and guidance of experienced engineers. Many companies also provide novice engineers with formal classroom training.

Throughout their careers, Petroleum Engineers enroll in continuing education programs and training programs to update their skills and keep up with advancements in their fields.

Special Requirements

All engineers who offer engineering services directly to the public or perform work that affects the life, health, or property of the public must be licensed as professional engineers (P.E.). All states, as well as Washington, D.C., and U.S. territories, have their own particular licensing requirements. For specific information, contact the board of engineering examiners for the area where you wish to practice. See Appendix II for a list of boards.

Experience, Special Skills, and Personality Traits

Entry-level candidates should have work experience related to the positions for which they apply. They may have gained their experience through internships, work-study programs, student research projects, or summer employment.

To be effective at their work, Petroleum Engineers need strong self-management, problem-solving, writing, and communication skills. In addition, they must have excellent teamwork and interpersonal skills, as they must work well with various people from diverse backgrounds.

Some personality traits that successful Petroleum Engineers share are being detail-oriented, analytical, creative, self-motivated, curious, tactful, and ethical.

Unions and Associations

Petroleum Engineers can join professional associations to take advantage of professional services and resources such as networking opportunities and continuing education programs. The Society of Petroleum Engineers, a national society, specifically serves the interests of this profession. For contact information, see Appendix III.

Tips for Entry

1. Contact people with whom you worked during your internships for advice about finding a job as well as for leads to job vacancies.
2. A willingness to relocate, including to other countries, may increase your chances of finding the job you want.
3. Check out company Web sites for employment opportunities. Many of them state how you may apply for a job.
4. Learn more about Petroleum Engineers on the Internet. You might start by visiting the Society of Petroleum Engineers Web site, http://www.spe.org. For more links, see Appendix IV.

WELDING ENGINEER

CAREER PROFILE

Duties: Support welding operations in product development, construction, manufacturing, research, and other engineering operations; perform duties as required

Alternate Title(s): Materials Joining Engineer; a title that reflects an engineering function such as Project Engineer

Salary Range: $44,000 to $113,000

Employment Prospects: Good

Advancement Prospects: Good

Prerequisites:

Education or Training—Bachelor's degree in welding engineering or another related field

Experience—Previous work experience generally required

Special Skills and Personality Traits—Leadership, problem-solving, decision-making, self-management, communication, interpersonal, and teamwork skills; responsible, self-motivated, adaptable, honest, and ethical

Special Requirements—Professional Engineer (P.E.) licensure may be required

CAREER LADDER

```
┌─────────────────────────────────┐
│     Senior Welding Engineer      │
└─────────────────────────────────┘

┌─────────────────────────────────┐
│        Welding Engineer          │
└─────────────────────────────────┘

┌─────────────────────────────────┐
│     Junior Welding Engineer      │
└─────────────────────────────────┘
```

Position Description

Some people say that welding is what keeps the world together. It is used every day to build and repair automobiles, aircraft, ships, and other forms of transportation. It plays a critical role in the manufacturing process of thousands of products. In addition, it is used for constructing buildings, bridges, dams, and other structures, as well as to join piping systems in pipelines, manufacturing facilities, refineries, and power plants. Welding is normally thought of as a process—that of permanently joining and fusing metal or nonmetal pieces solidly together. However, it is more than a process, it is an engineering discipline known as welding engineering.

Welding Engineers are responsible for supporting the welding operations that are part of product development, construction, manufacturing, research, and other engineering operations. Their job requires a knowledge and background from multiple disciplines such as material science, electrical engineering, and mechanical engineering. They apply the principles of science, mathematics, and engineering to solving welding problems related to the design, testing, production, quality control, maintenance, and other aspects of welded products. (Welded products range from microelectronic devices and computers to robots, industrial machinery, off-road vehicles, bridges, high-rise buildings, undersea pipelines, and space probes.)

These engineers are experts in the various types of welding processes used to join materials together, such as gas tungsten arc, electron beam, laser, resistance, plasma, sound wave, and robotic welding processes. Some Welding Engineers are experts in other methods of joining materials, such as soldering, brazing, adhesive bonding, and some micro-joining processes. These engineers are sometimes known as materials joining engineers.

Welding Engineers must be highly knowledgeable about the properties of various metallic and nonmetallic materials—such as steel, stainless steel, nickel, aluminum alloys, titanium, plastics, ceramics, and composites—and understand how different materials are affected in the welding process. Because most welding processes use electricity as their energy source, Welding Engineers have a strong understanding of how electricity, electrical power, and electrical circuits work. In addition, they are experienced in structural, machine, and production design; manufacturing processes; and nondestructive testing and evaluations.

Welding Engineers are involved in various engineering activities. They assist product development teams by providing input toward the joint design of a product, selecting materials for the product, and determining which welding processes would be appropriate for the product and its fabrication. These engineers also provide technical assistance to sales and technical services departments.

Some Welding Engineers are engaged in conducting basic research to generate new knowledge and understanding about welding processes or welding phenomena. Others use the findings of basic researchers to discover new or improved welding equipment, processes, techniques, or procedures.

Welding Engineers perform a variety of tasks, which vary according to their position and skill level. For example, they may be responsible for:

- developing or improving welding processes, techniques, and equipment
- developing welding procedures to guide welders as well as production operations about specification restrictions, complex and unusual welding methods, and other matters
- assessing new product concepts and designs and providing input on their manufacturability
- defining welding processes for new and current products
- performing failure analysis on prototypes, products, or structures to determine what went wrong and making recommendations for fixing the problems
- preparing documentation for new or revised welding procedures
- testing and evaluating new welding equipment
- coordinating inspections to ensure that welds, welding procedures, and welding equipment conform to appropriate welding codes and standards
- establishing initiatives to improve the quality of welding operations
- staying abreast of new developments in the welding field and determining how they can be applied to improve production processes
- conferring with engineering personnel to exchange project information, offering technical advice about welding concerns, troubleshooting problems, or discussing other work matters
- training welding personnel
- preparing correspondence, technical reports, and required paperwork

Welding Engineers may specialize in any number of ways. They may become experts in specific welding processes (such as laser welding and microjoining processes), certain materials (such as steels, aluminum alloys, or composites), and particular industries (such as automotive, aerospace, or petrochemicals). Experienced engineers also specialize in one or more engineering specialties, such as research, design, management, or consulting.

These engineers work in offices and laboratories, as well as spend some time on production floors or at construction sites. They generally work a 40-hour week but work additional hours as needed to complete tasks or meet deadlines.

Salaries

Salaries for Welding Engineers vary, depending on such factors as their education, experience, employer, industry, and geographical location. Specific salary information for this occupation is unavailable, but an idea can be obtained by looking at the salaries for engineers in general. According to the November 2004 *Occupational Employment Statistics* survey by the U.S. Bureau of Labor Statistics, the estimated annual salary for most engineers not listed separately in the survey ranged between $44,040 and $113,000.

Employment Prospects

Welding Engineers work in many industries—construction, defense, aerospace, automotive, manufacturing, energy, mining, chemicals, and computer industries, to name just a few. They are employed by private companies, contracting firms, consulting firms, government agencies, research institutes, and colleges and universities.

Job openings generally become available as Welding Engineers retire, advance to higher positions, or transfer to other occupations. According to some experts, there is a high demand for Welding Engineers in the United States as well as worldwide. Some companies meet their needs for Welding Engineers by employing and retraining individuals who were educated in nonwelding disciplines.

Advancement Prospects

As Welding Engineers gain experience, they are assigned to more complex projects as well as receive increasingly greater responsibilities. They may advance in any number of ways, depending on their ambitions and interests. They may become technical specialists or consultants; they may become researchers or instructors; or they may move into the business areas of an organization, such as marketing, technical sales, or finance. Those with managerial and administrative ambitions may pursue such positions as supervisory, project, and chief engineers. In addition, they may advance to executive officer positions within their organization. To advance to higher positions, they are usually required to possess a master's or doctoral degree.

Engineers with entrepreneurial ambitions can become independent consultants or owners of firms that offer technical or consulting services.

Education and Training

Minimally, a bachelor's degree in welding engineering, welding technology, metallurgical engineering, materials science and engineering, manufacturing engineering, mechanical engineering, or another related field is needed for individuals to obtain entry-level positions. A master's or doctoral degree is usually required for them to advance to careers in management, consulting, research, or teaching.

As of 2005, Ohio State University and LeTourneau University of Longview, Texas, are the only American institutions that offer a welding engineering (Ohio State) or a materials joining (LeTourneau) program that is accredited by ABET, Inc.

Employers typically provide entry-level engineers with training programs, which may include both on-the-job training and formal classroom training. New engineers work under the supervision and direction of experienced engineers.

Throughout their careers, Welding Engineers enroll in continuing education programs and training programs to update their skills and keep up with advancements in their fields.

Special Requirements

All engineers who offer engineering services directly to the public or perform work that affects the life, health, or property of the public must be licensed as professional engineers (P.E.) where they practice. Every U.S. state and territory, as well as Washington, D.C., has its own licensing requirements. For specific information, contact the board of engineering examiners for the area where you wish to practice. See Appendix II for a list of boards.

Experience, Special Skills, and Personality Traits

Applicants do not need prior work experience for entry-level positions, but having experience is preferable. Recent graduates may have gained their experience through internships, work-study programs, student research projects, or summer employment. Having experience within an employer's industry is also preferable.

Welding Engineers need strong leadership, problem-solving, decision-making, and self-management skills for their job. In addition, they need effective communication, interpersonal, and teamwork skills, as they must work well with various people from diverse backgrounds. Being responsible, self-motivated, adaptable, honest, and ethical are some personality traits that successful Welding Engineers have in common.

Unions and Associations

Many Welding Engineers belong to local, state, and national societies to take advantage of networking opportunities, continuing education programs, and other professional services and resources. The American Welding Society and the Society of Manufacturing Engineers are two professional associations at the national level that Welding Engineers might join. For contact information, see Appendix III.

Tips for Entry

1. Although it is not a requirement to become a Welding Engineer, learn the basics of welding to get a better understanding of the technology. You might obtain formal training through a high school, vocational school, or community college welding program.
2. To enhance their employability, some Welding Engineers obtain professional certification from a recognized organization such as the American Welding Society.
3. Directly contact employers for whom you want to work. If a company has no current vacancies, ask if you may come in for an informational interview to learn more about the company and the role Welding Engineers play there.
4. Use the Internet to learn more about Welding Engineers and the welding industry in general. You might start by visiting the American Welding Society Web site, http://www.aws.org. For more links, see Appendix IV.

ENGINEERING SPECIALTIES

RESEARCH ENGINEER

CAREER PROFILE

Duties: Perform applied or basic research; plan, conduct, and evaluate experiments; perform duties as required

Alternate Title(s): A title that reflects an engineering discipline such as Mechanical Engineer

Salary Range: $33,000 to $124,000

Employment Prospects: Good

Advancement Prospects: Good

Prerequisites:

Education or Training—A master's or doctoral degree in an engineering discipline or a related field

Experience—Previous work and research experience generally required

Special Skills and Personality Traits—Interpersonal, problem-solving, organizational, communication, writing, and self-management skills; persistent, dedicated, organized, enthusiastic, flexible, and creative

Special Requirements—Professional engineer (P.E.) licensure may be required

CAREER LADDER

```
┌─────────────────────────────────┐
│   Senior Research Engineer       │
└─────────────────────────────────┘

┌─────────────────────────────────┐
│     Research Engineer            │
└─────────────────────────────────┘

┌─────────────────────────────────┐
│  Assistant Research Engineer     │
└─────────────────────────────────┘
```

Position Description

Research Engineers carry out engineering research within their discipline (such as civil, mechanical, electrical, computer, chemical, materials, biomedical, and aerospace engineering). These professionals use the basic principles and knowledge of science, mathematics, and engineering to study and develop useful and applicable technologies for the good of mankind. They may be employed in private, academic, governmental, and nonprofit research laboratories.

Most Research Engineers, especially in private labs, are involved in applied research. They conduct studies to specifically create new or improved products, devices, structures, and processes. For example, chemical Research Engineers might be involved in the development of new medicines, synthetic fabrics, or oil refinery processes.

Some Research Engineers engage in basic research to increase knowledge in their particular areas of interest. For example, biomedical Research Engineers might work on projects related to biology and medicine to gain further understanding of how certain biological systems work.

The nature of research in any area (for example, nanotechnology, artificial intelligence, biomechanics, or construction) is so diverse that projects are usually completed by interdisciplinary teams of engineers and scientists. Teams also consist of engineering technologists and technicians as well as other research and administrative support staff. Additionally, industrial Research Engineers work with members from marketing, quality assurance, and other departments to ensure that they develop products that meet their customers' needs and requirements.

Research Engineers use various research techniques and approaches. They may perform laboratory work, literature searches, case studies, and fieldwork. They usually work on several projects at a time. Hence, they perform a wide range of duties, which vary every day. For example, they might be involved in:

• planning or developing projects
• designing or conducting experiments
• developing or scheduling tests
• collecting, analyzing, or reporting data

- designing devices, test instrumentation, computer models, or software programs
- preparing protocols, summaries, patent applications, or reports
- brainstorming ideas or discussing the progress of projects with co-workers
- preparing proposals, technical papers, or presentations
- attending professional conferences
- planning and organizing their work schedules
- inspecting or repairing lab equipment
- maintaining a safe work environment
- supervising junior or student researchers, technicians, and other staff

Novice researchers perform routine tasks under the guidance of experienced Research Engineers. They are usually given assignments in which problems are well defined and in which they use standard practices and techniques to conduct experiments and tests. As researchers gain experience, they receive increasingly difficult assignments and become capable of working more independently. They may be assigned the responsibility of supervising junior researchers, technicians, and other staff.

Senior Research Engineers typically act as technical leads or consultants on projects. (The primary researcher is called the principal investigator.) These professionals perform such duties as planning and developing research; overseeing and coordinating projects; devising new or improved engineering approaches and research techniques; making decisions on technical methods and problems; organizing and overseeing meetings; serving as key contributors on proposals, reports, papers, and presentations; and supervising, training, and evaluating staff members.

Research Engineers work in offices, laboratories, and production sites. Sometimes their studies require working in the field, such as at construction sites, in mines, or along shorelines. Some researchers are involved in projects that require working and living in remote locations for several days, weeks, or months. For example, researchers in ocean engineering might conduct field expeditions that require living and working on research ships. Many Research Engineers travel to other cities, states, and countries to attend meetings and conferences.

Salaries

Salaries for Research Engineers vary, depending on such factors as their education, experience, employer, and geographical location. According to the November 2004 *Occupational Employment Statistics* survey by the U.S. Bureau of Labor Statistics (BLS), the estimated annual salary ranged between $32,840 and $98,790 for engineering occupations in general. The estimated annual salary for most postsecondary engineering teachers, which include those

who also conduct research, ranged between $39,430 and $124,140.

Employment Prospects

Research Engineers are employed by local, state, and federal governmental agencies. (The National Aeronautics Administration, the Environmental Protection Agency, and the National Science Foundation are a few examples of federal agencies.) They also find employment with governmental, academic, and nonprofit laboratories. In addition, Research Engineers work for private companies—from start-up firms to large, established corporations—in practically all industries.

Most job openings become available as Research Engineers transfer to other jobs, advance to higher positions, or retire. The BLS states that job opportunities for engineers, in general, are favorable because the number of engineering graduates is expected to be about the same as the number of jobs that will become available through 2014.

Many researchers with academic, governmental, and nonprofit employers are appointed for one or more years, depending on the nature of the research project. When a project ends, a researcher may continue employment if other projects and funding are available.

Advancement Prospects

Advancement opportunities lead to such positions as project engineer, principal investigator, program manager, laboratory director, and executive officer. Doctoral degrees are often required for researchers to obtain top management positions.

Education and Training

Most employers hire applicants who possess a master's or doctoral degree in an engineering discipline, mathematics, physical science, or another field related to the job for which they apply. For some entry-level research positions, employers may hire applicants with a bachelor's degree if they have qualifying work experience.

Novice researchers typically receive on-the-job training while working under the guidance and supervision of experienced engineers. Some employers also provide formal classroom training programs.

Special Requirements

All engineers who offer engineering services directly to the public or perform work that affects the life, health, or property of the public must be licensed as professional engineers (P.E.). Every U.S. state and territory, as well as Washington, D.C., has its own requirements for licensure. For specific information, contact the board of engineering examiners for the area where you wish to practice. See Appendix II for a list of boards.

Experience, Special Skills, and Personality Traits

Employers typically seek candidates who have work and research experience related to the position that they offer. Entry-level applicants may have gained their experience through internships, work-study programs, academic research projects, fellowships, or summer employment.

Research Engineers need strong interpersonal, problem-solving, and organizational skills for their work. In addition, they must demonstrate excellent communication and writing skills. Exceptional self-management skills, such as the ability to work independently, meet deadlines, and follow and understand directions, are also important. Being persistent, dedicated, organized, enthusiastic, flexible, and creative are some personality traits that successful Research Engineers share.

Unions and Associations

Many Research Engineers are members of professional associations that serve the interests of their particular disciplines. By joining local, state, or national societies, they can take advantage of networking opportunities, continuing education programs, and other professional services and resources. For names and contact information of various engineering societies, see Appendix III.

Tips for Entry

1. To see if research is something you might like to do, obtain a research assistantship or volunteer to work on a professor's research project.
2. Many professional associations have student chapters. Join one, and participate in its activities.
4. Use the Internet to learn more about a prospective employer. Many companies, research laboratories, governmental agencies, and other employers have Web sites. Many of them also post information about current research projects.

DEVELOPMENT ENGINEER

CAREER PROFILE

Duties: Coordinate and perform various activities in the development of new products from their conception to the launching of their full production; perform duties as required

Alternate Title(s): Product Development Engineer, Process Development Engineer; a title that reflects an engineering discipline such as Mechanical Engineer

Salary Range: $33,000 to $99,000

Employment Prospects: Good

Advancement Prospects: Good

Prerequisites:

Education or Training—Bachelor's degree in engineering

Experience—Previous work experience generally required

Special Skills and Personality Traits—Leadership, teamwork, interpersonal, problem-solving, critical-thinking, time management, communication, writing, and computing skills; creative, persistent, self-motivated, flexible, adaptable, detail-oriented, and collaborative

Special Requirements—Professional engineer (P.E.) licensure usually required

CAREER LADDER

```
┌─────────────────────────────┐
│      Senior Engineer        │
└─────────────────────────────┘

┌─────────────────────────────┐
│          Engineer           │
└─────────────────────────────┘

┌─────────────────────────────┐
│       Junior Engineer       │
└─────────────────────────────┘
```

Position Description

Everything we use today—computers, communication systems, appliances, air-conditioning units, cars, airplanes, medicine, medical devices, packaged food, toys, sporting goods, gardening equipment, industrial machines, automated systems, construction materials, and so forth—began as an idea. Companies may take several months to several years to turn an idea into a final product that is ready to be sold on the market. This process of creating new products—or new services, formulations, applications, or systems—is known as product development. The engineers who are specifically involved in this engineering specialty are known as Development Engineers.

Development Engineers are expected to have a firm understanding of what customers need and want, and to come up with products that would be cost effective for their company. These engineers apply the principles and techniques of engineering, science, mathematics, and business to solve problems as they occur within the product development cycle.

The product development cycle involves several stages, and Development Engineers may be assigned to support any one of those phases. At the exploratory stage, Development Engineers are members of teams made up of representatives from engineering, manufacturing, marketing, finance, and other technical and nontechnical divisions. These teams consider new research findings and technologies, as well as consumer trends and their competition, to generate ideas for original products or improved versions of existing products.

In the feasibility stage of product development, teams determine whether a potential product idea is possible and practical. Development Engineers are engaged in gathering information and performing analyses to answer such questions as: Is there a market for the product? How large a market is it? What kind of competition would there be? Can the product be made? How would the company produce it? How much would it cost? How much would customers be willing to pay for it? How does the product fit in with the company's overall product lines? Would the product be profitable for the company?

In the next phase, usually known as the development stage, Development Engineers participate in various activities. They assist in defining the overall project. They help establish project objectives, plans, schedules, and costs. They may be involved in developing manufacturing (or operations) plans, marketing plans for launching the product, or test plans for the evaluation of prototypes.

Development Engineers are also involved in defining the new product. With design teams, these engineers work on establishing the design parameters, creating designs, and deciding which designs best meet specifications. These engineers may actually perform design work or provide technical expertise and support to the design engineers and others on the design team.

Testing and validation of a selected product design is the next phase of the product development cycle. Development Engineers oversee the making of a prototype, or model, of a product design. They are also responsible for coordinating or performing standardized tests to ensure that the prototype meets the customers' requirements, product specifications, and all applicable governmental regulations.

The final stage of product development is known as the launch phase—the manufacturing of the product for sale. Prior to this phase, many Development Engineers are concerned with optimizing the production processes for the new product. These engineers are often known as process development engineers. They may perform such activities as determining what equipment and processes are needed to produce the product; designing required tools, equipment, buildings, and processes; improving manufacturing techniques; and developing implementation plans for new equipment and processes.

Development Engineers interface with many people on a continual basis. In addition to working closely with other engineers, they work with managers, professionals, technicians, scientists, and other personnel from different departments. For example, they may work with staff from research, design, manufacturing, purchasing, packaging, distributing, marketing, and sales divisions. Development Engineers also have frequent contact with vendors, suppliers, consultants, contractors, and governmental agencies, among others. They communicate with co-workers and others in person, over the phone, by correspondence, and through e-mail.

Product Development Engineers normally have a 40-hour week schedule. They put in additional hours as needed to complete their tasks and to meet deadlines.

Salaries

Development Engineers earn a salary according to their job level (such as entry-level or journey-level). Their salaries vary depending on such factors as their education, experi-

ence, engineering discipline, employer, industry, and geographical location. According to the November 2004 *Occupational Employment Statistics* survey by the Bureau of Labor Statistics (BLS), the estimated annual salary for most engineers ranged between $32,840 and $98,790.

Employment Prospects

Most job openings become available as engineers are promoted, transfer to other occupations, or retire. Job growth for this occupation is predicted to increase by 9 to 17 percent through 2014, according to the BLS. Job opportunities in general should be favorable because the number of engineering graduates is expected to be about the same as the number of job openings.

Advancement Prospects

As Development Engineers gain experience, they are assigned to more complex projects as well as receive increasingly greater responsibilities. They may advance in any number of ways, depending on their ambitions and interests. They may become technical specialists, or move into the business areas of an organization, such as marketing, technical sales, or finance.

Those with managerial and administrative ambitions and talents may seek engineering management positions. In addition, they may pursue executive officer positions within their organization. Engineers with entrepreneurial ambitions can become independent consultants or owners of firms that offer technical or consulting services.

Education and Training

Applicants for entry-level positions need at least a bachelor's degree in their engineering discipline or another related field. Many engineers hold an advanced degree. Those seeking to advance further in management or to move to other career paths such as consulting, research, or teaching generally need a master's or doctoral degree.

Entry-level engineers typically receive on-the-job training while working under the guidance and supervision of experienced engineers. Novice engineers may also be required to participate in formal classroom instruction.

Throughout their careers, engineers enroll in continuing education and training programs to update their skills and keep up with advancements in their fields.

Special Requirements

All engineers who perform work that affects the public safety and welfare, or who provide engineering services directly to the public, must be licensed professional engineers (P.E.). Licensing requirements differ in each state and territory, as well as in Washington, D.C. For specific information, contact the board of engineering examiners for the area where you wish to practice. See Appendix II for a list of boards.

Experience, Special Skills, and Personality Traits

Employers often hire applicants who have no professional experience for entry-level positions, although they prefer to employ applicants with relevant experience. Many recently hired graduates have obtained experience through internships, work-study programs, student research projects, and summer employment.

Development Engineers need strong leadership, teamwork, and interpersonal skills for their line of work. They also need effective problem-solving, critical-thinking, time management, communication, and writing skills. Having competent computing skills is also essential.

Some personality skills that successful Development Engineers share include being creative, persistent, self-motivated, flexible, adaptable, detail-oriented, and collaborative.

Unions and Associations

Many engineers join professional associations to take advantage of various professional services and resources such as networking opportunities, continuing education programs, certification, and current research findings. Development Engineers might join the Product Development and Management Association, a society that serves the particular interests of this engineering specialty.

They can also join engineering societies that serve their particular disciplines such as the Institute of Electrical and Electronics Engineers, the Biomedical Engineering Society, or the ASME International. In addition, they can join special-interest societies such as the National Society of Professional Engineers or the American Indian Science and Engineering Society. For contact information for all of the above organizations, see Appendix III.

Tips for Entry

1. Many employers prefer to hire candidates who can use computer-aided design (CAD) systems.
2. A willingness to relocate may improve your chances of obtaining the job you want. Some companies pay for relocation costs for new employees.
3. Before you take a job offer, be sure it is from a company with whom you want to work. Do you agree with the company's mission? Do you think you will have the opportunity to grow professionally in the way that you want? Do you see yourself staying with the company for a while?
4. Use the Internet to learn more about the field of product development. You might start by visiting the Product Development and Management Association Web site, http://www.pdma.org. For more links, see Appendix IV.

DESIGN ENGINEER

CAREER PROFILE

Duties: Create designs for new or improved products, structures, processes, or systems; perform duties as required

Alternate Title(s): Product Design Engineer, Process Design Engineer; a title that reflects an engineering discipline such as Aerospace Engineer or Electronics Engineer

Salary Range: $33,000 to $99,000

Employment Prospects: Good

Advancement Prospects: Good

Prerequisites:

Education or Training—Bachelor's degree in engineering

Experience—Previous work experience generally required

Special Skills and Personality Traits—Analytical, problem-solving, decision-making, communication, writing, leadership, interpersonal, teamwork, and self-management skills; innovative, creative, detail-oriented, dedicated, self-motivated, reliable, diplomatic, and flexible

Special Requirements—Professional engineer (P.E.) licensure may be required

CAREER LADDER

```
+-------------------------------+
|        Senior Engineer        |
+-------------------------------+

+-------------------------------+
|           Engineer            |
+-------------------------------+

+-------------------------------+
|   Associate or Junior Engineer  |
+-------------------------------+
```

Position Description

Engineering design is an important function in the development of new or improved products—computer chips, appliances, medical equipment, farm machinery, aircraft, buildings, dams, roads, amusement park rides, water treatment facilities, heating systems, chemical processes for manufacturing plants, telecommunication systems, software applications, research tools, and so on. The engineers who are involved in this engineering specialty are known as Design Engineers. They are responsible for taking concepts and information for specific problems and creating design solutions, which may result in components, devices, machinery, structures, processes, or systems.

Design Engineers are assigned to work on one or more projects at a time. Design projects may be for products or systems that companies plan to sell or they may be for tools, components, or processes that are needed for other research and development projects. A design project may last several weeks, months, or years, depending on its complexity.

A design project team is usually composed of engineers, engineering technologists, engineering technicians, and others. Design Engineers apply the principles and techniques of their particular discipline (such as aerospace, chemical, geotechnical, marine, or petroleum engineering), as well as those of mathematics and science to solve design problems. Their design solutions may be in the form of drawings or mathematical equations.

Design Engineers generally begin a project by reviewing and understanding the requirements that customers need in a product or process. They next determine the design specifications that will satisfy those requirements. For example, engineers who are working on a product design must determine such things as the product's size, shape, and structure, along with the specific methods and materials that are needed to make it. Upon completing a list of specifications, Design Engineers then define the design problem that they need to solve.

Typically, Design Engineers come up with several design alternatives. They analyze and evaluate each design and select the one that best fits the customer's requirements. In determining the best design, they must take into consideration a number of factors besides function and performance. They think about the aesthetics, reliability, efficiency, safety, and cost of each design. Additionally, they consider the ethics and social impact a product may have on people's lives and the environment. Product designers also address how well a product can endure testing as well as look at issues that may come up in manufacturing it.

Design Engineers use computers to help them develop their designs. In addition to design software, these engineers work with computer-aided design (CAD) systems that allow them to create computer models and simulate various aspects of their design to see how different parts work together. These engineers also confer with various people, such as vendors, subject matter experts, and customers, to obtain information needed for their projects.

Most Design Engineers are engaged in the development process of a design until a prototype or final product has been fabricated. For example, they may be involved in obtaining materials for building a prototype, making it, and testing it to make sure it meets the exact specifications.

Design Engineers work in private companies, governmental agencies, and research institutes, as well as in architectural and engineering services firms that offer contractual or consulting services.

Engineering design is one of several engineering job functions in which many engineers are engaged. Not all Design Engineers stay in this specialty throughout their careers. Many gain experience working in one or more other specialties, such as testing, analysis, project management development, or sales; they may choose to later specialize in other functions or return to design work.

Design Engineers mostly work in office settings. On occasion they travel to plant facilities, laboratories, construction sites, or other job sites to perform their duties. They usually work a 40-hour week and put in additional hours as needed to complete tasks and meet deadlines.

Salaries

Design Engineers earn a salary according to their job level (such as entry-level or journey-level). Their salaries will vary, depending on various factors, such as their education, experience, engineering discipline, employer, industry, and geographical location. According to the November 2004 *Occupational Employment Statistics* survey by the Bureau of Labor Statistics, the estimated annual salary for most engineers ranged between $32,840 and $98,790.

The National Society of Professional Engineers reported in *The Engineering Income and Salary Survey 2005* that the average total annual income for professional engineers who worked in design was $62,204.

Employment Prospects

Opportunities for Design Engineers vary from employer to employer. As new projects are started, employers may choose to assign engineers from among their personnel or hire new staff or employ contractual workers.

Advancement Prospects

Many engineers begin their careers in design. Those choosing to stay in this engineering specialty can advance to supervisory and project management positions.

Engineers, in general, can advance according to their ambitions and interests. They can become technical specialists and consultants in their fields; they can pursue engineering management positions; or they can seek opportunities in such non-technical areas as sales, marketing, or human resources. Becoming researchers or college instructors are two other career advancement options for engineers. Furthermore, engineers can become independent consultants or owners of technical or consulting firms.

Education and Training

Minimally, Design Engineers possess a bachelor's degree in their engineering discipline or another related field. Many engineers hold an advanced degree. Those seeking to advance into management or move to other career paths such as consulting, research, or teaching generally need a master's or doctoral degree. Engineers must possess a doctorate to teach engineering in colleges and universities.

Entry-level engineers typically receive supervision and guidance from their supervisors and other experienced engineers.

Special Requirements

All engineers who perform work that affects the public safety and welfare, or who provide engineering services directly to the public must be licensed professional engineers (P.E.). Licensing requirements differ in each state and territory, as well as in Washington, D.C. For specific information, contact the board of engineering examiners for the area where you wish to practice. See Appendix II for a list of boards.

Some employers require entry-level engineers to be licensed engineers-in-training (E.I.T.), the first level of the P.E. licensure. They may hire strong candidates without licenses on the condition that they obtain the proper license within a certain time.

Experience, Special Skills, and Personality Traits

Although they prefer to hire candidates with relevant experience, many employers hire applicants without professional experience to entry-level design positions. Many recently-hired graduates have obtained experience through internships, work-study programs, student research projects, and summer employment.

Design Engineers need strong analytical, problem-solving, decision-making, communication, and writing skills for their work. They also need effective leadership, interpersonal, and teamwork skills, as they must be able to work well with various people from different backgrounds. In addition, they should have excellent self-management skills, such as being able to work independently, meet deadlines, follow and understand directions, prioritize multiple tasks, and handle stressful situations.

Some personality traits that successful Design Engineers share include being innovative, creative, detail-oriented, dedicated, self-motivated, reliable, diplomatic, and flexible.

Unions and Associations

Almost all engineering professions are served by one or more professional societies, at the local, state, or national level. For example, the American Institute of Chemical Engineers, the American Academy of Environmental Engineers, the Society of Manufacturing Engineers, the Structural Engineering Institute, and the Biomedical Engineering Society are just a few national societies that serve different engineering disciplines. In addition, engineers can join special-interest societies such as the National Society of Professional Engineers or the National Society of Black Engineers. By joining a professional association, engineers can take advantage of networking opportunities, continuing education programs, certification, and other professional services and resources. (For contact information for the above organizations, see Appendix III.)

Tips for Entry

1. While you are in high school and college, start exploring the industries in which you think you would like to work. For example, you can go on plant or company tours, or check out museums that have industrial exhibits. Also obtain internships or summer employment in different industries.
2. Take a basic drawing course.
3. Go over your résumé before submitting it to a prospective employer. Does it clearly show how you are qualified for the position for which you are applying? If not, then revise your résumé so that your experiences and skills relate to the job.
4. Check out newspaper want ads. Large bookstores often carry daily or Sunday editions of newspapers from major U.S. cities.
5. Use the Internet to learn about prospective employers. Many organizations have Web sites on which they post their job vacancies as well as instructions for applying for work.

ANALYTICAL ENGINEER

CAREER PROFILE

Duties: Perform engineering analysis of product designs while using mathematical models; perform duties as required

Alternate Title(s): A title that reflects an engineering discipline such as Electrical Engineer or Aerospace Engineer

Salary Range: $33,000 to $99,000

Employment Prospects: Good

Advancement Prospects: Good

Prerequisites:

Education or Training—Bachelor's degree in an engineering discipline

Experience—Previous work experience generally required

Special Skills and Personality Traits—Supervisory, interpersonal, teamwork, organizational, writing, communication, and self-management skills; flexible, self-motivated, cooperative, persistent, and creative

Special Requirements—Professional engineer (P.E.) licensure may be required for journey-level positions

CAREER LADDER

```
┌─────────────────────────────┐
│      Senior Engineer        │
└─────────────────────────────┘

┌─────────────────────────────┐
│         Engineer            │
└─────────────────────────────┘

┌─────────────────────────────┐
│      Junior Engineer        │
└─────────────────────────────┘
```

Position Description

When designs are created for new products, companies want to make sure they are safe, sound, and reliable before proceeding further in their development. Analytical Engineers perform these complex and sophisticated analyses and evaluations. These engineering analytical experts not only support design teams in creating quality designs but also help companies reduce the cost and time of developing new products.

Along with applying engineering and science principles and methods, Analytical Engineers use mathematical modeling to assess potential problems with designs. Their job is to construct mathematical equations that describe the components of a problem and their relationship to each other. They assign different values to the variables in those equations to get an idea of how various solutions will work. Through their mathematical models, these engineers can examine whether designs meet performance, reliability, durability, safety, and other requirements.

Analytical Engineers perform various types of analyses, such as structural or thermal analysis, depending on the needs of the design projects. They also use different analytical approaches appropriate to the type of designs that they examine. These engineers utilize hand calculations, common computer tools such as calculation software and spreadsheet programs, and computer modeling applications that allow them to simulate, validate, and optimize products.

Although every project varies, Analytical Engineers generally follow a similar analytical process with each assignment. They begin by creating a plan that involves defining the purpose and scope of the analysis, what approaches would best achieve their objectives, and what information is needed to perform the analysis. Next, they gather necessary data from design engineers, project managers, and others, which they use to develop their mathematical model. In most complex cases, Analytical Engineers create and run a computer model to perform the analysis.

Analytical Engineers then examine, interpret, and evaluate the results of the analysis to form conclusions and make recommendations to improve the performance of the design, to solve any reliability issues, and to add value to the design.

Finally, these engineers prepare technical reports that are concise, comprehensive, and easy to understand. Analytical Engineers are expected to complete their assignments within a certain budget and time frame.

In addition to analyzing designs for products, Analytical Engineers may be assigned to examine designs for new or modified manufacturing processes. They also provide analytical support to engineering teams who are concerned with failures or breakdowns in products or manufacturing processes. Furthermore, Analytical Engineers participate in or lead teams that are engaged in developing new analytical methods and techniques utilizing state-of-the art technology.

Their job involves frequent contact with a variety of people within their company. For example, Analytical Engineers interact with professionals, technicians, managers, and other personnel within any stage of the production development and manufacturing cycles.

Analytical Engineers work 40 hours a week but put in additional hours as required to meet deadlines. Engineers who work for consulting firms typically travel to client sites to meet with clients as well as to perform necessary tasks.

Salaries

Salaries for Analytical Engineers vary, depending on such factors as their education, experience, job level, employer, industry, and geographical location. Specific salary information for this occupation is unavailable. However, the estimated annual salary for most engineers overall ranged between $32,840 and $98,790, according to the November 2004 *Occupational Employment Statistics* survey by the Bureau of Labor Statistics (BLS).

Employment Prospects

Analytical Engineers are employed in many industries, including aerospace, automotive, electronics, medical, pharmaceutical, chemicals, telecommunications, and energy industries, among others. Some work for engineering consulting firms that offer engineering analysis services. Most job openings become available as engineers are promoted, transfer to other occupations, or retire. Employers will create additional positions to fill growing needs.

Overall, new job growth for engineers is generally expected to increase by 9 to 17 percent through 2014, according to the BLS. However, job opportunities should continue to be favorable because the number of engineering graduates is expected to be about the same as the number of job openings in the coming years. Some experts report that a large number of engineers will be eligible for retirement in the next several years.

Advancement Prospects

Analytical Engineers generally can advance according to their ambitions and interests. They can become technical specialists and consultants in their fields; they can pursue engineering management positions; or they can move into such non-technical areas as sales, marketing, or human resources. Becoming researchers or college instructors are two other career advancement options for engineers. Furthermore, they can become independent consultants or owners of technical or consulting firms.

Education and Training

Educational requirements vary for entry-level positions among employers. Minimally, applicants must possess a bachelor's degree in an engineering discipline, mathematics, physics, or another related field. Some employers prefer to hire applicants who possess a master's degree.

Entry-level engineers are usually given on-the-job training while working under the supervision and guidance of experienced engineers. Some companies also provide novice engineers with formal classroom instruction.

Those seeking to advance further in management or to careers in consulting and research usually need a master's or doctoral degree. Engineers must possess a doctorate to teach in colleges and universities.

Special Requirements

Employers may require that journey-level Analytical Engineers possess a professional engineer (P.E.) license.

In general, engineers must be licensed if they offer engineering services directly to the public or perform work that affects the life, health, or property of the public. Every U.S. state and territory, as well as Washington, D.C., has its own requirements for P.E. licensure. For specific information, contact the board of engineering examiners for the area where you wish to practice. See Appendix II for a list of boards.

Experience, Special Skills, and Personality Traits

Employers usually hire applicants who have one or more years of experience performing engineering analysis work and who can demonstrate the ability to use engineering analysis software and methods. Recent graduates may have gained their experience through internships, work-study programs, student research projects, postdoctoral training, or part-time employment.

Analytical Engineers need excellent supervisory, interpersonal, and teamwork skills, as they must be able to work well with various engineers, managers, and others from diverse backgrounds. Analytical Engineers also need effective organizational, writing, and communication skills. Other essential skills are self-management skills, which include the abilities to work independently, handle stressful situations, meet deadlines, prioritize multiple tasks, and follow and understand instructions. Being flexible, self-motivated, cooperative, persistent, and creative are some personality traits that successful Analytical Engineers have in common.

Unions and Associations

Many engineers are members of professional associations to take advantage of various professional services and resources such as networking opportunities, continuing education programs, certification, and publications. Analytical Engineers may join engineering societies that serve their particular disciplines such as the ASME International (formerly the American Society of Mechanical Engineers), the Biomedical Engineering Society, the SAE International (formerly the Society of Automotive Engineers), or the American Institute of Aeronautics and Astronautics. For contact information, see Appendix III.

Tips for Entry

1. Many employers prefer to hire candidates with strong academic records.
2. Before going to a job interview, become familiar with the types of products or services that a prospective employer offers. Also learn as much as you can about the company's operations.
3. Keep up with new technologies for performing engineering analysis.
4. Use the Internet to learn more about potential employers. To find a company Web site, as well as articles and other pertinent information about the company, enter its name into a search engine.

REGULATORY AFFAIRS (RA) ENGINEER

CAREER PROFILE

Duties: Ensure that companies are in compliance with all applicable laws and regulations as well as with regulatory guidelines relating to development, testing, manufacturing, and marketing practices; perform duties as required

Alternate Title(s): Regulatory Engineer, Licensing Engineer, Compliance Engineer

Salary Range: $33,000 to $99,000

Employment Prospects: Good

Advancement Prospects: Good

Prerequisites:

    Education or Training—Bachelor's degree in an engineering or science discipline

    Experience—Previous work experience generally required

    Special Skills and Personality Traits—Organizational, planning, time management, writing, computer, communication, presentation, negotiating, and interpersonal skills; analytical, detail-oriented, cooperative, diplomatic, diligent, and flexible

    Special Requirements—Professional engineer (P.E.) licensure may be required

CAREER LADDER

```
┌─────────────────────────┐
│     Senior Engineer     │
└─────────────────────────┘

┌─────────────────────────┐
│        Engineer         │
└─────────────────────────┘

┌─────────────────────────┐
│     Junior Engineer     │
└─────────────────────────┘
```

Position Description

Many industries, including the food, cosmetics, pharmaceutical, biotechnology, medical device, medical diagnostic, chemicals, telecommunications, transportation, energy, utilities, and environmental industries, among others, are regulated to ensure that companies produce safe and effective consumer goods and services. Hence, most, if not all, companies hire Regulatory Affairs (RA) Engineers or other RA professionals to make sure that the companies are in compliance with the required laws and regulations.

RA Engineers have backgrounds in chemical engineering, biomedical engineering, electrical engineering, and other disciplines that are related to the industries in which they work. They apply engineering principles and methods to solving problems to ensure that development, testing, manufacturing, and marketing practices meet all applicable laws and regulations as well as regulatory guidelines. These engineers are concerned with different regulatory agencies at the local,

state, and federal levels. Many of them also review, understand, and interpret the regulatory processes of foreign countries where their companies market products or services.

These engineers are involved in product development projects from the conception of a product or service to its launch as a commercial venture. Their job is to review, understand, interpret, and apply all applicable laws, regulations, and regulatory guidelines from various regulatory agencies. For example, at the federal level, RA Engineers might deal with such regulatory agencies as the U.S. Food and Drug Administration, the Nuclear Regulatory Commission, the Environmental Protection Agency, the U.S. Department of Transportation, or the Occupational Safety and Health Administration.

RA Engineers are assigned to provide support and guidance to several projects at a time. They advise project managers and team members about pertinent governmental requirements that would affect the development or manufacture of proposed products. RA Engineers also assist in developing strategies and participating in activities to ensure that processes and practices comply with regulatory requirements.

RA Engineers are also responsible for the submission of formal documents to regulatory agencies. They coordinate the compilation of all information and materials that are required for licensing, registrations, applications, and compliance reports, as well as produce the submission packages. For example, an RA Engineer at a medical device company might prepare an application package for new product approval to the U.S. Food and Drug Administration. (This agency must approve all new medicines, treatments, medical devices, and other products before they can be sold to consumers.) These engineers also act as their company's representatives and meet with officers from regulatory agencies as needed to answer questions regarding their company's products, processes, and practices.

In addition, RA Engineers are responsible for keeping up-to-date with new or proposed changes in laws and regulations as well as regulatory procedures that apply to their industry domestically and internationally. They also evaluate new regulatory guidelines and determine how they apply to their company's processes and products. These engineers inform RA Managers or other appropriate personnel about any necessary changes that the company needs to make.

RA Engineers perform a wide range of tasks that vary each day, such as:

- research regulatory questions for project members
- review technical documents for regulatory submissions
- evaluate and prepare comments on proposed legislation, regulations, or guidelines
- respond to questions from regulatory agencies
- negotiate submission issues with regulatory reviewers for product approvals
- train company personnel about regulatory requirements, industrial standards, or protocols
- attend meetings with project teams
- complete required forms and paperwork
- prepare correspondence or reports
- maintain records
- stay familiar with the technical and scientific background of their company's products

Their job involves constant contact with a variety of people within their company. For example, RA Engineers interact with professionals, technicians, and managers in research, development, production, and packaging groups to obtain necessary information to complete regulatory forms.

RA Engineers work 40 hours a week but put in additional hours as needed to complete tasks and meet deadlines.

Salaries

Salaries for Regulatory Affairs Engineers vary, depending on various factors, such as their education, experience, job level, employer, industry, and geographical location. According to the November 2004 *Occupational Employment Statistics* survey by the Bureau of Labor Statistics, the estimated annual salary for most engineers ranged between $32,840 and $98,790.

Employment Prospects

In addition to being employed by private companies, RA Engineers are hired by government agencies, academic institutions, and consulting firms that offer regulatory affairs services.

Opportunities for RA Engineers should continually be favorable, as companies need skilled professionals to help them stay abreast with and in compliance with laws and regulations which are constantly changing and becoming more complex. Most job openings become available as engineers are promoted, transfer to other occupations, or retire. Employers will create additional positions as their companies grow and expand.

Advancement Prospects

As RA Engineers gain experience, they are assigned to more complex projects as well as receive increasingly greater responsibilities. Depending on their ambitions and interests, they can advance in any number of ways. They can become technical specialists. They can rise through the ranks as supervisors, managers, or executives. Another option for them is to move into marketing, technical sales, finance, or another business area. In addition, they can become researchers or teachers. Engineers with entrepreneurial ambitions can become independent consultants or owners of firms that offer consulting services in regulatory affairs.

Engineers usually need a master's or doctorate degree to advance to careers in management, consulting, research, or teaching.

Education and Training

Applicants for entry-level RA Engineer positions need at least a bachelor's degree in an engineering or science discipline. Some employers in such industries as medical device and electronic industries usually prefer to hire applicants with appropriate engineering degrees.

Entry-level engineers typically receive on-the-job training while working under the supervision and guidance of experienced engineers. Novice engineers may also be given formal classroom instruction.

Throughout their careers, RA Engineers enroll in continuing education programs and training programs to update their skills and keep up with advancements in their fields.

Special Requirements

Some employers require that journey-level RA Engineers possess professional engineer (P.E.) licensure.

In general, engineers who provide engineering services directly to the public or who perform work that affects the public safety and welfare must be licensed engineers. Licensing requirements differ in each state and territory, as well as in Washington, D.C. For specific information, contact the board of engineering examiners for the area where you wish to practice. See Appendix II for a list of boards.

Experience, Special Skills, and Personality Traits

Entry-level candidates should have work experience related to the positions for which they apply. They may have gained their experience through internships, work-study programs, student research projects, or part-time employment. Many employers prefer to hire candidates who have prior experience in their industry.

RA Engineers need strong organizational, planning, time management, and writing skills for their job. Having strong computer skills, which include word processing, spreadsheet, and database development skills, is also essential. In addition, these engineers must have excellent communication, presentation, negotiating, and interpersonal skills in order to work well with many people from diverse backgrounds.

Some personality traits that successful RA Engineers share include being analytical, detail-oriented, cooperative, diplomatic, diligent, and flexible.

Unions and Associations

Many RA Engineers join professional associations to take advantage of networking opportunities, continuing educa- tion programs, certification, and various other professional services and resources. The Regulatory Affairs Professionals Society serves the interests of those engineers who work within the health-care sector.

These engineers can also join societies that serve specific engineering disciplines, such as the Institute of Electrical and Electronics Engineers, the Biomedical Engineering Society, the American Nuclear Society, the American Academy of Environmental Engineers, or the American Society of Agricultural and Biological Engineers. For contact information for all of the above organizations, see Appendix III.

Tips for Entry

1. Take courses to develop your communication, project management, and financial management skills.
2. At some companies, the job application process involves passing a thorough background check as well as a medical exam and drug screening.
3. Many engineers enter the regulatory affairs field after working several years in other engineering specialties.
4. Network with regulatory affairs professionals to find out about available job opportunities.
5. Use the Internet to learn more about regulatory affairs engineering. To get a list of Web sites, enter the keywords *regulatory engineering or regulatory affairs engineering* in a search engine. To learn about some links, see Appendix IV.

TEST ENGINEER

CAREER PROFILE

Duties: Carry out tests and evaluations on devices, products, processes, or systems; perform duties as required

Alternate Title(s): A title that reflects a specialty such as Systems Test Engineer, Quality Assurance Test Engineer, Software Test Engineer, or Flight Test Engineer

Salary Range: $33,000 to $99,000

Employment Prospects: Fair

Advancement Prospects: Good

Prerequisites:

Education or Training—Bachelor's degree in engineering

Experience—Previous work experience generally required

Special Skills and Personality Traits—Teamwork, interpersonal, communication, analytical, problem-solving, and writing skills; creative, self-motivated, detail-oriented, inquisitive, reliable, confident, and flexible

Special Requirements—Professional engineer (P.E.) licensure may be required

CAREER LADDER

```
┌─────────────────────────────┐
│      Senior Engineer        │
└─────────────────────────────┘

┌─────────────────────────────┐
│         Engineer            │
└─────────────────────────────┘

┌─────────────────────────────┐
│ Associate or Junior Engineer│
└─────────────────────────────┘
```

Position Description

All products—airplanes, ships, cars, appliances, electronics, computers, software, computer games, Web sites, medicines, food products, cosmetics, and so on—need to be tested before they are placed on the market. Businesses and manufacturers want to make sure that their products are free of defects and that they satisfy the requirements of their customers. Hence, they employ Test Engineers to perform this engineering function. These engineers test new products as well as existing products. They also are involved in testing prototypes.

Test Engineers are experts in developing and conducting tests to verify that products meet all design specifications. They make sure that products (or prototypes) work as they are designed. In addition, they test products for their performance, reliability, safety, and other factors. They perform their tests in the types of settings in which the products would be used, and they operate or use the products in the manner that customers would use them.

These engineers are trained in specific disciplines, such as biomedical engineering, aerospace engineering, electronics engineering, mechanical engineering, structural engineering, or environmental engineering. They are knowledgeable about the products that they evaluate. They understand how a product or system, such as a blood pressure machine, stereo system, automobile, or roller coaster are built and should function, and they understand the problems that can cause products or systems to fail in their performance.

Test Engineers are responsible for planning each test, according to standard formats. They gather necessary information from design and production groups to develop appropriate tests. They may work with automated test equipment, or computerized machines, to conduct many of their tests. When they have completed their tests, these engineers write comprehensive reports that describe the test procedures and results.

They perform a variety of tasks, which vary each day. For example, some of their tasks include:

- writing test procedures, methods, or protocols
- developing models for testing for safety and efficacy
- implementing automated test strategies
- developing automated test scripts and architectures
- evaluating test tools

- analyzing test cases
- preparing progress reports
- completing required paperwork for quality standards
- gathering information
- developing software to use for testing
- reviewing design documents
- making recommendations for new test equipment
- creating schedules for testing
- reading literature to remain current with technological developments and testing issues

Senior engineers may be assigned to lead and supervise less experienced Test Engineers.

Test Engineers often work on two or more projects at a time. They may deal with projects at different stages. They are expected to complete their projects in a timely manner, and sometimes are required to turn projects around quickly. Their job requires them to work closely with other Test Engineers as well as engineers from product design engineering groups, manufacturing departments, and other groups.

Test Engineers normally work a 40-hour week. They put in additional hours as needed to complete their various tasks or to meet deadlines.

Salaries

Test Engineers earn a salary according to their job level (such as entry-level or journey-level). Their salaries vary depending on such factors as their education, experience, engineering discipline, employer, industry, and geographical location. According to the November 2004 *Occupational Employment Statistics* survey by the Bureau of Labor Statistics (BLS), the estimated annual salary for most engineers ranged between $32,840 and $98,790.

According to *The Engineering Income and Salary Survey 2005* by the National Society of Professional Engineers, the average total annual income for professional engineers who worked in testing was $68,769.

Employment Prospects

Job opportunities are available to fill both permanent and contractual positions. Most openings will become available as engineers are promoted, transfer to other occupations, or retire. Employers will create additional positions as their needs grow and expand.

The employment rate for engineers overall is expected to increase by 9 to 17 percent through 2014, according to the BLS. However, job opportunities in general should be favorable because the number of engineering graduates is expected to be about the same as the number of job openings.

Advancement Prospects

Test Engineers may advance in any number of ways, depending on their ambitions and interests. They can become tech-

nical specialists and consultants as well as pursue supervisory and management positions. Entrepreneurial engineers can become independent consultants or owners of technical or consulting firms.

Some Test Engineers seek opportunities in other engineering specialties, such as design, research, teaching, or project management.

Education and Training

Minimally, Test Engineers possess a bachelor's degree in their engineering discipline or another related field. Many engineers hold an advanced degree. Those seeking to advance further in management or to follow other career paths in such areas as consulting, research, or teaching generally need a master's or doctoral degree.

Entry-level engineers typically receive supervision and guidance from their supervisors and other experienced engineers.

Special Requirements

Employers may require professional engineer (P.E.) licensure for some positions. They may hire strong candidates without a license on the condition that they obtain it within a certain time period.

In general, engineers who perform work that affects the public safety and welfare or who provide engineering services directly to the public must be licensed professional engineers. Licensing requirements differ in each state and territory, as well as in Washington, D.C. For specific information, contact the board of engineering examiners for the area where you wish to practice. See Appendix II for a list of boards.

Experience, Special Skills, and Personality Traits

Many employers hire applicants who have no professional experience for entry-level design positions. They prefer to hire candidates with relevant experience. Many recently hired graduates have obtained experience through internships, work-study programs, student research projects, and summer employment.

Test Engineers need effective teamwork, interpersonal, and communication skills, as they must be able to work well with colleagues, managers, and others from diverse backgrounds. In addition, they should have strong analytical, problem-solving, and writing skills. Being creative, self-motivated, detail-oriented, inquisitive, reliable, confident, and flexible are some personality traits that successful Test Engineers share.

Unions and Associations

Many Test Engineers belong to local, state, or national professional associations to take advantage of networking opportunities, continuing education programs, and other professional services and resources. Some national societies include the American Society of Test Engineers, the International Test and Evaluation Association, and the ASTM International. For contact information, see Appendix III.

Tips for Entry

1. Some companies hire entry-level Test Engineers for temporary or contractual positions. Sometimes temporary positions can lead to permanent positions.
2. Keep up with technologies to maintain your competitive edge.
3. Contact the human resources department of companies or agencies that interest you to learn about current job vacancies and their selection process. If no position is available, ask to whom you can send your résumé for future job openings.
4. Use the Internet to find out more about Test Engineers. You might start by visiting the American Society of Test Engineers Web site, http://www.astetest.org. For more links, see Appendix IV.

PRODUCTION ENGINEER

CAREER PROFILE

Duties: Coordinate the activities and resources that are involved in manufacturing products; perform duties as required

Alternate Title(s): A title that reflects a particular engineering discipline such as Biomedical Engineer

Salary Range: $33,000 to $99,000

Employment Prospects: Good

Advancement Prospects: Good

Prerequisites:

Education or Training—Bachelor's degree in an engineering discipline

Experience—Previous work experience generally required

Special Skills and Personality Traits—Administrative, time management, customer service, writing, communication, leadership, interpersonal, and teamwork skills; tactful, self-motivated, energetic, ethical, organized, versatile, flexible, and creative

CAREER LADDER

```
┌─────────────────────────────┐
│       Senior Engineer       │
└─────────────────────────────┘

┌─────────────────────────────┐
│        Civil Engineer       │
└─────────────────────────────┘

┌─────────────────────────────┐
│       Junior Engineer       │
└─────────────────────────────┘
```

Position Description

Manufacturers strive to fill customers' orders for their products—which may be packaged food, appliances, computers, avionics components, chemicals, vehicles, or other goods—in a timely manner while keeping costs down. These companies hire Production Engineers to coordinate the activities and resources that are involved in manufacturing their products, and to ensure that the overall production process flows smoothly and efficiently from start to finish.

Production Engineers are sometimes confused with manufacturing engineers. Although both of these types of engineers are involved in the manufacturing process, they each play different roles. While Production Engineers are concerned with manufacturing processes and flows, manufacturing engineers are involved with the tools and techniques that are needed to fabricate the products.

Production Engineers are usually assigned to oversee the day-to-day operation of a specific manufacturing process. They are responsible for organizing the human, material, and monetary resources for their workstations, departments, or divisions in a manner that is most cost-effective for their companies. These engineers apply engineering, scientific, and mathematical principles and methods to solve technical problems regarding products, processes, and plant layouts.

Production Engineers are responsible for staying on schedule with customer orders. It is also their job to make sure that products are made according to specifications. Sometimes customers require a modification in a product's design. Production Engineers must then determine what changes must be made to the manufacturing processes and equipment, and implement the necessary adaptations.

They continually assess the manufacturing processes to find solutions that can increase productivity and efficiency, as well as improve quality and reduce costs. They are concerned with a variety of factors such as labor, raw materials, facility layout, production rates, safety, quality control, and operating efficiency. In addition, they are involved in the selection and installation of new equipment, machinery, and systems as well as the development of new or improved manufacturing processes.

Production Engineers are also responsible for troubleshooting problems and issues as they arise during manufacturing. For example, Production Engineers might investigate and resolve what caused the production of low quality products.

These engineers typically manage several projects and activities at a time, which are all geared toward improving the quality and cost of products and manufacturing processes. Their days are varied because they perform a wide range of tasks. For example, they might:

- plan a new project, which includes identifying technical requirements, staffing, equipment, and facility needs, and establishing a schedule and budget
- prepare or direct the preparation of system layouts, drawings, and schematics
- participate in the development of long-range plans for manufacturing facilities
- research, evaluate, and recommend improvements for safety, worker efficiency, waste reduction, use of equipment, or other matters
- monitor their assigned unit for compliance with company policies and procedures as well as with appropriate laws and regulations
- oversee the installation of new equipment and check the quality of its performance before using it for large-scale production
- write standard operating procedures for new equipment or manufacturing processes
- review bid proposals from vendors for the purchase of new processing equipment
- prepare reports, correspondence, or required paperwork
- coordinate safety activities for employees
- stay up-to-date with developments in manufacturing processes and technology by reading literature, by attending professional and trade conferences, or through other means

Production Engineers work closely with other engineers, as well as with managers, technicians, craftspeople, assemblers, and others. They also interact frequently with engineering teams and others from various departments.

Production Engineers divide their time between their offices and production areas. While working on the production floor, these engineers may be exposed to loud noise, moving parts, fumes, and toxic chemicals. Hence, they are required to wear appropriate protective clothing and equipment.

They work a 40-hour week and put in additional hours as necessary to complete their tasks or to meet production deadlines. Those engineers who work in plants that operate around the clock may be assigned to rotating shifts.

Salaries

Production Engineers earn a salary according to their job level (such as entry-level or journey-level). Their earnings vary, depending on various factors, such as their education, experience, engineering discipline, employer, industry, and geographical location. According to the November 2004 *Occupational Employment Statistics* survey by the Bureau of Labor Statistics (BLS), the estimated annual salary for most engineers ranged between $32,840 and $98,790.

The National Society of Professional Engineers reported in *The Engineering Income and Salary Survey 2005* that the average total annual income for professional engineers who worked in production was $70,999.

Employment Prospects

Most job openings will become available as engineers are promoted, transfer to other occupations, or retire. Employers will create additional positions to fill growing needs.

In general, the job growth for engineers overall is expected to increase by 9 to 17 percent through 2014, according to the BLS. Job opportunities should continue to be favorable because the number of engineering graduates is expected to be about the same as the number of job openings in these coming years. Some experts report that a large number of engineers will become eligible for retirement in the next several years.

Advancement Prospects

Engineers can advance according to their ambitions and interests. They can become technical specialists and consultants in their fields; they can pursue engineering management positions; or they can seek opportunities in such non-technical areas as sales, marketing, or human resources. Other career advancement options include becoming researchers or college instructors. Furthermore, engineers can become independent consultants or owners of technical or consulting firms.

Education and Training

Minimally, Production Engineers must possess a bachelor's degree in production, manufacturing, industrial, or another related engineering field. Many engineers hold an advanced degree. Those seeking to advance further in management or to follow other career paths such as consulting, research, or teaching need a master's or doctoral degree.

Entry-level Engineers typically receive supervision and guidance from their supervisors and other experienced engineers.

Throughout their careers, engineers enroll in continuing education and training programs to update their skills and keep up with technological advancements.

Experience, Special Skills, and Personality Traits

Entry-level candidates should have work experience related to the positions for which they apply. They may have gained their experience through internships, work-study programs, student research projects, or part-time employment.

To perform well at their job, Production Engineers need excellent administrative, time management, customer service, writing, and communication skills. They must also have effective leadership, interpersonal, and teamwork skills in order to deal with various people—managers, professionals, technicians, and others—from diverse backgrounds. Being tactful, self-motivated, energetic, ethical, organized, versatile, flexible, and creative are some personality traits that successful Production Engineers share.

Unions and Associations

Production Engineers can join professional associations to take advantage of networking opportunities, continuing education programs, and other professional services and resources. Various engineering societies are available. They can join special-interest societies such as the Society of Manufacturing Engineers, the SAE International (formerly the Society of Automotive Engineers), the Society of Women Engineers, or the Society of Hispanic Professional Engineers. They can also join societies that serve their particular engineering discipline, such as the Institute of Electrical and Electronics Engineers, the American Academy of Environmental Engineers, or the International Society of Food Engineering. For contact information for these organizations, see Appendix III.

Tips for Entry

1. Develop strong communication and writing skills by taking such courses as English, speech, and journalism.
2. Join a student chapter of a professional association. Participate in activities and meetings to start building a network of contacts.
3. Contact a company's human resource department to find out to whom you can send a résumé. Be sure you get the person's complete name and job title. Also make sure you have the correct spelling of his or her name.
4. Use the Internet to learn more about becoming an engineer. You might start by visiting these Web sites: Junior Engineering Technical Society, http://www.jets.org; and Engineering Education Service Center, http://www.engineeringedu.com. For more links, see Appendix IV.

SALES ENGINEER

CAREER PROFILE

Duties: Provide technical assistance to customers about products or services; develop and maintain a customer base; perform duties as required

Alternate Title(s): Field Consultant, Sales Representative

Salary Range: $42,000 to $119,000

Employment Prospects: Good

Advancement Prospects: Good

Prerequisites:

Education or Training—Bachelor's degree in an engineering or science discipline

Experience—Previous work experience generally required

Special Skills and Personality Traits—Analytical, problem-solving, writing, communication, customer service, interpersonal, teamwork, and self-management skills; friendly, enthusiastic, persuasive, enterprising, resourceful, and detail-oriented

CAREER LADDER

```
┌─────────────────────────────────┐
│      Senior Sales Engineer      │
└─────────────────────────────────┘

┌─────────────────────────────────┐
│          Sales Engineer         │
└─────────────────────────────────┘

┌─────────────────────────────────┐
│ Junior or Associate Sales Engineer │
└─────────────────────────────────┘
```

Position Description

Sales is an essential business activity for all manufacturers, and for most, if not all of them, it is also an important engineering function. Many components, devices, equipment, machinery, and systems are so highly complex that customers often need help deciding what to buy. Customers may be businesses, government agencies, the military, universities, research institutes, or the general public. Professionals called Sales Engineers are responsible for helping their customers to determine which products and services would provide the best solutions to their problems.

Sales Engineers are not salespeople, but they do work closely with salespeople. Their role is to provide technical assistance to salespeople to help make sales. Most Sales Engineers have engineering or science backgrounds. They may be recent engineering graduates as well as professional engineers who have chosen to work in this engineering specialty. Sales Engineers apply the theories and principles of engineering to the technical problems faced by customers. Although Sales Engineers do not sell, it is their job to persuade customers that their company's products and services fit the customers' specific needs.

Sales Engineers usually deal with customers face-to-face. They describe products and services that meet their customers' requirements. They explain how the products or services work, what they can do, and why they can solve their customers' problems. Sales Engineers answer questions as well as give demonstrations to show the usefulness of products or services.

When customers make their purchases, Sales Engineers train them on how to use the products or services. Sales Engineers also make follow-up calls and visits with their customers to see how they are doing with the products or services they have purchased. Furthermore, they handle any technical problems or issues that their customers may have as products are installed or as services are provided.

Sales Engineers are assigned to cover territories, or geographical regions. Their territories may consist of several cities, states, or countries. Sales Engineers are also responsible for developing and maintaining their customer base by establishing trusting relationships, which involves understanding their customers' business requirements, issues, and other needs. In addition, Sales Engineers help the research and development, production, or other teams at their company develop new or improved products by providing them with pertinent information about their customers.

Sales Engineers perform a variety of tasks, which vary each day. For example, they might:

- prepare product demonstrations
- read literature or attend workshops to learn about new products
- assist in the development of engineering specifications for current and future products
- develop sales plans and strategies
- identify potential customers within their territory
- make appointments to meet with customers
- arrange for technical service or field service engineers to handle specific problems that customers are having with products
- prepare expense account forms or other required paperwork
- keep up-to-date with emerging technologies, industry news and trends, and the latest developments in competing products and services
- promote products while working in company booths at trade shows, conferences, and marketing events

Sales Engineers generally work a 40-hour week but put in additional hours as needed to meet with customers. Many Sales Engineers have flexible work schedules to allow for arranging appointments that are more convenient for customers. They often travel by vehicle or airplane to meet with customers and sometimes must be away from their home office for several days or weeks at a time.

Salaries

Salaries for Sales Engineers vary, depending on such factors as their education, experience, employer, industry, and geographical location. They may earn salaries as well as receive a commission or bonus. (Commissions are based on a percentage of the amount of sales an individual makes.) According to the November 2004 *Occupational Employment Statistics* survey by the U.S. Bureau of Labor Statistics (BLS), the estimated annual salary for most Sales Engineers overall ranged between $42,420 and $118,830.

The National Society of Professional Engineers reports in *The Engineering Income and Salary Survey 2005* that the average total annual income for professional engineers who worked in sales was $86,163.

Sales Engineers who work for manufacturers are usually reimbursed for their expenses for transportation, lodging, meals, and entertaining customers.

Employment Prospects

In addition to working for manufacturers, Sales Engineers are employed by wholesale distributors and manufacturer's agent firms—independent companies that sell products from different suppliers.

Job openings generally become available as Sales Engineers transfer to other occupations, advance to higher positions, or retire. Employers will create additional positions as their needs expand. The employment growth for Sales Engineers is predicted to increase by 9 to 17 percent through 2014, according to the BLS. Because sales are dependent on such factors as the health of the economy and consumers' preferences, the number of available job opportunities fluctuates each year.

Advancement Prospects

Sales Engineers can be promoted to supervisory and managerial positions. They can also move into marketing and rise through the ranks in that field. Many Sales Engineers measure their success by earning higher incomes and receiving sales accounts or territories.

Sales engineers with technical backgrounds may pursue other engineering specialties, such as development, design, production, quality, or research.

Education and Training

In general, entry-level applicants must possess at least a bachelor's degree, preferably in an engineering or science discipline.

Entry-level Sales Engineers typically receive on-the-job training while working under the supervision and guidance of experienced engineers. Some companies also provide formal classroom training programs.

Throughout their careers, Sales Engineers enroll in continuing education programs and training programs to keep up with technical advancements in their fields, as well as to update their technical and sales skills.

Experience, Special Skills, and Personality Traits

Many employers hire recent engineering graduates without any sales experience as entry-level Sales Engineers because they have the required technical background. They generally look for candidates who are quick learners and have a positive personality. Candidates who have previous sales experience are more desirable to employers.

To perform well at their job, Sales Engineers must have effective analytical, problem-solving, writing, communication, customer service, interpersonal, and teamwork skills. In addition, they need strong self-management skills, including the ability to work independently, handle stressful situations, and prioritize multiple tasks. Being friendly, enthusiastic, persuasive, enterprising, resourceful, and detail-oriented are some personality traits that successful Sales Engineers have in common.

Unions and Associations

Many Sales Engineers join professional associations that serve their particular engineering disciplines to take advantage of professional services and resources, such as networking opportunities, continuing education programs, and publications. Some also join engineering societies that have special foci, such as the Society of Women Engineers, the National Society of Black Engineers, the Society of Hispanic Professional Engineers, or the National Society of Professional Engineers. For contact information for these organizations, see Appendix III.

Tips for Entry

1. While in high school or college, obtain a part-time or summer job in sales to see if it is a field that might interest you.
2. Read a job announcement carefully. Do you have any of the requirements that an employer desires in a candidate? Be sure you mention them on your résumé, as well as on your job application.
3. Many companies visit college campuses to recruit for entry-level positions. Check with your campus career center or engineering department for announcements. If you are interested in certain companies, contact their human resources department to see if, and when, they plan to visit your campus.
4. Use the Internet to learn more about prospective employers, as well as positions that are currently available. To find a Web site for an organization, enter the organization's name in a search engine.

FIELD SERVICE ENGINEER

CAREER PROFILE

Duties: Install, maintain, and repair products and systems at customer sites; perform other duties as required

Alternate Title(s): Field Engineer, Technical Services Engineer, Field Service Representative

Salary Range: $33,000 to $99,000

Employment Prospects: Good

Advancement Prospects: Good

Prerequisites:

Education or Training—Bachelor's degree in an engineering discipline or another related field; on-the-job training

Experience—Previous work experience preferred

Special Skills and Personality Traits—Customer relations, interpersonal, communication, problem-solving, trouble-shooting, teamwork, writing, and self-management skills; self-motivated, creative, dedicated, organized, cooperative, detail-oriented, and friendly

CAREER LADDER

```
┌─────────────────────────────┐
│      Senior Engineer        │
└─────────────────────────────┘

┌─────────────────────────────┐
│         Engineer            │
└─────────────────────────────┘

┌─────────────────────────────┐
│  Associate or Junior Engineer │
└─────────────────────────────┘
```

Position Description

Computers, information technology systems, medical devices, laboratory equipment, avionics components, boilers, pumps, construction equipment, farm machinery, automated systems, control systems, communication systems, and security systems are only a few examples of products and systems with which customers may need technical assistance at their workplaces or homes. At many companies, this engineering role is performed by Field Service Engineers who provide various preventative and repair services.

Field Service Engineers come from different engineering backgrounds, such as electronics engineering, mechanical engineering, environmental engineering, biomedical engineering, aerospace engineering, acoustical engineering, or petroleum engineering. Along with their backgrounds and extensive company training, they are knowledgeable about customers' products or systems. They understand how a product or system is built, how it works, and what it is capable of doing. They also have a firm grasp on why a product or system may not perform properly.

Field Service Engineers provide different types of technical services, which they are expected to deliver efficiently and in a timely manner. They install products or systems, or oversee their installation, at customer sites. These engineers test the products or systems to ensure their quality and that they are working properly. Field Service Engineers also demonstrate to customers how to operate the products or systems for their particular uses. Customers might also request these engineers to train specific employees.

Field Service Engineers are also assigned to perform maintenance service on customers' products or systems to ensure their continued effective performance. These are regularly scheduled inspections done at customer sites. Field Service Engineers evaluate the current conditions of devices, equipment, machinery, or systems and service them accordingly. The engineers also identify problems or potential problems, which they describe to customers along with offering their suggestions for fixing the problems.

Additionally, Field Service Engineers are called out to customer sites to resolve technical problems that customers are having with their products or systems. These engineers review performance reports and documentation from customers, as well as inspect the products or systems to determine the nature, size, and source of the problem. The engineers then recommend to customers what repairs, replacements, or other corrective actions should be made. Engineers make all necessary repairs, and if repairs cannot be made on location, they make the necessary arrangements for products, systems, or parts to be returned to the factory. When Field Service Engineers cannot resolve any technical problems, they consult with engineering personnel at the home office.

As representatives of their companies, Field Service Engineers are responsible for providing a high level of customer satisfaction and for building strong customer relationships. These engineers work closely with customers to determine the best technical solutions for their customers' problems. For example, they advise customers on ways to improve the performance of their products or systems.

Field Service Engineers perform a variety of tasks in the course of their work. They study and interpret operations or maintenance manuals, specifications, blueprints, schematics, and other documentation. They prepare work schedules, maintain daily work logs, write reports, and complete expense account forms. They respond to customers' technical queries by phone or fax, as well as through e-mail or correspondence. These engineers also provide input into the development of new or improved products or systems. In addition, they are expected to stay abreast of emerging technologies as well as with industry news and trends. Many senior engineers are assigned to supervise technicians or junior engineers with installing, testing, repairing, and servicing equipment and systems.

Field Service Engineers are usually part of a company's technical services department. They travel to customer sites, which may be offices, laboratories, physical plants, factories, refineries, construction sites, greenhouses, or shipyards. They usually travel by car or plane, sometimes visiting other cities, states, and even countries. Their assignments may require that they stay in hotel rooms overnight or for several nights a week.

Field Service Engineers usually work a 40-hour schedule. They put in additional hours as needed to complete their duties. Some field engineers are on call 24 hours a day to offer customer support.

Salaries

Salaries for Field Service Engineers vary, depending on such factors as their education, experience, employer, industry, and geographical location. According to the November 2004 *Occupational Employment Statistics* survey by the U.S. Bureau of Labor Statistics (BLS), the estimated annual salary for most engineers ranged between $32,840 and $98,790.

Employment Prospects

Job growth for engineers overall is expected to increase by about 9 to 17 percent through 2014, according to the BLS.

However, job opportunities should continue to be favorable, because the number of engineering graduates is expected to be about the same as the number of job openings.

Most job openings become available as Field Service Engineers transfer to other occupations, advance to higher positions, or retire. Employers will create additional positions as their needs expand.

Advancement Prospects

Field Service Engineers may advance in any number of ways, depending on their ambitions and interests. They can become technical specialists and consultants as well as pursue supervisory and management positions. Entrepreneurial engineers can become independent consultants or owners of technical or consulting firms.

Field Service Engineers can also seek opportunities in other engineering specialties, such as design, testing, research, or production.

Education and Training

Most employers prefer to hire candidates for entry-level positions who have a bachelor's degree in an engineering discipline or another related field. Some employers may hire applicants with an associate degree if they have qualifying work experience.

Employers typically provide entry-level engineers with training programs, which may include both on-the-job training and formal classroom training. New engineers work under the supervision and direction of experienced engineers.

Experience, Special Skills, and Personality Traits

Applicants do not need prior work experience for entry-level positions, but it is usually preferred by employers. Entry-level candidates may have gained relevant experience through internships, work-study programs, student research projects, or employment.

Because they must work well with colleagues, managers, customers, and others from diverse backgrounds, Field Service Engineers need excellent customer relations, interpersonal, and communication skills. In addition, these engineers need strong problem-solving, trouble-shooting, teamwork, and writing skills. They also need effective self-management skills, including the ability to work independently, meet deadlines, handle stressful situations, and prioritize multiple tasks.

Some personality traits that successful Field Service Engineers share include being self-motivated, creative, dedicated, organized, cooperative, detail-oriented, and friendly.

Unions and Associations

Field Engineers can join professional associations at the local, state, or national level to take advantage of networking opportunities, continuing education programs, and other professional services and resources. There are various engineering societies that serve different engineering disciplines or special interests. A few national societies include the Institute of Electrical and Electronics Engineers, the Association for Computing Machinery, the American Institute of Aeronautics and Astronautics, the American Society of Agricultural and Biological Engineers, and the Society of Women Engineers. For contact information for these organizations, see Appendix III.

Tips for Entry

1. Some companies prefer that applicants fill out online application forms at their Web sites.
2. You may increase your job opportunities by being willing to relocate.
3. You want a prospective employer to know how well you are qualified for the position you are seeking. Carefully go over a job announcement, then write your résumé so that it provides clear examples of jobs, work assignments, or duties that you have performed that match what the employer is seeking.
4. Not sure of what engineering field to enter? Use the Internet to learn more about your options. You might start by visiting these Web sites: A Sightseer's Guide to Engineering (by the National Society of Professional Engineers), http://www.engineeringsights.org; and ASEE Engineering K-12 Center (by the American Society for Engineering Education), http://www.engineeringk12.org. For more links, see Appendix IV.

FACILITIES ENGINEER

CAREER PROFILE

Duties: Be involved in the planning, design, construction, operation, maintenance, and renovation of facilities as well as their systems and equipment; perform duties as required

Alternate Title(s): Operations Engineer, Plant Engineer, Maintenance Engineer

Salary Range: $33,000 to $99,000

Employment Prospects: Good

Advancement Prospects: Good

Prerequisites:

   Education or Training—Bachelor's degree in an engineering discipline

   Experience—Previous work experience generally required

   Special Skills and Personality Traits—Leadership, interpersonal, communication, report-writing, analytical, problem-solving, and organizational skills; diplomatic, courteous, self-motivated, persistent, honest, trustworthy, cooperative, innovative, and detail-oriented

   Special Requirements—Professional engineer (P.E.) licensure may be required

CAREER LADDER

```
┌─────────────────────────────┐
│      Senior Engineer        │
└─────────────────────────────┘

┌─────────────────────────────┐
│          Engineer           │
└─────────────────────────────┘

┌─────────────────────────────┐
│      Junior Engineer        │
└─────────────────────────────┘
```

Position Description

Hospitals, schools, nuclear plants, airports, government buildings, military installations, research facilities, corporate buildings, manufacturing plants, and shopping malls are just a few examples of institutional, health-care, business, commercial, and industrial operations that are a major concern of Facilities Engineers.

These hands-on engineers are responsible for ensuring that everything from the physical infrastructures to the equipment and systems needed to run facilities are all working effectively, efficiently, and safely at all times. In factories, energy plants, wastewater treatment centers, and similar operations, Facilities Engineers also care for the equipment and systems that are used to manufacture products or provide services.

Their job requires them to be involved in the planning, design, construction, operation, maintenance, and renovation of buildings and their systems and equipment. These engineers apply a range of engineering principles and methods to solve a variety of problems. They have an understanding and proficiency in electrical systems, mechanical systems, control systems, structural engineering, construction management, architectural engineering, and safety engineering, among other areas.

Facilities Engineers are engaged in a wide range of activities, which vary depending on their position, experience, and skills levels. They are assigned to projects that may involve one or several buildings. They are responsible for making sure that completed projects meet all requirements and budgets as well as comply with building and engineering codes. The following are some of the project areas to which these engineers may be assigned:

- project design—engineers develop and design projects involving new construction, installation, renovation, or modification of buildings and systems
- construction operations—engineers assist or provide the oversight and project management for construction work of facilities

- installation operations—engineers assist or oversee the installation and testing of utilities systems and components for electricity, communications, data networks, gas, oil, water, compressed air, and so on
- maintenance—engineers manage the maintenance planning, strategies, and practices required to ensure that facilities, systems, and equipment are working at a full productive level that is cost effective for their employers
- environmental controls—engineers are concerned with environmental issues and problems related to noise control, air quality, water quality, solid waste handling, and hazardous waste
- security and fire protection operations—engineers are involved in such activities as maintaining physical security systems; establishing employee and visitor control identification systems; designing, installing, and maintaining fire protection and security systems; and developing emergency response and recovery plans
- safety operations—engineers manage a safety workplace program that includes safety instruction for employees and regularly-scheduled safety inspections of facilities, grounds, equipment, and systems
- regulatory compliance—engineers perform necessary activities to make sure that the facilities, systems, and equipment meet all appropriate local, state, and federal laws and regulations

In addition to their engineering activities, Facilities Engineers are responsible for coordinating (or assisting with the coordination of) daily operations. They perform a wide range of administrative and supervisory duties. Hence, they are proficient in project administration and management as well as in such business activities as strategic planning, estimating, budgeting, purchasing, financial management, personnel development, organization planning, and labor relations.

Facilities Engineers' workdays are far from routine. They perform a wide range of tasks that vary every day, such as:

- inspect work in progress or work that has been completed
- prepare plans, specifications, and cost estimates for a new project
- review construction drawings and specifications submitted by technicians
- analyze building designs and make recommendations for improvements
- update documentation for buildings, systems, or equipment
- troubleshoot mechanical or electrical problems
- process work requests
- prepare cost estimates for a project
- plan and schedule work for a project
- select vendors for equipment purchases
- negotiate business contracts with a supplier, vendor, contractor, or consultant

- oversee work of contractors
- handle personnel matters
- plan safety training program for employees
- complete daily operating logs
- prepare reports, such as for works in progress, about departmental or plant activities, or for feasibility studies
- oversee the maintenance of records for blueprints, construction material costs, and governmental compliance reports

Novice Facilities Engineers typically work under the guidance and supervision of senior engineers. Their focus is to develop their skills and their understanding of the rules, regulations, standards, and practices of their area of concern. As they gain experience and knowledge, they receive more complex assignments and are able to exercise greater levels of authority. They may work as lead persons in certain assignments while directing the activities of other engineers and technicians.

Senior Facilities Engineers are more actively involved with the decision-making process and are likely to be team leaders. Their decisions are made without direct supervision. Senior engineers are more aware of program needs and work independently in response to those needs. For example, they are expected to implement departmental customer service and partnership concepts.

Facilities Engineers divide their time between working in offices and in the field. Many of them occasionally work in wet, cold, hot, or other unfavorable weather conditions. Engineers in industrial settings perform many of their duties on the production floor and in shop areas.

Facilities Engineers, in all settings, interface with many people on a regular basis and might communicate with them in person, by phone or letters, or through e-mail. Facilities Engineers work closely with other engineers as well as with architects, managers, technicians, crafts people, and other staff. They also have frequent contact with members of other departments in their organization, as well as with vendors, contractors, engineering consultants, governmental officials, and the general public.

Facilities Engineers work a 40-hour week but put in additional hours as needed.

Salaries

Facilities Engineers earn a salary according to their job level (such as entry-level or journey-level). Their salaries vary, depending on various factors, such as their education, experience, engineering discipline, employer, industry, and geographical location. According to the November 2004 *Occupational Employment Statistics* survey by the Bureau of Labor Statistics (BLS), the estimated annual salary for most engineers ranged between $32,840 and $98,790.

Employment Prospects

Most job openings become available as engineers are promoted, transfer to other occupations, or retire. New job growth for engineers overall is predicted to increase by 9 to 17 percent through 2014, according to the BLS. However, job opportunities in general should be favorable because the number of engineering graduates is expected to be about the same as the number of job openings. Experts in the field report that a large number of engineers will become eligible for retirement in the coming years.

Advancement Prospects

Junior Facilities Engineers can advance to senior positions in project engineering, design engineering, or other technical areas. They can also fill managerial and administrative positions as site managers and executive-level officers.

Some Facilities Engineers pursue other career paths by becoming technical specialists, consultants, researchers, or college instructors. Entrepreneurial engineers can become independent consultants or owners of technical or consulting firms.

Education and Training

Minimally, a bachelor's degree in an engineering discipline is needed for applicants to obtain entry-level positions. A master's or doctoral degree is usually required for engineers to advance to careers in management, consulting, research, or teaching.

Employers typically provide entry-level engineers with training programs, which may include both on-the-job training and formal classroom training. New engineers work under the supervision and direction of experienced engineers.

Throughout their careers, Facilities Engineers enroll in continuing education programs and training programs to update their skills and keep up with advancements in their fields.

Special Requirements

All engineers who perform work that affects the public safety and welfare, or who provide engineering services directly to the public, must be licensed engineers. Licensing requirements differ in each state and territory, as well as in Washington, D.C. For specific information, contact the board of engineering examiners for the area where you wish to practice. See Appendix II for a list of boards.

Experience, Special Skills, and Personality Traits

Employers seek candidates who can demonstrate their ability to work in a multidisciplinary environment. Entry-level candidates should have work experience related to the positions for which they apply. They may have gained their experience through internships, work-study programs, student research projects, or part-time employment. Having experience in the industry is preferred.

To perform well at their job, Facilities Engineers need excellent leadership, interpersonal, communication, report-writing, analytical, problem-solving, and organizational skills. Being diplomatic, courteous, self-motivated, persistent, honest, trustworthy, cooperative, innovative, and detail-oriented are some personality skills that Facilities Engineers share.

Unions and Associations

Many engineers join professional associations to take advantage of various professional services and resources such as networking opportunities, continuing education programs, certification, and current research findings. Facilities Engineers might join a society that serves the particular interests of this engineering specialty, such as the Association for Facilities Engineering or the Association of Energy Engineers.

They can also join engineering societies that serve their particular disciplines such as the ASME International, the American Nuclear Society, the National Fire Protection Association, or the American Society of Civil Engineers. In addition, they can join special-interest societies such as the National Society of Professional Engineers or the Society of Women Engineers. For contact information for all of the above organizations, see Appendix III.

Tips for Entry

1. Take some business courses. Talk with Facilities Engineers and managers for course recommendations.
2. Some employers hire only candidates who are U.S. citizens or foreign individuals who have U.S. permanent resident status.
3. When you are doing a job search, take advantage of the resources at your college career center. Most centers assist alumni as well as students.
4. Use the Internet to learn more about facilities engineering. You might start by visiting these Web sites: Association for Facilities Engineering (AFE), http://www.afe.org; and AFE–St. Louis Chapter, http://www.afestlouis.org. For more links, see Appendix IV.

PROJECT ENGINEER

CAREER PROFILE

Duties: Manage and coordinate engineering projects; may perform design or other engineering functions on assigned projects; perform other duties as required

Alternate Title(s): A title that reflects a particular discipline such as Chemical Engineer

Salary Range: $39,000 to $126,000

Employment Prospects: Good

Advancement Prospects: Good

Prerequisites:

    Education or Training—Bachelor's degree in an engineering field

    Experience—Several years of work experience

    Special Skills and Personality Traits—Leadership, organizational, problem-solving, writing, interpersonal, teamwork and communication skills; patient, friendly, diplomatic, detail-oriented, innovative, resourceful, disciplined, dedicated, and flexible

    Special Requirements—Professional engineer (P.E.) licensure may be required

CAREER LADDER

```
┌─────────────────────────────┐
│       Senior Engineer       │
└─────────────────────────────┘

┌─────────────────────────────┐
│          Engineer           │
└─────────────────────────────┘

┌─────────────────────────────┐
│  Associate or Junior Engineer │
└─────────────────────────────┘
```

Position Description

Engineers work on many projects throughout their careers. For example, they may be involved in building homes or repairing roads, designing robotic machinery or creating amusement park rides, developing medical devices or researching methods to make human tissues, improving processes for refining oil or producing food products, creating new system software or redesigning computer hardware, or upgrading water treatment plants or designing hazardous waste dumps.

Almost all engineering projects are a team effort. The project team is usually composed of several engineers from different disciplines, as well as technicians and support staff. Scientists and mathematicians are often part of engineering projects as well. But only one engineer, the Project Engineer, is responsible for the success or failure of a project. He or she is in charge of the day-to-day management and coordination of an engineering project.

Engineering projects may take several days, weeks, months, or years to complete. They may range in cost from a few thousand dollars to billions of dollars. Project Engineers are responsible for delivering a project according to schedule and within its budget. In addition, Project Engineers make sure that their projects meet all technical specifications.

Project Engineers may be responsible for one or more projects, which are assigned by their supervisors. They work with their supervisors to decide who will work on a project and what resources will be needed for the project. Goals, budgets, and schedules are usually determined before projects are assigned to Project Engineers.

It is the job of Project Engineers to plan the work for their teams. They assign tasks, coordinate the work of team personnel, and monitor the progress of their work. Project Engineers may also perform some tasks. Project Engineers work with team members to address and resolve problems as they occur; however, all final decisions are made by the Project Engineers. These team leaders provide their supervisors with regular status reports on their projects.

On large complex projects, several Project Engineers are often assigned to be in charge of certain aspects. The different Project Engineers are supervised and guided by a project manager.

Project Engineers perform a variety of tasks, which vary each day. Some of their tasks include:

- assisting in the preparation of plans, specifications, and estimates for a new project
- researching project design requirements
- reviewing and approving work done by project team members
- making sure work complies with technical specifications as well as governmental laws and regulations
- investigating routine problems
- meeting with consultants, contractors, staff, the general public, or others to discuss the progress of their project
- leading project meetings
- preparing correspondence, memorandums, forms, or reports
- maintaining an accurate and up-to-date record of project activities

Project Engineers usually work in office settings, but on occasion they must go to laboratories, industrial plants, field sites, or other job sites to perform their duties. Their job requires them to interact with a variety of people—project team members, staff personnel, decision makers, subject-matter experts, and so forth—on a daily basis. They are sometimes under pressure to complete projects on tight schedules.

Project Engineers work a 40-hour week schedule. On occasion, they must work evenings and weekends to meet deadlines and complete various tasks. They sometimes travel to another city, state, or country to attend meetings with clients and perform other duties. This may require working there for several days or weeks at a time.

Salaries

Salaries for Project Engineers vary, depending on various factors, such as their education, experience, engineering discipline, employer, industry, and geographical location. For example, the U.S. Bureau of Labor Statistics (BLS) reported, in its November 2004 *Occupational Employment Statistics* survey, the following estimated annual salary ranges for most engineers in these engineering disciplines:

- aerospace engineer, $56,190 to $114,950
- agricultural engineers, $38,840 to $91,000
- biomedical engineers, $43,490 to $113,070
- chemical engineers, $48,990 to $112,790
- civil engineers, $43,530 to $97,650
- computer hardware engineers, $51,190 to $125,800
- electrical engineers, $47,430 to $110,330
- environmental engineers, $41,570 to $99,120
- mechanical engineers, $44,240 to $100,400
- mining engineers, $42,150 to $119,110

According to *The Engineering Income and Salary Survey 2005* by the National Society of Professional Engineers, the average total annual income for professional engineers who worked in project management was $82,592.

Employment Prospects

Job growth for engineers is predicted to increase by 9 to 17 percent through 2014, according to the BLS. However, job opportunities in general should be favorable because the number of engineering graduates is expected to be about the same as the number of job openings. (For information about specific disciplines, refer to those profiles in this book.)

Most job openings become available as engineers are promoted, transfer to other occupations, or retire. Opportunities for Project Engineers vary from employer to employer. As new projects are started, employers may choose to assign engineers from among their personnel or hire engineers, either temporarily or on a permanent basis, for project engineer positions.

Advancement Prospects

As Project Engineers gain experience, they are assigned to manage larger and more complex projects. They can rise through the management and administrative ranks as project managers, unit managers, division managers, and executives. Some Project Engineers pursue non-technical positions in such areas as sales, marketing, or human resources.

Other Project Engineers pursue other career options by becoming technical specialists, consultants, researchers, or college instructors. Entrepreneurial engineers can become independent consultants or owners of technical or consulting firms.

Education and Training

Project Engineers possess at least a bachelor's degree in their engineering discipline. Many hold an advanced degree. Those seeking to advance further in management or to follow other career paths, such as consulting, research, or teaching, generally need a master's or doctoral degree.

Novice Project Engineers typically receive supervision and guidance from their supervisors and other experienced engineers.

Special Requirements

Many employers require entry-level Project Engineers to be licensed as either a professional engineer (P.E.) or as an engineer-in-training (E.I.T.). They may hire strong candidates without a license on the condition that they obtain the proper license within a certain time.

All engineers who perform work that affects the public safety and welfare or who provide engineering services directly to the public must be licensed engineers. Licensing requirements differ in each state and territory, as well as in Washington, D.C. For specific information, contact the board of engineering examiners for the area where you wish to practice. See Appendix II for a list of boards.

Experience, Special Skills, and Personality Traits

Project Engineers usually have been promoted from such positions as design or operations engineers. They typically have several years of work experience, and demonstrate expertise in their areas of work.

Project Engineers must have excellent leadership, organizational, problem-solving, and writing skills for their work. Having strong interpersonal, teamwork and communication skills is also essential, as they must be able to maintain cooperative working relationships among team members, managers, and others who come from different backgrounds. Being patient, friendly, diplomatic, detail-oriented, innovative, resourceful, disciplined, dedicated, and flexible are some personality traits that successful Project Engineers share.

Unions and Associations

Many Project Engineers are members of professional associations that serve their particular engineering disciplines. For example, civil and environmental engineers may belong to the American Society of Civil Engineers, electrical engineers may join the Institute of Electrical and Electronics Engineers, and mechanical engineers may be members of ASME International. Project Engineers are also eligible to join groups that serve the interests of engineering managers in general, such as the International Association for Management of Technology. (For contact information for these organizations, see Appendix III.) By joining a professional association, engineers can take advantage of networking opportunities, continuing education programs, certification, and other professional services and resources.

Tips for Entry

1. Take a course in public speaking or acting to help prepare you for dealing and communicating with both technical and non-technical people.
2. While in college, participate in an internship program at a company or government agency that you might be interested in working for after graduation. Many employers hire recent graduates who completed an internship with them.
3. Become proficient in word processing, spreadsheet, presentation, and other software that you would use for administrative tasks such as preparing budgets, writing reports, and making presentations.
4. Some technical consulting firms hire recent graduates and train them to be Project Engineers.
5. Use the Internet to learn more about prospective employers. To find a Web site for an organization, as well as other relevant Web sites, enter the organization's name in a search engine.

ENGINEERING MANAGER

CAREER PROFILE

Duties: Oversee technical operations on a daily basis; plan, direct, and coordinate work activities of employees; perform duties as required

Alternate Title(s): Project Manager, Senior Manager, Department Manager, Plant Engineer, Engineering Director, Chief Engineer

Salary Range: $64,000 to $146,000

Employment Prospects: Good

Advancement Prospects: Good

Prerequisites:

Education or Training—Bachelor's degree; an advanced degree preferred

Experience—Several years of work experience in product development and manufacturing

Special Skills and Personality Traits—Leadership, management, business administration, analytical, organizational, problem-solving, writing, communication, interpersonal, teamwork, and self-management skills; inspiring, persuasive, cooperative, reliable, honest, ethical, persistent, decisive, and flexible

Special Requirements—Professional engineer (P.E.) licensure may be required

CAREER LADDER

```
┌─────────────────────────────────────┐
│ Executive Manager or Chief Engineer  │
└─────────────────────────────────────┘

┌─────────────────────────────────────┐
│        Department, Division, or       │
│            District Manager           │
└─────────────────────────────────────┘

┌─────────────────────────────────────┐
│        Program or Unit Manager        │
└─────────────────────────────────────┘

┌─────────────────────────────────────┐
│            Project Manager            │
└─────────────────────────────────────┘
```

Position Description

Engineering projects, programs, units, divisions, facilities, and all other technical operations are expected to run smoothly and efficiently every day. The engineers who are responsible for overseeing these operations are generally known as Engineering Managers. They are responsible for planning, directing, and coordinating the work activities of professionals, technicians, and support personnel on a daily basis. These managers also seek solutions to problems and issues that affect the quality, efficiency, and profitability of their organizations.

Engineering Managers work in all types of industries, including construction, utilities, aerospace, automotive, electronics, computer, biotechnology, chemicals, energy, telecommunications, medical, pharmaceutical, food, agricultural, and transportation industries, among others. They are employed by businesses and manufacturers, contracting firms and consulting companies, government agencies and nonprofit organizations, and research institutes and academic institutions. Their focus may be on managing activities concerned with basic or applied research, product development, manufacturing processes, materials management, oversight of facilities, workforce reliability, product quality, or other areas.

The work of these managers involves the application of engineering, science, and mathematics to solve a wide range of technical problems and issues. In addition, Engineering Managers utilize knowledge of business and management principles such as strategic planning, resource allocation, production methods, leadership technique, and coordination of people and resources.

Many Engineering Managers have specific professional titles that reflect the types of operations that they oversee. Project managers are responsible for directing and coordinating the activities of projects that organizations initiate for research, product development, construction, and other purposes. Plant managers are in charge of the planning, operation, and maintenance of facilities as well as the systems and equipment within those structures. The managers who are responsible for particular groups within an organization are referred to by such titles as unit supervisor, department manager, and regional manager, whereas executive managers may be called chief engineers, engineering directors, vice president of engineering, or another title.

Regardless of their position or rank, all Engineering Managers are responsible for planning, directing, monitoring, and controlling the work of groups of employees. Some managers work with employees directly, while other managers oversee lower-level managers who supervise workers on their team or in their unit. All managers are responsible for ensuring that projects and programs run on schedule and within their budgets. Engineering Managers, in particular, make sure that their assignments are in compliance with organizational policies and standards as well as with all appropriate laws and regulations.

Engineering Managers develop work plans for a variety of activities. This includes creating goals, objectives, and strategies, as well as establishing work procedures and policies. Managers continually evaluate many plans, which involves keeping abreast of new technological and market developments and revising plans accordingly. These managers also prepare and coordinate schedules and budgets for the various work activities under their helm.

Engineering Managers assign employees to specific tasks and provide them with proper supervision and guidance. These managers monitor the job performance of their staff as well as provide their employees with necessary training that may be in the form of on-the-job training or formal classroom instruction. Depending on their organization and position, Engineering Managers may have the power to hire, promote, or fire employees. Usually in organizations that have several management layers, lower-level managers may only make recommendations to higher managers or executive officers.

In addition to their staff, Engineering Managers work closely with others in their organizations. They interface with managers from technical and business departments to coordinate work activities. For example, an Engineering Manager might work with staff from development, production, packaging, marketing, finance, and other departments to discuss ideas for new products. Engineering Managers also confer with higher levels of management to discuss current and future activities. Further, Engineering Managers have frequent contact with vendors, suppliers, contractors, regulatory officers, customers, and others.

Engineering Managers perform a wide range of tasks on their job, which vary daily. For example, they:

- develop or revise plans for work activities
- develop and implement work policies, standards, procedures, and priorities
- prepare budgets and schedules for upcoming projects
- troubleshoot problems as they arise
- develop training programs for employees
- participate in the recruitment or hiring of new employees
- review proposal bids from vendors, suppliers, contractors, or consultants
- direct the negotiation of contracts
- make decisions about buying, modifying, repairing, and maintaining equipment
- prepare correspondence, paperwork, technical reports, and other documents

Engineering Managers are expected to keep up-to-date with new technologies and developments in their fields as well as stay abreast of current management practices. They read professional and trade publications, attend trade shows and professional conferences, and enroll in workshops, seminars, and courses.

Engineering Managers mostly work in offices. Some of them may also spend time working in laboratories, in plant facilities, at construction sites, or other work sites where they may be exposed to loud noise, moving parts, fumes, and toxic chemicals. Hence, they are required to wear appropriate protective clothing and equipment.

Engineering Managers are often under constant stress when handling negotiations, dealing with conflict, meeting deadlines, and attending to other matters. They usually put in more than 40 hours a week to complete their duties. They sometimes travel to other cities or states to attend professional meetings and conferences.

Salaries

Salaries for Engineering Managers vary, depending on such factors as their education, experience, position, employer, and geographical location. According to the November 2004 *Occupational Employment Statistics* (OES) survey by the U.S. Bureau of Labor Statistics (BLS), the estimated annual salary for most Engineering Managers ranged between $64,230 and $145,600.

Employment Prospects

The BLS reported in its November 2004 OES survey that an estimated 188,620 Engineering Managers were employed in the United States. The highest level of employment for these managers was in the architectural and engineering services industry. Other major industries were the federal government, the electronic instrument manufacturing industry, the aerospace product and parts manufacturing industry, and the semiconductor and electronic component manufacturing industry.

Job openings generally become available as Engineering Managers retire, advance to higher positions, or transfer to other jobs. Additional positions will be created as companies grow and expand, as well as when new firms start up. According to the BLS, employment growth for this occupation should increase by 9 to 17 percent through 2014.

Advancement Prospects

Engineering Managers can advance in any number of ways, according to their ambitions and interests. They can rise through the technical management ranks. They can also seek promotion to executive-level positions. In addition, they can pursue non-technical management positions in such areas as marketing, sales, or human resources.

Another career path for Engineering Managers is to become independent consultants or owners of firms that offer technical or management consulting services. Engineering Managers may also pursue teaching and research careers in academia.

Education and Training

Educational requirements vary from employer to employer. Minimally, engineers must possess a bachelor's degree in their discipline to become Engineering Managers. Most employers prefer to hire candidates who hold an advanced degree (master's or doctorate). The advanced degree may be in one's technical field or in engineering management. Those seeking non-technical management jobs may improve their employability by possessing a master's in business administration (MBA).

Throughout their careers, Engineering Managers enroll in continuing education and training programs to update their skills and keep up with advancements in their fields.

Special Requirements

All engineers who perform work that affects the life, health, or property of the public or offer engineering services directly to the public must be licensed as professional engineers (P.E.). Each state and territory, as well as Washington, D.C., has its own licensing requirements. For specific information, contact the board of engineering examiners for the area where you wish to practice. See Appendix II for a list of boards.

Experience, Special Skills, and Personality Traits

Engineers usually have several years of work experience before they are promoted to managerial positions. Employers typically select job candidates who demonstrate their ability to lead and motivate people as well as have strong technical backgrounds.

To perform well at their job, Engineering Managers must have effective leadership, management, and business administration skills. Their work requires that they have excellent analytical, organizational, problem-solving, and writing skills. They also need strong communication, interpersonal,

and teamwork skills, as they must work well with colleagues, supervisors, executive officers, technicians, vendors, and various others from diverse backgrounds. Further, Engineering Managers need excellent self-management skills, including such abilities as handling stressful situations calmly, working independently, meeting deadlines, and prioritizing multiple tasks.

Some personality traits that successful Engineering Managers share include being inspiring, persuasive, cooperative, reliable, honest, ethical, persistent, decisive, and flexible.

Unions and Associations

Engineering Managers can join various professional societies to take advantage of networking opportunities, continuing education programs, certification, publications, and other professional resources and services. A few national societies that serve the interests of different engineering managers are the American Society for Engineering Management, the IEEE Engineering Management Society, and the International Association for Management of Technology.

Many managers also belong to engineering societies that serve their particular disciplines or special interests, such as:

- American Indian Science and Engineering Society
- American Institute of Chemical Engineers
- American Society for Engineering Education
- American Society of Agricultural and Biological Engineers
- American Society of Civil Engineers
- ASM International
- ASME International (formerly the American Society of Mechanical Engineers)
- Institute of Electrical and Electronics Engineers
- Institute of Industrial Engineers
- Institute of Transportation Engineers
- National Society of Black Engineers
- National Society of Professional Engineers
- Society of Manufacturing Engineers
- Society of Women Engineers

For contact information for these organizations, see Appendix III.

Tips for Entry

1. Does your company offer an educational program for its employees? Take advantage of it to obtain a master's degree in engineering management or business administration.
2. To enhance their employability, some Engineering Managers obtain professional certification from societies to which they belong.
3. You can learn more about engineering management on the Internet. To get a list of Web sites, enter the keywords *engineering management or engineering managers* in a search engine. To learn about some links, see Appendix IV.

ENGINEERING CONSULTANT

CAREER PROFILE

Duties: Offer consulting services to individuals and organizations; provide advice about or solutions to engineering issues and problems; perform duties as required

Alternate Title(s): Management Consultant; a title that reflects a particular field, such as Chemical Engineering Consultant

Salary Range: $42,000 to $141,000

Employment Prospects: Good

Advancement Prospects: Fair

Prerequisites:

Education or Training—Bachelor's degree, minimum

Experience—Several years of work experience within field

Special Skills and Personality Traits—Leadership, analytical, problem-solving, writing, time-management, interpersonal, teamwork, communication, business, and customer service skills; ethical, trustworthy, detail-oriented, self-motivated, self-disciplined, assertive, and creative

Special Requirements—Professional engineer (P.E.) licensure usually required

CAREER LADDER

```
┌─────────────────────────────────────┐
│          Senior Consultant           │
└─────────────────────────────────────┘

┌─────────────────────────────────────┐
│        Engineering Consultant        │
└─────────────────────────────────────┘

┌─────────────────────────────────────┐
│  Junior Consultant or Professional,  │
│  Specialist, Manager, or Executive   │
└─────────────────────────────────────┘
```

Position Description

When organizations need engineering expertise that they lack within their ranks, they normally seek Engineering Consultants. These professional men and women have many years of experience working in their engineering fields and have lots of knowledge about their engineering specialties.

Engineering Consultants offer their services as resources and advisors to help clients improve their organizations' structure, efficiency, or profits. Clients may range from individuals to institutions, from start-up firms to established corporations, from local, state, or federal government agencies to foreign governments, from the military to nongovernmental agencies. Clients generally prefer to hire consultants than to take on new staff, because it is more cost-effective to employ specialists on a temporary basis. In addition, consultants are not influenced by organizational politics and thus can perform their jobs more objectively.

Consultants may be salaried employees of engineering consulting firms or they may be independent practitioners. They work for clients on a contractual basis, and provide specific consulting services for a period that may last several days, weeks, months, or years.

Many Engineering Consultants are technical consultants. They provide advice about nonmanagement activities as well as diverse issues within their particular disciplines. They are contracted to provide assistance within the context of such engineering functions as development, analysis, design, testing, production, regulatory affairs, or project management. For example, a geotechnical consultant might provide a local agency with assistance on the design of earthquake retrofitting projects; an environmental consultant might help an oil refinery comply with governmental regulations; and an industrial engineer might develop ways to help an insurance company improve the efficiency of its personnel.

Some Engineering Consultants offer management consulting services. Their specialty is providing business advice. They analyze and evaluate specific business problems and recommend practical solutions to managers. For example, management consultants might help clients reorganize their corporate structure, improve their operations, remain competitive within their existing markets, or sell their company.

Other Engineering Consultants offer litigation or expert witness services to attorneys who may be handling civil, criminal, or administrative cases. These consultants help attorneys investigate and understand technical issues that they confront in their cases. As expert witnesses, they may be asked to provide sworn testimony at depositions, trials, hearings, or arbitrations for one of two purposes: to give an expert opinion about an issue or fact, or to provide sufficient information so that the judges and juries can understand specific technical issues.

Engineering Consultants sometimes work on several projects at a time. They work alone or with other consultants. They also work closely with their clients' managers, engineers, and other personnel. These consultants usually have the autonomy to plan their work details and make decisions regarding how they perform their work. They provide their clients with regular oral or written updates of their progress and seek approval for each stage of a project before going on to the next one. Engineering Consultants are responsible for completing required studies, reports, and paperwork, as well as maintaining accurate records of their work activities.

Many consultants are involved in business development for their firms, in which they generate new work or new clients. For example, they prepare bid proposals that describe how their firm plans to handle clients' proposed projects, make presentations to potential clients, and attend trade conferences and shows to promote their firm's business.

Independent consultants are responsible for overseeing their business operations. They perform various administrative tasks such as developing office policies, establishing consulting fees, billing clients, paying taxes and bills, updating business licenses, keeping accurate business records, and maintaining office equipment.

Engineering Consultants generally have flexible work schedules, which may include working early morning or evening hours as well as on weekends. It is normal for them to work more than 40 hours a week to complete their various duties. Their work can be stressful, particularly when they must meet tight deadlines. Depending on the type of project and the tasks they perform, Engineering Consultants may work in offices or laboratories, at manufacturing plants or operations facilities, or construction sites or other outdoor settings.

Consultants frequently travel to meet clients at their offices or to work at their clients' worksites. Clients may be based in other cities, states, or countries. Thus, consultants may be required to work and live there for several days or weeks at a time.

Salaries

Earnings for Engineering Consultants vary, depending on such factors as their education, experience, specialty, position (staff, self-employed, or business owner), and geographical location. Many consultants receive additional compensation in the form of performance-based bonuses, profit sharing, or stock ownership.

Specific information for engineering consultants is unavailable, but they generally earn salaries similar to other engineers. The U.S. Bureau of Labor Statistics (BLS) reported in its November 2004 *Occupational Employment Statistics* survey the following estimated annual salary ranges for most engineers in these engineering disciplines:

- aerospace engineers, $56,190 to $114,950
- biomedical engineers, $43,490 to $113,070
- chemical engineers, $48,990 to $112,790
- civil engineers, $43,530 to $97,650
- computer hardware engineers, $51,190 to $125,800
- electrical engineers, $47,430 to $110,330
- environmental engineers, $41,570 to $99,120
- industrial engineers, $43,220 to $95,690
- mechanical engineers, $44,240 to $100,400
- petroleum engineers, $49,240 to $140,850

According to *The Engineering Income and Salary Survey 2005* by the National Society of Professional Engineers, the average total annual income for professional engineers who worked in consulting was $79,967.

Gross earnings for independent contractors and business owners depend on the amount of business they have generated, from which they subtract the cost of running their businesses. Independent contractors might charge clients hourly rates or flat fees for projects.

Employment Prospects

Job opportunities are available throughout the United States, particularly in large metropolitan areas. However, the job competition is keen, according to the BLS, because many college graduates and experienced professionals are attracted to the prestige, independent work, high salaries, and good benefits that come with consulting work. The BLS further reports a strong demand for environmental and safety consulting due to the constant changes in environmental and workplace safety laws and regulations.

Advancement Prospects

Staff consultants can rise through the ranks as associates, consultants, managers, and partners. Many seek positions with other firms to earn higher pay, obtain more complex assignments, or be promoted to higher positions. After years of experience, entrepreneurial consultants become self-employed as independent contractors or form their own consulting firms.

Education and Training

Engineering consulting firms hire candidates who possess at least a bachelor's degree in an appropriate field. Candidates who have a master's or doctoral degree are desirable by some firms.

Novice consultants typically receive on-the-job training while working under the supervision and guidance of senior consultants.

Throughout their careers, Engineering Consultants enroll in continuing education and training programs to update their skills and keep up with advancements in their fields.

Special Requirements

Engineering Consultants are usually required to be licensed professional engineers (P.E.). Every state, along with each U.S. territory and Washington, D.C., requires engineers to be licensed if their work affects the public safety and welfare or if they offer their services directly to the public. Licensure requirements vary in the different states. For specific information, contact the board of engineering examiners for the area where you wish to practice. See Appendix II for a list of boards.

Consultants who own their firms must also possess the proper business licenses. For information, contact local government offices.

Experience, Special Skills, and Personality Traits

Engineering Consultants have several years of work experience, with expertise in the various concepts, practices, and procedures of their specialties and fields.

Many engineering consulting firms hire college graduates for entry-level positions. They usually seek candidates who have gained some work experience through internships, work-study programs, or employment,

To be effective as consultants, engineers need excellent leadership, analytical, problem-solving, writing, and time-management skills. Because they must work well with clients, colleagues and others from diverse backgrounds, they must have strong interpersonal, teamwork, and communication skills. Having good business and customer service skills is also important.

Some personality traits that successful Engineering Consultants have in common are being ethical, trustworthy, detail-oriented, self-motivated, self-disciplined, assertive, and creative.

Unions and Associations

Many Engineering Consultants are members of professional associations that provide networking opportunities, continuing education programs, publications, and other professional services and resources. They belong to societies that serve their particular disciplines such as the American Society of Civil Engineers, the ASME International (formerly the American Society of Mechanical Engineers), the American Institute of Chemical Engineers, or the Institute of Electrical and Electronics Engineers. Many consultants also join special-interest engineering societies such as the Society of Women Engineers, the Society of Hispanic Professional Engineers, the American Society for Engineering Education, or the National Society of Professional Engineers. For contact information for all these organizations, see Appendix III.

Tips for Entry

1. Talk with Engineering Consultants to learn more about their work, as well as how they got into consulting.
2. In college, obtain an internship in an engineering consulting firm. Along with gaining valuable experience, you can get an idea if consulting is the type of work you would like to get into.
3. Develop a network of contacts, which includes colleagues as well as former teachers and employers.
4. You can learn more about engineering consulting on the Internet. To get a list of Web sites, enter the keywords *engineering consulting or engineering consultants* in a search engine. To learn about some links, see Appendix IV.

FORENSIC ENGINEER

CAREER PROFILE

Duties: Provide expert evaluation and opinions on technical issues related to legal and legal-related matters; conduct investigations and tests; perform duties as required

Alternate Title(s): Forensic Consultant; a title that reflects an engineering discipline such as Geotechnical Engineer or Agricultural Engineer

Salary Range: $43,000 to $141,000

Employment Prospects: Fair

Advancement Prospects: Good

Prerequisites:

Education or Training—Bachelor's or advanced degree in an engineering discipline

Experience—Several years of work experience in a specialty

Special Skills and Personality Traits—Research, note-taking, presentation, interpersonal, communication, and writing skills; honest, ethical, curious, innovative, self-motivated, competent, and detail-oriented

Special Requirements—Professional engineer (P.E.) licensure required

CAREER LADDER

```
┌─────────────────────────────┐
│   Senior Forensic Engineer   │
└─────────────────────────────┘

┌─────────────────────────────┐
│      Forensic Engineer       │
└─────────────────────────────┘

┌─────────────────────────────┐
│          Engineer            │
└─────────────────────────────┘
```

Position Description

What caused a levee to break? Why did the freeway collapse during the storm? Was a person's death caused by a defect in his heart stents? How did contaminants get into a water supply? Who is the rightful patent owner of a new invention? Technical issues such as these are often part of legal matters that require engineering expertise. Professional engineers who are involved in performing legal investigations and offering expert evaluations and opinions to attorneys, insurance companies, government agencies, corporations, and others are known as Forensic Engineers.

These engineers are acknowledged experts in their fields—civil engineering, structural engineering, traffic engineering, wastewater engineering, chemical engineering, control systems engineering, avionics engineering, automotive engineering, or other engineering discipline or subspecialty. They apply engineering principles and techniques, as well as science and mathematics, to the examination of technical issues that are part of criminal cases, civil suits, insurance claims, patent infringements, contract disputes, regulatory matters, and other legal matters. They investigate accidents, crashes, structural failures, fires, explosions, environmental spills, and other natural and human-made disasters.

Forensic Engineers conduct forensic investigations with scientific precision. Their goal is to determine only the facts. They are expected at all times to remain impartial and unbiased about the subject matter that they examine.

Their job involves reviewing police reports, eyewitness statements, expert reports, and other materials for background information. They may inspect sites where accidents, catastrophes, or losses occurred, as well as examine all available physical evidence. They may perform tests on products or structures to evaluate them for failure or defects. They may also reproduce events in laboratory settings to determine what has happened. They may perform standardized tests on products to evaluate them for failure or defects. Forensic Engineers document every step of their inspections with written notes, photographs, and videotapes.

Forensic Engineers analyze and interpret their data and form objective conclusions, which may or may not be favorable for their clients. Forensic Engineers prepare reports of their findings and conclusions in language that nontechnical individuals can understand. Their reports must be written clearly and concisely, yet comprehensively, as they may be used in pretrial proceedings, trials, and settlement negotiations, as well as in administrative hearings, alternative dispute resolution conferences, and other legal hearings.

Forensic Engineers are sometimes retained by lawyers to provide testimony at depositions and trials as expert witnesses. Unlike ordinary witnesses, expert witnesses can testify on issues based on their opinions, which are formed on the evaluations they have made on evidence related to a case. As expert witnesses, Forensic Engineers may also be called up to provide technical explanations to help judges and juries understand specific issues in a case.

In order to qualify as an expert witness, Forensic Engineers must be able to demonstrate to lawyers and the courts that they have sufficient experience and skills to address the issues within a particular case. Usually, their qualifications are determined by their education, experience, membership in professional organizations, and the professional materials (articles or books) that they have published.

Many attorneys also hire Forensic Engineers to provide various litigation consulting services. For example, they may assist lawyers by helping them understand the technical subject matter involved in a case so that the lawyers can fully understand the issues. Engineers may also be asked to identify technical issues and facts within a case, formulate a list of questions that lawyers would ask witnesses in cross examination, find expert witnesses, or prepare demonstrative evidence (such as diagrams, models, or computer animation) for a trial.

Forensic Engineers occasionally work more than 40 hours a week to complete tasks and meet deadlines. Their assignments may require them to travel to other cities or states.

Salaries

Earnings for Forensic Engineers vary, depending on such factors as their education, experience, specialty, position (staff, self-employed, or business owner), and geographical location. Specific salary information for this occupation is unavailable, but they generally earn salaries similar to other experienced engineers. The U.S. Bureau of Labor Statistics reported in its November 2004 *Occupational Employment Statistics* survey the following estimated annual salary ranges for most engineers in these engineering disciplines:

- aerospace engineers, $56,190 to $114,950
- biomedical engineers, $43,490 to $113,070
- chemical engineers, $48,990 to $112,790
- civil engineers, $43,530 to $97,650
- computer hardware engineers, $51,190 to $125,800
- electrical engineers, $47,430 to $110,330
- mechanical engineers, $44,240 to $100,400
- petroleum engineers, $49,240 to $140,850

Gross earnings for independent contractors and business owners depend on the amount of business they have generated, from which they subtract the cost of running their businesses. Independent contractors might charge clients hourly rates or flat fees for projects.

Employment Prospects

Forensic Engineers are mostly employed by small forensic engineering firms or are self-employed. Some are employed by government agencies and large corporations. Others work on a part-time basis while working full-time as engineers or academicians.

Opportunities for experienced, credible, and ethical Forensic Engineers are good, as they are constantly needed to explain technical matters for legal and legal-related cases.

Advancement Prospects

Staff Forensic Engineers can advance through the ranks from junior consultants to principal consultants. They can also be promoted to supervisory and management positions. Entrepreneurial engineers pursue their ambitions to become independent consultants or owners of forensic engineering firms.

Independent practitioners and company owners measure their success by earning higher incomes and becoming highly recognized for their expertise and professionalism.

Education and Training

Forensic engineering is not a specific engineering discipline, hence no colleges or universities offer a college degree in this field. However, several universities offer graduate courses in forensic engineering as electives.

Minimally, Forensic Engineers need to hold a bachelor's degree in an engineering or science discipline. Many of these engineers possess either a master's or doctoral degree, which is preferred by many clients.

Throughout their careers, Forensic Engineers enroll in continuing education and training programs to update their skills and keep up with advancements in their fields.

Special Requirements

Forensic Engineers are required to be licensed Professional Engineers (P.E.), as they offer their services directly to the public. Licensure requirements vary in the different states, as well as in the territories and Washington, D.C. For specific information, contact the board of engineering examiners for the area where you wish to practice. See Appendix II for a list of boards.

Engineers who own their firms must possess the proper business licenses. For information, contact local government offices.

Experience, Special Skills, and Personality Traits
To become Forensic Engineers, individuals must have several years of work experience in their fields. They must have technical competency in their specialties, and must be knowledgeable about legal procedures.

To perform well at their job, Forensic Engineers need strong research, note-taking, presentation, and interpersonal skills. Because they must be able to present technical ideas clearly and succinctly to nontechnical people, these engineers need excellent communication and writing skills.

Some personality traits that successful Forensic Engineers share include being honest, ethical, curious, innovative, self-motivated, competent, and detail-oriented.

Unions and Associations
Many Forensic Engineers join local, state, or national professional associations to take advantage of networking opportunities, continuing education programs, publications, and other professional services and resources. Some national societies that serve the specific interests of these engineers are the National Academy of Forensic Engineers, the American Academy of Forensic Sciences, and the American College of Forensic Examiners.

These engineers also belong to engineering societies that serve their particular disciplines such as the American Society of Civil Engineers, the Structural Engineering Institute, the American Institute of Aeronautics and Astronautics, the ASME International (formerly the American Society of Mechanical Engineers), the American Institute of Chemical Engineers, or the Institute of Electrical and Electronics Engineers.

Forensic Engineers are also eligible to join special focus engineering societies such as the National Society of Professional Engineers, the National Society of Black Engineers, or the Society of Women Engineers.

For contact information for all the above organizations, see Appendix III.

Tips for Entry
1. While in high school or college, start learning about forensic engineering and forensics in general. Many books are written on these subjects. Check your school or local library for available titles.
2. As a professional, you might join Toastmasters, a nonprofit group that helps professionals develop their public speaking and leadership skills.
3. If you plan to become an independent consultant, take some small business courses to help you succeed.
4. Some ways you can build up your professional credibility as a Forensic Engineer are to publish technical articles, give presentations at professional conferences and meetings, and conduct workshops in forensic engineering methods.
5. You can learn more about forensic engineering on the Internet. To get a list of Web sites, enter the keywords *forensic engineering* or *forensic engineers* in a search engine. To learn about some links, see Appendix IV.

ENGINEERING TECHNOLOGISTS AND TECHNICIANS

ENGINEERING TECHNOLOGIST

CAREER PROFILE

Duties: Assist engineers in solving technical problems in all phases of engineering projects; perform duties as required

Alternate Title(s): A title that reflects a specialty, such as Food Technologist or Construction Engineering Technologist

Salary Range: $24,000 to $78,000+

Employment Prospects: Fair

Advancement Prospects: Fair

Prerequisites:

　Education or Training—Bachelor's degree in engineering technology; on-the-job training

　Experience—Previous work experience preferred

　Special Skills and Personality Traits—Problem-solving, communication, writing, interpersonal, teamwork, and self-management skills; creative, practical, responsible, ethical, cooperative, and self-motivated

　Special Requirements—Professional engineer (P.E.) licensure may be required

CAREER LADDER

```
┌─────────────────────────────────────┐
│   Senior Engineering Technologist    │
└─────────────────────────────────────┘

┌─────────────────────────────────────┐
│      Engineering Technologist        │
└─────────────────────────────────────┘

┌─────────────────────────────────────┐
│ Engineering Technologist (entry-level) │
└─────────────────────────────────────┘
```

Position Description

Not all technical staff members on project teams are engineers. Some of them are Engineering Technologists, and they play key roles in the completion of all kinds of engineering projects.

Engineering Technologists work in the range of professions that rank between engineers and skilled craftspeople. Their responsibilities are closest to those of engineers. They are involved with the same fields of endeavor as engineers, such as civil engineering or mechanical engineering, as well in specific areas—avionics, electronics, robotics, the environment, and so forth. Like engineers, Engineering Technologists have a background in scientific and engineering theory, but their approach to using their knowledge is more practical, or applications oriented, than that of engineers. These professionals use the principles of science, mathematics, and engineering to solve technical problems that arise in all phases of engineering projects—design, research and development, testing, construction, production, sales, inspection, and maintenance.

Engineering Technologists assist engineers with developing product or project designs. They help to refine designs so that they function properly, utilize materials that are on hand, and adhere to appropriate mathematical, scientific, and engineering principles. Technologists have a more intimate knowledge of the materials and equipment that are needed to produce technical products. They are often required to use computer-aided design (CAD) equipment.

Technologists who work in the area of research and development help engineers by setting up equipment, conducting experiments, collecting data, and recording the results of their experiments. They construct prototypes of new products for testing in controlled laboratory or field environments. They are also involved with the testing of finished products.

In the area of production, Engineering Technologists assist in deciding upon the best methods to manufacture goods. They suggest ways to maximize productivity by putting efficient work flow procedures into operation, by eliminating unneeded production steps, or by changing the layouts of manufacturing facilities. They inspect, test, and monitor products as they are fabricated, and contribute to quality assurance processes.

In all aspects of engineering projects, Engineering Technologists may become the frontline supervisors of engineering teams after gaining experience with technical duties. In their supervisory capacity, they work under the direction of managing engineers to oversee the activities of technicians and other staff members, as well as prepare work schedules and encourage increased productivity from the team. They may also be in charge of such engineering projects as large construction projects and oversee a crew of construction workers. As supervisors, they keep an eye open for safety and environmental concerns and identify ways to resolve or eliminate problems.

These professionals may specialize by working in specific engineering fields, such as in chemical, aerospace, civil, electrical and electronics, environmental, mechanical, manufacturing, petroleum, mining, and industrial engineering. They may also work within subfields of these areas. They also may specialize in specific engineering functions, such as manufacturing operations, power generation, project planning, plant operations, quality assurance, testing, sales, and technical service.

Engineering Technologists complete various tasks in the course of their day-to-day work. For example, they:

- use CAD systems to modify or improve engineering designs
- prepare and conduct experiments
- conduct tests and evaluate results
- collect data from research or testing procedures
- make prototypes of new products
- inspect products for flaws or imperfections
- prepare reports and paperwork

Engineering Technologists work for a wide range of industries in the technology sector. They are more likely to work in those enterprises that are concerned with such engineering endeavors as manufacturing, implementation, applications, or sales rather than in companies that deal with the engineering work of conceptual design or research.

These professionals work with other people in team situations and in other professional relationships. Most Engineering Technologists work 40 hours per week but may occasionally work extra hours to complete projects or meet deadlines. They work in laboratories, offices, or industrial settings. They may be exposed to chemical, equipment, or toxic material hazards.

Salaries

Salaries for Engineering Technologists vary, depending on such factors as their education, experience, job duties, employer, industry, and geographical location. Specific information for this occupation is unavailable. They normally earn more than engineering technicians, whose annual salary generally ranges between $24,000 and $78,000.

Employment Prospects

Job openings mostly become available as Engineering Technologists transfer to other jobs, advance to higher positions, retire, or leave the workforce for various reasons. Opportunities are more favorable for technologists who keep up with new technologies and need less job training.

The demand for different engineering technology specialties is dependent on the industrial and business needs of local communities. Keep in mind that the job market overall for Engineering Technologists fluctuates with the state of the economy. For example, fewer jobs are available when the economy is facing a downturn.

Advancement Prospects

As Engineering Technologists gain experience, they are assigned to more complex projects as well as receive increasingly greater responsibilities. Those with supervisory and administrative skills may advance to such positions. Some of them move into positions in marketing, technical sales, and other business areas.

Some Engineering Technologists pursue advanced degrees in engineering technology to pursue teaching and research careers.

Education and Training

Engineering Technologists usually possess a bachelor's degree in engineering technology. Many of them earned their degree in a specific discipline, such as civil engineering technology, mechanical engineering technology, construction engineering technology, manufacturing engineering technology, or environmental engineering technology.

Like engineering programs, engineering technology programs are difficult academic programs. Engineering technology programs differ from engineering programs in that they provide students with less theory course work and more hands-on laboratory experience.

Many engineers prefer to hire candidates who have graduated from an engineering technology program that is accredited by ABET, Inc. (formerly known as the Accreditation Board for Engineering and Technologies).

Employers typically provide entry-level technologists with on-the-job training while working under the supervision and direction of experienced engineers. Many employers also give their new personnel formal classroom instruction.

Throughout their careers, Engineering Technologists enroll in continuing education and training programs to update their skills and keep up with advancements in their fields.

Special Requirements

In some states, Engineering Technologists can become licensed as professional engineers, but they are restricted to perform only certain activities. Employers in these states may prefer to hire Engineering Technologists who possess P.E. or engineer-in-training (E.I.T.) licenses. The P.E. licensure process consists of two stages. At the first level, qualifying individuals become E.I.Ts. After working several years under the supervision of licensed engineers, E.I.T.s become eligible to apply for the P.E. license.

In general, engineers who offer engineering services directly to the public or perform work that affects the life, health, or property of the public must be licensed as professional engineers. Licensing requirements vary with different states (as well as the territories and Washington, D.C.). For specific information, contact the board of engineering examiners for the jurisdiction where you wish to practice. See Appendix II for a list of boards.

Experience, Special Skills, and Personality Traits

In general, applicants do not need any prior work experience to obtain entry-level positions, although it is preferable that they have relevant experience. They may have gained their experience through internships, work-study programs, student research projects, or part-time employment.

Engineering Technologists must have effective problem-solving, communication, and writing skills to perform their various duties. Strong interpersonal and teamwork skills are also essential, as technologists must work well with colleagues, engineers, technicians, managers, and others from diverse backgrounds. In addition, Engineering Technologists need excellent self-management skills, including the ability to work independently, meet deadlines, handle stressful situations, follow and understand instructions, and prioritize multiple tasks.

Some personality traits that successful Engineering Technologists share are being creative, practical, responsible, ethical, cooperative, and self-motivated.

Unions and Associations

Many Engineering Technologists belong to professional associations to take advantage of networking opportunities, continuing education programs, job banks, and other professional services and resources. Many of them are members of the American Society of Certified Engineering Technicians, a national society that serves the specific interests of Engineering Technologists.

Many also join societies that serve their particular discipline. For example, some of the different engineering societies are:

- American Academy of Environmental Engineers
- American Institute of Aeronautics and Astronautics
- American Institute of Chemical Engineers
- American Society of Agricultural and Biological Engineers
- American Society of Civil Engineers
- ASME International (formerly the American Society of Mechanical Engineers)
- Biomedical Engineering Society
- Institute of Electrical and Electronics Engineers
- Institute of Industrial Engineers

For contact information for these organizations, see Appendix III.

Tips for Entry

1. While you are in high school, take math and science courses to prepare you for the course work you will be taking in an engineering technology program. Writing and public speaking courses are also helpful.
2. Research your college choices carefully. Be sure the college you pick offers the engineering technology discipline in which you want to specialize.
3. Some employers prefer to hire candidates who hold professional certification that is granted by the National Institute for Certification in Engineering Technologies (NICET). For more information about technologist certification, visit the NICET Web site, http://www.nicet.org.
4. Learn more about Engineering Technologists on the Internet. You might start by visiting the American Society of Certified Engineering Technicians Web site, http://www.ascet.org. For more links, see Appendix IV.

ENGINEERING TECHNICIAN

CAREER PROFILE

Duties: Provide technical support to engineers, scientists, and others; may be involved in research, product development, manufacturing, or another area; perform duties as required

Alternate Title(s): A title that reflects a specialty such as Aerospace Engineering Technician

Salary Range: $24,000 to $78,000

Employment Prospects: Good

Advancement Prospects: Fair

Prerequisites:

Education or Training—Associate degree in engineering technology; on-the-job training

Experience—Previous work experience generally required

Special Skills and Personality Traits—Communication, teamwork, interpersonal, reading, writing, math, computer, and self-management skills; creative, practical, cooperative, curious, detail-oriented, reliable, and adaptable

CAREER LADDER

```
┌─────────────────────────────────────┐
│   Senior Engineering Technician      │
└─────────────────────────────────────┘

┌─────────────────────────────────────┐
│      Engineering Technician          │
└─────────────────────────────────────┘

┌─────────────────────────────────────┐
│ Engineering Technician (entry-level) │
└─────────────────────────────────────┘
```

Position Description

Engineers design and build many wonderful and useful systems, machines, and structures, but such projects are often complex and require team effort. Without the other members of their teams, these projects would take much longer for engineers to complete. Among the skilled workers that comprise engineering teams are Engineering Technicians.

Engineering Technicians assist engineers, scientists, and engineering technologists in all phases of engineering work. These technical staffers are the hands-on experts who perform such tasks as installing, repairing, and testing. They solve technical problems, build and set up equipment, conduct experiments and record the results, collect data, make calculations, assist in design work, fabricate prototypes, and work in the area of quality control.

Some of their work overlaps that of engineering technologists, but their levels of education, expertise, job responsibilities, and salary ranges differ for the most part. For example, their entry-level qualifications are different: technicians have associate's degrees, whereas technologists have bachelor's degrees. Technologists help to design equipment and figure out how to use it; technicians do the

installing, testing, using, and repairing of the equipment. Technologists often supervise technicians. Technicians are more apt to do physically demanding work.

Engineering Technicians are knowledgeable about how to construct structures, build machines, and make various other items. They are adept at using tools and computers, including computer-aided design (CAD) equipment. Their mathematical background is in arithmetic, algebra, geometry, and statistics. They also have some knowledge of physics. Technicians draw and use blueprints, schematic drawings, and models. They know how to design, use, and repair machines. They understand manufacturing processes.

These skilled workers are employed in most of the engineering fields. Their job titles reflect their specific area of engineering concern. They specialize as civil engineering technicians, electronics engineering technicians, industrial engineering technicians, or mechanical engineering technicians, for example. In each of these fields, they fulfill such functions as installing, testing, and maintaining equipment; inspecting machines; conducting studies and tests; analyzing results; planning ways to improve production processes; calibrating equipment; diagnosing equipment malfunctions;

recording and interpreting test data; helping to develop new products; estimating project costs; conducting studies; inspecting facilities; and drawing sketches of parts for manufactured products.

Engineering Technicians begin their careers by performing routine tasks under the supervision and direction of engineers, scientists, technologists, or senior technicians. With experience, they perform more complex tasks with minimal supervision, and may become supervisors.

Engineering Technicians perform a wide range of tasks, many of which are specific to their occupation. During their careers, they:

- review blueprints or instructions for projects
- draw sketches according to specifications
- set up tests for prototypes or finished products
- use computers to analyze, interpret, and record test data
- develop testing methods or techniques
- modify equipment in compliance with specifications or test results
- communicate with team members about design changes
- assess which materials are needed for a project
- draw diagrams of work procedures
- follow engineering designs to make prototypes
- maintain and repair test instruments
- evaluate prototypes or finished products for quality
- prepare written reports
- observe workers' use of equipment and their on-the-job performance
- assist customers

Jobs for these technicians are found in many industries wherever engineering teams are needed. Engineering Technicians may work indoors at laboratories, offices, and factories, or at such outdoor settings as construction sites. They may be exposed to hazardous equipment or materials and may be required to wear protective gear.

Civil engineering technicians may travel to construction sites. Industrial technicians may work day, evening, or night shifts. Most of these skilled workers put in 40-hour workweeks. On occasion they are required to work overtime to meet deadlines.

Salaries

Salaries for Engineering Technicians vary, depending on such factors as their education, experience, employer, industry, and geographical location. The U.S. Bureau of Labor Statistics (BLS) reported in its November 2004 *Occupational Employment Statistics* survey the following estimated annual salary ranges for most Engineering Technicians in these disciplines:

- aerospace engineering technicians, $34,810 to $74,740
- civil engineering technicians, $24,130 to $58,460

- electrical and electronic engineering technicians, $29,050 to $69,090
- electro-mechanical technicians, $28,460 to $64,310
- environmental engineering technicians, $24,280 to $64,520
- industrial engineering technicians, $29,590 to $78,300
- mechanical engineering technicians, $29,040 to $67,070
- all other engineering technicians, $30,550 to $72,190

Employment Prospects

Major employers of Engineering Technicians include architectural and engineering services firms; local, state, and federal government agencies; and electronic components and accessories companies. The BLS reported in its November 2004 OES survey that over 513,000 Engineering Technicians were employed in the United States.

Employment growth for Engineering Technicians is expected to increase by 9 to 17 percent through 2014, according to the BLS. Job growth varies within the different specialties, as well as in the different industries. For example, employment of environmental engineering technicians is expected to increase by 18 to 26 percent, partly due to increased demand for environmental protection and partly due to increased recognition of these technicians as a separate occupation.

In addition to job growth, opportunities will become available as Engineering Technicians transfer to other jobs, advance to higher positions, retire, or leave the workforce for various reasons. Keep in mind that the job market for Engineering Technicians fluctuates with the economy. During recessions, many employers hire fewer employees and sometimes lay off personnel.

Advancement Prospects

Engineering Technicians can advance to senior or supervisory positions. Most of these technicians realize advancement by earning higher wages and receiving more complex assignments. Those interested in becoming engineers, architects, or engineering technologists can earn appropriate college degrees.

Education and Training

Employers usually prefer to hire applicants for entry-level positions who possess at least an associate's degree in engineering technology.

Individuals can earn an associate's degree in engineering technology from a two-year college or a bachelor's degree from a four-year college or a university. Graduates of four-year programs are usually hired for engineering technologist positions, which are applied engineering jobs.

Entry-level Engineering Technicians typically receive on-the-job training while working under the guidance and supervision of experienced personnel. Some employers also provide technicians with formal classroom instruction.

Throughout their careers, these technicians enroll in continuing education programs and training programs to update their skills and keep up with advancements in their fields.

Experience, Special Skills, and Personality Traits

Although prior work experience is not needed for entry-level positions, employers prefer to hire candidates who have some related experience. Entry-level candidates may have gained their experience through internships, work-study programs, or employment. Having previous experience within an employer's industry is also preferable.

Engineering Technicians must have excellent communication, teamwork, and interpersonal skills, as they need to work well with colleagues, managers, professionals, and others from diverse backgrounds. In addition, they need strong reading, writing, math, and computer skills for their job. Engineering Technicians should also have self-management skills, such as the ability to work independently, handle stressful situations, meet deadlines, and prioritize multiple tasks.

Some personality traits that Engineering Technicians have in common include being creative, practical, cooperative, curious, detail-oriented, reliable, and adaptable.

Unions and Associations

Engineering Technicians can join local, state, or national professional associations to take advantage of networking opportunities, continuing education programs, certification, and other professional resources and services. For example, some technicians belong to the American Society of Certified Engineering Technicians, a national society that specifically serves the interests of Engineering Technicians. For contact information, see Appendix III.

Tips for Entry

1. While you are in high school, take science and math courses to prepare you for your college training in engineering technology.

2. Many employers prefer to hire candidates who earned a degree from a program accredited by ABET, Inc.

3. Research engineering technology programs carefully. What kind of job placements have they made? Do they offer the type of training you want? Do they have courses related to the engineering specialty in which you want to work? How qualified are their instructors? What kind of job placement assistance do they provide? What are the facilities like? How up-to-date is their technology?

4. Enhance your employability by keeping up with new technologies.

5. Use the Internet to learn more about Engineering Technicians. You might start by visiting the American Society of Certified Engineering Technicians Web site, http://www.ascet.org. For more links, see Appendix IV.

DRAFTER

Duties: Create blueprints or mechanical drawings from design specifications; perform duties as required

Alternate Title(s): Computer-Aided Design and Drafting (CADD) Technician, CADD Operator; A title that reflects a specialty, such as Mechanical Drafter

Salary Range: $25,000 to $81,000

Employment Prospects: Fair

Advancement Prospects: Fair

Prerequisites:

Education or Training—High school diploma; on-the-job training

Experience—Previous work experience generally required

Special Skills and Personality Traits—Drawing, math, computer, problem-solving, teamwork, interpersonal and communication skills; detail-oriented, dependable, persistent, and self-motivated

```
┌─────────────────────────┐
│      Senior Drafter     │
└─────────────────────────┘

┌─────────────────────────┐
│         Drafter         │
└─────────────────────────┘

┌─────────────────────────┐
│      Junior Drafter     │
└─────────────────────────┘
```

Position Description

Drafting, or mechanical drawing, is a type of drawing characterized by precision and accuracy. Every manufactured item begins as a design or mechanical drawing. Buildings, highways, bridges, and other structures are also designed and meticulously drawn before construction begins. These drawings are also known as blueprints. Men and women called Drafters create them from design specifications provided by engineers, architects, and designers.

Drafters make all manufacturing and building possible. Their completed blueprints show objects or buildings from various angles. They are drawn exactly to scale and include written specifications such as angles, dimensions, and other measurements. They show how the various components of a product or structure fit together. Engineers use these mechanical drawings to precisely construct their finished products exactly as they had visualized them. A project may require only one drawing or hundreds of drawings, depending on the complexity of the product or structure.

Drafters understand mathematics and other technical principles and apply them to their work. Traditionally, they made blueprints by hand with the aid of pencils, pens, rulers, T-squares, protractors, compasses, and other drafting

tools while sitting at drawing tables. Today, most Drafters use computer-aided design and drafting (CADD) systems to create their work. CADD systems allow Drafters to create drawings electronically and store them on computer disks or hard drives. They can quickly make changes to their drawings or duplicate them with these systems. Some Drafters work on networked systems that enable several people to work on different parts of a complex drawing. They print their drawings on laser or inkjet printers unless the work is large. In that case, Drafters use machines called pen plotters or electrostatic plotters. Occasionally they print drawings on photographic film.

Drafters may specialize in several ways. They may utilize certain skills or use specific computer applications. They may work in particular industries or choose to work on specific types of engineering projects. For example:

- aeronautical drafters create engineering drawings to be used in the manufacturing of airplanes or missiles, along with their related components
- architectural drafters draw architectural and structural features; they may specialize in certain structures such as office buildings or homes

- civil drafters create drawings and maps to be used in major construction projects such as highways, flood control projects, wastewater systems, and bridges
- electrical drafters prepare diagrams for wiring systems in buildings and the electrical power distribution system
- electronics drafters draw and diagram the components and circuitry of electronic devices
- mechanical drafters create drawings and assembly diagrams of machines and machine parts
- pipeline drafters make drawings that are used by the oil and gas industries to build their refineries, lay out their oilfields, and create piping systems

All Drafters are expected to consistently produce accurate and properly detailed work. They are also responsible for maintaining their skills and working relationships. Furthermore, Drafters complete certain tasks on a regular basis. For example, they:

- prepare preliminary sketches of designs before working on final drawings
- check such specifications as product dimensions, materials, and how product components relate to each other
- confer with engineers to change drawings as needed
- troubleshoot problems for co-workers
- produce statistical charts and graphs
- keep up-to-date with developments in CADD software
- read building code books to stay current with regulations
- write project reports and other documents, including correspondence with clients
- perform calculations when creating or modifying drawings

Drafters work for engineering and architectural service companies. They also work in the manufacturing industry for companies that produce machines, fabricated metals, electrical equipment, and other manufactured goods.

They work in office settings, where they must sit and concentrate at drawing tables or computer terminals for long time intervals. Their close-up work and long hours at computer terminals may make them susceptible to eyestrain or repetitive motion injuries.

Drafters may work on several projects simultaneously. They work with other drafters and office personnel, as well with engineers or architects. Civil Drafters occasionally leave the office to visit construction sites.

Forty-hour weeks are standard with Drafters. Some of them may routinely put in as many as 55 hours each week. Some of them work part time.

Salaries

Salaries for Drafters vary, depending on such factors as their education, experience, employer, and geographical location. The U.S. Bureau of Labor Statistics (BLS) reported in its November 2004 *Occupational Employment Statistics* survey the following estimated annual salary ranges for most drafters in these disciplines:

- architectural and civil drafters, $25,960 to $59,100
- electrical and electronics drafters, $29,110 to $73,160
- mechanical drafters, $28,210 to $68,110
- all other drafters, $25,230 to $81,450

Employment Prospects

According to the BLS's November 2004 OES survey, nearly 230,000 Drafters were employed in the United States. Architectural and civil Drafters held over 40 percent of the drafting jobs. Mechanical Drafters held about 76,000 jobs, while electrical and electronics Drafters held almost 32,000 jobs.

Job openings usually become available as Drafters transfer to other jobs, are promoted, retire, or leave the workforce for various reasons. Opportunities for the various drafting specialties vary from location to location, as the demand is dependent upon the needs of local industry.

Job growth for this occupation, as reported by the BLS, is expected to increase slowly—by 0 to 8 percent—through 2014. Drafters who have postsecondary training and are experienced in CADD systems should have the best opportunities, according to some experts in the field.

Drafters are mostly employed in industries that are highly influenced by the state of the economy. For example, when the economy is experiencing a downturn, employers hire fewer Drafters, and oftentimes lay off personnel.

Advancement Prospects

Most Drafters realize advancement by earning higher wages and receiving more complex assignments. Drafters with leadership skills may be promoted to supervisory and management positions. With additional training and experience, drafters can also advance to designer positions. Those interested in becoming engineers, architects, or engineering technologists can pursue appropriate college degrees. Entrepreneurial Drafters can eventually become independent practitioners or owners of contracting or consulting firms.

Education and Training

Minimally, Drafters need to possess at least a high school or general equivalency diploma. Many of them also have an associate degree in drafting technology or another related field.

Most employers prefer to hire applicants for entry-level or journey positions who have completed postsecondary training programs in drafting, which are offered by community colleges, private technical schools, colleges, or universities. Many also accept applicants who obtained their technical training while serving in the military.

Employers typically provide Drafters with on-the-job training while working under the supervision and guidance of experienced personnel. Some companies also give trainees formal classroom instruction.

Throughout their careers, Drafters enroll in continuing education programs and training programs to update their skills and keep up with advancements in their fields.

Experience, Special Skills, and Personality Traits

In general, applicants do not need prior work experience to obtain entry-level positions, but many employers prefer applicants who have some practical experience. They may have gained experience through internships, work-study programs, or part-time employment. Many employers also seek applicants who have backgrounds in computer-aided design and drafting techniques.

Drafters need adequate drawing, math, computer, problem-solving, and teamwork skills for their job. They also must have effective interpersonal and communication skills, as they work closely with colleagues, managers, professionals, and others from diverse backgrounds. Some personality traits that successful Drafters share include being detail-oriented, dependable, persistent, and self-motivated.

Unions and Associations

Drafters can join professional societies at the local, state, or national level to take advantage of networking opportunities, continuing education programs, certification, and other professional services and resources. For example, the American Design Drafting Association International is a national organization that serves the interests of this profession. For contact information, see Appendix III.

Tips for Entry

1. Are you in high school? Find out if your school offers a youth apprenticeship program that places juniors and seniors in paid work-experience settings. They receive on-the-job training in a specific occupation such as drafting.

2. Some employers offer apprenticeships in drafting to young people who are at least 16 years old and possess a high school or general equivalency diploma. An apprenticeship program usually lasts for a few years. Apprentices, or trainees, are hired for full-time employment that consists of on-the-job training and classroom instruction. To find out what may be available in your community, talk to a high school or community college counselor. You might also be able to get information from a job counselor at your state employment services office.

3. Some drafters enhance their employability by obtaining the professional certification granted by the American Design Drafting Association International.

4. Use the Internet to learn more about Drafters. You might start by visiting the American Design Drafting Association International Web site, http://www.adda.org. For more links, see Appendix IV.

SURVEYOR

CAREER PROFILE

Duties: Take accurate measurements of areas on the surface of the earth for creating maps, establishing boundaries, building roads, and other purposes; perform duties as required

Alternate Title(s): Land Surveyor; a title that reflects a specialty such as GIS Analyst or Forensic Surveyor

Salary Range: $25,000 to $74,000

Employment Prospects: Fair

Advancement Prospects: Fair

Prerequisites:

    Education or Training—A degree or certificate in surveying or another related field; on-the-job training

    Experience—Previous work experience generally preferred

    Special Skills and Personality Traits—Math, computer, research, communication, interpersonal, and teamwork skills; precise, detail-oriented, collaborative, productive, honest, adaptable, discreet, and punctual

    Special Requirements—Professional surveyor (P.S.) licensure required

CAREER LADDER

```
┌─────────────────────────────┐
│      Senior Surveyor        │
└─────────────────────────────┘

┌─────────────────────────────┐
│         Surveyor            │
└─────────────────────────────┘

┌─────────────────────────────┐
│      Surveyor Trainee       │
└─────────────────────────────┘
```

Position Description

Surveyors quietly contribute greatly to our society, and are vital to several engineering fields, including civil engineering in particular. These professionals measure areas of our planet from vantage points above the earth, on the ground, and below its surface; from the highest mountains to the bottoms of the oceans; from rural areas to city neighborhoods. Their measurements are used to create maps, establish boundaries, and accurately build roads, buildings, and other structures.

Surveying is an ancient profession. The Egyptians used surveying techniques to build the great pyramids and establish farm boundaries. Over the centuries, and particularly over recent decades, Surveyors have refined their techniques and the technologies of surveying. As a consequence, today's Surveyors take more accurate measurements with such sophisticated equipment as satellites and computers.

The most important tool that Surveyors use is called the total station. It includes the small telescope on a tripod that most of us readily recognize. The telescope is equipped with an electronic laser device that measures distances. The laser beam is aimed at a prism atop a pole situated at a target point; the prism reflects the beam back to the total station, where the beam's elapsed travel time is recorded. The entire apparatus can pivot both horizontally and vertically. Some of these devices can calculate differences in elevation.

Occasionally, Surveyors use a steel tape to specify distances. They also use the Global Positioning System (GPS) to measure distances. GPS satellites send signals that indicate where they are in relation to specific points on earth where receivers are placed. Computers use the data from these receivers to determine the distance between two points. Surveyors also make use of such technologies as aerial photography and geographic information systems (GIS).

These professionals use mathematics to perform their work. They are well versed in algebra, basic calculus, geometry, and trigonometry. They are also knowledgeable about legal issues pertaining to surveys, property, and contracts. They are adept with handling sensitive equipment. Surveyors are occasionally required to testify as expert witnesses in courts or other legal venues. Architects, cartographers, and other professionals use their services. They may find employment opportunities in the fields of business, research, computers, mapmaking, and so forth.

Surveyors may specialize in specific types of surveying. Some of these specialists are:

- topographic surveyors, who measure the shape of land features (such as valleys and mountains) and map their locations
- hydrographic surveyors, who measure and map the shape of underwater features
- geodesists, who ascertain the size and shape of our planet to obtain precise measurements of the Earth's surface for the purpose of creating accurate maps
- construction surveyors, who take measurements at all types of construction sites
- mine surveyors, who take surveys for mine locations, subways, underground facilities, and tunnels
- boundary surveyors, who measure, mark, and map boundary lines for property owners
- remote sensing analysts, who monitor changes in land features by using data gathered from satellite and aerial systems
- GIS analysts, who use geographic information systems to develop maps for special purposes, such as for deciding where to build new roads
- forensic surveyors, who assist in legal and legal-related cases where precise measurements are needed to resolve issues pertaining to such matters as crimes, lawsuits, and industrial or automobile accidents

Surveyors plan and schedule fieldwork and direct the work of survey parties. They select previously established reference points and precisely locate key features of the survey area. They record the results of their surveys, confirm their data's accuracy, and prepare maps and reports. They research legal records for previous survey work in pertinent locations. Surveyors communicate regularly with engineers, architects, clients, and other people involved in their projects. They estimate the cost of the jobs with which they are involved. They supervise and train survey technicians and assistants. They ensure that the work they perform is accurate and complete in every detail so that engineers have complete information.

Surveyors work in indoor and outdoor settings, depending on their principal area of concern. They often work alone when compiling documentation but frequently work with technicians and assistants when conducting surveys.

Surveying can be strenuous work. They often stand for long intervals. They frequently must walk long distances or hike up hills while toting heavy instruments and related equipment. Surveyors often have long commutes to their work sites. They may be required to relocate temporarily.

They usually work 40 hours per week but may work longer hours when weather conditions are optimal for fieldwork.

Salaries
Salaries for Surveyors vary, depending on such factors as their education, experience, employer, and geographical location. According to the November 2004 *Occupational Employment Statistics* (OES) survey by the U.S. Bureau of Labor Statistics (BLS), the estimated annual salary for most Surveyors ranged between $25,030 and $73,580.

Employment Prospects
The BLS reported in its November 2004 OES survey that an estimated 51,960 Surveyors were employed in the United States. The highest levels of employment for this occupation were found in the architectural and engineering services industry, which employed over 75 percent of all Surveyors. The next largest employers were local government, state government, and the construction industry. Surveyors also find employment in federal agencies such as the U.S. Geological Survey, the Bureau of Land Management, and the Army Corps of Engineers. Others work for the mining, oil, construction, and utility industries. Some Surveyors are self-employed.

The BLS reports that job growth for this occupation should increase by 9 to 17 percent through 2014. Opportunities are expected to grow in such nontraditional areas as natural resource exploration, mapping, urban planning, and emergency preparedness. In addition, Surveyors will be needed to replace those who retire, are promoted, or transfer to other occupations.

Advancement Prospects
As Surveyors gain experience, they are assigned to more complex projects as well as receive increasingly greater responsibilities. Some advance by becoming technical specialists, while others are promoted to supervisory and management positions, which usually involve less fieldwork. Individuals with entrepreneurial ambitions can become independent consultants or owners of technical or consulting firms.

Education and Training
Several formal surveyor-training options are available. Individuals can enroll in a one-, two-, or three-year program in surveying or surveying technology that is offered by a community college, vocational school, or private institute. Upon completion of a program, students earn either a certificate or an associate's degree. Another option for individuals is to pursue a bachelor's degree in surveying.

With the recent technological advances in the field, many employers prefer to hire candidates who possess bachelor's degrees. Also, keep in mind that more states are requiring that licensed Surveyors have a bachelor's degree in surveying, civil engineering, or another related field.

Entry-level Surveyors typically receive on-the-job training while working under the supervision and guidance of experienced personnel.

Throughout their careers, Surveyors enroll in continuing education programs and training programs to update their skills and keep up with advancements in their fields.

Special Requirements

Surveyors are required to possess professional surveyor (P.S.) licensure where they practice. In some jurisdictions, another title such as land surveyor (L.S.) or professional land surveyor (P.L.S.) is used. Every state and territory, as well as Washington, D.C., has its own licensing requirements. In general, applicants must meet educational and experience requirements as well as pass a written examination. For specific information contact the board of surveying examiners for the area where you wish to practice. See Appendix II for a list of boards.

Experience, Special Skills, and Personality Traits

Entry-level candidates should have work experience related to the positions for which they apply. They may have gained their experience through internships, work-study programs, or part-time employment.

To perform well at their job, Surveyors must have effective math, computer, and research skills. They also need strong communication skills, including the ability to use hand signals. In addition, Surveyors need excellent interpersonal and teamwork skills, as they must work well with colleagues, managers, professionals, and others from diverse backgrounds. Being precise, detail-oriented, collaborative, productive, honest, adaptable, discreet, and punctual are some personality traits that successful Surveyors share.

Unions and Associations

Many Surveyors belong to local, state, or national societies to take advantage of networking opportunities, continuing education programs, certification, and other professional services and resources. At the national level, Surveyors might join such professional associations as the American Congress on Surveying and Mapping, the National Society of Professional Surveyors, the American Association for Geodetic Surveying, or the National Association of County Surveyors. For contact information, see Appendix III.

Tips for Entry

1. While you are in high school, get a part-time or volunteer position as a surveying assistant to get an idea of a Surveyor's job and whether it is one you would like to have.
2. Enhance your employability by keeping up with technologies as they emerge.
3. Contact employers directly about current or future job vacancies.
4. Learn more about Surveyors on the Internet. You might start by visiting these Web sites: American Congress on Surveying and Mapping, http://www.acsm.net; and Land Surveyor Reference Page, http://www.lsrp.com. For more links, see Appendix IV.

ALTERNATIVE CAREERS FOR ENGINEERS

PROFESSOR

CAREER PROFILE

Duties: Provide instruction in engineering or engineering technology courses; may conduct basic or applied research; perform duties as required

Alternate Title(s): Instructor, Assistant Professor, Associate Professor

Salary Range: $39,000 to $124,000

Employment Prospects: Fair

Advancement Prospects: Fair

Prerequisites:

   Education or Training—Doctoral degree

   Experience—Previous teaching experience needed; professional experience may be required for engineering technology instructional positions

   Special Skills and Personality Traits—Interpersonal, communication, presentation, management, and organizational skills; creative, inspirational, enthusiastic, dedicated, flexible, and self-motivated

CAREER LADDER

```
┌─────────────────────────────┐
│          Professor          │
└─────────────────────────────┘


┌─────────────────────────────┐
│     Associate Professor     │
└─────────────────────────────┘


┌─────────────────────────────┐
│     Assistant Professor     │
└─────────────────────────────┘


┌─────────────────────────────┐
│          Instructor         │
└─────────────────────────────┘
```

Position Description

Engineering and engineering technology Professors teach the future generations of engineers, technologists, and technicians. They are responsible for educating college and university students who are seeking degrees in their fields of interest, such as civil, chemical, aerospace, biomedical, industrial, electrical, or mechanical engineering or engineering technology.

Engineering Professors are engaged in training various types of engineers. These educators work in four-year colleges and universities where they teach courses in undergraduate and graduate programs. Students who complete undergraduate engineering programs earn bachelor's degrees, while students in graduate programs earn master's and doctoral degrees.

Engineering technology Professors are involved in training students to become technicians and technologists—essential members of the engineering team. These instructors work in two-year colleges (also known as community colleges or technical colleges) and four-year colleges. In two-year colleges, students can earn an associate degree in an engineering technology field, such as mechani-

cal technology or aerospace technology. At the four-year college level, students can earn a bachelor's degree in their chosen field.

Professors are assigned to teach courses that are part of a prescribed curriculum within their department. For each of their courses, Professors are responsible for developing a course syllabus that outlines the topics that they will be teaching. Their responsibilities also include preparing class lectures and lab work.

The format of their classes varies with each course. For example, a Professor might facilitate graduate students in small seminars, while another professor might lecture to hundreds of students in a large lecture hall. Some professors use cable, closed-circuit television, or the Internet to provide instruction to students.

Professors perform a variety of teaching duties, which vary each day. Preparing lectures, planning laboratory experiments, creating examinations, and grading student papers are a few examples of their various tasks. Professors also supervise students with their research projects. In addition, Professors hold regularly scheduled office hours to meet with students to advise them about academic and career matters. Many Professors also improve communication with students through the use of electronic mail and their own Web sites, where the Professors post schedules, class notes, and other pertinent information.

Many Professors, particularly at four-year colleges and universities, are also responsible for conducting research in their areas of interest. They might engage in basic research projects to gain new knowledge and understanding about subject matter, or they might be involved in applied research, which is the application of basic research to create or improve products, structures, processes, and systems. Some of their research duties include designing experiments, performing tests, gathering and analyzing data, preparing reports, planning work schedules, attending meetings, and supervising research and lab assistants. They are also expected to publish the results of their research through scholarly journals, books, or electronic media.

Research Professors are responsible for seeking funding for their projects, which covers overhead costs, staff salaries, buying equipment and supplies, and so forth. This involves such tasks as identifying funding sources (such as government agencies and private corporations) and preparing grant proposals. Professors often collaborate on projects with colleagues from within their discipline, as well as from other disciplines.

All Professors, from two-year colleges to research universities, are required to perform service on and off campus. Many Professors work with student organizations. Many of them serve on academic or administrative committees that handle policies, curriculum, budgets, hiring, and other departmental or institutional matters. In addition, many Professors serve on committees, boards, panels, commissions, and other advisory groups to community agencies, government agencies, nonprofit organizations, corporations, and other institutions.

Professors are expected to stay up-to-date with developments in their field. They network with colleagues; read current books, journals, and other publications; and participate in professional conferences.

Professors have a flexible work schedule and typically work more than 40 hours a week. They often work evenings and weekends to perform their various teaching, research, and service duties.

Salaries

Salaries for Professors vary, depending on such factors as their education, experience, employer, and geographical location. Part-time or adjunct instructors typically earn less than full-time Professors. According to the November 2004 *Occupational Employment Statistics* (OES) survey by the U.S. Bureau of Labor Statistics (BLS), the estimated annual salary for most Professors ranged between $39,430 and $124,140.

Many Professors receive additional earnings through consulting work, writing articles and books for publication, and teaching courses for professional associations or other organizations.

Employment Prospects

The BLS reported in its November 2004 OES survey that about 34,410 engineering teachers were employed in colleges and universities in the United States.

The job growth for postsecondary teachers is predicted to increase by 27 percent or more through 2014, according to the BLS. Keep in mind that this refers to postsecondary teachers in all academic disciplines in two-year colleges, four-year colleges, and universities. In addition to job growth, Professors will be needed to replace those who retire, advance to higher positions, or transfer to other occupations. Some experts report that more opportunities should be available in the next few years as many professors are becoming eligible for retirement.

Competition is tight for tenure-track positions. Opportunities are better for limited-term appointments. In recent years, colleges and universities have been hiring part-time (or adjunct) instructors to teach one to three courses per term.

Advancement Prospects

Tenure-track faculty begin their careers as instructors or assistant professors. After serving a specific number of years, their academic, research, and service records are reviewed to determine if they should be granted tenure. When Professors are granted tenure, they cannot be fired without just cause and due process. With tenure, assistant professors can rise through the ranks as associate professors and full professors. Those with managerial and administrative ambitions can seek positions as department chairs, academic deans, administrative directors, provosts, and presidents.

Education and Training

Engineering Professors must possess doctoral degrees in their chosen fields to teach in four-year colleges and universities, especially for tenure-track positions. Schools sometimes hire strong applicants with master's degrees for hard-to-fill or temporary positions. A master's degree is the minimum requirement to teach in two-year colleges, but many professors have doctoral degrees.

Students are required to dedicate several years of academic of work to earn a doctoral degree. First, students earn a bachelor's degree in an engineering program that usually takes four to five years to complete. Next, they earn a master's degree, which may be a one- or two-year program, and then complete a doctorate program, which may be another four to seven years of study. Doctoral candidates must complete a dissertation on original research within their major field of study.

Many doctoral graduates spend two or more years completing postdoctoral training before accepting a permanent position.

Experience, Special Skills, and Personality Traits

Employers seek applicants who show that they have the capacity to be both excellent teachers and researchers. Applicants should have previous teaching experience, which they may have gained as graduate teaching assistants, lecturers, or adjunct instructors. Depending on the employer, applicants for positions in engineering technology programs may be required to have several years of professional experience.

Engineering Professors need excellent interpersonal, communication, and presentation skills, as they must work effectively with students, colleagues, administrators, community leaders, and the general public. Having strong management and organizational skills is also essential. Some personality traits that successful engineering Professors share include being creative, inspirational, enthusiastic, dedicated, flexible, and self-motivated.

Unions and Associations

Engineering Professors belong to various societies at the local, state, and national levels to take advantage of networking opportunities, publications, and other professional resources and services. Many are members of the American Society for Engineering Education, which serves the interests of engineering educators. In addition, engineering Professors join societies that serve their particular disciplines, such as the American Society of Agricultural and Biological Engineers, the American Institute of Chemical Engineers, or the Institute of Electrical and Electronics Engineers.

Some Professors are members of special-focus associations such as the Society of Women Engineers, the National Society of Black Engineers, the Society of Hispanic Professional Engineers, and the National Society of Professional Engineers. Furthermore, engineering Professors may join such academic societies as the National Association of Scholars and the American Association of University Professors.

For contact more information for all of the organizations, see Appendix III.

Tips for Entry

1. The Preparing Future Faculty (PFF) program provides graduate students with opportunities to gain teaching experience in academic settings. For further information, visit the PFF Web site at http://www.preparing-faculty.org.
2. Many colleges and universities maintain a list of qualified candidates for adjunct or temporary positions. Once you are on a list, contact the school frequently. Sometimes schools need to hire staff immediately to replace instructors who have taken permanent teaching positions.
3. Check with professional societies about academic job announcements. Many of them post job listings at their Web sites.
4. Use the Internet to learn more about teaching in higher education. You might start by visiting these Web sites: American Society for Engineering Education, http://www.asee.org; and The Chronicle of Higher Education, http://chronicle.com. To learn about other links, see Appendix IV.

ATTORNEY

CAREER PROFILE

Duties: Manage clients' personal and business legal affairs; provide clients with legal advice; represent clients before courts and administrative hearings; perform duties as required

Alternate Title(s): Lawyer; Associate, Partner; a title that reflects a practice specialty such as Patent Attorney or Employment Lawyer

Salary Range: $48,000 to $146,000 +

Employment Prospects: Good

Advancement Prospects: Good

Prerequisites:

    Education or Training—Juris doctorate (J.D.); a bachelor's degree in any field

    Experience—Completion of a law clerkship preferred

    Special Skills and Personality Traits—Writing, communication, research, interviewing, interpersonal, and self-management skills; trustworthy, persistent, creative, analytical, and flexible

    Special Requirements—Be a licensed attorney; must be registered to practice before federal courts or administrative offices

CAREER LADDER

```
┌─────────────────────────────────────┐
│  Senior Associate, Senior Staff      │
│  Attorney, or Solo Practitioner      │
└─────────────────────────────────────┘

┌─────────────────────────────────────┐
│      Associate or Staff Attorney     │
└─────────────────────────────────────┘

┌─────────────────────────────────────┐
│         Junior Associate or          │
│         Junior Staff Attorney        │
└─────────────────────────────────────┘
```

Position Description

Many engineers, as well as engineering graduates, transfer their training and backgrounds into successful careers as Attorneys. The practice of law covers a wide range of areas, such as intellectual property law, patent law, corporate law, family law, employment law, tax law, criminal law, aviation law, cyberspace law, nuclear law, and environmental law. Attorneys usually concentrate on practicing in one or more areas of law.

Attorneys advise clients—who may be individuals, small businesses, large corporations, nonprofit organizations, government agencies, educational institutions, or others—of their legal rights and obligations. They perform a variety of legal services for their clients. For example, they draft wills, set up trust funds, review business contracts, lobby legislators, negotiate settlements, provide mediation, and defend their clients in court. Because Attorneys handle personal and business legal matters for their clients, they establish a special relationship with each client and are obligated to put each client's interest above their own.

In addition to specializing in practice areas, many Attorneys specialize as transactional or litigation lawyers. Transactional lawyers help clients with legal transactions such as business contracts, insurance claims, estate planning, property sales, and company mergers. Litigation lawyers, on the other hand, represent clients in court trials, administrative hearings, or alternative conflict resolution procedures. As litigation specialists, they are responsible for preparing cases for trials or hearings, developing legal strategies, handling negotiations and settlements, and, if necessary, appealing court decisions.

Attorneys are employed in different settings. Many work as associates or partners in law firms, which usually specialize in several practice areas. Some Attorneys work in corporate legal departments as in-house counsels. These lawyers have only one client—their employer, which may be a private company, government agency, educational institution, or nonprofit organization.

Many Attorneys work for local, state, and federal government agencies in various capacities, such as staff attorney, prosecutor, and public defender. Some lawyers are employed by public-interest organizations. They might work with legal assistance programs, which provide legal services to individuals on limited incomes, or with citizen action groups and social advocacy organizations for whom they advocate for legal reforms or specific social issues on behalf of the general public.

Other Attorneys are solo practitioners; they are self-employed. Unlike attorneys in law firms or corporate departments, solo practitioners can determine their own work schedule, the size of their caseload, and what types of new cases they will take. As small business owners, solo practitioners are responsible for their own office management and for generating new business.

Attorneys perform a variety of duties, which vary from day to day. For example, some of their tasks include communicating with clients, conducting research, reviewing legal documents, writing legal correspondence, and drafting legal documents. They are also responsible for keeping up with laws and regulations pertinent to their practice areas. In addition, many lawyers supervise paralegals, legal secretaries, and other legal support staff.

Many Attorneys perform pro bono (free) legal services from time to time on behalf of economically disadvantaged individuals.

Attorneys often work long and irregular hours to meet deadlines and complete tasks on their various clients' cases.

Salaries

Salaries for Attorneys vary, depending on such factors as their experience, position, practice area, employer, and geographical location. In general, government lawyers and solo practitioners earn less than associates and partners in large law firms. According to the November 2004 *Occupational Employment Statistics* (OES) survey by the U.S. Bureau of Labor Statistics (BLS), the estimated annual salary for most Attorneys ranged between $48,630 and $145,600.

The NALP's *2005 Associate Salary Survey* reported that median salaries for first year associates ranged from $67,500 (in firms with two to 25 lawyers) to $125,000 (in firms of more than 500 lawyers); and for eighth-year associates, from $109,000 to $181,500.

Employment Prospects

The BLS reports that job growth for Attorneys should increase by 9 to 17 percent through 2014. Much of the growth is expected to be for salaried positions. The job competition is strong for both entry-level and experienced positions in the different law settings—law firms, government

agencies, courts, corporations, and public interest. Among entry-level candidates, opportunities are best for those who have graduated from the top law schools with excellent academic records.

Advancement Prospects

In law firms, Attorneys rise through the ranks from junior associate to partner. As partners, Attorneys receive a share of the profits earned by their law firms. In government and corporate settings, Attorneys can advance to supervisory, managerial, and administrative positions.

Many Attorneys seek advancement by pursuing positions at other firms or organizations that offer higher pay, greater responsibilities, or more prestige. The top goal for some Attorneys is to become successful solo practitioners.

Attorneys can also follow other legal career paths to become judges, law professors, FBI special agents, politicians, lobbyists, and business executives.

Education and Training

Attorneys must have a juris doctor (J.D.) degree, which is granted after completing three or four years of law school. Many state bars require that Attorneys earn their J.D. degree from law schools accredited by the American Bar Association. Admission requirements vary among law schools, but all schools require that applicants possess a bachelor's degree (in any field) and submit their Law School Admission Test (LSAT) scores.

The competition to get into law school is strong, especially for the top schools such as Yale Law School, Harvard Law School, Stanford Law School, Columbia University School of Law, University of Chicago Law School, and Northwestern University School of Law. Law schools typically select applicants whose LSAT scores, undergraduate work, work experience, and other factors demonstrate an aptitude for the study of law.

Law students take required courses, such as contracts, torts, and constitutional law, during their first year and then choose elective courses in different areas of law during their last years of study. Students obtain practical experience by participating in legal clinics, moot courts, and practice trials.

Most employers provide their lawyers with in-house training and education programs. Many law firms have programs that team junior associates with experienced staff members.

Special Requirements

Attorneys must be licensed to practice law before a state court. Each state in the United States (as well as Washington, D.C., and each territory) has its own requirements for passing its state bar and maintaining licensure. For information, contact the state board of bar examiners that covers the jurisdiction where you wish to practice.

Attorneys who practice before federal courts or administrative offices, such as the U.S. Patent and Trademark Office, must be registered. Qualifications for bar admissions vary with the different federal courts and administrative offices.

Experience, Skills, and Personality Traits
Employers usually prefer to hire candidates for entry-level positions who have completed law clerkships in law firms, court systems, government agencies, or corporate legal departments. They also look for candidates who have strong backgrounds or training in the practice areas in which they will be working. For example, an intellectual property or patent law firm would usually prefer to hire candidates who have engineering (or science) training or background.

Attorneys must have excellent writing, communication, research, and interviewing skills to be effective in their work. Having strong interpersonal and self-management skills is also important. Being trustworthy, persistent, creative, analytical, and flexible are some personality traits that successful Attorneys share.

Unions and Associations
In many states, Attorneys are required to join their state bar association. Many professional associations serve the diverse interests of Attorneys at the local, state, and national levels. Membership in these societies is voluntary. As members of an association, Attorneys can take advantage of networking opportunities, continuing education programs, and other professional resources and services.

Professional societies that specifically serve the general interests of Attorneys include the American Bar Association, the National Lawyers Association, and the National Association of Women Lawyers. The American Intellectual Property Law Association, the National Association of Patent Practitioners, the National Employment Lawyers Association, and the Association of Trial Lawyers of America are a few examples of societies that serve the interests of Attorneys in specific practice areas.

Tips for Entry
1. Take courses in high school and college that can help you develop strong writing, reading, researching, speaking, and critical thinking skills.
2. Employers sometimes offer positions to law school graduates who have served clerkships with them.
3. Contact the human resources department of an organization to find out about job vacancies and selection procedures.
4. Learn as much as you can about a prospective employer and key people (such as partners) before going to a job interview. If the organization has a Web site, be sure to check all the links there.
5. Use the Internet to learn more about lawyers and becoming one. Some Web sites you might visit are: American Bar Association, http://www.abanet.org; and Hieros Gamos, http://www.hg.org. To learn about other links, see Appendix IV.

POLICY ANALYST

CAREER PROFILE

Duties: Conduct research on science and technology issues and problems and provide analyses to policy makers; perform duties as required

Alternate Title(s): Science and Technology Policy Analyst, Engineering Policy Analyst, Technology Policy Analyst; a title that reflects a specialty such as Environmental Policy Analyst, Budget Analyst, or Legislative Analyst

Salary Range: $36,000 to $96,000

Employment Prospects: Good

Advancement Prospects: Good

Prerequisites:

    Education or Training—Master's or doctoral degree in an engineering, science, or related field; fellowships

    Experience—Experience in or substantive knowledge about an engineering field; previous work experience in public policy generally preferred

    Special Skills and Personality Traits—Analytical, critical thinking, information management, communication, writing, research, teamwork, interpersonal, and networking skills; diplomatic, friendly, enthusiastic, curious, creative, objective, self-motivated, and collaborative

CAREER LADDER

```
┌─────────────────────────────────────┐
│         Senior Policy Analyst        │
└─────────────────────────────────────┘

┌─────────────────────────────────────┐
│            Policy Analyst            │
└─────────────────────────────────────┘

┌─────────────────────────────────────┐
│    Research Assistant or Associate   │
└─────────────────────────────────────┘
```

Position Description

What types of research should the government fund? If certain regulations were done away with, how would the environment be affected? How do you improve security against bioterrorism? What can be done to encourage more students to consider a career in engineering? Science and technology (S&T) questions such as these are addressed every day by policy makers in public, private, nonprofit, and nongovernmental organizations. They must make critical decisions, create laws, develop plans of actions, and establish policies about a wide range of S&T problems and issues, even though they do not have a technical background.

Helping policy makers create the most effective S&T policies for their organization—whether it be a small public-interest group or a large national government—are S&T Policy Analysts. These professionals are experts in such areas as energy, environmental protection, food supplies, nuclear waste disposal, nanotechnology, telecommunica-

tions, intellectual property, homeland security, defense, space exploration, genetic engineering, public health, engineering education, and international economic development. Many S&T Policy Analysts are in fact former engineers, scientists, and mathematicians. It is their job to educate policy makers about technical subject matter. Policy Analysts break down complex issues and problems and provide policy makers with accurate information and useful analyses so that they can make wise decisions.

S&T Policy Analysts work at the local, state, and federal levels of government for legislators, regulatory agencies, and other governmental agencies. They also work for private corporations, academic institutions, research institutes, think tanks, nonprofit organizations, public-interest groups, consulting firms, professional and trade associations, and other organizations that are concerned with science and technology policy. Some Policy Analysts are independent consultants.

Policy Analysts are assigned to projects on which they may work alone or with others. They are expected to complete and deliver their assignments on a timely basis. In addition, they must perform their assignments in an objective manner. In other words, they cannot put their own beliefs or ideas into their studies.

Their work involves much research on the issues or problems assigned to them. Before gathering information, Policy Analysts define and plan their projects according to the objectives of the policy makers. Next, they start gathering data. They read literature that may be in printed materials, in electronic databases, or on the Internet. They research pertinent laws, regulations, and policies. They also consult with various experts about the different aspects of the issue; these experts may be academicians, professionals, government officials, staff members, or researchers.

They sort through the information to determine which is most relevant and important to the issue or problem they are studying. Policy Analysts review, analyze, and interpret the information after which they begin to formulate potential solutions as well as anticipate possible consequences that may result from implementing their solutions. Policy Analysts then prepare concise written or oral reports of their findings and recommendations. They make sure that technical information is stated in terms that policy makers and other non-technical clients can easily understand.

Policy Analysts usually work in office settings. Their job requires them to interact with a variety of people—project team members, staff personnel, decision makers, subject-matter experts, and so forth—on a daily basis. They are sometimes under pressure to complete projects on tight schedules. It is not uncommon for them to work more than 40 hours a week to meet project deadlines.

Salaries

Salaries for Policy Analysts vary, depending on such factors as their education, experience, employer, and geographical location. Specific salary information for this occupation is unavailable, but Policy Analysts generally earn salaries similar to operation research analysts. The estimated annual salary for most operation research analysts ranged between $36,560 and $96,420, according to the U.S. Bureau of Labor Statistics in its November 2004 *Occupational Employment Statistics* survey.

Employment Prospects

The science and technology policy occupation is small. However, job opportunities are favorable for science and technology Policy Analysts, especially if they have a strong engineering or science background, according to some experts in the field. Traditionally, Policy Analysts in this area have not usually had any technical background, but because of rapid growth in technological development, employers seek technical candidates who can help them make sound decisions in many areas, such as military defense, national security, space exploration, environmental protection, public health, and telecommunications.

Along with opportunities in private, public, and nonprofit sectors in the United States, Policy Analysts can find employment in other countries that need assistance with addressing various science and technology policy issues. Job openings typically become available as Policy Analysts are promoted, retire, or transfer to other jobs. Employers will create additional positions to meet growing needs, as long as funding is available.

Advancement Prospects

Policy Analysts usually begin their careers as research assistants or policy assistants. From these positions, they can rise through the ranks as Policy Analysts to technical consultant to project director to senior professional staff positions. Those interested in policy-making positions can seek such positions as executive director or vice president, while those interested in teaching future policy professionals can become instructors in colleges and universities. Entrepreneurial individuals can become independent consultants or owners of consulting firms.

Policy Analysts typically move back and forth among government, industry, and academia, think tanks, and other organizations as they pursue their careers. A doctoral degree is usually needed for Policy Analysts to advance to senior-level positions or to have a career in higher education.

Education and Training

Entry-level applicants for science and technology Policy Analyst positions must hold at least a master's degree. They may have earned a degree in engineering, science, mathematics, computer science, or another technical field; or they may have earned a degree in public policy, science and technology studies, public administration, economics, business administration, or another related field.

Increasingly more universities are offering a science and technology policy program in which students can earn a master's or doctoral degree. In some schools, the S&T policy program is offered as a concentration within the field of public policy or public administration programs.

Recent graduates as well as engineers who have worked several years in their field obtain one or more fellowships to gain practical policy training. They may work in Congress, federal regulatory agencies, state executive offices, nongovernmental organizations, research and policy institutes, private corporations, or other settings. Fellowships usually last one or two years.

Throughout their careers, Policy Analysts enroll in continuing education programs to update their skills and keep up with advancements in their fields.

Experience, Special Skills, and Personality Traits

Employers typically seek candidates for entry-level positions who have practical experience (or substantive knowledge) in one or more technical fields, such as space, the environment, nanotechnology, or biomedical engineering. Candidates should also have a basic background in policy science and a familiarity with issues affecting policies in their fields of interest.

To be effective at their jobs, Policy Analysts must have superior analytical, critical thinking, information management, communication, writing, and research skills. Having excellent teamwork, interpersonal, and networking skills is also essential, as Policy Analysts must work well with colleagues, managers, clients, politicians, executive officers, and others from diverse backgrounds. Being diplomatic, friendly, enthusiastic, curious, creative, objective, self-motivated, and collaborative are some personality traits that successful Policy Analysts share.

Unions and Associations

Professional associations provide their members with the opportunity to network with colleagues as well as to take advantage of various professional resources and services such as job banks, publications, and current research findings. Many science and technology Policy Analysts are members of the American Association for the Advancement of Science and other engineering and science societies that serve their particular areas of interests. Many also belong to the Association for Public Policy Analysis and Management, which serves the general interests of policy profes-

sionals and institutions. (For contact information for these organizations, see Appendix III.)

Tips for Entry

1. In high school, you can gain valuable experience by participating in student government. If your local government office offers an internship program, take advantage of it. Congress and many state legislatures also have page programs for high school juniors and seniors.

2. As an undergraduate student, obtain an internship that exposes you to public policy activities. For example, Congress and state legislatures offer internship programs for undergraduate students to work in legislators' offices.

3. As a professional, you can get an idea if public policy may be for you by volunteering to serve on a policy committee in your professional association. Many employers have hired candidates who completed a policy fellowship with them. Among the many organizations that have policy fellowship programs is the American Association for the Advancement of Science (AAAS). For information, visit the AAAS Science and Technology Policy Fellowships webpage at http://fellowships.aaas.org.

4. Use the Internet to learn more about the field of science and technology policy. You might start by visiting these Web sites: The National Academies, http://www.nationalacademies.org; and U.S. Office of Science and Technology Policy, http://www.ostp.gov. For more links, see Appendix IV.

MANAGEMENT CONSULTANT

CAREER PROFILE

Duties: Provide business advice and solutions to clients on a consulting basis; conduct research and data analysis; perform other duties as required

Alternate Title(s): Management Analyst, Research Associate

Salary Range: $38,000 to $121,000

Employment Prospects: Excellent

Advancement Prospects: Good

Prerequisites:

Education or Training—A bachelor's degree for research associate positions; an advanced degree for junior consultants

Experience—Industry and management experience preferred

Special Skills and Personality Traits—Interpersonal, social, teamwork, leadership, time management, problem-solving, analytical, writing, and communication skills; friendly, self-motivated, hard-working, creative, curious, detail-oriented, assertive, and ethical

CAREER LADDER

```
┌─────────────────────────────────────┐
│     Senior Management Consultant     │
└─────────────────────────────────────┘

┌─────────────────────────────────────┐
│       Management Consultant          │
└─────────────────────────────────────┘

┌─────────────────────────────────────┐
│       Junior Consultant or           │
│       Research Associate             │
└─────────────────────────────────────┘
```

Position Description

Many individuals with engineering backgrounds have moved into successful careers as management analysts, or Management Consultants. They use their problem-solving skills to come up with creative solutions for helping organizations improve their structure, efficiency, or profits. Management Consultants offer their services on a contractual basis. Most of them are associates or partners of companies that offer management consulting services. Others are self-employed as independent contractors.

Management Consultants assist clients from small start-up firms to large established corporations as well as educational institutions, nonprofit organizations, government agencies, and foreign governments. They are experts in a wide array of business functions, such as business strategies, finance, marketing, human resources, manufacturing processes, environmental management, information technology, and electronic commerce. They may be involved in such projects as: reorganizing a client's organizational structure, determining the best location for a client to open a business, developing strategies for entering new marketplaces, examining the reasons a client's business is earning low profits, or designing new information technology systems.

Many organizations hire management consultants for various reasons. For example, they may not have staff members who can handle the problems, or they wish to hire additional personnel only on a temporary basis. Because they are not part of their clients' workforce, Management Consultants are able to remain objective and not be influenced by company politics.

Depending on the nature and complexity of a project, Management Consultants might be assigned to work on a project alone or as part of a team of consultants. They work closely with their clients' managers, and generally use the same procedure to handle every project. They first identify and assess their clients' problems and then conduct research, which involves reviewing materials and records from both internal and external sources, interviewing managers and staff members, and administering surveys and market studies.

After collecting sufficient data, the consultants analyze and interpret the information to develop recommendations and solutions for their clients. The consultants complete their process by preparing and submitting written or oral reports of their findings and recommendations. Clients sometimes retain Management Consultants to implement the solutions that they have suggested.

Novice consultants are typically assigned routine tasks while working under the guidance of senior personnel. As they gain experience, they are given greater responsibilities, such as handling a project on their own. Along with supervising junior consultants and other staff, senior consultants are involved in business development. They continually seek out new clients, as well as maintain strong relationships with existing clients.

Many Management Consultants specialize in a particular industry, as well as in certain functions. For example, an engineering Management Consultant might specialize in the planning, management, and restructuring of companies within the utilities industry.

Management Consultants work 40 hours per week but sometimes put in as much as 50 to 60 hours or more per week in order to complete tasks and meet deadlines. They divide their time between their offices and their clients' work sites, which may require traveling to other cities, states, or countries and spending several days or weeks there to perform their duties.

Salaries

Salaries for Management Consultants vary, depending on such factors as their education, experience, employer, and geographical location. The U.S. Bureau of Labor Statistics (BLS) reported in its November 2004 *Occupational Employment Statistics* (OES) survey that the estimated annual salary for most management analysts ranged between $37,990 and $121,390. The estimated annual mean wage for those working in management and technical consulting services was $89,070.

Employment Prospects

Management Consultants are employed by both small and large management consulting firms that may offer services to all or specific industries. Some firms also specialize in offering consulting services in only a few business functions. In addition, Management Consultants can find employment with companies that offer management consulting along with other business services. They can also find staff positions as management analysts with government agencies.

Job opportunities are available throughout the United States, particularly in large metropolitan areas. According to the BLS, the job growth for management analysts should increase by 18 to 24 percent through 2014, especially in large consulting firms that have international expertise and in firms that specialize in such areas as engineering,

biotechnology, information technology, health care, human resources, and marketing. Additionally, Management Consultants will be needed to replace individuals who transfer to other occupations, retire, or advance to higher positions.

Competition for available positions is strong because many college graduates and experienced professionals are attracted to the prestige, independent work, high salaries, and good benefits that come with the Management Consultant job.

Advancement Prospects

Management Consultants rise through the ranks as research associates (or junior consultants), consultants, managers, and partners. Having an advanced degree may be needed to obtain supervisory and management positions. Those with entrepreneurial ambitions become independent consultants or start their own consulting firms.

Education and Training

The research associate and junior consultant positions are both entry level at most firms. In general, research associates need at least a bachelor's degree, while junior consultants must possess a master's or doctoral degree. Many employers hire candidates who possess a master's in business administration; many also seek candidates who have a doctorate in an engineering or a science discipline.

Novice consultants receive on-the-job training while working under the guidance and supervision of senior Management Consultants. Some large firms also provide formal classroom training programs that last several weeks or months.

Throughout their careers, Management Consultants enroll in continuing education and training programs to update their skills and keep up with advancements in their fields.

Experience, Special Skills, and Personality Traits

Employers hire candidates who have several years of work experience in their field that also includes some management experience. Many firms hire recent college graduates (with bachelor's or advanced degrees) to entry-level positions. They should have work experience related to the positions for which they apply; they may have gained such experience through internships, work experience programs, or summer employment.

Because they must be able to work well with clients, colleagues, and others from diverse backgrounds, Management Consultants need excellent interpersonal, social, and teamwork skills. Their job also requires that they have effective leadership, time management, problem-solving, analytical, writing, and communication skills. Some personality traits that successful Management Consultants have in common are being friendly, self-motivated, hard-working, creative, curious, detail-oriented, assertive, and ethical.

Unions and Associations

Many Management Consultants belong to professional associations to take advantage of networking opportunities, continuing education programs, and other professional services and resources. Two national societies that serve the interests of Management Consultants include the Institute of Management Consultants USA and the Professional and Technical Consultants Association. For contact information, see Appendix III.

Tips for Entry

1. Volunteering to do management consulting work with nonprofit organizations is a way to gain practical work experience.
2. Keep up with the latest developments in management consulting, as well as with current management issues.
3. Before going to a job interview, find out what will be involved. (You might contact the human resources department or a consultant who works at a company.) Along with answering questions about yourself and your experience, you may be asked to solve mock business problems as well as to make a presentation.
4. To enhance their employability, some Management Consultants obtain professional certification that is granted by the Institute of Management Consultants USA. For more information, visit its Web site at http://www.imcusa.org.
5. Use the Internet to learn more about management consulting. To get a list of Web sites, enter the keywords *management consulting* or *management consultants* in a search engine. To learn about some links, see Appendix IV.

MARKETING MANAGER

CAREER PROFILE

Duties: Plan and coordinate marketing strategies; supervise staff; perform other duties as required

Alternate Title(s): Product Marketing Manager

Salary Range: $47,000 to $146,000

Employment Prospects: Good

Advancement Prospects: Fair

Prerequisites:

Education or Training—Bachelor's degree in any field

Experience—Previous work experience in industry as well as in marketing

Special Skills and Personality Traits—Communication, interpersonal, teamwork, leadership, analytical, presentation, business writing, and computer skills; creative, flexible, enthusiastic, tactful, self-motivated, and decisive

CAREER LADDER

```
┌─────────────────────────────┐
│     Marketing Director      │
└─────────────────────────────┘

┌─────────────────────────────┐
│     Marketing Manager       │
└─────────────────────────────┘

┌─────────────────────────────┐
│  Associate Marketing Manager │
└─────────────────────────────┘
```

Position Description

Some engineers decide to move into the field of marketing where they are still involved in the development and manufacturing of products (such as medical devices or avionics equipment) and services (such as construction services) for companies. However, instead of fulfilling such engineering functions as research, analysis, design, testing, or production, they are helping firms create and promote the types of products and services that the target customers will want to buy. Many engineers who switched careers have taken on the complex role of Marketing Managers.

These professionals are responsible for planning and coordinating marketing strategies and tactics that would result in successful sales of their firm's products and services. Marketing, however, is not about making sales. It is the process of coordinating and managing all business activities that identify the consumer demand for a company's products and services, persuade the targeted customers that they want to buy such products and services, and deliver the specific products and services to them. Hence, when companies are developing new products and services, Marketing Managers are involved in answering questions such as these: Who will buy our products or services? What does our target market want? How do we make our products or services

attractive so that they will be bought? How much should we charge? What is the best way to package them? How should we promote them?

It is the Marketing Managers' job to identify the potential markets (consumers, retailers, manufacturers, government, and so forth) for their company's products and services. They also determine what the demand is for their company's products and services, as well as compare it with the demand for similar products and services that are produced by their competitors. In addition, Marketing Managers develop strategies for pricing products and services. This involves determining how much customers or clients would be willing to pay, while still allowing companies to be profitable.

Marketing Managers work closely with both technical and business managers to ensure the success of their marketing visions for companies. For example, they work with product development managers to create the products and services that customers want from information that is gathered through market research, which may include surveys of and interviews with a sample of the target market. Marketing Managers also collaborate with advertising, promotions sales, and public relations managers to design the most effective and efficient strategies of selling products and services. In small companies, Marketing Managers are often responsible for overseeing all of these activities.

Marketing Managers also monitor trends among their company's targeted customer base to get an idea of any new products and services that may stimulate their interest, or if current products and services should be modified in some way to maintain its base as well as to attract new buyers.

Some Marketing Managers are known as product, or brand, managers. They direct and coordinate all the business and marketing efforts for one or more brands that their company produces. Some product managers are in charge of an entire category of brands. These managers are responsible for how well their brand succeeds or fails in the marketplace.

Marketing Managers are responsible for supervising and managing a staff of marketing and administrative personnel. They perform a wide range of tasks on their job, which vary daily. For example, Marketing Managers might:

- examine the market potential of a new business opportunity
- evaluate marketing strategies and modify them accordingly
- create or monitor budgets
- develop promotional materials, such as brochures, articles, direct mail materials, and content for a company Web site
- review marketing materials, proposals, and presentations for accuracy and errors
- plan exhibits for trade shows, conferences, and client meetings
- conduct market research
- participate in sales meetings
- identify training needs for marketing and technical staff

Marketing Managers work 40 hours a week but sometimes work evenings and weekends to meet deadlines and complete tasks. Some travel may be required of them to attend meetings and professional conferences.

Many U.S. companies do business worldwide, and usually assign experienced Marketing Managers to oversee international marketing projects. These professionals may be required to relocate in foreign cities or travel often between their home office in the United States and foreign cities. They are also expected to be familiar with the culture and languages of the countries in which the products or services will be sold.

Salaries

Salaries for Marketing Managers vary, depending on such factors as their education, experience, employer, and geographical location. According to the November 2004 *Occupational Employment Statistics* (OES) survey by the U.S. Bureau of Labor Statistics (BLS), the estimated annual salary for most Marketing Managers ranged between $47,100 and $145,600. The estimated annual mean wage for those managers working in the architectural and engineering services industry was $93,470.

Employment Prospects

The BLS reported in its November 2004 OES survey that an estimated 172,300 Marketing Managers were employed throughout all industries in the United States. The job growth for marketing managers, in general, is predicted to increase by 18 to 26 percent through 2014 because of the intense competition for selling products and services to consumers in the United States as well as around the world, according to the BLS. Keep in mind that job growth varies in each industry. For example, job growth in many manufacturing industries is expected to decline.

In addition to job growth, opportunities will become available as Marketing Managers retire, are promoted, or transfer to other occupations.

Advancement Prospects

Marketing Managers can rise through the ranks to become top executive officers. Entrepreneurial individuals can become independent consultants or owners of marketing firms.

Some Marketing Managers pursue advancement by earning higher salaries, receiving greater responsibilities, and gaining professional recognition. This generally requires moving from one organization to the next.

Education and Training

Minimally, Marketing Managers must possess a bachelor's degree, which may be in any field. Industrial employers generally prefer to hire applicants who possess a bachelor's degree in an engineering or science discipline. Most employers prefer to hire candidates who also possess a master's degree in business administration with an emphasis in marketing.

Throughout their careers, Marketing Managers enroll in continuing education and training programs to update their skills and keep up with advancements in their fields.

Experience, Special Skills, and Personality Traits

Employers generally seek candidates who have several years of experience in their industry. Candidates should also have previous marketing experience.

Marketing Managers need excellent communication, interpersonal, teamwork, and leadership skills to work well and effectively with colleagues, staff, managers, and clients. In addition, they must have strong analytical, presentation, and business writing skills. They must also be computer proficient. Being creative, flexible, enthusiastic, tactful, self-motivated, and decisive are some personality traits that successful Marketing Managers have in common.

Unions and Associations

Marketing Managers can join professional associations to take advantage of networking opportunities, certification, continuing education programs, and other professional services and resources. The American Marketing Association and the Sales and Marketing Executives International are two national societies that serve the general interests of this profession. Marketing Managers who work for architectural, engineering, and construction consulting firms may join the Society for Marketing Professional Services. For contact information for these organizations, see Appendix III.

Tips for Entry

1. To find out if marketing may be a field that interests you, enroll in one or more marketing courses in college.

2. Many Marketing Managers are promoted into their position from such positions as sales representative, promotions specialist, purchasing agent, or public relations specialist. Promotional opportunities are usually better in large companies.

3. The ability to communicate in a foreign language may open up employment opportunities in many rapidly growing areas around the country, especially in cities with large Spanish-speaking populations.

4. Use the Internet to learn more about the marketing field. You might start by visiting the American Marketing Association Web site at http://www.marketingpower.com. For more links, see Appendix IV.

TECHNICAL WRITER

CAREER PROFILE

Duties: Create scientific, technical, or clinical materials for training, educational, marketing, and other purposes; perform duties as required

Alternate Title(s): Technical Communicator, Documentation Specialist, Information Developer, Web Designer

Salary Range: $33,000 to $88,000

Employment Prospects: Good

Advancement Prospects: Good

Prerequisites:

Education or Training—Bachelor's degree in any field

Experience—Previous work experience or training in subject areas; previous publishing experience

Special Skills and Personality Traits—Communication, organizational, research, presentation, interpersonal, customer service, teamwork, and self-management skills; tactful, diplomatic, enthusiastic, detail-oriented, flexible, persistent, and creative

CAREER LADDER

```
┌─────────────────────────────────┐
│   Senior Technical Writer or     │
│     Independent Contractor       │
└─────────────────────────────────┘

┌─────────────────────────────────┐
│        Technical Writer          │
└─────────────────────────────────┘

┌─────────────────────────────────┐
│ Junior or Assistant Technical Writer │
└─────────────────────────────────┘
```

Position Description

Technical writing is a career path that many individuals with engineering training have taken. Technical Writers work in practically every industry—aviation, biotechnology, computing, construction, energy, government, manufacturing, medicine, petroleum, transportation, and so on. Their job is to communicate complex scientific, technical, or clinical information in clear and accurate language that technical or nontechnical readers can understand.

They create a wide range of technical materials that are used for training, educational, marketing, and other purposes. Materials are produced in a variety of media and formats, such as print, video, CD-ROM, and Web sites. Some examples of work in which Technical Writers may be involved are:

- user, repair, or maintenance manuals for consumer products
- safety and operating guides for employees
- technical specifications or installation procedures
- help systems that are part of software or online tutorials
- catalogs and parts lists
- proposals for grants or contractual projects
- environmental impact statements
- content for Web sites
- in-house materials such as training manuals, employee handbooks, company newsletters, and annual reports
- press releases, brochures, and other promotional materials about an organization's services, products, or achievements
- journal or magazine articles, technical reports, or scientific papers

Some Technical Writers are employed in full-time or part-time positions, while others are hired on a contractual basis through technical writing services. Some writers are self-employed, or independent contractors. Regardless of their job status, Technical Writers develop materials on a work-for-hire basis. Their employers or clients own the final products and can take full credit for their creation.

Technical Writers usually begin a writing project by meeting with the technical team, marketing managers, clients, or others to learn about the project's purpose, objectives, and audiences. The writers also find out what is needed in terms of format, length, deadlines, and other matters.

Once they know a project's requirements, Technical Writers plan and structure their project. Next, they gather, sort, and organize information about their subject matter to learn as much as they can. Along with studying literature, they interview professionals, technicians, and others for relevant information. Their research work may require traveling to workplaces such as laboratories and factories. They also conduct their research at libraries and on the Internet.

After preparing an outline of their project, Technical Writers begin writing a first draft of their work. They make sure that they are presenting the technical information in a clear and logical manner, as well as complying with specific standards and guidelines. They submit their drafts to editors or project reviewers who go over the draft and make corrections as well as suggestions for improving the copy. Technical Writers then make revisions and prepare the final draft for publication. Some writers are also involved in the production phase of a project. For example, they might select or create graphics and illustrations for the project, or participate in the project's design and layout.

Technical Writers use a variety of tools for their projects, including personal computers, printers, scanners, and other electronic equipment. They are familiar with various applications such as word processing, page layout, graphic, spreadsheet, and desktop publishing software.

Self-employed Technical Writers are also responsible for the daily management of their businesses. They perform various administrative duties, such as negotiate contracts, manage schedules and budgets, bill clients, pay taxes and bills, and maintain office equipment and supplies. Furthermore, they set aside time to generate new business. It is common for freelance writers to obtain jobs in other cities and states without ever meeting their clients face to face. They communicate with their clients, as well as deliver their work, by means of mail, overnight delivery services, telephone, and the Internet.

Self-employed writers typically have a more flexible work schedule than staff writers. Both staff and freelance writers work long and irregular hours to meet deadlines and complete their various tasks.

Salaries

Earnings for Technical Writers vary, depending on such factors as their education, experience, employer, job status, and geographical location. According to the November 2004 *Occupational Employment Statistics* survey by the U.S. Bureau of Labor Statistics (BLS), the estimated annual salary for most Technical Writers ranged between $32,950 and $87,520.

Employment Prospects

Staff and contractual opportunities for Technical Writers are available throughout the United States. Along with private companies, they can find employment with government agencies, nonprofit organizations, advertising agencies, educational institutions, technical writing services, and temporary job agencies.

The BLS reports that the job market for writers and editors in general should increase by 9 to 17 percent through 2014. Opportunities for Technical Writers should continue to be favorable because of constant developments in science and technology and the need to communicate technical information to both technical and nontechnical readers. In addition to job growth, Technical Writers will be needed to replace those who retire, transfer to other jobs, advance to higher positions, or leave the workforce.

Advancement Prospects

Supervisory and managerial positions as team leaders, project managers, and department supervisors are available to Technical Writers. They can also advance to marketing, training, and consulting positions. Some Technical Writers seek advancement by means of earning higher wages, receiving more complex assignments, and gaining professional recognition.

Education and Training

Most employers require applicants to possess a bachelor's degree, which usually may be in any field. Many Technical Writers have a bachelor's or advanced degree in English, journalism, engineering, computer science, or science. Some Technical Writers have earned a college degree or professional certificate in technical writing or technical communication.

Throughout their careers, Technical Writers enroll in continuing education and training programs to update their skills. Many also keep up with technology through independent study, attending professional conferences, and enrolling in courses.

Experience, Skills, and Personality Traits

Employers usually seek candidates who have previous technical writing experience, preferably in the subjects about which they will be writing. Some employers hire novice writers if they have qualifying technical training or work experience. Candidates are also expected to have publishing experience, as well as be familiar with word processing, page layout, HTML, desktop publishing, and other software.

To work effectively as Technical Writers, individuals need excellent communication, organizational, research, and presentation skills. They also must have strong interpersonal, customer service, and teamwork skills, as they work with many people with diverse backgrounds. In addition, Technical Writers need strong self-management skills, including the ability to meet deadlines, handle stressful situations, work independently, and follow and understand instructions. Being tactful, diplomatic, enthusiastic, detail-oriented, flexible, persistent, and creative are some personality traits that successful Technical Writers share. Furthermore, they are quick learners and can handle criticism about their work.

Unions and Associations

Technical Writers can join professional associations to take advantage of networking opportunities, continuing education programs, publications, and other professional services and resources. Some national societies that serve the interests of Technical Writers include the Society for Technical Communication, the National Writers Union, the Editorial Freelancers Association, the Professional Communication Society (part of the Institute of Electrical and Electronic Engineers), and the Special Interest Group on Design of Communication (a part of the Association for Computing Machinery). For contact information, see Appendix III.

Tips for Entry

1. Build a portfolio of your best writing samples that you can bring to your job interviews. Include manu-

als, specifications, proposals, market communications, and other technical materials that you have created as an employee, volunteer, or student.

2. To gain work experience, you might volunteer to write proposals or other technical documents for nonprofit organizations. You might also obtain writing jobs through temporary agencies.

3. Potential employers (or clients, if you are an independent contractor) can get an idea of your experience, skills, talents, and interests through your own Web site.

4. Check the classified ads under *technical writer and writer* in large daily newspapers. Also look at company display ads as well. Writing positions are sometimes advertised with engineers and programmer positions.

5. Use the Internet to learn more about Technical Writers. You might start by visiting the Society for Technical Communication Web site, http://www.stc.org. For more links, see Appendix IV.

PATENT EXAMINER

CAREER PROFILE

Duties: Examine patent applications and determine whether they should be issued a patent; perform duties as required

Alternate Title(s): None

Salary Range: $25,000 to $86,000

Employment Prospects: Fair

Advancement Prospects: Fair

Prerequisites:

Education or Training—Bachelor's degree in a qualifying engineering or science discipline

Experience—No work experience required

Special Skills and Personality Traits—Writing, communication, decision-making, interpersonal, teamwork, and self-management skills; analytical, focused, diligent, unbiased, reliable, courteous, and tactful

CAREER LADDER

```
┌─────────────────────────────┐
│    Senior Patent Examiner    │
└─────────────────────────────┘

┌─────────────────────────────┐
│       Patent Examiner        │
└─────────────────────────────┘

┌─────────────────────────────┐
│  Patent Examiner (Entry-Level)  │
└─────────────────────────────┘
```

Position Description

When individuals or groups invent new or improved devices, machines, processes, medicines, designs, plant varieties, and so on, they usually apply for a patent to protect their property rights. Patents are legal documents that give patent holders the exclusive rights to sell their inventions. If anyone else wishes to use, sell, or import a patented invention, he or she must first get permission from the patent holder. In the United States, the U.S. Patent and Trademark Office (USPTO) is the federal office that has the authority to issue patents, which are usually granted for a term of 20 years.

The USPTO employees who are responsible for examining patent applications are called Patent Examiners. They determine whether or not applicants should be granted patents for their inventions. It is the Patent Examiners' job to review applications objectively, completely, and in a timely manner.

Patent Examiners are assigned to technical centers that cover different disciplines, such as biotechnology, chemical engineering, agricultural engineering, computer architecture, semiconductors, optics, biomedical engineering, and mechanical engineering. As patent applications are received, they are assigned to the examiners, who specialize in the technical field that relates to the inventions.

Patent applications are detailed written descriptions and drawings of inventions that describe how they are made as well as how they are used. The applications also consist of a set of claims that defines the specific uses of inventions that belong exclusively to the invention owners.

Patent Examiners follow standard procedures to review patent applications. For example, they check that applications have been classified correctly and, if not, determine in which category the applications belong. The examiners also make sure that applications and the claimed inventions follow standard formats and rules, as well as comply with patent laws and regulations.

Their work involves conducting technical research and performing legal analyses. These examiners study relevant subject matter and technologies to fully understand the description and claims of inventions. In addition, Patent Examiners make a careful search through U.S. and foreign patents, patent applications, and other literature to determine if inventions are indeed new and useful. If they find other patent applications that claim the same inventions, Patent Examiners may start a proceeding to determine the rightful claimant.

After completing a careful examination, Patent Examiners decide whether an application is to be accepted or rejected. They can reject one, some, or all claims that are made on an application. Patent Examiners notify applicants or their representatives (attorneys or patent agents) through standard written forms. Along with rejected applications, Patent Examiners provide their reasons for not granting a patent. Applicants may choose to respond to get the examiners to reconsider their application.

USPTO Patent Examiners work 40 hours a week. They sometimes put in additional hours to complete their tasks. The USPTO offers a flexible work schedule, which allows examiners to set their own work hours and days.

Salaries

Salaries for USPTO Patent Examiners vary, depending on such factors as their education, experience, pay level, and geographical location. The USPTO usually hires Patent Examiners at the GS-5, GS-7, or GS-9 level on the general schedule (GS), the pay schedule for most federal employees. They can be promoted up to the full-performance level of GS-13. In 2006, the annual basic pay for the GS-5 to GS-13 levels ranged from $25,195 to $85,578. Employees in metropolitan areas, such as Washington, D.C., earn additional pay for living in an area with a higher cost of living.

Employment Prospects

The USPTO headquarters is located in Alexandria, Virginia. USPTO Patent Examiners, along with employees with technical and legal training, make up over half of USPTO's workforce, which in 2005 was over 6,500 employees. Opportunities in general are available as Patent Examiners are promoted, retire, or transfer to other jobs. The agency hires only U.S. citizens for Patent Examiner positions.

Advancement Prospects

Supervisory and management opportunities are available, but limited. Many Patent Examiners pursue career growth through wage increases and increased complexity of new assignments.

Education and Training

Minimally, applicants for entry-level positions must possess a bachelor's degree in computer science or in an engineering or science discipline that the USPTO requires. For example, in 2005, the qualifying engineering disciplines were electrical, chemical, ceramic, textile, transportation, construction, materials, metallurgy, mechanical, agricultural, computer hardware, and software engineering. Applicants with a master's degree may qualify at the GS-9 level for entry-level positions.

The USPTO sometimes hires candidates without a college degree for entry- level positions, if they have qualifying technical experience.

New examiners complete a few weeks of formal classroom instruction. They also receive on-the-job training while working under the guidance and supervision of experienced Patent Examiners. The USPTO provides examiners with continued classroom instruction, workshops, and other training programs throughout their careers to gain new knowledge and skills for their job.

Experience, Skills, and Personality Traits

Applicants for entry-level positions do not need any previous work experience to qualify at the GS-5 level, as long as they possess a bachelor's degree. They may qualify at the GS-7 level with one year of professional experience and at the GS-9 level with two years of professional experience.

Patent Examiners need strong writing, communication, and decision-making skills. They must also have adequate interpersonal and teamwork skills. They should also have excellent self-management skills, such as the ability to meet deadlines, handle stressful situations, work independently, understand and follow instructions, and prioritize multiple tasks. Being analytical, focused, diligent, unbiased, reliable, courteous, and tactful are some personality traits that successful Patent Examiners have in common.

Unions and Associations

The Patent Office Professional Association represents USPTO Patent Examiners in contract negotiations. This labor union seeks to get the best terms in regards employee benefits, and working conditions. For contact information, see Appendix IV.

Tips for Entry

1. The USPTO offers several programs for college students to gain practical experience. Work experience and internship programs are available during the summer as well as throughout the school year.
2. Throughout the year the USPTO participates in job fairs or similar events to recruit potential candidates. To learn if it may be coming to your campus, check with your college career center.
3. Be ready to answer questions about your training, experience, and technical aptitude on both the job application and in your job interview.
4. Use the Internet to learn more about USPTO and Patent Examiners. You might start by visiting the USPTO Web site at http://www.uspto.gov. To learn about other links, see Appendix IV.

APPENDIXES

APPENDIX I
EDUCATION AND TRAINING RESOURCES ON THE INTERNET

In this appendix, you will find World Wide Web sources for education and training programs pertaining to some of the occupations in this book. To learn about programs for other occupations, talk with school or career counselors as well as with professionals. You can also look up schools in college directories produced by the Princeton Review or other publishers, which may be found in your school or public library.

Note: All Web site addresses were current at the time this book was written. If a URL is no longer valid, enter the title of the Web site or the name of the organization or individual into a search engine to find the new URL.

GENERAL RESOURCES
The following Web sites provide links to various academic programs at colleges and universities in the United States.

- GradSchools.com, http://www.gradschools.com
- Peterson's, http://www.petersons.com
- Peterson's Graduate Planner http://www.petersons.com/graduate_home.asp
- The Princeton Review, http://www.princetonreview.com
- "Web U.S. Higher Education," a listing of two-year colleges, four-year colleges, and universities (maintained by the University of Texas at Austin), http://www.utexas.edu/world/univ
- WorldWideLearn, http://www.worldwidelearn.com

To find academic programs for the different engineering disciplines, check out the following links:

- ABET, Inc., http://www.abet.org
- All Engineering Schools, http://www.allengineeringschools.com
- American Society for Engineering Education, http://www.asee.org
- Women in Engineering Programs and Advocates Network, http://www.wepan.org

ACOUSTICAL ENGINEERING
The Acoustical Society of America has a directory of graduate programs in acoustics at http://asa.aip.org/asagrad/gpdir.cm.html.

AGRICULTURAL ENGINEERING
The American Society of Agricultural and Biological Engineers has a listing of international academic programs in agricultural, food, and biological engineering at http://www.asabe.org/membership/students/intlacademic.html.

AIR QUALITY ENGINEERING
- The Air And Waste Management Association provides a listing of undergraduate and graduate programs in the air, waste, and environmental fields at http://www.awma.org/education/highereducation.asp.
- A database of college programs in air quality can be found at EnviroEducation.com: The Environmental Education Directory. The URL is http://www.enviroeducation.com.

AQUACULTURAL ENGINEERING
A database of college programs in aquaculture and aquacultural engineering can be found at EnviroEducation.com: The Environmental Education Directory. Its URL is http://www.enviroeducation.com.

ARCHITECTURAL ENGINEERING
The Architectural Engineering Institute has a listing of architectural engineering programs at http://www.aeinstitute.org/education/abet_ae.cfm.

AUTOMOTIVE ENGINEERING
SAE International has a listing of schools that offer a master's degree in automotive engineering at http://students.sae.org/chapters/choosecollege.htm.

BIOLOGICAL ENGINEERING
- The American Society of Agricultural and Biological Engineers has a listing of international academic programs in biological engineering at http://www.asabe.org/membership/students/intlacademic.html.
- The Institute of Biological Engineering has a listing of academic programs in biological engineering and related areas at http://www.ibeweb.org/academic/index.cgi.
- The Great Western Library Alliance (at Iowa State University) has a listing of biological engineering programs at http://www.lib.iastate.edu/other/gwla/schools.html.

BIOMEDICAL ENGINEERING

- The Institute of Biological Engineering has a listing of biomedical engineering programs at http://www.ibeweb.org/academic/index.cgi.
- The Whitaker Foundation provides a database of biomedical engineering programs at http://bmes.seas.wustl.edu.

CERAMICS ENGINEERING

- The American Ceramic Society has a listing of colleges and universities that have programs in materials science and engineering, ceramic engineering, and metallurgical engineering at http://www.ceramics.org/education/colleges.asp.
- The Minerals, Metals and Materials Society sponsors the Materials Science and Engineering Career Resource Center (http://www.crc4mse.org). It lists colleges and universities that offer degree programs in materials, metallurgical, and ceramic engineering at http://www.crc4mse.org/resources/colleges.html.

CHEMICAL ENGINEERING

- The American Chemical Society has a database of master's degree programs for chemistry-based programs, such as chemical engineering, at http://acswebapplications.acs.org/applications/masters_survey/browse.cfm.
- The American Institute of Chemical Engineering has a list of chemical engineering programs at http://www.aiche.org/Students/Careers/Accred Universities.aspx

CIVIL ENGINEERING

The American Society of Civil Engineering provides a listing of civil engineering programs at http://www.asce.org/community/educational/instlist.cfm.

COMPUTER ENGINEERING

- ABET, Inc. provides a database of accredited computing programs in the United States at http://www.abet.org.
- The Computing Research Association has a database of doctoral programs called *CRA Forsythe List*, in computing and computing-related disciplines at http://www.cra.org/reports/forsythe.html.
- The Electrical and Computer Engineering Department at the University of Missouri at Rolla provides a listing of electrical and computer engineering programs at http://www.ece.umr.edu/links/schools/school_list.html.

CONSTRUCTION ENGINEERING

The Construction Management Association of America provides a listing of construction programs at http://cmaanet.org/college_univ.php.

DRAFTING

American Design Drafting Association International provides a listing of drafting programs. Go to http://www.adda.org, then click on the *Certified Schools* link.

ELECTRICAL ENGINEERING/ELECTRONICS ENGINEERING

The Electrical and Computer Engineering Department at University of Missouri at Rolla provides a listing of electrical and computer engineering programs at http://www.ece.umr.edu/links/schools/school_list.html.

ENGINEERING TECHNOLOGY

ABET, Inc. provides a database of accredited engineering technology programs in the United States at http://www.abet.org.

ENVIRONMENTAL ENGINEERING

A database of college programs in environmental engineering can be found at EnviroEducation.com: The Environmental Education Directory. The URL is http://www.enviroeducation.com.

FIRE PROTECTION ENGINEERING

- CareersinFireProtection.com (by the Society of Fire Protection) has a guide to schools that offer fire protection engineering programs. The URL is http://www.careersinfireprotectionengineering.com/careerguideinfo.htm.
- The Society of Fire Protection has a listing of fire protection engineering programs at http://www.sfpe.org/profession.aspx.

FLIGHT TEST ENGINEERING

The Society of Flight Test Engineers has a list of flight test-related training courses at its Web site. Go to http://www.sfte.org, then click on the *Education* link.

FOOD ENGINEERING

The American Society of Agricultural and Biological Engineers has a listing of international academic programs in food engineering at http://www.asabe.org/membership/students/intlacademic.html.

FOREST ENGINEERING

- The Council on Forest Engineering has a list of forest engineering departments at http://www.cofe.org/index files/Page395.htm.
- EnviroEducation.com, the Environmental Education Directory, offers a database to search for forestry programs at http://www.enviroeducation.com.

GEOTECHNICAL ENGINEERING

The World-Wide Web Virtual Library of Geotechnical Engineering provides a listing of geotechnical engineering programs at http://www.ejge.com/GVL/USA.htm.

HUMAN FACTORS ENGINEERING

The International Ergonomics Association has a listing of academic programs in human factors at http://www.iea.cc/directory/programs/wus.cfm.

INDUSTRIAL ENGINEERING
The World-Wide Web Virtual Library: Industrial Engineering has a listing of industrial engineering programs at http://www2.isye.gatech.edu/www-ie/academic.

LAW
The America Bar Association has a database of accredited law schools at http://www.abanet.org/legaled/approvedlawschools/approved.html.

MARKETING
The American Marketing Association has a listing of doctoral degree programs in marketing at http://www.marketingpower.com/content16594C5188.php. Alternatively, you can go to its home page (http://www.marketingpower.com), and click on the *Academic Resources* link, then on the *Career* link.

MATERIALS ENGINEERING/METALLURGICAL ENGINEERING
- The American Ceramic Society has a listing of colleges and universities that have programs in materials science and engineering, ceramic engineering, and metallurgical engineering. The URL is http://www.ceramics.org/education/colleges.asp.
- The Minerals, Metals and Materials Society sponsors the Materials Science and Engineering Career Resource Center (http://www.crc4mse.org). It lists colleges and universities that offer degree programs in materials, metallurgical, and ceramic engineering at http://www.crc4mse.org/resources/colleges.html.

MINING ENGINEER
The Mining and Metallurgical Society of America has a listing of mining engineering programs at http://www.mmsa.net/educ.htm.

NAVAL ENGINEERING
The Society of Naval Architects and Marine Engineers has a listing of naval architecture, marine engineering, and ocean engineering programs at http://www.sname.org/careers.htm.

NUCLEAR ENGINEERING
The American Nuclear Society provides a listing of nuclear engineering programs at http://www.ans.org/links/vc-edu.

PETROLEUM ENGINEERING
The Society of Petroleum Engineering has a listing of petroleum engineering programs. Go to http://www.spe.org, and click on the *Young Members* link. Then, click on the *Petroleum Engineering and Technical Schools* link.

PLANNING
- The Association of Collegiate Schools of Planning provides a listing of planning programs at http://www.acsp.org/org/links_to_planning_schools.htm.
- The American Planning Association provides a listing of doctoral programs in planning at http://www.planning.org/institutions/phd.html.

POLICY (SCIENCE AND TECHNOLOGY)
The American Association for the Advancement of Science provides a database of graduate programs in science and technology at http://www.aaas.org/spp/sepp. (The database is called the *Guide to Graduate Education in Science, Engineering, and Public Policy.*)

REHABILITATION ENGINEERING
The Rehabilitation Engineering and Assistive Technology Society of North America provides a list of rehabilitation engineering and assistive technology program at http://www.resna.org/ProfResources/ProfessDevel/atprogs.htm.

SURVEYING
The American Congress on Surveying and Mapping has a list of surveying programs at http://www.acsm.net/college.html.

SYSTEMS ENGINEERING
The International Council on Systems Engineering has a listing of systems engineering programs at http://www.incose.org/educationcareers/academicprogramdirectory.aspx.

TECHNICAL COMMUNICATIONS
The Society for Technical Communications has a database of college and universities offering programs in technical communication at http://www.stc.org/edu/academic Database01.asp.

WASTE MANAGEMENT ENGINEERING
- The Air And Waste Management Association provides a listing of undergraduate and graduate programs in the air, waste, and environmental fields. The URL is http://www.awma.org/education/highereducation.asp.
- A database of college programs in waste management can be found at EnviroEducation.com: The Environmental Education Directory. Its URL is http://www.enviroeducation.com.

WASTEWATER ENGINEERING
A database of college programs in wastewater can be found at EnviroEducation.com: The Environmental Education Directory. The URL is http://www.enviroeducation.com.

WATER RESOURCES ENGINEERING
A database of college programs in water resources can be found at EnviroEducation.com: The Environmental Education Directory. The URL is http://www.enviroeducation.com.

PAYING FOR YOUR EDUCATION
Scholarships, grants, student loans, and other financial aid programs are available to help you pay for your postsecondary education. These programs are sponsored by government agencies, professional and

trade associations, private foundations, businesses, and other organizations. For example, the National Society of Professional Engineers offers scholarships to high school students who plan to major in an engineering discipline as well as to undergraduate students who are enrolled in engineering programs. Be sure to contact organizations that serve your particular interests. You can find contact information for many professional associations in Appendix III.

To learn more about financial assistance programs, talk with your high school guidance counselor or college career counselor. You might also consult college catalogs, as they usually include financial aid information. In addition, you might visit or contact the financial aid office at the college where you plan to attend or are attending now. Lastly, check out these Web sites for financial aid information:

- Engineering Education Service Center, http://www.engineeringedu.com/scholars.html
- FinAid, http://www.finaid.org

- Information for Parents and Students (by the National Association of Student Financial Aid Administrators), http://www.studentaid.org
- National Action Council for Minorities in Engineering, http://www.nacme.org/scholarships
- National Science Foundation Graduate Research Fellowship Program, http://www.nsfgradfellows.org
- Student Aid on the Web (U.S. Department of Education Federal Student Aid), http://www.studentaid.ed.gov

APPENDIX II
STATE LICENSING AGENCIES FOR PROFESSIONAL ENGINEERS AND PROFESSIONAL SURVEYORS

This appendix provides contact information and Web site addresses for state government agencies that are responsible for licensing professional engineers and professional surveyors. These licensing agencies establish high standards for these professions to help protect the public's health, safety, and welfare. The 50 states—as well as the U.S. territories and Washington, D.C.—all have unique requirements for engineers and surveyors to obtain professional licenses.

Note: All Web addresses were accessible while this book was being written. If a URL no longer works, you may be able to find a new one by entering the name of the state and the licensing agency into a search engine.

PROFESSIONAL ENGINEERS

Not all engineers are required to be licensed as professional engineers. For example, many industrial engineers do not need to possess the professional engineer (P.E.) license. States require that engineers (such as consultants) who offer engineering services directly to the public or who are involved in engineering projects, such as construction, that affect the life, health, or property of the public must be licensed.

Many engineers who work in fields that do not require licensure choose to obtain their licenses to demonstrate that they have accomplished the high standards of their profession. P.E. licensure is granted in the different engineering disciplines, such as civil engineering, structural engineering, electrical engineering, and fire protection engineering.

To become a professional engineer, an individual must fulfill requirements that take several years to complete. Each jurisdiction establishes its own set of qualifications for P.E. licensure but, in general, an individual must meet the following requirements:

- possess a bachelor's degree that was granted by a university or college engineering program accredited by ABET, Inc. (formerly known as the Accreditation Board for Engineering and Technology)
- pass the "Fundamentals of Engineering" (F.E.) exam, the first exam in the licensure process, to be granted an engi-

neering-in-training (E.I.T.) or engineering intern (E.I.) license
- gain several years of practical experience while working under the supervision of licensed professional engineers
- pass the "Principles and Practice of Engineering" exam in his or her engineering discipline

For more general information about becoming a professional engineer, visit the following Web sites: National Society of Professional Engineers, http://www.nspe.org; and Professional Engineering Licensure (by the National Council of Examiners for Engineering and Surveying), http://www.engineeringlicense.com.

PROFESSIONAL SURVEYORS

The 50 states, the U.S. territories, and Washington, D.C. all require practicing surveyors within their jurisdiction to be licensed. In most states, licensed surveyors are known by the title professional surveyor (P.S.). In some jurisdictions, licensed surveyors may go by the title land surveyor (L.S.), professional land surveyor (P.L.S.), or professional surveyor and mapper (P.S.M.).

The qualifications that individuals need for obtaining the P.S. license vary with each jurisdiction. In general, individuals must meet minimum educational and work experience requirements. Increasingly more licensing boards are requiring that individuals possess a bachelor's degree from a college or university surveying program accredited by ABET, Inc.

The licensing process involves two stages. At the first level, individuals must pass the "Fundamentals of Surveying" (F.S.) exam to obtain the surveying intern (S.I.) or surveyor-in-training (S.I.T.) license. These licensed interns then gain practical experience while working under licensed, professional surveyors. After completing the work experience requirement for their jurisdiction, individuals can then take the "Principles and Practice of Surveying" examination. Upon successful completion of the second test, individuals become eligible for licensure.

LICENSING BOARDS

ALABAMA

State Board of Licensure for Professional Engineers and Land Surveyors
100 North Union Street, Suite 382
Montgomery, AL 36104
Mailing address:
P.O. Box 304451
Montgomery, AL 36130
Phone: (334) 242-5568
Fax: (334) 242-5105
http://www.bels.state.al.us

ALASKA

State Board of Registration for Architects, Engineers and Land Surveyors
333 Willoughby, Ninth Floor
Juneau, AK 99811
Mailing address:
P.O. Box 110806
Juneau, AK 99811
Phone: (907) 465-1676
Fax: (907) 465-2974
http://www.dced.state.ak.us/occ/pael.htm

ARIZONA

State Board of Technical Registration
1110 West Washington Street, Suite 240
Phoenix, AZ 85007
Phone: (602) 364-4930
Fax: (602) 364-4931
http://www.btr.state.az.us

ARKANSAS

State Board of Registration for Professional Engineers and Land Surveyors
623 Woodlane Drive
Little Rock, AR 72201
Mailing address:
P.O. Box 3750
Little Rock, AR 72203
Phone: (501) 682-2824
Fax: (501) 682-2827
http:www.arkansas.gov/pels

CALIFORNIA

Board for Professional Engineers and Land Surveyors
2535 Capitol Oaks Drive, Suite 300
Sacramento, CA 95833
Phone: (866) 780-5370 or (916) 263-2222
Fax: (916) 263-2246
http://www.dca.ca.gov/pels

COLORADO

Board of Licensure for Professional Engineers and Professional Land Surveyors
1560 Broadway, Suite 1300
Denver, CO 80202
Phone: (303) 894-7788
Fax: (303) 894-7790
http://www.dora.state.co.us/engineers_surveyors

CONNECTICUT

State Board of Examiners for Professional Engineers and Land Surveyors
165 Capitol Avenue
Hartford, CT 06106
Phone: (860) 713-6145
http://www.ct.gov/dcp (then click on the *View License Categories* link)

DELAWARE

Delaware Association of Professional Engineers
56 West Main Street, Suite 208
Christiana, DE 19702
Phone: (302) 368-6708
Fax: (302) 368-6710
http://www.dape.org

State Board of Professional Land Surveyors
Cannon Building, Suite 203
861 Silver Lake Boulevard
Dover, DE 19904
Phone: (302) 744-4532
Fax: (302) 739-2711
http://www.dpr.delaware.gov/boards/land surveyors

DISTRICT OF COLUMBIA

Board of Professional Engineers and Land Surveyors
Department of Consumer and Regulatory Affairs
941 North Capitol Street NE
Washington, DC 20002
Phone: (877) 374-1156 or (202) 442-4320
http://dcra.dc.gov/dcra (first click on the *Business Resources* link, then the *Occupational Licensing* link)

FLORIDA

Board of Professional Engineers
2507 Callaway Road, Suite 200
Tallahassee, FL 32303
Phone: (850) 521-0500
Fax: (850) 521-0521
http://www.fbpe.org

Board of Professional Surveyors and Mappers
1940 North Monroe Street
Tallahassee, FL 32399
Phone: (850) 487-1395
http://www.myflorida.com/dbpr/pro/surv/sm_index.shtml

GEORGIA

State Board of Registration for Professional Engineers and Land Surveyors
237 Coliseum Drive
Macon, GA 31217
Phone: (478) 207-2440
Fax: (478) 207-1363
http://www.sos.state.ga.us/plb/pels

GUAM

Guam Board of Registration for Professional Engineers, Architects and Land Surveyors
718 North Marine Drive
Unit D, Suite 208
Upper Tumon, GU 96913
Phone: (671) 646-3115/3138
Fax: (671) 649-9533
http://www.guam-peals.org

HAWAII

Board of Professional Engineers, Architects, Surveyors and Landscape Architects
P.O. Box 3469
Honolulu, HI 96801
Phone: (808) 586-3000
Fax: (808) 586-2707
http://www.hawaii.gov/dcca/areas/pvl/boards/engineer

IDAHO

Board of Professional Engineers and Professional Land Surveyors
5535 West Overland Road
Boise, ID 83705
Phone: (208) 373-7210
Fax: (208) 373-7213
http://www.ipels.idaho.gov

ILLINOIS

Board of Professional Engineers
Department of Financial and Professional Regulation
320 West Washington Street
Springfield, IL 62786
Phone: (217) 785-0877
http://www.idfpr.com/dpr/WHO/pe.asp

Structural Engineering Board
Department of Financial and Professional Regulation
320 West Washington Street
Springfield, IL 62786
Phone: (217) 782-8556
http://www.idfpr.com/dpr/WHO/se.asp

Land Surveyors Licensing Board
Department of Financial and Professional Regulation
320 West Washington Street
Springfield, IL 62786
Phone: (217) 782-8556
http://www.idfpr.com/dpr/WHO/lansv.asp

INDIANA

State Board of Registration for Professional Engineers
402 West Washington Street, Room W072
Indianapolis, IN 46204
Phone: (317) 234-3022
http://www.in.gov/pla/bandc/engineers

State Board of Registration for Professional Land Surveyors
402 West Washington Street, Room W072
Indianapolis, IN 46204
Phone: (317) 234-3022
http://www.in.gov/pla/bandc/surveyors

IOWA

Engineering and Land Surveying Board
1920 SE Hulsizer Road
Ankeny, IA 50021
Phone: (515) 281-4126
Fax: (515) 281-7411
http://www.state.ia.us/engls

KANSAS

State Board of Technical Professions
900 SW Jackson, Suite 507
Topeka, KS 66612
Phone: (785) 296-3053
http://www.kansas.gov/ksbtp

KENTUCKY

State Board of Licensure for Professional Engineers and Land Surveyors
Kentucky Engineering Center
160 Democrat Drive
Frankfort, KY 40601
Phone: (800) 573-2680 or (502) 573-2680
Fax: (502) 573-6687
http://kyboels.ky.gov

LOUISIANA

Professional Engineering and Land Surveying Board
9643 Brookline Avenue, Suite 121
Baton Rouge, LA 70809
Phone: (225) 925-6291
Fax: (225) 925-6292
http://www.lapels.com

MAINE

Professional Engineers Licensure Board
Augusta Airport Terminal Building, Second Floor
Augusta, ME 04330
Mailing address:
92 State House Station
Augusta, ME 04333
Phone: (207) 287-3236
Fax: (207) 626-2309
http://www.maine.gov/
   professionalengineers

Board of Licensure for Professional Land Surveyors
Mailing address:
35 State House Station
Augusta, ME 04333
Phone: (207) 624-8522
Fax: (207) 624-8637
http://www.state.me.us/pfr/olr/categories/
   cat24.htm

MARYLAND

State Board for Professional Engineers
500 North Calvert Street, Room 308
Baltimore, MD 21202
Phone: (410) 230-6322
Fax: (410) 333-0021
http://www.dllr.state.md.us/license/
   occprof/profeng.html

State Board for Professional Land Surveyors
500 North Calvert Street, Room 308
Baltimore, MD 21202
Phone: (410) 230-6322
Fax: (410) 333-0021
http://www.dllr.state.md.us/license/
   occprof/lsurvyr.html

MASSACHUSETTS

Board of Registration of Professional Engineers and Land Surveyors
Division of Professional Licensure
239 Causeway Street, Suite 500
Boston, MA 02114
Phone: (617) 727-9957
http://www.mass.gov/dpl/boards/en

MICHIGAN

Board of Professional Engineers
P.O. Box 30018
Lansing, MI 48909
Phone: (517) 241-9253
http://www.michigan.gov/engineers

Board of Professional Surveyors
P.O. Box 30018
Lansing, MI 48909
Phone: (517) 241-9253
http://www.michigan.gov/surveyors

MINNESOTA

State Board of Architecture, Engineering, Land Surveying, Landscape Architecture, Geoscience and Interior Design
85 East Seventh Place, Suite 160
St. Paul, MN 55101
Phone: (651) 296-2388
Fax: (651) 297-5310
http://www.aelslagid.state.mn.us

MISSISSIPPI

Board of Licensure for Professional Engineers and Surveyors
239 North Lamar, Suite 501
Jackson, MS 39201
Mailing address:
P.O. Box 3

Jackson, MS 39205
Phone: (601) 359-6160
Fax: (601) 359-6159
http://www.pepls.state.ms.us

MISSOURI

State Board for Architects, Professional Engineers, Land Surveyors and Landscape Architects
3605 Missouri Boulevard, Suite 380
Jefferson City, MO 65102
Mailing address:
P.O. Box 184
Jefferson City, MO 65102
Phone: (573) 751-0047
Fax: (573) 751-8046
http://pr.mo.gov/apelsla.asp

MONTANA

Board of Professional Engineers and Land Surveyors
P.O. Box 200513
301 South Park Avenue, Fourth Floor
Helena, MT 59620
Phone: (406) 841-2351
Fax: (406) 841-2309
http://www.engineer.mt.gov

NEBRASKA

Board of Engineers and Architects
301 Centennial Mall South, Sixth Floor
P.O. Box 95165
Lincoln, NE 68509
Phone: (402) 471-2021
Fax: (402) 471-0787
http://www.ea.state.ne.us

Board of Examiners for Land Surveyors
555 North Cotner Boulevard, Lower Level
Lincoln, NE 68505
Phone: (402) 471-2566
Fax: (402) 471-3057
http://www.sso.state.ne.us/bels

NEVADA

State Board of Engineers and Land Surveyors
1755 East Plumb Lane, Suite 135
Reno, NV 89502
Phone: (775) 688-1231
Fax: (775) 688-2991
http://www.boe.state.nv.us

NEW HAMPSHIRE

Board of Licensure for Professional Engineers
57 Regional Drive
Concord, NH 03301
Phone: (603) 271-2219
Fax: (603) 271-6990
http://www.state.nh.us/jtboard/pe.htm

Board of Licensure for Land Surveyors
57 Regional Drive
Concord, NH 03301
Phone: (603) 271-2219
Fax: (603) 271-6990
http://www.state.nh.us/jtboard/ls.htm

NEW JERSEY

State Board of Professional Engineers and Land Surveyors
124 Halsey Street, Sixth Floor
Newark, NJ 07102
Mailing address:
P.O. Box 45015
Newark, NJ 07101
Phone: (973) 504-6460
http://www.state.nj.us/lps/ca/nonmedical/pels.htm

NEW MEXICO

Board of Licensure for Professional Engineers and Surveyors
4001 Office Court Drive, Suite 902–904
Santa Fe, NM 87507
Phone: (505) 827-7561
Fax: (505) 827-7566
http://www.state.nm.us/pepsboard

NEW YORK

State Board for Engineering and Land Surveying
89 Washington Avenue
Albany, NY 12234-1000
Phone: (518) 474-3817, ext. 250
http://www.op.nysed.gov/pe.htm

NORTH CAROLINA

Board of Examiners for Engineers and Surveyors
4601 Six Forks Road, Suite 310
Raleigh, NC 27609
Phone: (919) 791-2000
Fax: (919) 791-2012
http://www.ncbels.org

NORTH DAKOTA

State Board of Registration for Professional Engineers and Land Surveyors
721 West Memorial Highway
P.O. Box 1357
Bismarck, ND 58502
Phone: (701) 258-0786
Fax: (701) 258-7471
http://www.ndpelsboard.org

NORTHERN MARIANA ISLANDS

Board of Professional Licensing
Commonwealth of Northern Mariana Islands
P.O. Box 502078
Saipan, Northern Mariana Islands 96950
Phone: (670) 234-5897
Fax: (670) 234-6040

OHIO

State Board of Registration for Professional Engineers and Surveyors
77 South High Street, Room 1698
Columbus, OH 43215
Phone: (877) OHIO ENG
or (614) 466-3651
Fax: (614) 728-3059
http://www.ohiopeps.org

OKLAHOMA

State Board of Licensure for Professional Engineers and Land Surveyors
Oklahoma Engineering Center, Room 120
201 NE 27th Street
Oklahoma City, OK 73105
Phone: (405) 521-2874
Fax: (405) 523-2135
http://www.pels.state.ok.us

OREGON

State Board of Examiners for Engineering and Land Surveying
728 Hawthorne Avenue NE
Salem, OR 97301
Phone: (503) 362-2666
Fax: (503) 362-5454
http://www.osbeels.org

PENNSYLVANIA

State Registration Board for Professional Engineers, Land Surveyors and Geologists
2601 North Third Street
Harrisburg, PA 17110
Mailing address:
P.O. Box 2649
Harrisburg, PA 17105
Phone: (717) 783-7049
Fax: (717) 705-5540
http://www.dos.state.pa.us/eng

PUERTO RICO

Board of Examiners of Engineers and Land Surveyors
Secretaria Auxiliar de Juntas Examinadoras
151 Fortaleza Street
Third Floor, Office 308
San Juan, PR 00902
Mailing address:
Secretaria Auxiliar de Juntas Examinadoras
Department of State
P.O. Box 9023271
San Juan, PR 00902
Phone: (787) 722-2122, ext. 232
Fax: (787) 722-4818

RHODE ISLAND

Board of Registration for Professional Engineers
One Capitol Hill, Third Floor
Providence, RI 02908
Phone: (401) 222-2565
Fax: (401) 222-5744
http://www.bdp.state.ri.us/peng

Board of Registration for Professional Land Surveyors
One Capitol Hill, Third Floor
Providence, RI 02908
Phone: (401) 222-2038
Fax: (401) 222-5744
http://www.bdp.state.ri.us/pls

SOUTH CAROLINA

Board of Professional Engineers and Land Surveyors
Kingstree Building
110 Centerview Drive, Suite 201
Columbia, SC 29210
Mailing address:
P.O. Box 11597
Columbia, SC 29211
Phone: (803) 896-4422
Fax: (803) 896-4427
http://www.llr.state.sc.us/POL/Engineers

SOUTH DAKOTA

Board of Technical Professions
2040 West Main Street, Suite 304
Rapid City, SD 57702
Phone: (605) 394-2510
Fax: (605) 394-2509
http://www.state.sd.us/dol/boards/engineer

TENNESSEE

State Board of Architectural and Engineering Examiners
Department of Commerce and Insurance
500 James Robertson Parkway
Nashville, TN 37243
Phone: (800) 256-5758 or (615) 741-3221
Fax: (615) 532-9410
http://www.state.tn.us/commerce/boards/ae

State Board of Examiners for Land Surveyors
500 James Robertson Parkway, Third Floor
Nashville, TN 37243
Phone: (615) 741-3611
Fax: (615) 741-5995
http://www.state.tn.us/commerce/boards/surveyors

TEXAS

Texas Board of Professional Engineers
1917 IH 35 South
Austin, TX 78741
Phone: (512) 440-7723
Fax: (512) 440-1414
http://www.tbpe.state.tx.us

Texas Board of Professional Land Surveying
Mailing address:
Building A, Suite 156
12100 Park 35 Circle
Austin, TX 78753
Phone: (512) 239-5263
Fax: (512) 239-5253
http://www.txls.state.tx.us/sect00/homepage.html

UTAH

Professional Engineers and Professional Land Surveyors Board
Division of Occupational and Professional Licensing
160 East 300 South, First Floor
Salt Lake City, UT 84114
Mailing address:
P.O. Box 146741
Salt Lake City, UT 84114
Phone: (801) 530-6628
Fax: (801) 530-6511
http://www.dopl.utah.gov/licensing/engineer_and_land_surveyor_sub_page.html

VERMONT

Board of Professional Engineering
81 River Street, Drawer 09
Montpelier, VT 05609
Phone: (802) 828-1380
Fax: (802) 828-2368
http://www.vtprofessionals.org/opr1/engineers

Board of Land Surveyors
81 River Street
Montpelier, VT 05609
Phone: (802) 828-1635
http://www.vtprofessionals.org/opr1/surveyors

VIRGINIA

Board for Architects, Professional Engineers, Land Surveyors, Certified Interior Designers and Landscape Architects
Department of Professional and Occupational Regulation
3600 West Broad Street
Richmond, VA 23230
Phone: (804) 367-8500
Fax: (804) 367-2475
http://www.state.va.us/dpor/ape_main.htm

VIRGIN ISLANDS

Board for Architects, Engineers and Land Surveyors
Department of Licensing and Consumer Affairs
Golden Rock Shopping Center
Christiansted, St. Croix
USVI 00820
Phone: (340) 773-2226

Fax: (340) 778-8250
http://www.usvi.org/dlca/licensing/archite
cts.html

WASHINGTON

**Board of Registration for Professional
Engineers and Land Surveyors**
Department of Licensing
405 Black Lake Boulevard, Building Two
Olympia, WA 98502
Mailing address:
P.O. Box 9025
Olympia, WA 98507
Phone: (360) 664-1575
Fax: (360) 664-2551
http://www.dol.wa.gov/engineers/
engfront.htm

WEST VIRGINIA

**State Board of Registration for
Professional Engineers**
300 Capitol Street, Suite 910
Charleston, WV 25301

Phone: (800) 324-6170 (304) 558-3554
Fax: (304) 558-6232
http://www.wvpebd.org

State Board of Professional Surveyors
2298 Sutton Lane
Flatwoods, WV 26621
Mailing address:
P.O. Box 390
Flatwoods, WV 26621
Phone: (304) 765-0315
Fax: (304) 765-0316

WISCONSIN

**Examining Board of Architects,
Landscape Architects, Professional
Engineers, Designers and Land
Surveyors**
Bureau of Business and Design
Professions
1400 East Washington Avenue
Madison, WI 53703
Mailing address:
P.O. Box 8935

Madison, WI 53708
Phone: (608) 266-5551
http://drl.wi.gov/boards/jal/index.htm

WYOMING

**Board of Registration for Professional
Engineers and Professional Land
Surveyors**
6920 Yellowtail Drive, Suite 100
Cheyenne, WY 82002
Phone: (307) 777-6155
Fax: (307) 777-3403
http://www.wrds.uwyo.edu/wrds/borpe/
borpe.html

APPENDIX III
PROFESSIONAL UNIONS AND ASSOCIATIONS

This appendix provides information about the professional organizations that are mentioned in the job profiles. You can contact these organizations, or visit their Web sites, to learn more about careers, job opportunities, training programs, conferences, professional certification, and other topics. Many of these organizations have student chapters. Most have branch offices throughout the United States; contact an organization's headquarters to find out if a branch is in your area.

To learn about other local, state, regional, and national professional societies and unions, talk with local professionals.

Note: Web site addresses change from time to time. If you come across an address that no longer works, you may be able to find an organization's new URL by entering its name into a search engine.

CIVIL ENGINEERING

American Academy of Environmental Engineers
130 Holiday Court
Suite 100
Annapolis, MD 21401
Phone: (410) 266-3311
Fax: (410) 266-7653
http://www.aaee.net

American Concrete Institute
38800 Country Club Drive
Farmington Hills, MI 48331
Phone: (248) 848-3700
Fax: (248) 848-3701
http://www.aci-int.org

American Planning Association
Chicago, Illinois office:
122 South Michigan Avenue, Suite 1600
Chicago, IL 40603
Phone: (312) 431-9100
Fax: (312) 431-9985
Washington, D.C., office:
1776 Massachusetts Avenue NW
Washington, DC 20036
Phone: (202) 872-0611
Fax: (202) 872-0643
http://www.planning.org

American Public Works Association
Kansas City, Missouri office:
2345 Grand Boulevard
Suite 700
Kansas City, MO 64108
Phone: (800) 848-APWA or
    (816) 472-6100
Fax: (816) 472-1610
Washington, D.C., office:
1401 K Street NW, 11th Floor
Washington, DC 20005
Phone: (202) 408-9541
Fax: (202) 408-9542
http://www.apwa.net

American Society of Civil Engineers
ASCE world headquarters:
1801 Alexander Bell Drive
Reston, VA 20191
Phone: (800) 548-2723 or
    (703) 295-6300
Fax: (703) 295-6222
Washington, D.C., office:
101 Constitution Avenue NW
Suite 375 East
Washington, DC 20001
Phone: 800-548-ASCE (2723), ext. 7850
http://www.asce.org

American Water Resources Association
Four West Federal Street
P.O. Box 1626
Middleburg, VA 20118
Phone: (540) 687-8390
Fax: (540) 687-8395
http://www.awra.org

American Wood Council
1111 19th Street NW
Suite 800
Washington, DC 20036
Phone: (202) 463-2766
Fax: (202) 463-2791
http://www.awc.org

Construction Management Association of America
7918 Jones Branch Drive
Suite 540
McLean, VA 22102
Phone: (703) 356-2622
Fax: (703) 356-6388
http://cmaanet.org

The Geo-Institute of the ASCE
1801 Alexander Bell Drive
Reston, VA 20191
Phone: (703) 295-6350
Fax: (703) 295-6351
http://www.geoinstitute.org

Institute of Transportation Engineers
1099 14th Street NW
Suite 300 West
Washington, DC 20005
Phone: (202) 289-0222
Fax: (202) 289-7722
http://www.ite.org

National Society of Professional Engineers
1420 King Street
Alexandria, VA 22314
Phone: (703) 684-2800
Fax: (703) 836-4875
http://www.nspe.org

Society of Women Engineers
230 East Ohio Street
Suite 400
Chicago, IL 60611
Phone: (312) 596-5223
http://www.swe.org

Structural Engineering Institute of ASCE
1801 Alexander Bell Drive
Reston, VA 20191
Phone: (800) 548-2723
http://www.seinstitute.org

ENVIRONMENTAL ENGINEERING

Air and Waste Management Association
One Gateway Center, Third Floor
420 Fort Duquesne Boulevard
Pittsburgh, PA 15222
Phone: (800) 270-3444
or (412) 232-3444
Fax: (412) 232-3450
http://www.awma.org

American Academy of Environmental Engineers
130 Holiday Court
Suite 100
Annapolis, MD 21401
Phone: (410) 266-3311
Fax: (410) 266-7653
http://www.aaee.net

American Institute of Chemical Engineers
Three Park Avenue
New York, NY 10016
Phone: (800) 242-4363 or (212) 591-8100
Fax: (212) 591-8888
http://www.aiche.org

American Society of Agricultural and Biological Engineers
2950 Niles Road
St. Joseph, MI 49085
Phone: (269) 429-0300
Fax: (269) 429-3852
http://www.asabe.org

American Society of Civil Engineers
ASCE world headquarters:
1801 Alexander Bell Drive
Reston, VA 20191
Phone: (800) 548-2723 or (703) 295-6300
Fax: (703) 295-6222
Washington, D.C., office:
101 Constitution Avenue NW
Suite 375 East
Washington, DC 20001
Phone: 800 548-ASCE (2723), ext. 7850
http://www.asce.org

American Water Resources Association
Four West Federal Street
P.O. Box 1626
Middleburg, VA 20118
Phone: (540) 687-8390
Fax: (540) 687-8395
http://www.awra.org

American Water Works Association
6666 West Quincy Avenue
Denver, CO 80235
Phone: (800) 926-7337 or (303) 794-7711
Fax: (303) 347-0804
http://www.awwa.org

National Society of Professional Engineers
1420 King Street
Alexandria, VA 22314
Phone: (703) 684-2800
Fax: (703) 836-4875
http://www.nspe.org

Society of Women Engineers
230 East Ohio Street
Suite 400
Chicago, IL 60611
Phone: (312) 596-5223
http://www.swe.org

Solid Waste Association of North America
1100 Wayne Avenue
Suite 700
Silver Spring, MD 20910
Mailing address:
P.O. Box 7219
Silver Spring, MD 20907
Phone: (800) 467-9262
Fax: (301) 589-7068
http://www.swana.org

CHEMICAL ENGINEERING

AACC International
3340 Pilot Knob Road
St. Paul, MN 55121
Phone: (651) 454-7250
Fax: (651) 454-0766
http://www.aaccnet.org

American Chemical Society
1155 16th Street NW
Washington, DC 20036
Phone: (800) 227-5558 or (202) 872-4600
Fax: (202) 776-4615
http://www.chemistry.org

American Institute of Chemical Engineers
Three Park Avenue
New York, NY 10016
Phone: (800) 242-4363 or (212) 591-8100
Fax: (212) 591-8888
http://www.aiche.org

American Society of Agricultural and Biological Engineers
2950 Niles Road
St. Joseph, MI 49085
Phone: (269) 429-0300
Fax: (269) 429-3852
http://www.asabe.org

Association of Consulting Chemists and Chemical Engineers
P.O. Box 297
Sparta, NJ 07871
Phone: (973) 729-6671
Fax: (973) 729-7088
http://www.chemconsult.org

Institute of Food Technologists
525 West Van Buren
Suite 1000
Chicago, IL 60607
Phone: (312) 782-8424
Fax: (312) 782-8348
http://www.ift.org

International Association for Food Protection
6200 Aurora Avenue
Suite 200W
Des Moines, IA 50322
Phone: (800) 369-6337 or (515) 276-3344
Fax: (515) 276-8655
http://www.foodprotection.org

International Society of Food Engineering
c/o Biological Systems Engineering
P.O. Box 646120
Washington State University

Pullman, WA 99164
Phone: (509) 335-6188
Fax: (509) 335-2722
http://www.bsyse.wsu.edu/isfe

National Society of Professional Engineers
1420 King Street
Alexandria, VA 22314
Phone: (703) 684-2800
Fax: (703) 836-4875
http://www.nspe.org

Society of Women Engineers
230 East Ohio Street
Suite 400
Chicago, IL 60611
Phone: (312) 596-5223
http://www.swe.org

MATERIALS ENGINEERING

American Ceramic Society
735 Ceramic Place
Suite 100
Westerville, OH 43081
Phone: (614) 890-4700
Fax: (614) 899-6109
http://www.ceramics.org

American Institute of Chemical Engineers
Three Park Avenue
New York, NY 10016
Phone: (800) 242-4363 or (212) 591-8100
Fax: (212) 591-8888
http://www.aiche.org

ASM International
9639 Kinsman Road
Materials Park, OH 44073
Phone: (800) 336-5152 (U.S. and Canada); (800) 368-9800 (Europe); or (440) 338-5151
Fax: (440) 338-4634
http://www.asminternational.org

ASTM International
100 Barr Harbor Drive
P.O. Box C700
West Conshohocken, PA 19428
Phone: (610) 832-9585
Fax: (610) 832-9555
http://www.astm.org

Materials Division, ASME International
http://divisions.asme.org/materials

Materials Engineering and Sciences Division, American Institute of Chemical Engineers
http://www.che.gatech.edu/MESD

Materials Research Society
506 Keystone Drive
Warrendale, PA 15086
Phone: (724) 779-3003
Fax: (724) 779-8313
http://www.mrs.org

Minerals, Metals, and Materials Society
184 Thorn Hill Road
Warrendale, PA 15086
Phone: (800) 759-4867 or (724) 776-9000
Fax: (724) 776-3770
http://www.tms.org

NACE International
1440 South Creek Drive
Houston, TX 77084
Phone: (800) 797-6223 or (281) 228-6200
Fax: (281) 228-6300
http://www.nace.org

National Society of Professional Engineers
1420 King Street
Alexandria, VA 22314
Phone: (703) 684-2800
Fax: (703) 836-4875
http://www.nspe.org

Society for Biomaterials
15000 Commerce Parkway, Suite C
Mt. Laurel, NJ 08054
Phone: (856) 439-0826
Fax: (856) 439-0525
http://www.biomaterials.org

Society of Plastics Engineers
14 Fairfield Drive
P.O. Box 403
Brookfield, CT 06804
Phone: (203) 775-0471
Fax: (203) 775-8490
http://www.4spe.org

Society of Women Engineers
230 East Ohio Street
Suite 400
Chicago, IL 60611
Phone: (312) 596-5223
http://www.swe.org

MECHANICAL ENGINEERING

American Society of Heating, Refrigerating and Air-Conditioning Engineers
1791 Tullie Circle NE
Atlanta, GA 30329
Phone: (800) 527-4723 or (404) 636-8400
Fax: (404) 321-5478
http://www.ashrae.org

ASME International
Three Park Avenue
New York, NY 10016
Phone: (800) 843-2763 or (212) 591-7722
Fax: (212) 591-7674
http://www.asme.org

National Society of Professional Engineers
1420 King Street
Alexandria, VA 22314
Phone: (703) 684-2800
Fax: (703) 836-4875
http://www.nspe.org

SAE International
World headquarters:
400 Commonwealth Drive
Warrendale, PA 15096
Phone: (724) 776-4841
Automotive headquarters:
755 West Big Beaver
Suite 1600
Troy, MI 48084
Fax: (248) 273-2494
Washington, D.C., office:
1828 L Street NW
Suite 906
Washington, DC 20036
Phone: (202) 463-7318
Fax: (202) 463-7319
http://www.sae.org

Society of Manufacturing Engineers
One SME Drive
P.O. Box 930
Dearborn, MI 48121
Phone: (800) 733-4763 or (313) 271-1500
Fax: (313) 425-3400
http://www.sme.org

Society of Women Engineers
230 East Ohio Street
Suite 400
Chicago, IL 60611
Phone: (312) 596-5223
http://www.swe.org

ELECTRICAL, ELECTRONICS, AND COMPUTER ENGINEERING

American Association for Artificial Intelligence
445 Burgess Drive, Suite 100
Menlo Park, CA 94025
Phone: (650) 328-3123
Fax: (650) 321-4457
http://www.aaai.org

American Institute of Aeronautics and Astronautics
1801 Alexander Bell Drive, Suite 500
Reston, VA 20191
Phone: (800) 639-AIAA or
(703) 264-7500
Fax: (703) 264-7551
Western office:
2221 Rosecrans Avenue
El Segundo, CA 90245
Phone: (310) 643-7510
Fax: (310) 643-7509
http://www.aiaa.org

Guidance, Navigation and Control Technical Committee, American Institute of Aeronautics and Astronautics
1801 Alexander Bell Drive, Suite 500
Reston, VA 20191
http://www.aiaa.org

Association for Computing Machinery
1515 Broadway, 17th Floor
New York, NY 10036
Phone: (800) 342-6626 or
(212) 869-7440
http://www.acm.org

Association of Information Technology Professionals
401 North Michigan Avenue
Suite 2400
Chicago, IL 60611
Phone: (800) 224-9371 or (312) 245-1070
Fax: (312) 527-6636
http://www.aitp.org

IEEE Computer Society
1730 Massachusetts Avenue NW
Washington, DC 20036
Phone: (202) 371-0101
Fax: (202) 728-9614
http://www.computer.org/portal/site/ieeecs

IEEE Control Systems Society
445 Hoes Lane
P.O. Box 1331
Piscataway, NJ 08855
Phone: (800) 678-4333 or (908) 562-5528
http://www.ieeecss.org

Institute of Electrical and Electronics Engineers (IEEE)
Three Park Avenue, 17th Floor
New York, NY 10016
Phone: (212) 419-7900
Fax: (212) 752-4929
http://www.ieee.org

Instrumentation, Systems, and Automation Society
67 Alexander Drive
Research Triangle Park, NC 27709
Phone: (919) 549-8411
Fax: (919) 549-8288
http://www.isa.org

National Association of Radio and Telecommunications Engineers
167 Village Street
Medway, MA 02053
Phone: (800) 89-NARTE or (508) 533-8333
Fax: (508) 533-3815
http://www.narte.org

National Society of Black Engineers
1454 Duke Street
Alexandria, VA 22314
Phone: (703) 549-2207
Fax: (703) 683-5312
http://www.nsbe.org

National Society of Professional Engineers
1420 King Street
Alexandria, VA 22314
Phone: (703) 684-2800
Fax: (703) 836-4875
http://www.nspe.org

Optical Society of America
2010 Massachusetts Avenue NW
Washington, DC 20036
Phone: (202) 223-8130
Fax: (202) 223-1096
http://www.osa.org

SAGE (a USENIX Association Special Interest Group)
2560 Ninth Street, Suite 215
Berkeley, CA 94710
Phone: (510) 528-8649
Fax: (510) 548-5738
http://www.sage.org

Society of Cable Telecommunications Engineers
140 Phillips Road
Exton, PA 19341
Phone: (800) 542-5040 or (610) 363-6888
Fax: (610) 363-5898
http://www.scte.org

Society of Manufacturing Engineers
One SME Drive
Dearborn, MI 48121
Phone: (800) 733-4763 or (313) 271-1500
Fax: (313) 425-3401
http://www.sme.org

Society of Women Engineers
230 East Ohio Street
Suite 400
Chicago, IL 60611
Phone: (312) 596-5223
http://www.swe.org

Special Interest Group on Software Engineering, Association for Computing Machinery
1515 Broadway, 17th Floor
New York, NY 10036
Phone: (212) 626-0613
Fax: (212) 302-5826
http://www.sigsoft.org

Technical Council on Software Engineering, IEEE Computer Society
IEEE Computer Society
Attn: TCSE
1730 Massachusetts Avenue NW
Washington, DC 20036
Phone: (202) 371-0101
http://www.tcse.org

AEROSPACE ENGINEERING

American Association for Artificial Intelligence
445 Burgess Drive, Suite 100
Menlo Park, CA 94025
Phone: (650) 328-3123
Fax: (650) 321-4457
http://www.aaai.org

American Astronautical Society
6352 Rolling Mill Place
Suite 102
Springfield, VA 22152
Phone: (703) 866-0020
Fax: (703) 866-3526
http://www.astronautical.org

American Institute of Aeronautics and Astronautics
1801 Alexander Bell Drive, Suite 500
Reston, VA 20191
Phone: (800) 639-AIAA or
(703) 264-7500
Fax: (703) 265-7551
Western office:
2221 Rosecrans Avenue
El Segundo, CA 90245
Phone: (310) 643-7510
Fax: (310) 643-7509
http://www.aiaa.org

ASME International
Three Park Avenue
New York, NY 10016
Phone: (800) 843-2763 or (212) 591-7722
Fax: (212) 591-7674
http://www.asme.org

Association for Computing Machinery
1515 Broadway, 17th Floor
New York, NY 10036
Phone: (800) 342-6626 or (212) 869-7440
http://www.acm.org

Institute of Electrical and Electronics Engineers
Three Park Avenue, 17th Floor
New York, NY 10016
Phone: (212) 419-7900
Fax: (212) 752-4929
http://www.ieee.org

National Society of Professional Engineers
1420 King Street
Alexandria, VA 22314
Phone: (703) 684-2800
Fax: (703) 836-4875
http://www.nspe.org

Society of Flight Test Engineers
44814 North Elm Avenue
Lancaster, CA 93534
Phone: (661) 949-2095
Fax: (661) 949-2096
http://www.sfte.org

Society of Hispanic Professional Engineers
http://www.shpe.org

Society of Women Engineers
230 East Ohio Street
Suite 400
Chicago, IL 60611
Phone: (312) 596-5223
http://www.swe.org

AGRICULTURAL AND BIOLOGICAL ENGINEERING

American Academy of Environmental Engineers
130 Holiday Court
Suite 100
Annapolis, MD 21401
Phone: (410) 266-3311
Fax: (410) 266-7653
http://www.aaee.net

American Fisheries Society
5410 Grosvenor Lane
Bethesda, MD 20814
Phone: (301) 897-8616
Fax: (301) 897-8096
http://www.fisheries.org

American Society of Agricultural and Biological Engineers
2950 Niles Road
St. Joseph, MI 49085
Phone: (269) 429-0300
Fax: (269) 429-3852
http://www.asabe.org

Aquacultural Engineering Society
c/o Freshwater Institute
P.O. Box 1889
Shepherdstown, WV 25443
Phone: (304) 876-2815
http://www.aesweb.org

Council on Forest Engineering
620 SW Fourth Street
Corvallis, OR 97333
Phone: (541) 754-7558
Fax: (541) 754-7559
http://www.cofe.org

National Society of Professional Engineers
1420 King Street
Alexandria, VA 22314
Phone: (703) 684-2800
Fax: (703) 836-4875
http://www.nspe.org

Society of American Foresters
5400 Grosvenor Lane
Bethesda, MD 20814
Phone: (866) 897-8720 or (301) 897-8720
Fax: (301) 897-3690
http://www.safnet.org

Society of Women Engineers
230 East Ohio Street
Suite 400
Chicago, IL 60611
Phone: (312) 596-5223
http://www.swe.org

World Aquaculture Society–U.S. Chapter
143 J.M. Parker Coliseum
Louisiana State University
Baton Rouge, LA 70803
Phone: (225) 578-3137
Fax: (225) 578-3493
http://ag.arizona.edu/azaqua/WAS/uschap.htm

BIOMEDICAL ENGINEERING

American Association for the Advancement of Science
1200 New York Avenue NW
Washington, DC 20005
Phone: (202) 326-6400
http://www.aaas.org

American Association of University Professors
1012 14th Street NW
Suite 500
Washington, DC 20005
Phone: (202) 737-5900
Fax: (202) 737-5526
http://www.aaup.org

American College of Clinical Engineering
5200 Butler Pike
Plymouth Meeting, PA 19462
Phone: (610) 825-6067
Fax: (480) 247-5040
http://www.accenet.org

American Institute for Medical and Biological Engineering
1901 Pennsylvania Avenue NW
Suite 401
Washington, DC 20006
Phone: (202) 496-9660
Fax: (202) 466-8489
http://www.aimbe.org

American Institute of Chemical Engineers
Three Park Avenue
New York, NY 10016
Phone: (800) 242-4363 or (212) 591-8100
Fax: (212) 591-8888
http://www.aiche.org

American Society of Biomechanics
http://www.asbweb.org

Association for the Advancement of Medical Instrumentation
1110 North Glebe Road
Suite 220
Arlington, VA 22201
Phone: (703) 525-4890
Fax: (703) 276-0793
http://www.aami.org

Biomedical Engineering Society
8401 Corporate Drive
Suite 140
Landover, MD 20785
Phone: (301) 459-1999
Fax: (301) 459-2444
http://www.bmes.org

IEEE Engineering in Medicine and Biology Society
445 Hoes Lane
Piscataway, NJ 08855
Phone: (732) 981-3433
Fax: (732) 465-6435
http://embs.gsbme.unsw.edu.au

National Association of Scholars
221 Witherspoon Street, Second Floor
Princeton, NJ 08542
Phone: (609) 683-7878
http://www.nas.org

Rehabilitation Engineering and Assistive Technology Society of North America
1700 North Moore Street, Suite 1540
Arlington, VA 22209
Phone: (703) 524-6686
TTY: (703) 524-6639
Fax: (703) 524-6630
http://www.resna.org

Tissue Engineering and Regenerative Medicine International Society
http://www.tesinternational.org

INDUSTRIAL, MANUFACTURING, AND SYSTEMS ENGINEERING

Aerospace Human Factors Association
c/o Aerospace Medical Association
320 South Henry Street
Alexandria, VA 22314
Phone: (703) 739-2240
Fax: (703) 739-9652
http://www.asma.org/Organization/ashfa

American Society for Quality
600 North Plankinton Avenue
Milwaukee, WI 53203
Mailing address:
P.O. Box 3005
Milwaukee, WI 53201
Phone: (800) 248-1946 or (414) 272-8575
Fax: (414) 272-1734
http://www.asq.org

Human Factors and Ergonomics Society
1124 Montana Avenue, Suite B
Santa Monica, CA 90403
Mailing address:
P.O. Box 1369
Santa Monica, CA 90406
Phone: (310) 394-1811
Fax: (310) 394-2410
http://www.hfes.org

IEEE Systems, Man, and Cybernetics Society
Three Park Avenue, 17th Floor
New York, NY 10016
Phone: (212) 419-7900
Fax: (212) 752-4929
http://www.ieeesmc.org

Institute of Industrial Engineers
3577 Parkway Lane
Suite 200
Norcross, GA 30092
Phone: (800) 494-0460 or (770) 449-0460
Fax: (770) 441-3295
http://www.iienet.org

International Council on Systems Engineering
2150 North 107th Street
Suite 205
Seattle, WA 98133
Phone: (800) 366-1164 or (206) 361-6607
Fax: (206) 367-8777
http://www.incose.org

International Society for Performance Improvement
1400 Spring Street
Suite 260
Silver Spring, MD 20910
Phone: (301) 587-8570
Fax: (301) 587-8573
http://www.ispi.org

National Society of Professional Engineers
1420 King Street
Alexandria, VA 22314

Phone: (703) 684-2800
Fax: (703) 836-4875
http://www.nspe.org

Society of Manufacturing Engineers
One SME Drive
Dearborn, MI 48121
Phone: (800) 733-4763 or (313) 271-1500
Fax: (313) 425-3401
http://www.sme.org

Special Interest Group on Computer-Human Interaction, Association for Computer Machinery
http://sigchi.org

MORE ENGINEERING DISCIPLINES

Acoustical Society of America
Two Huntington Quadrangle
Suite 1NO1
Melville, NY 11747
Phone: (516) 576-2360
Fax: (516) 576-2377
http://asa.aip.org

American Geological Institute
4220 King Street
Alexandria, VA 22302
Phone: (703) 379-2480
Fax: (703) 379-7563
http://www.agiweb.org

American Institute of Mining, Metallurgical, and Petroleum Engineers
8307 Shaffer Parkway
Littleton, CO 80127
Mailing address:
P.O. Box 270728
Littleton, CO 80127
Phone: (303) 948-4255
Fax: (303) 948-4260
http://www.aimeny.org

American Nuclear Society
555 North Kensington Avenue
La Grange Park, IL 60526
Phone: (708) 352-6611
Fax: (708) 352-0499
http://www.ans.org

American Society of Heating, Refrigerating and Air-Conditioning Engineers
1791 Tullie Circle NE
Atlanta, GA 30329

Phone: (800) 527-4723 or (404) 636-8400
Fax: (404) 321-5478
http://www.ashrae.org

American Society of Naval Engineers
1452 Duke Street
Alexandria, VA 22314
Phone: (703) 836-6727
Fax: (703) 836-7491
http://www.navalengineers.org

American Society of Safety Engineers
1800 East Oakton Street
Des Plaines, IL 60018
Phone: (847) 699-2929
Fax: (847) 768-3434
http://www.asse.org

American Welding Society
550 NW LeJeune Road
Miami, FL 33126
Phone: (800) 443-9353 or (305) 443-9353
http://www.aws.org

Architectural Engineering Institute of ASCE
1801 Alexander Bell Drive
Reston, VA 20191
Phone: (703) 295-6393
http://www.aeinstitute.org

Association of Environmental and Engineering Geologists
P.O. Box 460518
Denver, CO 80246
Phone: (303) 757-2926
Fax: (303) 757-2969
http://www.aegweb.org

ASME International
Three Park Avenue
New York, NY 10016
Phone: (800) 843-2763 or (212) 591-7722
Fax: (212) 591-7674
http://www.asme.org

Audio Engineering Society
60 East 42nd Street, Room 2520
New York, NY 10165
Phone: (212) 661-8528
Fax: (212) 682-0477
http://www.aes.org

Environmental and Engineering Geophysical Society
1720 South Bellaire
Suite 110
Denver, CO 80222
Phone: (303) 531-7517
Fax: (303) 820-3844
http://www.eegs.org

Geological Society of America
P.O. Box 9140
Boulder, CO 80301
Phone: (888) 443-4472 or 303 357-1071
Fax: (303) 357-1070
http://www.geosociety.org

Illuminating Engineering Society of North America
120 Wall Street, Floor 17
New York, NY 10005
Phone: (212) 248-5000
Fax: (212) 248-5017 or (212) 248-5018
http://www.iesna.org

Institute of Electrical and Electronics Engineers
Three Park Avenue, 17th Floor
New York, NY 10016
Phone: (212) 419-7900
Fax: (212) 752-4929
http://www.ieee.org

Institute of Noise Control Engineering of the USA
210 Marston Hall
Ames, IA 50011
Phone: (515) 294-6142
Fax: (515) 294-3528
http://www.inceusa.org

International Institute of Acoustics and Vibration
http://www.iiav.org

International Society of Explosives Engineers
30325 Bainbridge Road
Cleveland, OH 44139
Phone: (440) 349-4400
Fax: (440) 349-3788
http://www.isee.org

Marine Technology Society
5565 Sterrett Place, Suite 108
Columbia, MD 21044
Phone: (410) 884-5330
Fax: (410) 884-9060
http://www.mtsociety.org

Mining and Metallurgical Society of America
476 Wilson Avenue
Novato, CA 94947
Phone: (415) 897-1380
http://www.mmsa.net

National Council of Acoustical Consultants
7150 Winton Drive, Suite 300
Indianapolis, IN 46268

Phone: (317) 328-0642
Fax: (317) 328-4629
http://www.ncac.com

National Fire Protection Association
One Batterymarch Park
Quincy, MA 02169
Phone: (617) 770-3000
Fax: (617) 770-0700
http://www.nfpa.org

National Society of Black Engineers
1454 Duke Street
Alexandria, VA 22314
Phone: (703) 549-2207
Fax: (703) 683-5312
http://www.nsbe.org

National Society of Professional Engineers
1420 King Street
Alexandria, VA 22314
Phone: (703) 684-2800
Fax: (703) 836-4875
http://www.nspe.org

Oceanic Engineering Society
http://www.oceanicengineering.org

Society for Mining, Metallurgy, and Exploration
8307 Schaffer Parkway
Littleton, CO 80127
Phone: (800) 763-3132 or (303) 973-9550
Fax: (303) 973-3845
http://www.smenet.org

Society of Fire Protection Engineers
7315 Wisconsin Avenue, Suite 620E
Bethesda, MD 20814
Phone: (301) 718-2910
Fax: (301) 718-2242
http://www.sfpe.org

Society of Manufacturing Engineers
One SME Drive
Dearborn, MI 48121
Phone: (800) 733-4763 or (313) 271-1500
Fax: (313) 425-3401
http://www.sme.org

Society of Naval Architects and Marine Engineers
601 Pavonia Avenue
Jersey City, NJ 07306
Phone: (800) 798-2188 or (201) 798-4800
Fax: (201) 798-4975
http://www.sname.org

Society of Petroleum Engineers
P.O. Box 833836
Richardson, TX 75083

Phone: (800) 456-6863 or (972) 952-9393
Fax: (972) 952-9435
http://www.spe.org

Society of Women Engineers
230 East Ohio Street
Suite 400
Chicago, IL 60611
Phone: (312) 596-5223
http://www.swe.org

**Structural Engineering Institute of
  ASCE**
1801 Alexander Bell Drive
Reston, VA 20191
Phone: (800) 548-2723
http://www.seinstitute.org

Women in Mining
P.O. Box 260246
Lakewood, CO 80226
Phone: (303) 298-1535
http://www.womeninmining.org

ENGINEERING SPECIALTIES

**American Academy of Environmental
  Engineers**
130 Holiday Court
Suite 100
Annapolis, MD 21401
Phone: (410) 266-3311
Fax: (410) 266-7653
http://www.aaee.net

**American Academy of Forensic
  Sciences**
410 North 21st Street
Colorado Springs, CO 80904
Phone: (719) 636-1100
Fax: (719) 636-1993
http://www.aafs.org

**American College of Forensic
  Examiners Institute of Forensic
  Science**
2750 East Sunshine Street
Springfield, MO 65804
Phone: (800) 423-9737 or (417) 881-3818
Fax: (417) 881-4702
http://www.acfei.org

**American Indian Science and
  Engineering Society**
2305 Renard SE
Suite 200
Albuquerque, NM 87106
Mailing address:
P.O. Box 9828
Albuquerque, NM 87119

Phone: (505) 765-1052
Fax: (505) 765-5608
http://www.aises.org

**American Institute of Aeronautics and
  Astronautics**
1801 Alexander Bell Drive, Suite 500
Reston, VA 20191
Phone: (800) 639-AIAA or
  (703) 264-7500
Fax: (703) 265-7551
Western office:
2221 Rosecrans Avenue
El Segundo, CA 90245
Phone: (310) 643-7510
Fax: (310) 643-7509
http://www.aiaa.org

**American Institute of Chemical
  Engineers**
Three Park Avenue
New York, NY 10016
Phone: (800) 242-4363 or (212) 591-8100
Fax: (212) 591-8888
http://www.aiche.org

American Nuclear Society
555 North Kensington Avenue
La Grange Park, IL 60526
Phone: (708) 352-6611
Fax: (708) 352-0499
http://www.ans.org

**American Society for Engineering
  Education**
1818 North Street NW
Suite 600
Washington, DC 20036
Phone: (202) 331-3500
Fax: (202) 265-8504
http://www.asee.org

**American Society for Engineering
  Management**
http://www.asem.org

**American Society of Agricultural and
  Biological Engineers**
2950 Niles Road
St. Joseph, MI 49085
Phone: (269) 429-0300
Fax: (269) 429-3852
http://www.asabe.org

American Society of Civil Engineers
ASCE world headquarters:
1801 Alexander Bell Drive
Reston, VA 20191
Phone: (800) 548-2723 or (703) 295-6300
Fax: (703) 295-6222
Washington, D.C., office:

101 Constitution Avenue NW
Suite 375 East
Washington, DC 20001
Phone: (800) 548-ASCE (2723), ext. 7850
http://www.asce.org

American Society of Test Engineers
P.O. Box 389
Nutting Lake, MA 01865
http://www.aste test.org

ASM International
9639 Kinsman Road
Materials Park, OH 44073
Phone: (800) 336-5152 (United States
  and Canada); (800) 368-9800
  (Europe); or (440) 338-5151
Fax: (440) 338-4634
http://www.asminternational.org

ASME International
Three Park Avenue
New York, NY 10016
Phone: (800) 843-2763 or (212) 591-7722
Fax: (212) 591-7674
http://www.asme.org

Association for Computing Machinery
1515 Broadway, 17th Floor
New York, NY 10036
Phone: (800) 342-6626 or (212) 626-0500
http://www.acm.org

Association for Facilities Engineering
8160 Corporate Park Drive
Suite 125
Cincinnati, OH 45242
Phone: (513) 489-2473
http://www.afe.org

Association of Energy Engineers
4025 Pleasantdale Road
Suite 420
Atlanta, GA 30340
Phone: (770) 447-5083
http://www.aeecenter.org

ASTM International
100 Barr Harbor Drive
P.O. Box C700
West Conshohocken, PA 19428
Phone: (610) 832-9585
Fax: (610) 832-9555
http://www.astm.org

Biomedical Engineering Society
8401 Corporate Drive
Suite 140
Landover, MD 20785
Phone: (301) 459-1999
Fax: (301) 459-2444
http://www.bmes.org

**IEEE Engineering Management
    Society**
http://www.ewh.ieee.org/soc/ems

**Institute of Electrical and Electronics
    Engineers**
Three Park Avenue, 17th Floor
New York, NY 10016
Phone: (212) 419-7900
Fax: (212) 752-4929
http://www.ieee.org

Institute of Industrial Engineers
3577 Parkway Lane
Suite 200
Norcross, GA 30092
Phone: (800) 494-0460 or (770) 449-0460
Fax: (770) 441-3295
http://www.iienet.org

Institute of Transportation Engineers
1099 14th Street NW
Suite 300 West
Washington, DC 20005
Phone: (202) 289-0222
Fax: (202) 289-7722
http://www.ite.org

**International Association for
    Management of Technology**
University of Miami
College of Engineering
P.O. Box 248294
Coral Gables, FL 33124
Phone: (305) 284-2344
Fax: (305) 284-4040
http://www.iamot.org

**International Society of Food
    Engineering**
c/o Biological Systems Engineering
P.O. Box 646120
Washington State University
Pullman, WA 99164
Phone: (509) 335-6188
Fax: (509) 335-2722
http://www.bsyse.wsu.edu/isfe

**International Test and Evaluation
    Association**
4400 Fair Lakes Court, Suite 104
Fairfax, VA 22033
Phone: (703) 631-6220
Fax: (703) 631-6221
http://www.itea.org

National Academy of Forensic Engineers
174 Brady Avenue
Hawthorne, NY 10532

Phone: (866) 623-3674
Fax: (877) 741-0633
http://www.nafe.org

National Fire Protection Association
One Batterymarch Park
Quincy, MA 02169
Phone: (617) 770-3000
Fax: (617) 770-0700
http://www.nfpa.org

National Society of Black Engineers
1454 Duke Street
Alexandria, VA 22314
Phone: (703) 549-2207
Fax: (703) 683-5312
http://www.nsbe.org

**National Society of Professional
    Engineers**
1420 King Street
Alexandria, VA 22314
Phone: (703) 684-2800
Fax: (703) 836-4875
http://www.nspe.org

**Product Development and
    Management Association**
15000 Commerce Parkway
Suite C
Mount Laurel, NJ 08054
Phone: (800) 232-5241 or (856) 439-9052
Fax: (856) 439-0525
http://www.pdma.org

**Regulatory Affairs Professionals
    Society**
11300 Rockville Pike
Suite 1000
Rockville, MD 20852
Phone: (301) 770-2920
Fax: (301) 770-2924
http://www.raps.org

SAE International
World headquarters:
400 Commonwealth Drive
Warrendale, PA 15096
Phone: (724) 776-4841
Automotive headquarters:
755 West Big Beaver
Suite 1600
Troy, MI 48084
Fax: (248) 273-2494
Washington, D.C., office:
1828 L Street NW
Suite 906
Washington, DC 20036
Phone: (202) 463-7318

Fax: (202) 463-7319
http://www.sae.org

**Society of Hispanic Professional
    Engineers**
http://www.shpe.org

Society of Manufacturing Engineers
One SME Drive
Dearborn, MI 48121
Phone: (800) 733-4763 or (313) 271-1500
Fax: (313) 425-3401
http://www.sme.org

Society of Women Engineers
230 East Ohio Street
Suite 400
Chicago, IL 60611
Phone: (312) 596-5223
http://www.swe.org

**Structural Engineering Institute of
    ASCE**
1801 Alexander Bell Drive
Reston, VA 20191
Phone: (800) 548-2723
http://www.seinstitute.org

ENGINEERING
TECHNOLOGISTS AND
TECHNICIANS

**American Academy of Environmental
    Engineers**
130 Holiday Court
Suite 100
Annapolis, MD 21401
Phone: (410) 266-3311
Fax: (410) 266-7653
http://www.aaee.net

**American Association for Geodetic
    Surveying**
Six Montgomery Village Avenue
Suite 403
Gaithersburg, MD 20879
Phone: (240) 632-9716
Fax: (240) 632-1321
https://www.aagsmo.org

**American Congress on Surveying and
    Mapping**
Six Montgomery Village Avenue
Suite 403
Gaithersburg, MD 20879
Phone: (240) 632-9716
Fax: (240) 632-1321
http://www.acsm.net

American Design Drafting Association International
105 East Main Street
Newbern, TN 38059
Phone: (731) 627-0802
Fax: (731) 627-9321
http://www.adda.org

American Institute of Aeronautics and Astronautics
1801 Alexander Bell Drive, Suite 500
Reston, VA 20191
Phone: (800) 639-AIAA or
   (703) 264-7500
Fax: (703) 265-7551
Western office:
2221 Rosecrans Avenue
El Segundo, CA 90245
Phone: (310) 643-7510
Fax: (310) 643-7509
http://www.aiaa.org

American Institute of Chemical Engineers
Three Park Avenue
New York, NY 10016
Phone: (800) 242-4363 or (212) 591-8100
Fax: (212) 591-8888
http://www.aiche.org

American Society of Agricultural and Biological Engineers
2950 Niles Road
St. Joseph, MI 49085
Phone: (269) 429-0300
Fax: (269) 429-3852
http://www.asabe.org

American Society of Certified Engineering Technicians
P.O. Box 1536
Brandon, MS 39043
Phone: (601) 824-8991
http://www.ascet.org

American Society of Civil Engineers
ASCE world headquarters:
1801 Alexander Bell Drive
Reston, VA 20191
Phone: (800) 548-2723 or (703) 295-6300
Fax: (703) 295-6222
Washington, D.C., office:
101 Constitution Avenue NW
Suite 375 East
Washington, DC 20001
Phone: (800) 548-ASCE (2723), ext. 7850
http://www.asce.org

ASME International
Three Park Avenue
New York, NY 10016
Phone: (800) 843-2763 or (212) 591-7722
Fax: (212) 591-7674
http://www.asme.org

Biomedical Engineering Society
8401 Corporate Drive
Suite 140
Landover, MD 20785
Phone: (301) 459-1999
Fax: (301) 459-2444
http://www.bmes.org

Institute of Electrical and Electronics Engineers
Three Park Avenue, 17th Floor
New York, NY 10016
Phone: (212) 419-7900
Fax: (212) 752-4929
http://www.ieee.org

Institute of Industrial Engineers
3577 Parkway Lane
Suite 200
Norcross, GA 30092
Phone: (800) 494-0460 or (770) 449-0460
Fax: (770) 441-3295
http://www.iienet.org

National Association of County Surveyors
http://www.naco.org/nacs

National Society of Professional Surveyors
Six Montgomery Village Avenue
Suite 403
Gaithersburg, MD 20879
Phone: (240) 632-9716
Fax: (240) 632-1321
http://www.acsm.net/nsps

ALTERNATIVE CAREERS FOR ENGINEERS

American Association for the Advancement of Science
1200 New York Avenue NW
Washington, DC 20005
Phone: (202) 326-6400
http://www.aaas.org

American Association of University Professors
1012 14th Street NW
Suite 500
Washington, DC 20005
Phone: (202) 737-5900
Fax: (202) 737-5526
http://www.aaup.org

American Bar Association
321 North Clark Street
Chicago, IL 60610
Phone: (800) 285-2221, (312) 988-5522,
   or (312) 988-5000
Washington, D.C., office:
740 15th Street NW
Washington, DC 20005
Phone: (202) 662-1000
http://www.abanet.org

American Institute of Chemical Engineers
Three Park Avenue
New York, NY 10016-5991
Phone: (800) 242-4363 or (212) 591-8100
Fax: (212) 591-8888
http://www.aiche.org

American Intellectual Property Law Association
2001 Jefferson Davis Highway
Suite 203
Arlington, VA 22202
Phone: (703) 415-0780
Fax: (703) 415-0786
http://www.aipla.org

American Marketing Association
311 South Wacker Drive
Suite 5800
Chicago, IL 60606
Phone: (800) AMA-1150 or
   (312) 542-9000
Fax: (312) 542-9001
http://www.marketingpower.com

American Society for Engineering Education
1818 N Street NW
Suite 600
Washington, DC 20036
Phone: (202) 331-3500
Fax: (202) 265-8504
http://www.asee.org

American Society of Agricultural and Biological Engineers
2950 Niles Road
St. Joseph, MI 49085
Phone: (269) 429-0300
Fax: (269) 429-3852
http://www.asabe.org

ASME International
Three Park Avenue
New York, NY 10016
Phone: (800) 843-2763 or (212) 591-7722
Fax: (212) 591-7674
http://www.asme.org

Association for Public Policy Analysis and Management
2100 M Street NW
Suite 610
Washington, DC 20036
Mailing address:
P.O. Box 18766
Washington, DC 20037
Phone: (202) 496-0130
Fax: (202) 496-0134
http://www.appam.org

Association of Trial Lawyers of America
1050 31st Street NW
Washington, DC 20007
Phone: (800) 424-2725 or (202) 965-3500
http://www.atla.org

Editorial Freelancers Association
71 West 23rd Street
Suite 1910
New York, NY 10010
Phone: (866) 929-5400 or (212) 929-5400
Fax: (866) 929-5439 or (212) 929-5439
http://www.the-efa.org

Institute of Electrical and Electronics Engineers
Three Park Avenue, 17th Floor
New York, NY 10016
Phone: (212) 419-7900
Fax: (212) 752-4929
http://www.ieee.org

Institute of Management Consultants USA
2025 M Street NW
Suite 800
Washington, DC 20036
Phone: (800) 221-2557 or (202) 367-1134
Fax: (202) 367-2134
http://www.imcusa.org

National Association of Patent Practitioners
4680-18-i Monticello Avenue, PMB 101
Williamsburg, VA 23188
Phone: (800) 216-9588
Fax: (757) 220-2231
http://www.napp.org

National Association of Scholars
221 Witherspoon Street, Second Floor

Princeton, NJ 08542
Phone: (609) 683-7878
http://www.nas.org

National Association of Women Lawyers
American Bar Center, MS 15.2
321 North Clark Street
Chicago, IL 60610
Fax: (312) 988-5491
http://www.nawl.org

National Employment Lawyers Association
44 Montgomery Street
Suite 2080
San Francisco, CA 94104
Phone: (415) 296-7629
Fax: (415) 677-9445
http://www.nelahq.org

National Lawyers Association
17201 East 40 Highway
Suite 207
Independence, MO 64055
Phone: (800) 471-2994
Fax: (816) 229-8425
http://www.nla.org

National Society of Black Engineers
1454 Duke Street
Alexandria, VA 22314
Phone: (703) 549-2207
Fax: (703) 683-5312
http://www.nsbe.org

National Society of Professional Engineers
1420 King Street
Alexandria, VA 22314
Phone: (703) 684-2800
Fax: (703) 836-4875
http://www.nspe.org

National Writers Union
113 University Place, Sixth Floor
New York, NY 10003
Phone: (212) 254-0279
Fax: (212) 254-0673
http://www.nwu.org

Patent Office Professional Association
http://www.popa.org

Professional and Technical Consultants Association
543 Vista Mar Avenue
Pacifica, CA 94044

Phone: (800) 74-PATCA or
(408) 971-5902
Fax: (650) 359-3089
http://www.patca.org

Professional Communication Society, Institute of Electrical and Electronic Engineers
http://www.ieeepcs.org

Sales and Marketing Executives International
P.O. Box 1390
Sumas, WA 98295
Phone: (312) 893-0751
Fax: (604) 855-0165
http://www.smei.org

Society for Marketing Professional Services
99 Canal Center Plaza
Suite 330
Alexandria, VA 22314
Phone: (800) 292-7677
Fax: (703) 549-2498
http://www.smps.org

Society for Technical Communication
901 North Stuart Street
Suite 904
Arlington, VA 22203
Phone: (703) 522-4114
Fax: (703) 522-2075
http://www.stc.org

Society of Hispanic Professional Engineers
http://www.shpe.org

Society of Women Engineers
230 East Ohio Street
Suite 400
Chicago, IL 60611
Phone: (312) 596-5223
http://www.swe.org

Special Interest Group on Design of Communication, Association for Computing Machinery
http://www.sigdoc.org

APPENDIX IV
RESOURCES ON THE WORLD WIDE WEB

In this appendix, you will find a listing of Web sites that can help you learn more about the various fields and specialties in engineering, as well as about the alternative career options that are available to engineers. In addition, you will find some Web resources that offer career and job search information.

Note: All Web site addresses were current at the time this book was written. If a URL is no longer valid, enter the web page title or the name of the organization or individual into a search engine to find the new address.

GENERAL INFORMATION

Open Directory Project
http://dmoz.org

U.S. Bureau of Labor Statistics
http://www.bls.gov

Wikipedia
http://www.wikipedia.com

World Book Online Reference Center
http://www.aolsvc.worldbook.aol.com/wb/Home

CAREER AND JOB INFORMATION

America's Job Bank
http://www.jobsearch.org

Career Prospects in Virginia
http://www.ccps.virginia.edu/career_prospects

Career Voyages
http://www.careervoyages.gov

Discover Engineering Online
http://www.discoverengineering.org

Engineering Careers, Jobs, and Employment Information
http://www.careeroverview.com/engineering-careers.html

Engineering Salary Calculator
http://www.engineersalary.com

Engineering Workforce Commission
http://www.ewc-online.org

GradNet
http://www.gradnet.iec.org

Graduating Engineer and Computer Careers Online
http://www.graduatingengineer.com

Iseek
http://www.iseek.org

Just Engineers.net
http://www.justengineers.net

Monster
http://www.monster.com

Occupational Employment Statistics
(U.S. Bureau of Labor Statistics)
http://www.bls.gov/oes

Occupational Outlook Handbook
(U.S. Bureau of Labor Statistics)
http://www.bls.gov/oco

O*Net OnLine
http://online.onetcenter.org

Partnership For Public Service
http://www.ourpublicservice.org

Sloan Career Cornerstone Center
http://www.careercornerstone.org

USA Jobs
(U.S. Office of Personnel Management)
http://www.usajobs.opm.gov

WetFeet.com
http://www.wetfeet.com

ENGINEERING—GENERAL INFORMATION

American Engineering Association
http://www.aea.org

Engineer Girl
http://www.engineergirl.org

Engineering and Mathematics
(The Riley Guide)
http://www.rileyguide.com/engin.html

Engineering Channel
(How Stuff Works)
http://science.howstuffworks.com/engineering-channel.htm

Engineering Central
http://www.engcen.com

Engineering.com
http://www.engineering.com

Engineering Education Service Center
http://www.engineeringedu.com

Engineering K-12 Center
(American Society for Engineering Education)
http://www.engineeringk12.org

The Engineering Tool Box
http://www.engineeringtoolbox.com

Engineers International
http://engineers-international.com

Engology.com
http://www.engology.com

Eng-Tips Forums
http://www.eng-tips.com

Future Scientists and Engineers of America
http://www.fsea.org

Junior Engineering Technical Society
http://www.jets.org

National Action Council for Minorities in Engineering
http://www.nacme.org

National Academy of Engineering
http://www.nae.edu

National Engineers Week
http://www.eweek.org

Progressive Engineer Online
http://www.progressiveengineer.com

A Sightseer's Guide to Engineering
http://www.engineeringsights.org

Tau Beta Pi
http://www.tbp.org

Theta Tau
http://www.thetatau.org

U.S. Council for International Engineering Practice
http://www.usciep.org

Women in Engineering Programs and Advocates Network
http://www.wepan.org

ACOUSTICAL ENGINEER

Acoustical Employment—Career Information
http://www.acoustics.org/emp.car.html

Acoustics.com
http://acoustics.com

International Society of Audiology
http://www.isa-audiology.org

World Forum for Acoustic Ecology
http://interact.uoregon.edu/MediaLit/WFAE/home/index.html

AEROSPACE ENGINEER

Aerospace Careers: Aeronautics and Astronautics
(Purdue University)
http://engineering.purdue.edu/AAE/Careers

Aviation Now.com
(Aviation Week)
http://www.aviationnow.com

Society of Professional Engineering Employees in Aerospace
http://www.speea.org

AGRICULTURAL ENGINEER

Agriculture Online
http://www.agriculture.com

Current Research Information System
(U.S. Department of Agriculture)
http://cris.csrees.usda.gov

Natural Resource, Agriculture, and Engineering Service
http://www.nraes.org

U.S. Department of Agriculture
http://www.usda.gov

AIR QUALITY ENGINEER

Air Now
http://cfpub.epa.gov/airnow

Air Subtopics
(U.S. Environmental Protection Agency)
http://www.epa.gov/ebtpages/air.html

Center for Clean Air Policy
http://ccap.org

Manufacturers of Emission Controls Association
http://www.meca.org

ANALYTICAL ENGINEER

FEA Portal
(Dermot Monaghan)
http://www.dermotmonaghan.com

NAFEMS
http://www.nafems.org

Practical Approaches to Engineering Analysis
(Integrated Technologies Engineering)
http://www.ite.com/~itekb/whitepaper/white_paper.htm

AQUACULTURAL ENGINEER

Aquaculture Information Center
(NOAA Central Library)
http://www.lib.noaa.gov/docaqua/frontpage.htm

Aquaculture Internet Resources
(Doug Ernst, Oregon State University)
http://biosys.bre.orst.edu/aquacult/aqualink.htm

National Aquaculture Association
http://www.nationalaquaculture.org

NOAA National Marine Fisheries Service
http://www.nmfs.noaa.gov

Sea Web
http://www.seaweb.org

ARCHITECTURAL ENGINEER

The Civil Engineering Portal— Architectural Engineering
http://www.icivilengineer.com/Architectural_Engineering

Greener Buildings
http://www.greenerbuildings.com

ATTORNEY

American Bar Association Career Counsel Pre-Law Toolkit
http://www.abanet.org/careercounsel/prelaw.html

Association of Patent Law Firms
http://www.aplf.org

Emplawyernet
http://www.emplawyernet.com

Intellectual Property Law Server
http://www.intelproplaw.com
Law and Policy Institutions Guide
http://www.lpig.org

Law School Admissions
(JD Admission.com)
http://www.law-school-admissions.com

Legal Career Center Network
http://www.thelccn.com

AUTOMOTIVE ENGINEER

Association of International Automobile Manufacturers
http://www.aiam.org

Automotive Industry Links
(Automotive Consulting Group)
http://www.autoconsulting.com/autolinks.htm

Automotive Research Center
http://arc.engin.umich.edu

Car•Body Design
http://www.carbodydesign.com

International Federation of Automotive Engineering Societies
http://www.fisita.com

AVIONICS ENGINEER

Avionics and Electronics
(Thirty Thousand Feet Aviation Directory)
http://www.thirtythousandfeet.com/avionics.htm

Avionics Engineering Center
(Ohio University)
http://www.ohio.edu/avionics

BIOCHEMICAL ENGINEER

Society for Biological Engineers
http://www.aiche.org/SBE

BIOMEDICAL ENGINEER

BIO.COM
http://bio.com

Biophysical Society
http://www.biophysics.org

Chemical and Biomedical Engineering Subject Portal
(Cleveland State University)
http://www.ulib.csuohio.edu/portals/chmeng-m.shtml

Institute of Biological Engineering
http://www.ibeweb.org

The Whitaker Foundation
http://www.whitaker.org

BIOSYSTEMS ENGINEER

Institute of Biological Engineering
http://www.ibeweb.org

CERAMIC ENGINEER

Association of American Ceramic Component Manufacturers
http://www.aaccm.org

Ceram
http://www.ceramres.co.uk

Ceramic Industry Magazine Online
http://www.ceramicindustry.com

United States Advanced Ceramics Association
http://www.advancedceramics.org

CHEMICAL ENGINEER

Cheresources.com
http://www.cheresources.com

The History of Chemical Engineering
(Wayne Pafko)
http://www.pafko.com/history/index.html

CHEMICAL PROCESS ENGINEER (PETROLEUM AND PETROCHEMICAL INDUSTRIES)

American Petroleum Institute
http://api-ec.api.org

Gas Processors Association
http://www.gasprocessors.org

Petrochemistry.net
http://www.petrochemistry.net

CIVIL ENGINEER

The Blue Book of Building and Construction
http://www.thebluebook.com

Civil Engineering Resources on the Internet
http://www.guideme.com/CivilEngineering.htm

Ultimate Civil Engineering Directory
http://www.tenlinks.com/engineering/civil

CLINICAL ENGINEER

American Medical Informatics Association
http://www.amia.org

Association for the Advancement of Medical Instrumentation
http://www.aami.org

Association of Medical Diagnostic Manufacturers
http://www.amdm.org

California Medical Instrumentation Association
http://www.cmia.org

Medical Device Manufacturers Association
http://www.medicaldevices.org

COMPUTER HARDWARE ENGINEER

ACM Queue
(Association for Computing Machinery)
http://acmqueue.com

Hardware
(Earth Web.com)
http://hardware.earthweb.com

CONSTRUCTION ENGINEER

Building Industry Directory and Information Resource
http://www.builderspace.com

Careers in Construction.com
http://www.careersinconstruction.com

Construction Web Links
http://www.constructionweblinks.com

CONTROL ENGINEER

American Automatic Control Council
http://www.a2c2.org

Dynamic Systems & Control Division
(ASME International)
http://divisions.asme.org/dscd

International Federation of Automatic Control
http://www.ifac-control.org

Measurement, Control and Automation Association
http://www.measure.org

DESIGN ENGINEER

Design Engineering
http://www.bizlink.com/designengineering.htm

Engineering Design
(Civil Engineering Department, Southern
    Illinois University)
http://civil.engr.siu.edu/intro/design.htm

Engineers Edge
http://www.engineersedge.com

DEVELOPMENT ENGINEER

Body of Knowledge
DRM Associates
http://www.npd-solutions.com/bok.html

Product Development Institute
http://www.prod-dev.com

DRAFTER

Drafting Jobs
http://drafting.jobs.jobsearchsite.com

efunda: engineering fundamentals
http://www.efunda.com

ELECTRICAL ENGINEER

IEEE Virtual Museum
http://www.ieee-virtual-museum.org

**The Institution of Engineering and
    Technology**
http://www.theiet.org

Web EE.com
http://www.web-ee.com

**WWW Virtual Library: Electrical and
    Electronics Engineering**
http://www.cem.itesm.mx/vlee

ELECTRONICS ENGINEER

Electronic Industries Alliance
http://www.eia.org

Electronics EE.com
http://www.electronicsee.com

EngPlanet Engineering Portal
http://www.engplanet.com

ENGINEERING
CONSULTANT

**American Council of Engineering
    Companies**
http://www.acec.org

EE Times: Career Center
(United Business Media)
http://eet.tech-engine.com

LexNotes—Expert Witnesses
http://www.lexnotes.com/sources/services
    /experts.shtml

ENGINEERING
MANAGER

Institute for Management Excellence
http://www.itstime.com

InformationWeek White Papers
http://whitepaper.informationweek.com

ENGINEERING
TECHNICIAN/
TECHNOLOGIST

Engineering Technology
(Rochester Institute of Technology)
http://www.rit.edu/~700www/et

**National Institute for Certification in
    Engineering Technologies**
http://www.nicet.org

The Technology Interface
(Jeff Beasley)
http://et.nmsu.edu/~etti

ENVIRONMENTAL
ENGINEER

Environmental Career Opportunities
http://www.ecojobs.com

The Environment Site.org
http://www.theenvironmentsite.org

**National Pollution Prevention Round
    Table**
http://www.p2.org

U.S. Environmental Protection Agency
http://www.epa.gov

FACILITIES ENGINEER

Maintenance Resources.com
http://www.maintenanceresources.com

Plant Engineering
http://www.manufacturing.net/ple

FIRE PROTECTION
ENGINEER

ETNEWS.ORG
http://www.etnews.org

Fire Protection Engineering
(Worcester Polytechnic Institute)
http://www.wpi.edu/Academics/Depts/Fire

Profession Links
(Society of Fire Protection Engineers)
http://www.sfpe.org/Profession/
    ProfessionLinks.aspx

U.S. Fire Administration
http://www.usfa.fema.gov

FLIGHT TEST ENGINEER

Baker Aviation Services
http://www.bakerav.com

National Test Pilot School
http://www.ntps.edu

777-200LR Worldliner
(Boeing)
http://www.boeing.com/commercial/
    777family/200LR

FOOD ENGINEER

Food Engineering Division
(Institute of Food Technologists)
http://www.ift.org/divisions/food_eng

FOODNET BASE
http://www.foodnetbase.com

Food Online
http://www.foodonline.com

Food Products Association
http://www.fpa-food.org

FORENSIC ENGINEER

**Engineering Forensics Research
    Institute**
(Rose-Hulman Institute of Technology)
http://www.rose-hulman.edu/~sutterer/
    EFRI/efri_home.htm

**Forensic Engineering: The Tay Bridge
    Disaster**
http://www.open2.net/forensic_
    engineering

Society of Forensic Engineers and Scientists
http://www.forensic-society.org

Technical Council on Forensic Engineering
(American Society of Civil Engineers)
http://asce_tcfe.tripod.com

FOREST ENGINEER

Forest Engineering at Oregon State University
http://www.cof.orst.edu/cof/fe

Forestry USA.com
http://www.forestryusa.com

Temperate Forest Foundation
http://www.forestinfo.org

GEOLOGICAL ENGINEER

American Association of Petroleum Geologists
http://www.aapg.org

American Geophysical Union
http://www.agu.org

GEO Community
http://www.geocomm.com

Geology and Mining Jobs and Professional Information
(Department of Geological and Mining Engineering and Sciences, Michigan Technological University)
http://www.geo.mtu.edu/geojobs/#pro

Mineral Resources Program
(U.S. Geological Survey)
http://minerals.usgs.gov

GEOTECHNICAL ENGINEER

The Civil Engineering Portal— Geotechnical Engineering
http://www.icivilengineer.com/Geotechnical_Engineering

Geo Institute Links
http://www.geoinstitute.org/static/relinks.cfm

U.S. Geological Survey
http://www.usgs.gov

HEATING, VENTILATING, AIR-CONDITIONING, AND REFRIGERATION (HVAC/R) ENGINEER

Air-Conditioning and Refrigeration Institute
http://www.ari.org

HVAC Excellence
http://www.hvacexcellence.org

HVAC Systems
(The Engineering Tool Box)
http://www.engineeringtoolbox.com/hvac-systems-t_23.html

HUMAN FACTORS ENGINEER

Cornell University Ergonomics Web
http://ergo.human.cornell.edu

Ergoworld
http://www.interface-analysis.com/ergoworld

FAA NAS Human Factors Group
http://hf.tc.faa.gov/value.htm

Human Factors Engineering Professional Network
http://www.iee.org/oncomms/pn/humanfactors/index.cfm

International Encyclopedia of Ergonomics and Human Factors
http://www.louisville.edu/speed/ergonomics

INDUSTRIAL ENGINEER

The Institute for Systems Research
(University of Maryland)
http://www.isr.umd.edu/ISR

Industrial Engineer Jobs
http://industrial.engineer.jobs.topusajobs.com

Institute of Operations Research and Management Science
http://www.informs.org

INFORMATION TECHNOLOGY (IT) ENGINEER

Datamation
http://itmanagement.earthweb.com

Information Technology Association of America
http://www.itaa.org

USENIX
http://www.usenix.org

MACHINERY SYSTEMS ENGINEER

North American Equipment Dealers Association
http://www.naeda.com

Worldwide Agricultural Machinery and Equipment Directory
http://www.agmachine.com

MANAGEMENT CONSULTANT

Association of Internal Management Consultants
http://www.aimc.org

Association of Management Consulting Firms
http://www.amcf.org

Careers in Consulting
http://www.careers-in-business.com/consulting/mc.htm

MANUFACTURING ENGINEER

Association for Manufacturing Excellence
http://www.ame.org

Manufacturing.net
http://www.manufacturing.net

MARKETING MANAGER

Guerrilla Marketing Online
http://www.gmarketing.com

Know This.com
http://www.knowthis.com

MATERIALS ENGINEER

Corrosion Doctors
http://www.corrosion-doctors.org

Exploring Materials Engineering
(San Jose State University)
http://www.engr.sjsu.edu/WofMatE

Materials Science and Engineering Laboratory
(National Institute of Standards and Technology)
http://www.msel.nist.gov

Nanotechnology News Network
http://www.nanonewsnet.com

MECHANICAL ENGINEER

Crank.com—The Mechanical Engineering Portal
http://icrank.com

Mechanical Design Engineering Resources on the World Wide Web
http://www.gearhob.com

Mechanical Engineer.com
http://www.mechanicalengineer.com

Mechanical Engineering Subject Portal
(Cleveland State University Library)
http://www.ulib.csuohio.edu/portals/meceng-m.shtml

METALLURGICAL ENGINEER

Steel Works
(American Iron and Steel Institute)
http://www.steel.org

The World Metals Information Network
http://www.amm.com

MINING ENGINEER

InfoMine
http://www.infomine.com

Minerals Engineering International Online
http://www.min-eng.com

Mining USA
http://www.miningusa.com

National Mining Association
http://nma.org

Open Pit Mine: Open Pit Mine Technology
http://technology.infomine.com/openpitmine

NASA ENGINEER

NASA Quest!
http://www.quest.arc.nasa.gov

NASA Sites
http://www.nasa.gov/about/sites/index.html

Space.com
http://www.space.com

Want to Work at NASA?
http://www.nasa.gov/about/career/index.html

NAVAL ENGINEER

American Shipbuilding Association
http://www.americanshipbuilding.com

Institute of Marine Engineering, Science and Technology
http://imarest.org

Marine Careers.net
(Sea Grant Program)
http://www.marinecareers.net

Martin's Marine Engineering Page
(Martin Ledue)
http://www.dieselduck.ca

Naval Engineering and Research Consortium
http://nerc.aticorp.org

NSnet
http://www.nsnet.com

NUCLEAR ENGINEER

Nuclear Energy Institute
http://www.nei.org

Nuclear Engineering Division
(ASME International)
http://divisions.asme.org/ned

Nuclear Engineering Virtual Library
(Department of Nuclear Energy, University of California, Berkeley)
http://www.nuc.berkeley.edu/main/vir_library.html

OCEAN ENGINEER

Center for Ocean Engineering
http://oe.mit.edu

Coastal and Ocean Engineering Jobs Database
http://www.cfd-online.com/Coastal_Jobs

Ocean Engineering Blog
http://oceanengineering.blogspot.com

Ocean Engineering Department
(Applied Physics Laboratory, University of Washington)
http://oe.apl.washington.edu

PATENT EXAMINER

Examiner Handbook to the U.S. Patent Classification System
http://www.uspto.gov/web/offices/pac/dapp/sir/co/examhbk

Patent Information Users Group
(The International Society for Patent Information)
http://www.piug.org

Patent and Trademark Office Society
http://www.ptos.org

PETROLEUM ENGINEER

Petroleum Engineer.com
http://www.petroleumengineer.com

Petroleum and Mining Job Portal
http://www.pmjobs.net

Women with Careers in Engineering
(Minerals, Management Service, U.S. Department of Interior)
http://www.gomr.mms.gov/homepg/lagniapp/womensc.html

POLICY ANALYST

Center for Science, Technology and Security Policy
http://www.aaas.org/programs/centers/cstsp/about.shtml

The Christine Mirzayan Science &
Technology Policy Graduate
Fellowship Program
http://www.nationalacademies.org/policyf
ellows/index.html
Technology Administration
(U.S. Department of Commerce)
http://www.technology.gov

State Science and Technology Institute
http://www.ssti.org

Law and Public Policy
(U.C. Berkeley Career Center)
http://career.berkeley.edu/LawPolicy/Law
Policy.stm

PRODUCTION ENGINEER

Best Manufacturing Practices
(BMP Center of Excellence)
http://www.bmpcoe.org

efunda: Engineering Processes
http://www.efunda.com/processes/
processes_home/process.cfm

Production Engineer
http://www.productionengineer.net

PROFESSOR

**Association of Environmental
Engineering and Science
Professors**
http://www.aeesp.org

PhDs.org
http://www.phds.org

**Resources in Science and Engineering
Education**
(Richard Felder)
http://www.ncsu.edu/felder-
public/RMF.html

PROJECT ENGINEER

Project Management Institute
http://www.pmi.org

QUALITY ENGINEER

Quality Engineering
(Department of Industrial and System
Engineering, University of Wisconsin)
http://www.engr.wisc.edu/ie/research/
qe.html

The Quality Portal
http://www.thequalityportal.com

REGULATORY AFFAIRS ENGINEER

**Center for the Study of Regulated
Industry**
http://robinson.gsu.edu/faculty/csri.html

Office of Regulatory Affairs
(U.S. Food and Drug Administration)
http://www.fda.gov/ora

REHABILITATION ENGINEER

**Rehabilitation Engineering Research
Centers**
http://www.ncddr.org/rpp/techaf/
techdfdw/rerc

**Rehabilitation Engineering Service
Delivery**
http://www.cs.wright.edu/bie/rehabengr/s
ervices/services.htm

RESEARCH ENGINEER

Engineering Information
http://www.ei.org

ROBOTICS ENGINEER

National Robotics Engineering Center
http://www.rec.ri.cmu.edu

Robotics Alliance Project
(NASA)
http://robotics.nasa.gov

Robotics Trends
http:www.roboticstrends.com

Robot Information Central
(Arrick Robotics)
http://www.robotics.com/robots.html

ROLLER COASTER ENGINEER

Coaster-World.com
http://www.coaster-world.com

Roller Coaster Web Sites
http://www.intel.com/education/projects/
wildride/learning/rctable.htm

Ultimate Roller Coaster.com
http://www.ultimaterollercoaster.com

SALES ENGINEER

**Manufacturers' Agents National
Association**
http://www.manaonline.org

SOFTWARE ENGINEER

**Software and Information Industry
Association**
http://www.siia.net

Software Engineering Institute
http://www.sei.cmu.edu

Sticky Minds.com
http://www.stickyminds.com

STRUCTURAL ENGINEER

Bridge Pros
http://www.bridgepros.com

**National Council of Structural
Engineers Association**
http://www.ncsea.com

**Structural Engineers Association
International**
http://www.seaint.org

**Structural Engineers Association of
California**
http://www.seaoc.org

SURVEYOR

County Surveyor's Links
(National Association of County
Surveyors)
http://www.naco.org/nacs/links.html

Measuring the World Around Us
http://www.surveyingcareer.com

Point of Beginning
http://www.pobonline.com

U.S. Geological Survey
http://www.usgs.gov

SYSTEMS ENGINEER

Institute for Systems Research
(University of Maryland)
http://www.isr.umd.edu

Systems Engineering Projects
http://www.syseng.net

TECHNICAL WRITER

General—Technical Writing
(The Civil Engineering Portal)
http://www.icivilengineer.com/General/Technical_Writing

Resources for Technical Writers
http://www.writerswrite.com/technical/techlink.htm

TECHWR-L
(Information in Focus, Inc.)
http://www.techwr=l.com/techwhirl

TELECOMMUNICATIONS ENGINEER

ATIS—Alliance for Telecommunications Industry Solutions
http://www.atis.org

Cable
(Dave Devereaux-Weber)
http://cable.doit.wisc.edu

National Association of Communication Systems Engineers
http://www.nacse.com

TelecomCareers.Net
http://www.telecomcareers.net

TEST ENGINEER

Test and Diagnostics Consortium
http://www.test-diagnostics.org

Test and Measurement World Online
http://www.reed-electronics.com/tmworld

TISSUE ENGINEER

National Tissue Engineering Center
http://www.ntec-online.com

Tissue Engineering Pages
http://www.tissue-engineering.net

Tissue Engineering's Web Watch
(Lee Weiss)
http://www.cs.cmu.edu/~webwatch

TRAFFIC ENGINEER

Traffic Stuff
(Richard C. Moeur)
http://www.richardcmoeur.com/trafstuf.html

TRANSPORTATION ENGINEER

Federal Highway Administration
(U.S. Department of Transportation)
http://www.fhwa.dot.gov

Intelligent Transportation Systems
(U.S. Department of Transportation)
http://www.its.dot.gov

Intelligent Transportation Society of America
http://www.itsa.org

U.S. Department of Transportation
http://www.dot.gov

URBAN PLANNER

International City Planners Network
http://city-planners-network.org

Planetizen: The Planning and Development Network
http://www.planetizen.com

PlannersWeb
http://www.plannersweb.com

WASTE MANAGEMENT ENGINEER

The Grass Roots Recycling Network
http://www.grrn.org

RadWaste.org
http://www.radwaste.org

Solid Waste
(The Civil Engineering Portal)
http://www.icivilengineer.com/Environmental_Engineering/Solid_Waste

SolidWaste.com
http://www.solidwaste.com

WASTEWATER ENGINEER

Water and Wastewater.com
http://www.waterandwastewater.com

Water Quality Association
http://www.wqa.org

WATER RESOURCES ENGINEER

The Groundwater Foundation
http://www.groundwater.org

Office of Water
(U.S. Environmental Protection Agency)
http://www.epa.gov/ow

Water Resources
(Open Directory Project)
http://dmoz.org/Science/Environment/Water_Resources

WELDING ENGINEER

EWI: Joining Technology
http://www.ewi.org

GLOSSARY

acoustics   The scientific study of sound and sound waves.

aeronautics   The study of flight as well as the operation of aircraft.

aerodynamics   The study of how air and other gases flow around aircraft and other objects.

aesthetics   The appreciation of beauty.

analytical skills   The abilities that a worker needs to critically examine and solve problems.

apparatus   Instrument, equipment, or machinery designed for a specific purpose.

application   The act of using engineering, scientific, or mathematical principles for a practical and specific purpose.

applied research   Scientific studies that are conducted for practical purposes, such as developing new products or technologies.

apprenticeship   The period of time that a person works under a skilled professional to learn a trade or craft.

artificial intelligence (AI)   Programs that allow computers to learn, reason, infer, and solve problems in order to complete certain tasks.

associate degree   The degree earned upon fulfilling the requirements of a two-year college program.

astronautics   The study of the construction and operation of spacecraft.

avionics   Electronic equipment designed for aircraft and spacecraft.

bachelor's degree   The degree earned upon fulfilling the requirements of a four-year college program.

background check   A thorough examination into an individual's background, which may include his or her educational, work, medical, financial, and criminal histories.

basic research   Scientific studies that are conducted to gain new knowledge and understanding about a particular topic.

biotechnology   The study and practice of using living cells and materials to create agricultural, diagnostic, pharmaceutical, and other products.

CAD   Computer-aided design; software used by engineers, architects, and others to help them with their drawing and designing tasks.

CADD   Computer-aided design and drafting; software used by engineers, technicians, and others to perform design and drafting tasks.

CAE   Computer-aided engineering; computer software and hardware used by engineers and others to help in the design, manufacture, handling, or distributon of products.

CAM   Computer-aided manufacturing; computer technology used to manage the processes for producing goods.

candidate   A person whom an employer is interested in hiring.

career   An individual's profession or occupation.

ceramics   Inorganic, nonmetallic materials such as clay, silica, or talc that can be molded into useful shapes to fulfill practical functions.

client   An individual or organization who uses the services of a professional.

code   A set of laws or rules that govern specific procedures within a profession.

communication skills   The speaking and listening abilities that workers need to perform their job.

compliance   Meeting the conditions required by a specific law, regulation, or policy.

component   A part of a unit or system.

computer hardware   All physical components of a computer; also all computer-related equipment such as printers and scanners.

computer model   A program that uses a mathematical equation to represent a particular problem; the program simulates how conditions in the problem may change when the variables in the equation are changed.

construction   The act of building houses, shopping complexes, roads, dams, and other structures and infrastructure.

consultant   An expert in his or her field who offers the services of his or her expertise to individuals and organizations for a fee.

consumer   An individual who buys products and services for his or her particular needs and wants.

contractor   An individual or company who is hired to perform specific tasks according to the terms of a written or oral agreement.

controls   Devices or systems designed to direct and regulate equipment, machinery, or systems.

critical thinking skills   The abilities to examine and analyze a situation and make sensible judgments on how to handle it.

data   Information, including facts and figures.

design   The drawing or other graphical description that shows how something is to be made.

detail-oriented   Paying close attention to the various parts of a task, project, or job.

development   The process in which a product or service is being planned and created.

device   An instrument or piece of equipment built for a particular purpose.

discipline   A field of study, such as mechanical engineering, industrial engineering, or geotechnical engineering.

doctorate (or doctoral degree)   An advanced degree; the degree earned upon fulfilling the requirements of a postgraduate program.

duties   Tasks or aspects of a job that a worker has been hired to do.

efficiency   Being able to do something well without unnecessary effort or expense.

E.I.T.   Engineer-in-training; a state license granted to an engineering intern.

engineering specialty   An engineering function such as design, research, or technical services.

engineering technology   The profession that applies scientific and engineering principles and techniques to solve technical problems.

entrepreneurial   Willing to take the risks of starting a new business.

entry-level position   A job that individuals can get with little or no experience.

EPA   Environmental Protection Agency; the U.S. agency that enforces federal environmental laws.

ergonomics   The study of the relationship between workers and their working environment and how to improve working conditions so that workers can work more efficiently.

estimated wages   An amount that is close to the actual pay a worker earns.

ethical   Behaving justly and honestly.

experience   Paid and volunteer work that an individual has done that is related to the position for which he or she applies.

expert witness   An individual whom a court recognizes as having the required knowledge, expertise, and credentials to address specific issues in a court trial.

FAA   Federal Aviation Administration; the U.S. agency that enforces federal aviation laws.

fabricate   To make or build something by putting different parts together.

facilities   Buildings used for a particular purpose.

failure analysis   The examination into how and why a product, process, or system broke down or could break down.

FDA   Food and Drug Administration; a branch of the U.S. Department of Health and Human Services that enforces federal food and drug laws.

field service   All the maintenance and repair activities that engineers perform for a customer at the customer's workplace or residence.

fire protection   The safeguarding of a building or complex with equipment and systems to control or extinguish fires.

flexible   Being able to handle changes.

forensic   Having to do with the application of science to the study of legal or regulatory matters.

GIS   Geographic information systems; the collection of geographic information that is stored in computer databases.

GPS   Global positioning system; the use of satellites to automatically pinpoint locations anywhere on Earth.

GS   General schedule; the pay schedule on which the salaries of many U.S. government workers are based.

human factors   The study of designing and arranging objects so that people can interact more efficiently and safely with them.

human resources   Personnel; the employees within an organization; also the department that is responsible for recruiting and hiring employees.

hydraulics   The study of practical applications of using liquids to perform mechanical tasks.

industry   A group of individuals and organizations engaged in the same kind of business enterprise.

information technology (IT)   The software and hardware used to store, protect, process, transmit, and retrieve information.

infrastructure   The public services and facilities needed to support communities, such as roads, schools, wastewater systems, telephone service, and power plants.

interdisciplinary   Involving engineers, scientists, and others from two or more fields.

internship   The period of working as a trainee or a low-level assistant in order to gain experience.

interpersonal skills   The abilities a worker needs to communicate and work well with others on the job.

jurisdiction   The area in which certain laws and regulations are applicable.

LAN   Local area network; a computer network that connects computers in an office building, college campus, or other local area.

laser   Acronym for light amplification by stimulated emission of radiation; a very intense beam of light that is formed within a crystal.

leadership skills   The abilities a worker needs to provide supervision and direction to other workers on a project or in a unit.

local government   A city or county government.

manufacturing process   The steps that are performed by workers and machinery to produce goods from raw materials into finished products.

marketing   The business activity of persuading potential customers that they want to buy certain products or services.

master's degree   An advanced degree; it is earned upon fulfilling the requirements of a one- or two-year graduate program.

mathematical model   A computational model used to describe a process or system; the equation represents the components in a problem and their relationship to each other.

modeling   The use of mathematical equations to simulate and predict what may happen.

nanotechnology   A technology that designs and produces very tiny materials, devices, and circuits made from single atoms and molecules.

NASA   National Aeronautics and Space Administration; the federal agency that oversees the U.S. space program.

networking   Making contacts with colleagues and other people who may provide you with resources such as information about job vacancies.

novice   A new or inexperienced worker.

optimize   To get the most out of something.

P.E.   Professional Engineer; the state license granted to an engineer who fulfills specific education and experience requirements.

personnel   Human resources; the employees who work in an organization; also the department that is responsible for recruiting and hiring new employees for an organization.

pharmaceutical   Involved in the manufacturing of medicines.

plant   A building or group of buildings where manufacturing processes take place; also a building (or buildings) where electric energy is made.

postdoctoral   Relating to academic work or research done after a doctoral degree has been awarded.

principle   A basic law, rule, or truth.

problem-solving skills   The abilities an engineer needs to analyze and evaluate problems and find ways to solve them.

process   A series of related steps, activities, or events that must occur in sequence in order for a task or job to be successfully completed.

product development   The stages that a company goes through to turn an idea into a final product that is ready to be sold on the market.

production   The manufacturing of goods.

professional association   An organization that serves the interests of a profession; its membership is made up of those particular professionals.

project management   The oversight and coordination of all the activities for an engineering project.

project manager   The engineer who directs and coordinates the activities of an engineering project.

protocol   A standard operating procedure.

prototype   The original model of a new design or product.

public works   Roads, highways, bridges, dams, water treatment centers, buildings, and structures that the government builds for public use.

qualifications   The experience and skills an individual needs to do a job for which he or she applies.

quality   Degree to which a product has all the required characteristics and is free of all defects.

quality control   All the activities involved in checking the quality of raw materials, products, packaging, and manufacturing processes.

regulation   A rule that a government agency establishes in order to fulfill the requirements of a law.

regulatory agency   A government agency that enforces a specific set of laws and regulations.

requirement   Something that is needed.

research and development   The process of developing new products or improving existing products for commercial purposes.

robotics   Devices or systems that perform physical tasks automatically.

seismic   Relating to vibrations in the Earth made by earthquakes or explosions.

self-management skills   The abilities a worker needs to perform his or her duties without constant supervision.

senior engineer   An engineer who has several years of work experience.

sensor   A device that detects and responds to heat, light, or other physical stimuli.

simulate   To create a representation, such as a computer model, of something.

software   Computer instructions, or programs, that allow computers to operate automatically; also applications that let computer users perform specific tasks such as word processing.

specification   A written description of the set of technical requirements for a product, service, process, or system.

start-up company   A new business or firm.

subdiscipline   A field of study that is part of a major area of study; for example, geotechnical engineering is a subdiscipline of civil engineering.

subject-matter expert   An individual who is highly knowledgeable in and experienced with a particular topic.

system   All the parts that work together to perform a specific job.

task   A duty or job that an employee must perform.

teamwork skills   The abilities an employee needs to work effectively as part of a group on a work project or in a unit.

technician   A worker who provides technical support to engineers and other professionals.

technique   A technical method for performing a task.

technologist   An engineer who is involved in the practical application of engineering, science, and mathematics.

technology   The application of science for practical purposes.

telecommunications   The telephone, radio, television, and computer systems that use wired or wireless electrical systems to transmit information.

thermodynamics   The study of the relationship among heat, work, and other forms of energy.

trade association   An organization that serves the interests of a particular industry; its membership is made up of companies within that industry.

transducer   A device that changes one type of energy into another.

URL   Universal Resource Locator: the address of a Web site on the Internet

USDA   United States Department of Agriculture.

USPTO   United States Patent and Trademark Office.

validate   To establish the logic or truth about something.

WAN   Wide area network; a computer network that connects computers over long distances through phone lines, satellites, or other means.

BIBLIOGRAPHY

A. PERIODICALS

Print and online publications are available for many of the various occupations described in this book. These include magazines, journals, newspapers, newsletters, webzines, and electronic news services. Listed below are just a few publications that serve the different engineering professions. Some publications are specifically geared toward readers who are interested in engineering careers.

You may be able to find some of the print publications at a public, school, or academic library. Many of the print magazines also allow limited free access to their articles on the Web. Some of the Web-based publications are free, whereas others require a subscription to access certain issues and other resources. Some publications offer free subscriptions to students or professionals.

Note: Web site addresses were current when this book was written. If a Web site address no longer works, you may be able to find its new address by entering the name of the publication into a search engine.

Air and Space
Smithsonian
P.O. Box 420113
Palm Coast, FL 32142
Phone: (800) 766-2149
http://www.airspacemag.com

Aviation Week and Space Technology
Phone: (800) 525-5003
http://www.aviationnow.com/avnow/
news/channel_awst.jsp

Career Cornerstone News
Sloan Career Cornerstone Center
http://www.careercornerstone.org/sccnew
s/sccsubs.htm

CE News.com
(for civil engineers and land surveyors)
http://www.cenews.com

Computer World
http://www.computerworld.com

Control Engineering
http://www.manufacturing.net/ctl

Design News
(for mechanical and design engineers)
http://www.designnews.com

Discover
Phone: (800) 829-9132
http://www.discover.com

Diversity/Careers in Engineering and Information Technology
http://www.diversitycareers.com

EC&M
(Electrical, Construction and Maintenance)
http://www.ecmweb.com

EE Times
Phone: (800) 577-5356
http://www.eet.com

Engineering News-Record (ENR)
McGraw-Hill Companies
Phone: (877) 876-8208
http://www.enr.com

Fire Engineering Magazine
Pennwell Publishing Company
http://fe.pennnet.com

Hispanic Engineer and Information Technology
Career Communications Groups
http://www.hispanicengineer.com

IEEE Spectrum
Institute of Electrical and Electronics Engineers
Phone: (866) 363-2304 or (615) 377-3322
http://www.spectrum.ieee.org

Invention and Technology
American Heritage
Phone: 777-1222 or (515) 247-7631
http://inventionandtechnology.com

Journal of Engineering Education
American Society for Engineering Education

P.O. Box 10819A
Chantilly, VA 20153
http://www.asee.org/about/publications/je
e/index.cfm

Mechanical Engineering
ASME International
Phone: (800) THE-ASME
http://www.memagazine.org

Minority Engineer
Equal Opportunity Publications, Inc.
http://www.eop.com/me.html

Modern Machine Shop
Gardner Publications, Inc.
6915 Valley Avenue
Cincinnati, OH 45244
Phone: (800) 950-8020
Fax: (513) 527-8801
http://www.mmsonline.com

Nuclear Engineering International
http://www.neimagazine.com

Nuts and Volts Magazine
Phone: (877) 525-2539 or (818) 487-4545
Fax: (818) 487-4550
http://www.nutsvolts.com

Occupational Outlook Quarterly Online
U.S. Bureau of Labor Statistics
http://www.bls.gov/opub/ooq/ooqhome.
htm

Popular Communications
CQ Communications, Inc.
Phone: (516) 681-2922
http://www.popular-communications.com

Popular Mechanics
P.O. Box 7170
Red Oak, IA 51591
Phone: (800) 333-4948
http://www.popularmechanics.com

Popular Science
P.O. Box 60001
Tampa, FL 33660
Phone: (800) 289-9399
http://www.popsci.com/popsci

The Pre-Engineering Times
Junior Engineering Technical Society
http://www.jets.org/publications/petimes.
  cfm

The American Surveyor
http://www.theamericansurveyor.com

Scientific American
Phone: (800) 333-1199
http://www.sciam.com

SERVO Magazine
T & L Publications, Inc.
Phone: (877) 525-2539 or (818) 487-4545
Fax: (818) 487-4550
http://www.servomagazine.com

Technology Review
Phone: (800) 877-5230 (386) 447-6352
http://www.techreview.com

Professional Surveyor Magazine
http://www.profsurv.com/newpsm

Today's Engineer Online
IEEE-USA

http://www.todaysengineer.org

WIRED
http://www.wired.com

Woman Engineer
Equal Opportunity Publications
http://www.eop.com/we.html

Zdnet
(Tech and White Papers for IT
  Professionals)
http://www.zdnet.com

HOW TO FIND MORE PERIODICALS

Here are some things you might do to find periodicals that are specific to a profession in which you are interested.

- Talk with librarians, educators, and professionals for recommendations.
- Check out professional and trade associations. Many of them publish journals, newsletters, magazines, and other publications.
- Visit an online bookstore, such as Amazon.com, to view the listings of magazines it has to offer for sale. Use such keywords as *engineering* or *technology* as well as keywords for specific disciplines. If the Web site does not have a particular search engine for magazines, be sure to add the word *magazines* to your keyword. (For example: *automotive engineering magazines*).
- You can also find listings of some engineering trade magazines at these Web sites: TechExpo, http://www. techexpo.com/tech_mag.html; and PITT Digital Library at the University of Pittsburgh (Library Research Guide for Engineers), http://www.library.pitt.edu/services/classes/ engineering/trade.html.

B. BOOKS

Listed below are some book titles that can help you learn more about careers in engineering, engineering technology, and alternative careers. To learn about other books that may be helpful, ask professionals—individuals and organizations—as well as librarians for suggestions.

Adams, James L. *Flying Buttresses, Entropy, and O-Rings: The World of an Engineer.* Cambridge, Mass.: Harvard University Press, 1993.

Baine, Celeste. *The Fantastical Engineer: A Thrillseeker's Guide to Careers in Theme Park Engineering.* Farmerville, La.: Bonamy Publishing, 2000.

Baine, Celeste. *Is There an Engineer Inside You? A Comprehensive Guide to Career Decisions in Engineering.* Second ed. Ruston, La.: Bonamy Publishing, 2002.

Basta, Nickholas. *Careers in High Tech.* Second ed. Lincolnwood, Ill.: VGM Career Horizons, NTC/Contemporary Publishing Group, 1997.

Basta, Nicholas. *Opportunities in Engineering Careers.* Second ed. Chicago, Ill.: VGM Career Horizons, McGraw-Hill Companies, 2002.

Camenson, Blythe. *Real People Working in Engineering.* Lincolnwood, Ill.: VGM Career Horizons, NTC/Contemporary Publishing Co., 1998.

Chen, Ann, ed. *Harvard Business School Guide to Careers in Marketing 2001.* Boston, Mass.: Harvard Business School Pub., 2000.

Chen, W.F., editor-in-chief. *The Civil Engineering Handbook.* Boca Raton, Fla.: CRC Press, 1995.

Cheshier, Stephen R. *Studying Engineering Technology.* Los Angeles: Discovery Press, 1998.

Committee on Science, Engineering, and Public Policy. *Careers in Science and Engineering: A Student Planning Guide to Graduate School and Beyond.* Washington, D.C.: National Academy Press, 1996.

Cook, John R., Jr., et al. *The Complete Guide to Environmental Careers in the 21st Century.* Washington, D.C.: Island Press, 1999.

Dakes, William C., et al. *Engineering Your Future.* Wildwood, Md.: Great Lakes Press, 1999.

Echaore-McDavid, Susan. *Career Opportunities in Aviation and the Aerospace Industry.* New York: Ferguson, Facts On File, Inc., 2005.

Echaore-McDavid, Susan. *Career Opportunities in Law and the Legal Industry*. New York: Checkmark Books, Facts On File, Inc., 2002.

Echaore-McDavid, Susan. *Career Opportunities in Law Enforcement, Security, and Protective Services*. New York: Checkmark Books, Facts On File, Inc., 2006.

Echaore-McDavid, Susan. *Career Opportunities in Science*. New York: Checkmark Books, Facts On File, Inc., 2003.

Farr, J. Michael, and Laurence Shatkin, eds. *The O*NET Dictionary of Occupational Titles*. Third ed. Indianapolis, Ind.: JIST Publishing, 2004.

Ferguson Editors. *Preparing for a Career in Engineering?* Chicago, Ill.: Ferguson Publishing Co., 1995.

Ferguson, Eugene. *Engineering and the Mind's Eye*. Cambridge, Mass.: MIT Press, 1994.

Ferguson Staff. *Ferguson's Careers in Focus: Transportation*. Chicago, Ill.: Ferguson Publishing Co., 2000.

Florman, Samuel C. *The Existential Pleasures of Engineering*. New York: St. Martin's Griffin, 1994.

Florman, Samuel C. *The Introspective Engineer*. New York: St. Martin's Griffin, 1996.

Garner, Geraldine. *Careers in Engineering*. Second ed. Chicago, Ill.: VGM Career Books, McGraw-Hill Companies, 2003.

Garner, Geraldine. *Great Jobs for Engineering Majors*. Chicago, Ill.: VGM Career Books, 2002.

Goldberg, Jan. *Careers for Scientific Types and Others with Inquiring Minds*. Lincolnwood, Ill.: VGM Career Horizons, NTC/Contemporary Publishing Group Inc., 2000.

Hagerty, Joseph D, and Louis F. Cohn. *Opportunities in Civil Engineering Careers*. Lincolnwood, Ill.: VGM Career Horizons, 1997.

Heisler, Sanford I., *The Wiley Engineer's Desk Reference*. Second ed. New York: John Wiley and Sons, Inc., 1998.

Heitzmann, William Ray. *Opportunities in Marine and Maritime Careers*. Lincolnwood, Ill.: VGM Career Horizons, NTC/Contemporary Publishing Group, 1997.

Henderson, Harry. *Career Opportunities in Computers and Cyberspace*. New York: Checkmark Books, Facts On File, Inc., 1999.

Hiam, Alexander. *Marketing for Dummies*. Foster City, Calif.: IDG Books, 1997.

Hoschette, John A. *Career Advancement and Surveying for Engineers*. New York: John Wiley and Sons, Inc., 1994.

Irwin, J. David. *On Becoming an Engineer: A Guide to Career Paths*. Piscataway, N.J.: IEEE Press, 1997.

Kahn, Jetty. *Women in Engineering Careers*. Mankato, Minn.: Capstone Press, 1999.

Kemper, John D., and Billy R. Sanders. *Engineers and Their Professions*. New York: Oxford University Press, 2001.

King, Joe. *Exploring Engineering*. Second ed. Upper Saddle River, N.J.: Prentice Hall, 2002.

Landis, Raymond D. *Studying Engineering*. Los Angeles: Discovery Press, 2000.

Macmillan Reference Editorial Staff and Frances A. Wiser (Project Director). *Career Information Center, 7th Edition: Engineering, Science and Technology*. New York: Macmillan Reference USA, 1999.

Maples, Wallace R. *Opportunities in Aerospace Careers*. Chicago, Ill.: VGM Career Books, McGraw-Hill Companies, Inc., 2003.

Maze, Stephanie, and Catherine O'Neill Grace. *I Want to Be . . . An Engineer*. San Diego, Calif.: Harcourt Brace & Co., 1997.

McGraw-Hill Companies. *Occupational Outlook Handbook, 2004–2005*. New York: VGM Career Books, McGraw-Hill Companies, 2005.

Morkes, Andrew, et al. *Ferguson's Careers in Focus: Engineering*. Second ed. Chicago, Ill.: Ferguson Publishing Co., 2003.

National Academy of Engineering. *The Engineer of 2020: Visions of Engineering in the New Century*. Washington, D.C.: National Academies Press, 2004. Available on the Web. http://books.nap.edu/books/0309091624/html.

National Academy of Engineering. *Frontiers of Engineering*. Washington, D.C.: National Academies Press, 2005. Available on the Web. http://www.nap.edu/books/0309095476/html.

Oakes, William C., et al. *Engineering Your Future*. Wildwood, Mo.: Great Lakes Press, 1999.

Pasternak, Ceel, and Linda Thornberg. *Cool Careers for Girls in Engineering*. Manassas Park, Va.: Impact Publications, 1999.

Peterson's Job Opportunities: Engineering and Computer Science. Austin, Tex.: Peterson's, A Division of Thomson Learning, 1999.

Petroski, Henry. *Invention by Design; How Engineers Get from Thought to Thing*. Cambridge, Mass.: Harvard University Press, 1998.

Petroski, Henry. *Paperboy: Confessions of a Future Engineer*. New York: Alfred A. Knopf, 2002.

Petroski, Henry. *Small Things Considered: Why There Is No Perfect Design*. New York: Alfred A. Knopf, 2003.

Roadstrum, W. H. *Being Successful as an Engineer*. Austin, Tex.: Engineering Press, 1998.

Rowh, Mark. *Opportunities in Technical Sales Careers*. Chicago, Ill.: VGM Career Books, a division of McGraw-Hill Co., 2002.

U.S. Bureau of Labor Statistics. *Career Guide to Industries, 2006–07 Edition*. Washington, D.C.: Bureau of Labor Statistics, 2006. Available on the Web. http://www.bls.gov/oco/cg/home.htm.

U.S. Bureau of Labor Statistics. *Occupational Outlook Handbook 2006–07 Edition*. Washington, D.C.: Bureau of Labor Statistics, 2006. Available on the Web. http://www.bls.gov/oco.

Walesh, Stuart G. *Engineering Your Future: Launching a Successful Entry-Level Technical Career in Today's Busi-*

ness Environment. Englewood Cliffs, N.J.: Prentice Hall, 1995.

Watlington, Amanda G., and Radeloff, Roger L. *Contract Engineering: Start and Build a New Career.* New York: McGraw-Hill, 1997.

Wetfeet, Inc. *Careers in Information Technology, 2005 Edition: Wetfeet Insider Guide.* San Francisco: Wetfeet, Inc., 2005

Wright, Paul H. *Introduction to Engineering.* Third ed. New York: John Wiley and Sons, 2002.

C. PAMPHLETS, BOOKLETS, AND OTHER MATERIALS

American Institute of Aeronautics and Astronautics. *Careers in Aerospace.* Reston, Va.: American Institute of Aeronautics and Astronautics.

American Nuclear Society. *Nuclear Technology Creates Careers.* LaGrange Park, Ill.: American Nuclear Society.

American Society for Engineering Education. *Engineering, Go For It!* Washington, D.C.: American Society for Engineering Education.

Biomedical Engineering Society. *Planning a Career in Biomedical Engineering.* Landover, Md.: Biomedical Engineering Society, 1999. Available on the Web. http://bmes.org/careers.asp.

Committee on Career Development. *Career Paths in Civil Engineering.* Reston, Va.: American Society of Civil Engineers. Available on the Web. http://www.asce.org/professional/careers.

Construction Management Association of America. *A Career in Construction Management.* McLean, Va.: Construction Management Association of America.

Partnership for Public Services. *Red, White and Blue Jobs: Engineering Jobs, Using Your Engineering Skills to Build a Stronger America.* Washington, D.C.: Partnership for Public Services. Available on the Web. http://www.ourpublicservice.org/workforusa (Click on the *For Students and Job Seekers* link).

INDEX